Judging Science

Judging Science
Scientific Knowledge and the Federal Courts

Kenneth R. Foster
Peter W. Huber

The MIT Press
Cambridge, Massachusetts
London, England

First MIT Press paperback edition, 1999

Set in Sabon by The MIT Press.
Printed and bound in the United States of America.

Library of Congress Cataloging-in-Publication Data

Foster, Kenneth R.
   Judging science : scientific knowledge and the federal courts / Kenneth R. Foster,
   Peter W. Huber
      p.   cm.
   Includes bibliographical references and index.
   ISBN 0-262-06192-9 (hardcover : alk. paper), 0-262-56120-4 (pb)
      1. Evidence, Expert—United States.   2. Forensic sciences—United States.
   3. Science and law.   I. Huber, Peter W. (Peter William), 1952–.   II. Title. ·
   KF8961.F67   1997
   347.73′67—dc20
   [347.30767]   96-36405
                                                                          CIP

If scientific, technical, or other specialized knowledge will assist the trier of fact to understand the evidence or to determine a fact in issue, a witness qualified as an expert by knowledge, skill, experience, training, or education, may testify thereto in the form of an opinion or otherwise.

—Rule 702, Federal Rules of Evidence

Conjectures that are probably wrong are of little use . . . in the project of reaching a quick, final, and binding legal judgment—often of great consequence—about a particular set of events in the past. We recognize that, in practice, a gatekeeping role for the judge, no matter how flexible, inevitably on occasion will prevent the jury from learning of authentic insights and innovations. That, nevertheless, is the balance that is struck by Rules of Evidence designed not for the exhaustive search for cosmic understanding but for the particularized resolution of legal disputes.

—*Daubert v. Merrell Dow Pharmaceuticals, Inc.*, 509 U.S. 579, 597 (1993) (Blackmun, joined by White, O'Connor, Scalia, Kennedy, Souter, and Thomas)

I do not doubt that Rule 702 confides to the judge some gatekeeping responsibility in deciding questions of the admissibility of proffered expert testimony. But I do not think it imposes on them either the obligation or the authority to become amateur scientists in order to perform that role.

—*Daubert v. Merrell Dow Pharmaceuticals, Inc.*, 509 U.S. 579, 600–601 (1993) (Rehnquist, joined by Stevens, dissenting in part)

Contents

Acknowledgements

We gratefully acknowledge the generous support of the Manhattan Institute for Policy Research. We thank many of our colleagues who provided both suggestions and feedback, with special thanks to John Fielder and Jonathan Koehler. Special thanks go to Laura Haefner, our assistant for editorial and research support, for her invaluable support in the creation and publication of this work. We are also grateful for the research assistance provided by Karin Albani, Danielle Briggs, and Gary Stahlberg. Finally, we thank Joyce Cannon for her excellent secretarial support in assembling the final manuscript.

Judging Science

1

Scientific Knowledge

What is scientific knowledge, and when is it reliable? These deceptively simple questions have been sources of endless controversy. Whether Creation Science should be taught in schools along with the theory of evolution turns on whether Creation Science—or evolution, for that matter—can fairly be called science rather than belief, faith, or something else. In the courtroom, the outcomes of criminal, paternity, first amendment, and civil liability cases (among others) often turn on scientific evidence, the reliability of which may be hotly contested. Scientists have been arguing for years about the risks or nonrisks of radon in the home, stilbestrol residues in food,[1] and other potential subtle causes of injury. Major policy disputes revolve around these issues. Sometimes, as with DNA testing in capital murder trials, the reliability of a claim presented as scientific is a matter of life and death.

In 1993, the U.S. Supreme Court handed down a landmark ruling on scientific evidence, *Daubert v. Merrell Dow Pharmaceuticals*.[2] "Faced with a proffer of expert scientific testimony," Justice Blackmun wrote for a seven-Justice majority, "the trial judge must determine . . . whether the expert is proposing to testify to (1) scientific knowledge that (2) will assist the trier of fact to understand or determine a fact in issue. . . . Many factors will bear on the inquiry, and we do not presume to set out a definitive checklist or test. But some general observations are appropriate."[3] The Court's "general observations" followed.

Chief Justice Rehnquist, joined by Justice Stevens, dissented. In a passage that says much about the *Daubert* controversy and about the purpose of this book, the Chief Justice wrote:

"General observations" by this Court customarily carry great weight with lower federal courts, but the ones offered here suffer from the flaw common to most such observations—they are not applied to deciding whether or not particular testimony was or was not admissible, and therefore they tend to be not only general, but vague and abstract. . . . Twenty-two amicus briefs have been filed in the case, and indeed the Court's opinion contains no fewer than 37 citations to amicus briefs and other secondary sources.

The various briefs filed in this case are markedly different from typical briefs . . . they deal with definitions of scientific knowledge, scientific method, scientific validity, and peer review—in short, matters far afield from the expertise of judges. . . .[4]

The *Daubert* majority did rely on some unusual authorities. Many of its references covered familiar legal territory—articles in law reviews, legal treatises, and advisory notes to the Federal Rules of Evidence.[5] But the Court went much further. It cited two of the twentieth century's most influential philosophers of science, Carl Gustav Hempel and Karl Raimund Popper, as well as John Ziman, a prominent physicist turned commentator on science. The Court cited the editors of influential medical journals. It also cited three amicus briefs filed on behalf of groups of scientists, quoting from two of them.[6] One of those groups comprised eighteen scientists, including six Nobel laureates,[7] with expertise in chemistry, physics, meteorology, epidemiology, environmental medicine, and teratology (the study of malformations). The second scientists' amicus brief had been filed on behalf of the American Association for the Advancement of Science and the National Academy of Sciences. A third group of scientists that filed with the Court included Stephen Jay Gould, a well-known author and paleontologist.

As Chief Justice Rehnquist noted in his dissent, Supreme Court opinions do not ordinarily rest on this kind of intellectual foundation. Few of the scientific sources cited by the majority would be readily at hand for most judges to consult, nor would the broader literature that those sources summarize and represent. Yet seven of the Justices agreed that the meaning of a key phrase in the Federal Rules of Evidence—"scientific knowledge"—cannot be given intelligent meaning without venturing beyond the standard law library into the domains of science and philosophy.

Bendectin Litigation

Bendectin, an effective remedy for morning sickness, was introduced in 1957 by the company that later became Merrell Dow Pharmaceuticals. Eventually more than 33 million women used the drug worldwide.

Box 1.1
Bendectin Litigation

Mekdeci v. Merrell Nat'l Laboratories (711 F.2d 1510 (11th Cir. 1983)), the first major Bendectin suit, was filed in 1977. After appeals, Merrell eventually prevailed. Many more claims were filed, however. U.S. District Chief Judge Carl B. Rubin of Cincinnati aggregated 750 pending Bendectin cases into a class action. Without admitting liability, Merrell offered $120 million in settlement of all pending and future claims. Most of the plaintiffs' lawyers agreed, but a small group of dissenters managed to torpedo the deal. Merrell then withdrew its settlement offer and went to trial; a jury returned a verdict in Merrell's favor and against the 1,100 claimants (in re *Richardson-Merrell, Inc. "Bendectin" Product Litigation*, 624 F. Supp. 1212 (S.D. Oh. 1985), aff'd, 857 F. 2d 290 (6th Cir. 1988), cert. denied sub nom, *Hoffman v. Merrell Dow Pharmaceuticals*, 488 U.S. 1006 (1989)).

In subsequent suits, Merrell sought unsuccessfully to avoid retrying the issue of causation again and again by invoking the doctrine of collateral estoppel. In the opening round of *Lynch v. Merrell-National Laboratories* (646 F. Supp. 856 (D. Mass. 1986), aff'd, 830 F.2d 1190 (1st Cir. 1987)), for example, the trial court granted summary judgment for Merrell on both causation and collateral estoppel grounds. The First Circuit Court of Appeals upheld the ruling, but only on the issue of causation.

In *Brock v. Merrell Dow Pharmaceuticals, Inc.* (874 F.2d 307 (5th Cir. 1989)), the Fifth Circuit concluded that epidemiologic studies constitute "the most useful and conclusive type of evidence" and, in cases of this type, "speculation unconfirmed by epidemiologic proof cannot form the basis for causation in a court of law." And in a Massachusetts Bendectin case (830 F.2d (1st Cir. 1987)), the First Circuit affirmed summary judgment for the defendant when the plaintiffs failed to present acceptable confirmatory data to support their experts' opinions on the issue of causation.

In another case (in re *Richardson-Merrell*, 624 F. Supp. 1212 (S.D. Ohio 1985)), as well as *Brock*, the evidence was not only admissible but, in the opinions of the two juries, it was sufficient to meet the burden of proof on the issue of causation. However, in affirming "judgment notwithstanding the verdict" in *Richardson* and in reversing the trial court's denial of the same in *Brock*, the appellate courts agreed that the opinions of the plaintiffs' expert witnesses were not sufficient to demonstrate causation by a preponderance of the evidence. "Judgment notwithstanding the verdict" is proper when there can be only one reasonable conclusion drawn from the evidence.

In both *Richardson* and *Brock*, the courts concluded that no reasonable jury could find on the basis of the evidence presented that Bendectin more likely than not caused the birth defects. These decisions, *Brock* in particular, reveal a closer scrutiny of the data and a willingness by the courts to look behind the experts' conclusions to analyze the adequacy of their foundations. In both cases, the courts concluded that neither *in vivo* nor *in vitro* animal studies nor chemical structure analysis data, alone or in combination, are capable of proving causation in human beings. Reanalyses of epidemiologic studies that resulted in statistically significant results were found insufficient to support a reasonable inference of causation.

Since *Mekdeci*, Bendectin cases have been litigated painstakingly, one by one. Merrell has won almost every case. (See Louis Lasagna and Sheila Shulman, Bendectin and the Language of Causation, in *Phantom Risk*, ed. K. Foster et al. (MIT Press, 1993).) Some juries have found for plaintiffs, however. (See David Bernstein, Daubert One Year Later (unpublished, 1994).) For example, a Washington, D.C., jury awarded young Mary Oxendine $750,000 (*Oxendine v. Richardson-Merrell*, No.1245-82 (D.C. Super. Ct. 1983), rev'd, *Oxendine v. Merrell Dow Pharmaceuticals, Inc.*, 506 A.2d 1100 (D.C. App. 1986) (mem. and order), vacated, No. 1245-82 (D.C. Super. Ct. Feb. 11, 1988), rev'd, 563 A.2d 330 (D.C. App.), cert. denied, 110 S. Ct. 1121 (1990), appeal after remand, 593 A.2d 1023 (1991)). (The award was overturned by the DC Superior Court in 1996.)

Daubert v. Merrell Dow Pharmaceuticals, Inc.[8] was one of more than a thousand lawsuits seeking recovery for birth defects allegedly produced by the mother's use of Bendectin during pregnancy (box 1.1).[9] Jason Daubert had been born with limb reduction, a rare birth defect which the plaintiffs attributed to his mother's use of Bendectin.

In November 1989, District Court Judge Earl Gilliam dismissed the *Daubert* case on summary judgment, citing serious deficiencies in the scientific evidence proffered by the plaintiffs' expert witnesses (box 1.2).[10] This trial court's decision was upheld in December 1991 by the Ninth Circuit Court of Appeals in an opinion written by Judge Alex Kozinski (box 1.3).[11] The U.S. Supreme Court then agreed to review the case.[12]

With its legal costs mushrooming, however, Merrell Dow had withdrawn Bendectin from the market on June 9, 1983. According to the American College of Obstetrics and Gynecology, Merrell Dow's decision "create[d] a significant therapeutic gap."[13] "We wouldn't bring Bendectin back," a Merrell Dow spokesman declared, even "if we won every lawsuit."[14]

The Science of Bendectin

The first report suggesting a link between Bendectin and birth defects came from Canada in 1969.[15] Other case reports and discussions of the possible teratogenic effects of the drug are scattered in the medical literature of

Box 1.2
William Daubert et al. v. Merrell Dow Pharmaceuticals, Inc.
source: 727 F. Supp. 570 (S.D. Cal. 1989) (Gilliam, J.)

In medical cases like this one, courts must "critically evaluate the reasoning process by which the experts connect data to their conclusions in order for courts to consistently and rationally resolve the disputes before them." . . . Absent a scientific understanding of the cause of the birth defects at issue in Bendectin cases, causation may be shown only through reliance upon epidemiological evidence. . . .

The federal courts have held that epidemiological studies are the most reliable evidence of causation in this area. Accordingly, expert opinion which is not based on epidemiological evidence is not admissible to establish causation because it lacks the sufficient foundation necessary under FRE 703. . . . Therefore, expert testimony concluding that Bendectin causes limb reduction defects which is generally based upon in vitro studies, chemical structure analyses and animal studies is insufficient to take the issue to the jury. The plaintiffs' experts must be competent to testify that some epidemiological study or recalculation shows a statistically significant relationship between the ingestion of Bendectin and birth defects and that this study forms the basis of their opinion. . . . In this case, the plaintiffs have failed to live up to the Brock mandate to provide some epidemiological evidence to support their claim that Bendectin is a teratogen. . . .

The defendants have introduced evidence that no epidemiological study ever performed has concluded that the use of Bendectin by pregnant women has a statistically significant association to birth defects in those women's children. . . . The plaintiffs' experts agree that none of the published studies show a statistically significant association between the use of Bendectin and birth defects. . . .

. . . [One of the witnesses] alleges that [his] "study" shows "a statistically significant association that is highly significant" . . . but his allegation and this evidence is insufficient to take this matter to a jury. . . . Similarly, Dr. Swan's unsupported allegation that the Jick data "statistically significantly associates Bendectin and limb defects" . . . is similarly insufficient.

The court feels that the strongest inference to be drawn for plaintiffs based on the epidemiological evidence is that Bendectin could possibly have caused plaintiffs' injuries, therefore summary judgment is proper against them.

the 1970s and the 1980s. Journals noted limb reductions, omphalocelegastroschisis (abnormality of the umbilicus and intestines), and neural-tube defects in children born to mothers who had taken Bendectin or one its various components during pregnancy.

Box 1.3
Daubert v. Merrell Dow Pharmaceuticals, Inc.
source: 951 F.2d 1128 (9th Cir. 1991) (and footnote 3) (A. Kozinski, J.)

For expert opinion based on a given scientific methodology to be admissible, the methodology cannot diverge significantly from the procedures accepted by recognized authorities in the field. If it does so diverge, it cannot be shown to be "generally accepted as a reliable technique," . . . and a district court must exclude it. If such evidence is admitted and materially affects the verdict, a judgment supported by this evidence cannot stand. . . .

Plaintiffs argue that reanalysis is a generally accepted scientific technique, so it follows that their experts were basing their opinions on a permissible methodology. But the reanalysis of epidemiological studies is generally accepted by the scientific community only when it is subjected to verification and scrutiny by others in the field. . . . Plaintiffs' reanalyses do not comply with this standard; they were unpublished, not subjected to the normal peer review process, and generated solely for use in litigation. It does not suffice that the expert's methodology meet some of the requirements imposed by the scientific community; it must meet all of the essential requirements. Selective borrowing from generally accepted scientific methodology does not satisfy *Solomon*'s rigorous standard. . . .

[The following is from footnote 3.] Scientific studies conducted in anticipation of litigation must be scrutinized much more carefully than studies conducted in the normal course of scientific inquiry. This added dose of skepticism is warranted, in part, because studies generated especially for use in litigation are less likely to have been exposed to the normal peer review process, which is one of the hallmarks of reliable scientific investigation. . . . For the convincing reasons articulated by our sister circuits, we agree with the district court that the available animal and chemical studies, together with plaintiffs' expert reanalysis of epidemiological studies, provide insufficient foundation to allow admission of expert testimony to the effect that Bendectin caused plaintiffs' injuries.

In September 1980, responding to such reports and to a request from the American College of Obstetrics and Gynecology, the Fertility and Maternal Health Drugs Advisory Committee of the U.S. Food and Drug Administration reviewed the available scientific information bearing on Bendectin's association with birth defects. The FDA invited experts to share their views on whether Bendectin was associated with increased risk for human birth defects and, if so, whether the benefits of its use outweighed the risks.

The committee concluded that existing data did not show an association between Bendectin and human birth defects. Two of the thirteen studies reviewed by the committee suggested a possible association, but these studies had been exploratory only and could not be taken to contradict the more focused, larger-scale epidemiologic studies. The committee decided that the available studies were sufficiently large to have detected a doubling of the overall malformation rate, but not large enough to rule out a doubling of any single malformation. It therefore recommended that the FDA monitor three ongoing epidemiologic studies and limit Bendectin use to patients for whom nondrug morning-sickness therapies had failed.[16]

Many Bendectin suits were filed in the late 1970s and the early 1980s. At that time there was still some debate in the medical literature about Bendectin's possible risks. A 1963 study by C. A. Bunde and D. M. Bowles[17] had found no risk, but a 1979 study by K. J. Rothman et al.[18] reported an odds ratio of 1.8 (nearly a doubling of the risk) for congenital heart disease. By the early 1990s, when *Daubert* would have come to trial, there was a much more extensive scientific record.

The literature on the human epidemiology of Bendectin is now voluminous. Lasagna and Shulman[19] and Brent[20] provide reviews. (For an excerpt from the latter, see box 1.4.) A few statistically significant correlations between the drug and birth defects have been reported in the literature,[21] but taken together the results are overwhelmingly negative.

Any fair assessment of how well courts handle scientific evidence must be based on the state of science at the time of the legal proceedings. The scientific record of Bendectin is much more extensive today than it was in the 1970s, but there have been no major shifts in scientific understanding. The large scientific record available today simply confirms what most epidemiologists would have inferred from the smaller scientific record a decade or two ago: If Bendectin poses any risks at all, they are very small.

Frye and *Daubert*

Several expert witnesses appeared repeatedly for the plaintiffs in the Bendectin cases, including *Daubert*. One key witness was Shanna Swan,[22] a well-credentialed epidemiologist working for the California Department of Health. She argued that data from epidemiologic studies supported the

Box 1.4
Bendectin Epidemiology

Robert L. Brent—a pediatrician, an expert on birth defects, and an occasional expert witness for the defense in Bendectin litigation—has recently published an extensive review of the Bendectin literature (Bendectin: Review of the medical literature of a comprehensively studied human nonteratogen and the most prevalent tortogen-litigen, *Reproductive Toxicology* 9 (1995): 337–349). Here we reprint two tables from that paper, summarizing the results of epidemiology studies related to Bendectin and congenital malformations. (The tables have been simplified from the originals published in Brent's paper. The reader is referred to the paper for references to the primary literature.)

The tables show cohort and case-control studies separately. In cohort studies, the investigators compare the incidence of birth defects in children of users and nonusers of Bendectin. In case-control studies, the investigator identifies a group of "cases" (children with a birth defect) and "controls" (normal children) and compares their mothers' use of the drug.

Table 1 presents the results of the cohort studies in terms of the relative risk and 95 percent confidence intervals. The relative risk is the ratio of the incidence of congenital malformations (of any type) in children exposed to the drug to the incidence in children whose mothers had not taken the drug during pregnancy. (A relative risk of 2 implies that the drug doubles the risk of birth defects.) The 95 percent confidence intervals are a measure of the uncertainty due to sampling error; according to the statistical test used, there is a 95 percent probability that the relative risk will lie within the confidence limits. If the 95 percent confidence intervals overlap 1, there is no statistically significant association.

None of the comparisons yielded statistically significant associations between the drug and birth defects. The "summary" line at the bottom of table 1 is a meta-analysis of several Bendectin studies, which was also negative.

Table 2 summarizes the case-control studies involving Bendectin. The results are expressed in terms of the odds ratio, which is a measure of the relative risk. Three of the 17 comparisons in the table resulted in statistically significant associations.

Particularly relevant to *Daubert* are two case-control studies involving limb-reduction defects. Neither reported an association between limb-reduction defects and the mothers' use of Bendectin.

The tables have been simplified from the originals published in Brent's paper. The reader is referred to that paper for the references to the primary literature.

Table 1
Bendectin and congenital malformation cohort studies.

Reference	Study group	Ex-posed total	Ex-posed mal-formed	Non-exposed total	Non-exposed mal-formed	Rela-tive risk	95% confid-ence interval
Heinonen et al., 1977	50,282	1,169	79	49,113	3,169	1.05	0.84–1.30
Fleming et al., 1981	22,977	620	31	22,357	1,208	0.93	0.65–1.31
Michaelis et al., 1983	1,748	874	18	874	19	0.95	0.50–1.79
Milkovich and van den Berg, 1976	10,205	628	14	9,577	343	0.62	0.37–1.06
Morelock et al., 1982	1,690	375	31	1,315	93	1.17	0.79–1.73
Aselton and Jick, 1983	5,254	1,364	2	3,890	4	1.43	0.26–7.78
Gibson et al., 1981	7,456	1,685	78	5,771	245	1.09	0.85–1.40
Jick et al., 1981	6,837	2,255	24	4,582	56	0.87	0.54–1.40
General Practitioner Research Group 1963	661	72	2	589	18	0.91	0.22–3.84
Newman and Correy, 1977	7,933	1,192	6	6,741	70	0.48	0.21–1.11
Smithels and Sheppard, 1978	3,426	1,173	28	1,713	31	0.89	0.54–1.51
Bunde and Bowles, 1963	4,436	2,218	11	2,218	21	0.52	0.25–1.08
Shiono and Klebanoff, 1989	31,564	2,720	51	28,793	520	1.00	0.8–1.40
Summary						0.95	0.62–1.45

Adapted from Einarson et al., 1988
A second meta-analysis was performed by McKeigue et al., 1994, with similar results.
T.R. Emerson, J.S. Leeder, and C. Koren. A method of meta-analysis of epidemiologic sudies. 22 Drug Intell. Chr. Pharmacol. 813–24 (1988).

Table 2
Bendectin case control studies.

Reference	Malformations	Odds ratio	Confidence limits	Significance
Greenberg et al., 1977[a]		0.84	0.62–1.17	–
Rothman et al., 1979[a]	Congenital heart disease	1.80	1.20–2.70	+
Zierler and Rothman, 1985[a]	Congenital heart disease	1.09	0.76–1.55	–
Golding et al., 1983[a]	Cleft lip and palate	2.88	1.19–6.96	+
Eskenazi and Braken, 1982[a]	Pyloric stenosis	4.33	1.75–10.75	+
Mitchell et al., 1981	Oral clefts cleft palate	0.90	0.50–1.50	–
	cleft lip and palate	0.60	0.40–0.80	–
		0.64	0.12–3.34	Oxford results
Elbourne et al., 1985	Oral clefts	0.37	0.09–1.44	Aberdeen results
				–
Mitchell et al., 1983	Pyloric stenosis	0.90	0.60–1.20	–
McCredie et al., 1984	Limb reduction defects	1.10	0.80–1.50	First trimester
		1.00	0.70–1.40	–
Cordero et al., 1981	Limb reduction defects	1.18	0.65–2.13	–
David, 1982	Poland anomaly			–
Bracken and Berg, 1983	Diaphragmatic hernia	1.60	0.30–8.70	–
Mitchell and Shapiro, 1983	Diaphragmatic hernia			–
Cordero et al., 1981	Diaphragmatic hernia	1.74	0.81–3.76	–

a. The first five case control studies were the only studies utilized in the meta analysis performed by Einarson et al. in 1988. The notation (positive + or negative –) in the last column indicates whether the authors concluded that their results were statistically significant. Robert L. Brent, Bendectin: Review of the medical literature of a comprehensively studied human nonteratogen and the most prevalent tortogen-litigen, Reproductive Toxicology 9 (1995): 337–349.

conclusion that Bendectin was linked with birth defects—despite conclusions to the contrary by the authors of those same studies and by the FDA. (Box 1.5 includes excerpts from Dr. Swan's *Daubert* affidavit. We discuss her testimony in detail in subsequent chapters.) A second key witness for Bendectin plaintiffs was Alan Done (box 1.6).

Until 1975, most federal courts would have had little trouble excluding Swan's testimony on the basis of the "*Frye* rule," which was grounded in the 1923 circuit court decision *Frye v. United States*. Until that time, expert testimony was admissible only when "the thing from which the deduction is made" had been "sufficiently established to have gained general acceptance in the particular field in which it belongs."[23] Swan's plainly had not. The Ninth Circuit Court of Appeals excluded it on that basis in the *Daubert* litigation, before the Supreme Court agreed to review the case.

The *Frye* rule came under attack in the 1960s and the 1970s, however. Some critics viewed it as delegating legal decisions to scientists. *Frye*, they argued, imposed an unfair burden on plaintiffs. "General acceptance," other critics argued, had substituted for real analysis of the reliability and validity of proffered testimony.

The Federal Rules of Evidence, codified in 1975, are the rules of evidence that federal judges apply today. Many, though not all, state courts revised their rules along similar lines. Three federal rules bear directly upon scientific evidence in court:

Rule 403 permits the exclusion of otherwise relevant evidence if its probative value is substantially outweighed by dangers of prejudice, confusion, misleading the jury, or wasting time.

Rule 702 states that trial testimony is admissible from any qualified scientific expert who possesses "scientific, technical, or other specialized knowledge [that] will assist the trier of fact [the jury] to understand the evidence or to determine a fact in issue."

Rule 703 provides that experts may base their opinions on data that might not be admissible as evidence, if those data are "reasonably relied upon by experts in the particular field in forming opinions or inferences upon the subject." This rule allows a scientific expert to rely on "hearsay evidence," which is not admitted when offered by ordinary witnesses.

For a time, some federal judges interpreted the 1975 rules as allowing almost any testimony said to be "scientific" to be presented to a jury. Criticism mounted. Some critics argued that courts were issuing decisions

Box 1.5
Affidavit of Shanna Helen Swan

submitted as part of Joint Appendix at 113, *Daubert v. Merrell Dow Pharmaceuticals, Inc.*, No. 92-102 (U.S. Dec. 2, 1992)

One would not rely solely on epidemiological studies that failed to show a statistical association at the 95% confidence level between a substance and a defect to determine that the substance does not cause the defect.

In order to understand epidemiology studies one must understand that the results can be positive, negative, or inconclusive. An inconclusive study is one that does reach traditional levels of statistical significance but does not have the statistical power to rule out appreciable relative risks. . . . In analyzing the validity of an epidemiological study one must analyze not only the chance of the error of a false positive . . . but also the "power" of the study, the chance of detecting an association if it exists. A confidence interval indicates that the true association level is somewhere in the range between the lower limit an[d] the higher limit of probability. The less sure one wants to be about the finding, the narrower is this range. . . . It is erroneous to conclude that merely because a confidence interval includes the number 1.0 that one can conclude from such data that there is no statistical association or no causation. . . .

. . . [I]n reviewing the various epidemiological studies on Bendectin, the most powerful study . . . only has approximately a 17.6% chance of finding a doubling of the rate of defects. The other studies are even less apt to find even a doubling. Even if one were to put all the studies together that involve the limbs, there would still be less than a 50% chance of finding a doubling of increased limb defects and only a minuscule chance of finding 50% increase or a 20% increase. In analyzing the various epidemiology studies, one quickly can see that the studies either have insufficient numbers, inappropriate control groups, inappropriate pooling of malformations, misclassification of exposure, or confounders. . . .

Having reviewed the epidemiological studies including, but not limited to Heinonen, Jick, Aselton, Morelock, Cordero, Eskenazi, McCredie . . . it is my opinion that one cannot conclude that there is in fact no statistical association between Bendectin an[d] limb reduction defects. More specifically one cannot draw a conclusion from those studies that Bendectin does not cause limb reduction defects.

Because limb defects are a rare occurrence, occurring less than one per one thousand live births, many thousands of births would be necessary in a controlled study to reveal even a 100% increase. The chances of finding a smaller increase such as a 10% or 20% would therefore be minuscule. That is one reason why an epidemiologist would not rely only on epidemiology studies in the face of other scientific data to suggest that a drug, such as Bendectin, does not cause birth defects. On the contrary, the prudent epidemiologist would he concerned about the public safety and when there is

> data consistent with increased risks, as with Bendectin, conclude that it is more probable than not that Bendectin is associated with birth defects.
>
> Rather, considering the foregoing studies, within a reasonable degree of certainty, based upon my education, training and experience, it is my opinion that considering all available data . . . that it is more likely than not that Bendectin is, in fact, associated with limb reduction defects. . . .
>
> . . . [S]o there be no question, it is my opinion within a reasonable degree of certainty, based on all of the available data, the Bendectin is associated with birth defects, including limb defects.

based on pseudo-scientific testimony that had little basis in reality.[24] Some courts gradually moved back toward stricter scrutiny of scientific evidence.[25]

At issue in *Daubert* was whether the *Frye* standard had survived the 1975 codification of the Federal Rules of Evidence. The Supreme Court carefully confined its discussion to scientific evidence of the kind presented in the *Daubert* litigation. Rule 702 makes reference to both "scientific" and other "technical or specialized" knowledge. The latter category of evidence, which might be presented by a physician diagnosing a specific patient or an engineer analyzing the collapse of a bridge, is subject to *Daubert* only insofar as it implicitly or explicitly relies on more general scientific principles.[26]

In *Daubert*, all nine Justices agreed that, insofar as "scientific knowledge" is concerned, *Frye* had been superseded by the new rules of evidence. But that narrow conclusion did not define what "scientific knowledge" means, and it certainly did not determine whether "scientific knowledge" and "general acceptance" mean much the same thing or two very different things. Indeed, the Justices split seven to two on how to interpret the new "scientific knowledge" standard.

This important threshold ruling in the *Daubert* opinion is easily overlooked or misunderstood. The first question before the Supreme Court—a strictly legal question—was whether the drafters of the 1975 Federal Rules of Evidence had intended to incorporate *Frye* explicitly into the new rules. The Court concluded they hadn't. A new phrase—"scientific knowledge"—had replaced "general acceptance." By analogy, the Supreme Court might conclude that the Securities Act of 1934 did not expressly incorporate prior common-law rules that prohibited the issuance of watered stock. This would not mean that the 1934 act therefore permitted stock-watering

Box 1.6
Affidavit of Alan K. Done

source: *DeLuca v. Merrell Dow Pharmaceuticals, Inc.*, Dkt. No. 870226(GEB) (D.N.J. Mar. 25, 1991)

It is my professional opinion, to a reasonable degree of medical and scientific certainty, that the congenital limb defect suffered by Amy Deluca was directly and proximately caused by ingestion of Bendectin by her mother, Cindy Deluca, early in the pregnancy from which this child issued. The factual bases for this opinion include my knowledge of the properties of Bendectin, the compatability of the timing of Bendectin exposure in this case with the particular defect, the fact that the defect is of the type for which there is substantial evidence of Bendectin causation, the absence of another more likely cause in this case, evidence of teratogenicity of Bendectin from animal teratogenicity and in-vitro mechanistic studies, and the ample evidence of human teratogenicity of Bendectin from the epidemiologic studies analyzed [in this case]. . . .

Acceptability of the methodology employed in reaching the opinions expressed above and summarized [in this case] is evident from the fact that it employs only analytic methods that are universally used and accepted by epidemiologists and statisticians. Contrary claims not withstanding, I did not utilize a unique or unusual methodology, but merely analyzed the data in a standardized manner, employing the same methods used by most of the authors of the published studies. This permitted a better evaluation of the magnitude of the association between Bendectin exposure and the occurrence of birth defects and the reasons why such association is not uniform among the studies. No one study can ever be the basis for a conclusion that a statistical association is tantamount to causation. Proof of causation can never come from epidemiologic studies, even with extensive replication. Whether an observed association means probable causation depends on the strength of the association (in this instance, increased risk), the regularity with which it is found, the biologic feasibility of causation, and an increased risk with higher dose. Assessment of the first two elements has been obscured somewhat relative to Bendectin and birth defects causation because numerous inconclusive studies (as opposed to negative) studies have been allowed by some others to weigh improperly against more powerful studies. The analysis presented . . . indicates that the considerable positive data are not refuted, but merely clouded by inconclusive other data.

frauds that were previously proscribed by other statutes or by the principles of common law; it would simply mean that after 1934 any such prohibitions would have to be found in the language of the new act rather than in the case law that it superseded.

The bulk of the *Daubert* opinion attempted to flesh out what "scientific knowledge" means under the Federal Rules of Evidence. The seven-Justice majority affirmed that under the 1975 rules federal trial judges have an important and continuing role as "gatekeepers"—a responsibility to screen testimony proffered as "scientific" rather than admit it uncritically for consideration by the jury.[27] The *Daubert* majority stated that legal "reliability" depends on the scientific "reliability" of the proffered testimony.[28] There must be a logically relevant connection between the expert's reasoning and the facts at issue in a case, the reasoning must be sound, and the scientific methodology must be reliable: "Proposed testimony must be supported by appropriate validation—i.e., 'good grounds,' based on what is known. . . . In a case involving scientific evidence, evidentiary reliability will be based upon scientific validity."[29]

The Supreme Court wrote at some length about the factors that judges should consider in their Rule 702 analyses. The *Daubert* opinion directs trial judges to determine whether a theory or a technique can be (or has been) tested, and whether it is falsifiable.[30] Peer review is to be weighed as an important, though not dispositive, factor.[31] Trial judges are to consider the "known or potential rate of error" of a scientific technique and the "existence and maintenance of standards controlling the technique's operation."[32] "General acceptance" within a scientific community is another important factor bearing on admissibility.[33] The Court noted that "the inquiry is a flexible one" and that "the focus, of course, must be solely on principles and methodology, not on the conclusions that they generate."[34]

Summing up its views in a short, concluding section, the Court wrote: "Vigorous cross-examination, presentation of contrary evidence, and careful instruction on the burden of proof are the traditional and appropriate means of attacking shaky but admissible evidence. . . . These conventional devices, rather than wholesale exclusion under an uncompromising 'general acceptance' test, are the appropriate safeguards where the basis of scientific testimony meets the standards of Rule 702."[35] This language is usually cited by those favoring looser standards of admissibility.[36] But the quoted sentence only reiterates that *Frye*'s focus on "general acceptance" is now replaced with *Daubert*'s focus on "reliable" and "valid" "scientific knowledge"—the standards of Rule 702. Standing alone, this single sentence from the Court's opinion simply begs the central question: How does a judge determine that scientific evidence is based on "the standards of Rule 702"? How different is that inquiry, in practice, from *Frye*'s?

All we know for sure is that the Court replaced a comparatively simple (arguably simplistic) test of *Frye* with a more nuanced and complex discussion. The relevant criteria enumerated by the *Daubert* Court center on the "reliability" and "validity" of proffered testimony. But the meaning of "validity" when used in connection with a general scientific proposition has a range of meanings among scientists, and scientists often have difficulty coming to agreement about the validity of particular theories. What validity may mean when used in reference to any one scientific paper or study can be still more difficult to answer. How are judges to decide on "scientific validity" when scientists and philosophers cannot agree on what those words mean, or when they apply, or how they might be applied to particular studies?

Rules of Evidence in Science and Law

The use of science in the courtroom raises two issues that seem different but are in fact related at a deeper level: scientific uncertainty and the misuse of science.

The first issue arises because science often cannot provide clear-cut answers to questions that have grave implications in the courts or in other branches of government. Risk assessment (the identification and quantification of risks to human health) is notoriously imprecise. The data are invariably mixed; they can be interpreted to support a range of positions by the various stakeholders. Making informed decisions about risk requires the interpretation of less-than-perfect epidemiological studies, high-dose animal studies of doubtful relevance to low-dose human exposures, or other evidence. Science can identify unequivocally the causes of relatively few diseases. On the whole, science has been abysmally unsuccessful in identifying the causes of specific birth defects, cancers, and other chronic diseases that are frequently the focuses of tort litigation. Thus, important social issues must often be decided on the basis of uncertain scientific evidence. "Validity" in science is not a binary attribute, like pregnancy. Grossly invalid data or theories can usually be identified for what they are. But often decisions about validity depend on the needs one has for the data. This is not to say that "truth" is relative, as a pernicious kind of postmodernism maintains. Rather, it is to say that science has limited ability to answer questions of great social importance.

The second issue—which one of us has called "junk science"[37]—arises when a witness seeks to present grossly fallacious interpretations of scientific data or opinions that are not supported by scientific evidence. Junk science is a legal problem, not a scientific one. It is cultivated by the adversarial nature of legal proceedings, and it depends on the difficulty many laypeople have in evaluating technical arguments.

In science, the ultimate test of the "validity" of a theory or of some data is time. Science is cumulative and, to a considerable extent, self-correcting. Scientists continually collect new data and propose new theories. Some will withstand the test of time, others will not. Bad science—grossly flawed data or theories—does not make it through peer review. If it does, it gets buried in the scientific literature, uncited and forgotten. Judges, however, cannot use these mechanisms to disapprove of science they do not trust.

Science and the law have completely different goals, and this may be why scientists and lawyers are so often frustrated by each other's undertakings. Science searches for a comprehensive understanding, which develops through a collective process involving many scientists. The procedures and objectives of a legal trial are quite different. A trial seeks to resolve a focused legal dispute in a finite period of time.

Scientists and lawyers differ by training, and often by temperament. Lawyers look for scientists who can firmly and compactly present scientific concepts to a jury of non-scientists, for purposes of advocacy. But a careful scientist will often be uncomfortable with a translation that is simple and blunt enough for the lawyers' purposes.

More important for this book, scientists approach the question of rules of evidence quite differently from lawyers. Scientists weigh evidence without formally distinguishing admissible from inadmissible evidence. That distinction is very important in the law. A legal trial must make a binary and (for the litigants' purposes) utterly final choice between one side and the other. The scientific arena is, in those respects, much less demanding.

The rules of evidence used by judges must be explicit, simple, and peremptory. Scientists can afford to rely on more varied, intuitive, and open-ended criteria.

When presented with evidence that is said to be valid, reliable science, a judge must make an up-or-down call on admissibility: either the evidence will be presented to the jury or it will not. The jury has the separate, more flexible job of "weighing" whatever evidence has been admitted. Decisions on "admissibility" may, and often do, determine the outcome of a trial, but that is beside the point. The decision the judge makes is not, in itself, directed at the parties to litigation. It is directed at discrete packages of testimony and evidence. The issue before a judge is not whether electromagnetic fields caused this plaintiff's cancer (for example), or whether such fields ever cause cancer; the issue for the judge is whether an expert is offering sufficiently reliable, solid, trustworthy evidence that they did and do. This perspective is much more familiar to lawyers than to scientists. Scientists do not have to make two-tiered calls at the threshold before digging deeper into the evidence and forming their conclusions about scientific issues.

Nor do scientists have to spend much time worrying about whether even to listen to other scientists. Most scientific journals screen what they publish, but any scientist can attend a symposium and buttonhole other scientists. The scientific community is strongly inclined toward letting new ideas be presented and debated. The legal presumption is against admitting expert testimony: a litigant may not simply walk an expert into court and put him on the stand without more ado. The burden is on the party offering expert testimony to first establish that it meets legal criteria of admissibility—criteria such as "reliability" and "validity," which are discussed in this book. This is a positive responsibility for the party presenting the testimony; the party opposing it need not do anything at all. The court must be satisfied that the testimony passes muster as "scientific knowledge." If the court simply has no idea whether it does, the testimony stays out.

Equally unfamiliar to many scientists is the idea that labeling evidence inadmissible is not the same as labeling it false. Judges applying the rules of evidence are not passing judgment on the ultimate truth of specific scientific propositions. They are ruling on whether a particular proposition, presented by a particular witness, is sufficiently reliable and well grounded to be admissible in this trial, at this point in time. Ordinary (nonscientist) witnesses are likewise forbidden to present "hearsay" testimony. The hearsay rules of evidence are not based on the plainly incorrect presumption that all gossip is always false. Gossip is often true. But judges concluded long ago that gossip, though sometimes true, isn't reliable enough to be presented to a jury in court. Scientific conjectures or speculations may turn out to be true too, but there is still good reason to exclude evidence of this character.

"Scientific Validity"

The problem of distinguishing science from nonscience has been explored in depth by scientists, philosophers, and sociologists.[38] In *Daubert* the Supreme Court referred to three different domains of human thought: the philosophy of science, the sociology of science, and science itself.

The first of these domains, the philosophy of science, emerged as a recognizable specialty late in the nineteenth century but has roots in several major and much older philosophical traditions. It was in this context that the *Daubert* Court cited Popper and Hempel.[39]

The second domain, science and technology studies, brings together a much more disparate group of scholars from disciplines such as psychology, sociology, history, and philosophy. They explore how social forces influence the development of science and how scientists make decisions, exercise judgment, and make mistakes. From this field, the *Daubert* Court cited the physicist John Ziman and the lawyer-sociologist Sheila Jasanoff.[40]

The third domain cited by the Court is science itself. The Court referred to this body of knowledge as separate from the first two. The Court used terms like "scientific validity" and "scientific reliability," and suggested that these are separate criteria that trial judges must weigh independently.

Science offers its own perspectives on these subjects. Popper's "critical rationalism" emphasizes the "falsifiability" of scientific theories. According to Popper, scientific propositions must be framed in ways that make possible contradiction, if they are false; scientific theories gain authority by withstanding the criticism of other scientists. This discourse is one that scientists themselves participate in. A separate, independent perspective on science, developed by cognitive psychologists (notably Amos Tversky and Daniel Kahneman), elucidates how people make accurate (or inaccurate) decisions under conditions of uncertainty. The Bayesian statistics behind these theories (which we discuss in detail in chapter 8) may seem esoteric to a lay reader, but they are certainly no more so than the writings of Hempel and Popper; and all these theories have been enormously influential.

Thinking and Deciding

The book is not a legal treatise; we do not dwell on the large law-review literature that addresses *Frye* or on the technical legal issues related to admissibility of specific types of scientific evidence.[41] Nor is this a philosophical treatise; we do not spend much time on Popper's technical philosophy (on falsification as a demarcation criterion of science) or on Thomas Kuhn's (on the scientific community). This book is, instead, an extended commentary on "scientific validity" and the law's rules of evidence. We attempt to explain the significance of the *Daubert* criteria in lay terms, providing key references to philosophical, scientific, and other sources and focusing on sources accessible to lay readers.

Our purpose is to explore a concrete, practical question: When should evidence that is framed as scientific be considered reliable enough to be presented to a jury? The second question we address is much broader: What is necessary or sufficient to establish "scientific validity" for more general purposes in scientific, regulatory, and other communities that use scientific evidence to make legal, social, and political decisions?

We discuss the *Daubert* criteria and how issues of scientific validity play out in the scientific and legal arenas. We also include brief selections from papers, most of them written by prominent scientists and philosophers, that bear on the issues of scientific validity and inference. These papers were not written as prescriptions for judges or lawyers; they are discussions from outside the legal community that bear on the terms, ideas, and standards alluded to in *Daubert*.

Judges plainly cannot surrender to scientists their responsibilities as gatekeepers of evidence, nor can they insist on impossibly high standards of scientific rigor. The general criteria outlined in *Daubert* are, however, similar to those that scientists use to evaluate scientific evidence. They are also similar to the criteria that any intelligent layperson would use to evaluate empirical claims about the world.

To illustrate the issues, we include excerpts of testimony proffered in *Daubert v. Merrell Dow Pharmaceuticals*[42] and other Bendectin cases. We also include a brief summary of some of the major scientific developments relative to the reproductive toxicity of Bendectin. We do not intend to re-argue *Daubert* or to offer unsolicited advice to the judges, lawyers, and juries who are still working on Bendectin cases. We use Bendectin simply to supply a concrete example of the much larger issues at stake in *Daubert*, and of the still larger issues at stake in every debate about scientific knowledge.

This book is organized around the criteria set out in *Daubert*. In chapter 2 we consider the issue of "fit"—whether a plausible theory relates specific facts to the larger factual issues in contention. In chapter 3 we discuss some of the philosophical questions that the Supreme Court raised in *Daubert*, particularly the concept of "falsification" of scientific claims. In chapter 4 we discuss the (sometimes spectacular) errors that scientists can make. Chapter 5 considers the issue of "reliability" in science and address what makes evidence reliable or unreliable in fields such as epidemiology and toxicology. In chapter 6 we explore the meaning of "scientific validity." In chapter 7 we address peer review and the problem of setting boundaries. In chapter 8 we consider a group of problems that bear on the hazards of confusion and prejudice in presenting science to a jury. In the concluding chapter we attempt to reconcile the law's need for workable rules of evidence with the views of scientific validity and reliability that emerge from scientific and other disciplines.

But we leave prescription to the last. As the psychologist Jonathan Baron points out in his book *Thinking and Deciding*, descriptive theory tells us how people "do" think when making decisions in the face of uncertainty.[43] Prescriptive theory tells us how they "should" think. Normative theory tries to identify rules of good thinking, to meet the needs of the thinker. Most of this book addresses the "do"—the ways that scientists go about their business, the ways in which they do or do not converge on answers, the ways in which they make mistakes, correct them, and pursue "reliability," "validity," and the scientific conception of "truth."

The goal of science is epistemic—to achieve "cosmic understanding," as the *Daubert* majority put it.[44] The goal of the judicial process is "the particularized resolution of legal disputes."[45] The task of a judge faced with questionable scientific testimony has little to do with questions of cosmic truth; the task is to apply the Federal Rules of Evidence evenhandedly, in a way that is faithful to the language of the rules and that makes sense in the very practical context of passing specific judgment on a specific claim. But these rules, as interpreted in *Daubert*, involve criteria that must derive, somehow, from science itself.

Judges can—and will—take their best shot at an answer. That best shot will get better as lawyers and judges gain a better understanding of how science works. An old formula holds that science is close reasoning pushed up against close observation. At that level, science is not so different from the law after all.[46]

2

Fit

Rule 702 . . . requires that the evidence or testimony "assist the trier of fact to understand the evidence or to determine a fact in issue." . . . The consideration has been aptly described . . . as one of "fit."

—*Daubert v. Merrell Dow Pharmaceuticals, Inc.*, 509 U.S. 579, 591 (1993)

The Supreme Court of the United States rarely alludes to astrology. Yet Justice Blackmun's majority opinion in *Daubert* does so at the very outset: ". . . evidence that the moon was full on a certain night will not assist the trier of fact in determining whether an individual was unusually likely to have behaved irrationally on that night."[1] On the other hand, "[t]he study of the phases of the moon . . . may provide valid scientific 'knowledge' about whether a certain night was dark. . . ."[2] The *Daubert* majority opinion repeats the point several times. Rule 702 requires that expert testimony "assist the trier of fact . . . to determine a fact in issue."[3] This requirement, according to *Daubert*, "requires a valid scientific connection to the pertinent inquiry as a precondition to admissibility."[4] Expert testimony must be "'sufficiently tied to the facts of the case that it will aid the jury in resolving a factual dispute.'"[5] The question is whether "reasoning or methodology properly can be applied to the facts in issue."[6] The issue is "fit."[7]

In law and science alike, fit is a matter of relevance—the extent to which an observation can be related, by a credible theory, to the issue at hand. A scientific fact may be reliable and accurate ("the moon was full"), but inferences made from it may be confusing or seriously misleading. Presented out of context or viewed from the wrong perspective, true facts may imply false conclusions. The moon may indeed have been full; however, when that fact is packaged into a story about astrological influences on human behavior, the true fact is being used to buttress or imply a false conclusion. The history of science records many instances of precise and accurate measurements' being piled up around false conclusions. In the nineteenth century, for example, conclusions about relative intelligence were backed up by painstaking comparisons of the skull volumes of people of different races.[8]

Fit clearly depends on the whole bundle—the observation together with the theory. Facts acquire meaning from the context of the theory (express or implied) in which they are presented, and in turn they determine what conclusions might be drawn from a theory.

Fit and Social Objectives

The presentation and acceptance of scientific facts occurs, first and last, in a social context. In that sense, scientific facts must fit the social objective at hand. This requirement is certainly obvious to lawyers, but it may demand judgments about science that may be unfamiliar to nonscientists.

Consider, for example, the U.S. Food and Drug Administration's approach to fit in connection with the approval of new drugs. Whether a chemical's biological effects are to induce a disease or a cure should make no difference from a purely scientific perspective; the interpretation of the evidence at hand should be much the same. But in practice there is a great difference. The FDA has the responsibility to confirm the efficacy of new drugs before they are put on the market. The agency insists that "efficacy" be demonstrated in terms related to the ultimate well-being of the patient— lower mortality or morbidity, fewer days in the hospital, fewer complications than with competing remedies, and so on. Showing that a drug affects some biochemical parameter in the body (as opposed to improving the clinical outcome of the patient) is usually not enough. The FDA takes the position that such data do not adequately fit the ultimate proposition, which is efficacious treatment of disease. The FDA thus rejects the implicit theory that a seemingly favorable biochemical change will entail an improved clinical outcome.

In May 1987, an FDA panel recommended against approving a New Drug Application for Activase (generically known as tissue plasminogen activator, or t-PA), which the drug's developer, Genentech, claimed would reduce heart damage immediately after a heart attack. Genentech had shown that t-PA dissolved blood clots and had the potential to reduce heart damage, but had not shown that the drug actually prolonged patients' lives. Without having many more details, the FDA approved the drug seven months later.[9] Merck ran into similar difficulties in connection with Lovastatin, a drug that lowers cholesterol, even though most doctors agree that the evidence is overwhelming that lowering cholesterol reduces the risk of heart disease.

As the t-PA example illustrates, regulators often make decisions that incorporate their own conclusions about underlying scientific facts. Sometimes these conclusions are contained in adjudications about a particular product and vendor—for example, an FDA panel independently reviewed the scientific evidence regarding the safety of Bendectin. (Bendectin is still approved for sale.) Sometimes the conclusions are contained in rules of more general applicability, such as the U.S. Occupational Safety and Health Administration's standards for exposure to benzene or cotton dust. But the scientific issues addressed (and perhaps seemingly resolved) in the regulatory arena can be put back into contention in civil or criminal litigation. The question then arises: How should courts handle testimony that attempts to link regulatory conclusions to the scientific controversy?

The answer is subtle. To begin with, common law has traditionally recognized a concept of "negligence per se." There is a strong (close to irrefutable) presumption that driving 60 miles per hour in a 30-mph zone is legally negligent. The speeding driver involved in an accident is not ordinarily permitted to argue that he wasn't really "negligent" because road conditions were very good, or that he was taking special care to offset the hazards inherent in his high speed. The law presumes that "ordinarily prudent" people do not violate established legal and regulatory norms, and the legal test of "negligence" is "ordinary prudence." Causality, however, is a separate and equally necessary element of proof. The negligence of driving 40 in a 30-mph zone doesn't cause one to be struck from the rear by another car that was going 60.

In general, then, proof of compliance with—or violation of—a regulatory standard proves a legal fact, but not a scientific one. Selling a drug banned by the FDA is irresponsible and illegal, but that does not tell us whether the drug causes birth defects or prevents them. OSHA may set exposure standards at levels intended to protect the most sensitive workers (pregnant women, for example), or may set them for purely precautionary reasons, without even being sure that any hazard exists. Another government agency may authorize the sale of alcohol, firearms, or tobacco. Legalizing the sale does not, of course, establish anything about scientific facts related to these products.

Congress does, of course, have the power to legalize the sale of dangerous products and to "preempt" any civil lawsuits that might have the practical effect of driving those same products off the market. Proof of these legal and regulatory facts may be quite appropriate, but only for legal purposes. So far as science itself is concerned, there is never a good fit—there is, indeed, never any fit at all—between social, political, or regulatory pronouncements and the facts at issue. Regulators can't create scientific facts, any more than legislatures can define the correct value of π.[10]

Fit and Scientific Paradigms

The question of fit arises frequently even within the strict confines of the scientific community. Many types of observations and theories bear on the proposition (still disputed by a few) that AIDS is caused by infection with the HIV virus. Virtually all scientists believe that the evidence overwhelmingly supports that conclusion, but there will always remain observations and theories that point in some other direction.

In *The Structure of Scientific Revolutions*, Thomas Kuhn points out that most scientists, most of the time, work within a generally accepted framework of theory and practice, which he calls a "paradigm."[11] This framework determines how a scientist will identify problems, and organize and interpret data. The paradigm determines what fits. That the phase of the moon determines human behavior and that brain size determines intelligence are long-dead paradigms.

Sometimes new paradigms arise that bring new connections to prominence. Kuhn calls these paradigm shifts "scientific revolutions." An example is the advent of the germ theory of disease, which highlighted the connection between the sanitary status of operating rooms and the mortality of patients after surgery.

The choice of scientific paradigm helps to determine how policy makers will judge the fit of an observation. In the eighteenth century, yellow fever was common in American cities. Physicians of the day attributed the disease to the "miasma" (vapors) given off by rotting organic matter and bad water. A devastating epidemic in 1793 impelled the city fathers of Philadelphia to order a general cleanup. They focused their attention on the rotting garbage that filled the city's streets and the Schuylkill and Delaware rivers (which bordered the city at that time). But several observers also noted the unusual numbers of mosquitos in the city. The fit between this observation and the disease came to be appreciated only much later.[12] Fortuitously, the cleanup programs led to the installation of a city water system, which eliminated water catch basins and thus reduced the number of breeding sites for mosquitos—the actual vectors of the disease.

There is thus a close link between fit and underlying theory. Most eighteenth-century doctors would have considered it obvious that unsanitary conditions were linked to the disease. To them, the link with mosquitos was speculative and unconvincing. Now that we have grasped a better theory for the cause of yellow fever, we no longer accept any direct, cause-and-effect connection between rotting refuse and yellow fever. In contrast, the causes of birth defects, spontaneous abortion, and chronic diseases such as cancer remain poorly understood, and the question of fit between exposure to environmental pollutants and such outcomes remains much more problematic.

Kuhn is occasionally cited by lawyers who argue that strange theories (from the viewpoint of conventional science) are merely new scientific paradigms that cannot be fairly judged by scientists who remain stuck in traditional ways of thinking. But Kuhn also pointed out that most new scientific paradigms fail.

Fit and the Emergence of Scientific Understanding

Scientific revolutions do occur, but most of the time scientific understanding emerges gradually from a collective body of research. Individual reports vary a great deal in quality and reliability. Some reported findings are so strong and convincing that they are accepted very quickly by the scientific community. Epidemiological studies that linked tobacco to lung cancer fall into that category. More commonly, with potential subtle risks, scientists are faced with a mass of data of uncertain reliability. Most connections that are well established today (e.g., that AIDS is caused by exposure to the HIV virus) came to be accepted only gradually, as scientific evidence accumulated. The evidence that underlies many socially charged issues, such as chronic illnesses that may be associated with silicone breast implants or with the "Gulf War Syndrome," remains weak and inconsistent.

With subtle environmental and technological risks, cause and effect are subtle and indirect, and explanatory theories are often speculative. How can one decide, in this context, what evidence fits? How can one assemble many different pieces of scientific evidence into a solved puzzle that presents an acceptably clear and understandable picture? What are the basic rules for arranging different types of evidence on the scientific table?

Various scientists have proposed decision rules for evaluating scientific data about health and disease that both determine the fit of scientific evidence and indicate how it is to be weighed. The bacteriologist Robert Koch proposed a set of postulates to use as a basis for inferring that a microorganism causes a disease; in box 2.1 Alfred Evans describes a modern version of these postulates. Other sets of prescriptive rules address inferences from epidemiologic studies. The most famous were proposed in a celebrated 1965 lecture by the epidemiologist Austin Bradford Hill.[13] (See box 2.2.) Variations on Hill's criteria have been proposed by other investigators, including Mervyn Susser.[14] (See box 2.3.) Koch's postulates became a textbook example of a scientific definition of fit and indeed were very productive. Most scientists would agree that evidence satisfying all Koch's postulates establishes a compelling case that a suspected etiologic agent is the actual cause of a disease, and Hill's criteria have also come to define the "gold standard" of epidemiologic proof. But neither Koch's nor Hill's criteria are necessary or sufficient conditions for inferring causation. They are, instead, very useful rules of thumb for assessing and evaluating the overall strength of a claimed association between exposure and illness. Both sets are demanding: by the time either set is fully satisfied, the cause-and-effect relationship will be a matter of textbook science and little controversy about the issue will remain.

Box 2.1
Causation and Disease: The Henle-Koch Postulates Revisited
Alfred S. Evans
source: *Yale Journal of Biology and Medicine* 49 (1976): 175

Criteria for Causation: A Unified Concept

1. Prevalence of the disease should be significantly higher in those exposed to the putative cause than in cases controls not so exposed.
2. Exposure to the putative cause should be present more commonly in those with the disease than in controls without the disease when all risk factors are held constant.
3. Incidence of the disease should be significantly higher in those exposed to the putative cause than in those not so exposed as shown in prospective studies.
4. Temporally, the disease should follow exposure to the putative agent with a distribution of incubation periods on a bell shaped curve.
5. A spectrum of host responses should follow exposure to the putative agent along a logical biologic gradient from mild to severe.
6. A measurable host response following exposure to the putative cause should regularly appear in those lacking this before exposure (i.e., antibody, cancer cells) or should increase in magnitude if present before exposure; this pattern should not occur in persons so exposed.
7. Experimental reproduction of the disease should occur in higher incidence in animals or man appropriately exposed to the putative cause than in those not so exposed; this exposure may be deliberate in volunteers, experimentally induced in the laboratory, or demonstrated in a controlled regulation of natural exposure.
8. Elimination or modification of the putative cause or of the vector carrying it should decrease the incidence of the disease (control of polluted water or smoke or removal of the specific agent).
9. Prevention or modification of the host's response on exposure to the putative cause should decrease or eliminate the disease (immunization, drug to lower cholesterol, specific lymphocyte transfer factor in cancer).
10. The whole thing should make biologic and epidemiologic sense.

The Henle-Koch postulates are a useful historical reference point but were not regarded as rigid criteria by Koch himself and should not be today. . . . New technology, better understanding of disease agents and of host responses, and the discovery of new "causes" will require changes in existing criteria.

Box 2.2
The Environment and Disease: Association or Causation?
Sir Austin Bradford Hill

source: *Proceedings of the Royal Society of Medicine* 58 (1965): 295–300

How . . . do we detect these relationships between sickness, injury and conditions of work? How do we determine what are physical, chemical and psychological hazards of occupation, and in particular those that are rare and not easily recognized?

Sometimes . . . we may be able to consider what *might* a particular environment do to man, and then see whether such consequences are indeed to be found. But more often than not we have no such guidance, no such means of proceeding. . . . [W]e see that the event B is associated with the environmental feature A, that, to take a specific example, some form of respiratory illness is associated with a dust in the environment. In what circumstances can we pass from this observed *association* to a verdict of *causation*? Upon what basis should we proceed to do so?

Disregarding then any such problem in semantics we have this situation. Our observations reveal an association between two variables, perfectly clear-cut and beyond what we would care to attribute to the play of chance. What aspects of that association should we especially consider before deciding that the most likely interpretation of it is causation?

(1) *Strength*:   . . . In thus putting emphasis upon the strength of an association we must, nevertheless, look at the obverse of the coin. We must not be too ready to dismiss a cause-and-effect hypothesis merely on the grounds that the observed association appears to be slight. . . .

(2) *Consistency*:   . . . Has it been repeatedly observed by different persons, in different places, circumstances and times?

(3) *Specificity*:   . . . If . . . the association is limited to specific workers and to particular sites and types of disease and there is no association between the work and other modes of dying, then clearly that is a strong argument in favour of causation.

(4) *Temporality*:   . . . Does a particular diet lead to disease or do the early stages of the disease lead to those peculiar dietetic habits? . . .

(5) *Biological gradient*:   . . . if the association is one which can reveal a biological gradient, or dose-response curve, then we should look most carefully for such evidence. . . .

(6) *Plausibility*:   It will be helpful if the causation we suspect is biologically plausible. . . .

(7) *Coherence*:   On the other hand the cause-and-effect interpretation of our data should not seriously conflict with the generally known facts of the natural history and biology of the disease. . . .

(8) *Experiment*:   For example, because of an observed association some preventive action is taken. Does it in fact prevent? . . .

(9) *Analogy*:   With the effects of thalidomide and rubella before us we would surely be ready to accept slighter but similar evidence with another drug or another viral disease in pregnancy.

Here then are nine different viewpoints from all of which we should study association before we cry causation. What I do not believe—and this has been suggested—is that we can usefully lay down some hard-and-fast rules of evidence that *must* be obeyed before we accept cause and effect. None of my nine viewpoints can bring indisputable evidence for or against the cause-and-effect hypothesis. . . .

Fit in the Regulatory Arena

The regulatory system has developed its own weight-of-evidence criteria for identifying hazards and quantifying risks. These guidelines, which offer detailed prescriptions for considering diverse kinds of data, bear on fit without explicitly using that term. For example, the U.S. Environmental Protection Agency's guidelines for carcinogen risk assessment[15] list a broad range of studies that the EPA considers pertinent to the identification of human carcinogens (substances that cause cancer). These include studies of physical-chemical properties, routes and patterns of exposure, structure-activity relationships, metabolic and pharmacokinetic properties, and toxicologic effects; short-term tests; long-term animal studies; and human epidemiological studies. The document also outlines an elaborate system for gauging the weight of evidence. The EPA classifies potential human carcinogens on a five-tier scale, not according to how strong a carcinogen a substance is but rather according to the strength of the evidence that a substance is a human carcinogen. The nature of the evidence that warrants classifying a substance in one of these categories is an issue of fit.

More pertinent to Bendectin litigation is the question of reproductive toxicity. Teratogenesis (development of a malformed fetus) is less well understood than carcinogenesis (development of cancer). The EPA's risk-assessment guidelines for teratogens are similar in spirit to its guidelines for carcinogens but less well developed. For example, the guidelines for developmental toxicity[16] list many kinds of studies that the agency considers pertinent to the identification of human teratogens, including laboratory animal studies, human studies (epidemiology), pharmacokinetics, and studies of molecular structure.

Box 2.3
Falsification, Verification, and Causal Inference in Epidemiology:
Reconsiderations in the Light of Sir Karl Popper's Philosophy
Mervyn Susser
source: *Causal Inference*, ed. K. Rothman et al. (Epidemiology Resources, 1988)

To infer that a factor does indeed produce a supposed effect, several criteria need to be deployed. . . . These are strength, consistency specificity, predictive performance and coherence. . . .

. . . The stronger an association, the more it supports a causal inference and is affirmative; the weaker an association, the more it is indeterminate. For a given exposure or outcome, incapacity for precise measurement may erode or render indeterminate a true and even strong association. . . .

. . . [S]pecificity . . . adds plausibility to a causal claim, but if absent does not detract from it. Specificity in the causes of a given effect is persuasive; specificity in the effects of a given cause usually less so. . . . Causal and outcome variables well-specified in terms of definition and measurement are essential to achieving both specificity and strength of association, and greater specificity will enhance strength. But specificity of the cause of a given outcome may be persuasive even in the presence of a weak association. . . .

. . . [I]n the case of a persisting null result, one can agree with Popper that consistency demands rejection of a hypothesis. . . . Yet to "prove" a negative is difficult because alternative qualifying hypotheses are so readily to hand; these render the criterion somewhat less decisive in falsification. In the case of a persisting positive result, . . . , [i]n my view, consistency is the most powerful verification available.

Predictive performance . . . requires that a hypothesis drawn from an observed association predicts a previously unknown fact or consequence, and must in turn be shown to lead to that consequence. . . .

When [predictive performance] clearly produces new knowledge, the *a priori* character of the prediction is strongly affirmative, the more so in that it provides little opportunity for post hoc reasoning and avoids many biases that lurk in situations of which the scientist has foreknowledge. . . . [I]n my view a failed prediction often leaves as much room for alternative explanations as a successful one, and therefore may carry no more force in falsifying a causal hypothesis than a success does in affirming one. To determine the success or failure of the prediction, however, all the criteria relevant to judging any association must be applied to the new association.

The criterion of coherence . . . requires that an association, to be used as an explanation, coheres with preconceptions about the outcome and about the suspect causal factor. . . .

. . . Coherence governs the overall plausibility of findings and ultimately enhances or destroys pre-existing theories. For a given result, coherence usually does no more than afford a modest affirmation of a hypothesis. A strong dose-response relation between causal factor and outcome, however, carries somewhat more affirmative weight than other dimensions of coherence. Incoherence shifts the balance towards rejection. One may also place weight on incoherence as an indicator of falsity where there is clear factual incompatibility between the findings of a study and pre-existing knowledge. Coherence counts most in the overall summing up of a multitude of data.

Conclusiveness in inferring causality—in epidemiology as with all studies in free-living human beings—is a desire more often than an accomplishment. . . . When it comes to negotiating the narrows and rapids of research, however, the formalities of philosophy need to be tempered by epidemiologic sense.

A later draft report from the EPA proposed a two-tier classification scheme for reproductive hazards.[17] One category consists of substances for which "sufficient evidence" (from animal or epidemiologic studies) exists for "the scientific community to judge that a causal relationship is or is not supported." Another category includes "situations for which there is less than the minimum sufficient evidence necessary for assessing the potential for reproductive toxicity. . . ." This level of complexity may be bureaucratic excess; however, in the absence of any clear understanding about the cause of cancer or reproductive toxicity, such weight-of-evidence schemes are about the best that can be done.

The EPA risk-assessment guidelines, together with Koch's postulates and Hill's criteria, offer only general guidelines for weighing evidence. Moreover, the EPA guidelines stress the importance of tacit criteria such as "biological consistency" and use of "good scientific judgment," rather than well-developed theories linking the observations and health outcomes. Thus, scientists have to form their judgments by weighing a mass of data, no single piece of which is likely to be dispositive. As one standard textbook explains, "epidemiologic and other evidence can accumulate to the point where a causal hypothesis becomes highly probable," but it is not possible to quantify "the degree of probability achieved by all the evidence for a specific hypothesis"; "an element of subjectivity remains."[18]

This "element of subjectivity" is, inevitably, a source of controversy. There is usually a spectrum of informed scientific opinion about matters related to health and disease, with a few individuals at either extreme end of the spectrum.

The EPA uses several different methods to deal with conflicting opinions of experts that implicitly lead to different ways of weighing discordant (nonfitting) bits of evidence. In some cases the agency dictates that "best scientific judgment" be used to assess an overall risk; then the "burden of proof for departure from previous approaches or interpretations should be low, therefore recognizing the range of valid scientific opinions on a particular topic."[19] This approach explicitly recognizes the different assessments of "fit" of discordant data by different scientists.

Alternatively, the EPA may demand an approach based on the consensus of scientific opinion, in which "discretion will be generally considered to be low and the burden of proof for departure from the stated preferences will be high, requiring new scientific data or novel approaches to analysis which gain strong peer support towards their adoption."[20] In this regulatory context, fit is determined by bureaucratic precedent.

Weight of Evidence and Rules of Evidence

Regulators setting policies for pollution or food safety clearly take a broader, more inclusive approach to evidence than scientists who are trying to establish definitive theories about the causes of disease. The "pure" scientist typically demands a high level of proof—that Koch's postulates are fulfilled, for example. To regulators, different standards of proof may suffice, depending on the social or political needs at hand.

How then should judges decide what kinds of evidence fit properly into which kinds of claims and cases? When it comes to scientific evidence in litigation, the legal process requires two stages of analysis. A trial judge must decide on the threshold "admissibility" of expert testimony; then the jury (or, in a nonjury trial, the judge, wearing a fact finder's hat) rules on "the weight of the evidence." But *Daubert* ties the threshold inquiry to such things as "fit," "falsifiability," "validity," and "reliability." For scientists, such terms acquire their meanings in the context of an overall body of scientific knowledge. In court, the overall body of evidence—or at least its formal presentation to the jury—comes in only after the judge has made a first-round ruling as to what will come in and what will not.

Daubert thus seems to require trial judges to survey the entire symphony of evidence before deciding which particular notes or movements will be kept in or left out. A rough parallel might be linking the admissibility of a confession to the ultimate innocence or guilt of a criminal defendant. To nonlawyers this may seem hopelessly circular, but only because they forget that legal fact finding relies on a two-stage, two-player decisional process in which the judge rules on evidentiary admissibility while the jury rules on evidentiary weight.

A paper published in response to *Daubert* by the toxicologist Joseph Rodricks falls squarely into this trap.[21] Rodricks largely ignores the text of *Daubert*. He describes instead the factors a toxicologist looks to in assessing causality. According to Rodricks, a toxicologist attempting to determine whether injury or disease was caused by exposure to a particular hazardous substance would ask three questions: (1) Can a particular chemical under any conditions cause a particular kind of harm? (2) Were the plaintiffs sufficiently exposed to the chemical to be harmed in that way? (3) Are other known alternative possible causes of the harm more likely to have caused it in this instance? Different experts may interpret scientific evidence quite differently, even while all of them reason and make inferences in ways broadly consistent with established principles of toxicology. According to Rodricks, "the real difficulty" for courts and for scientists lies in "characterizing the degree of validity associated with particular scientific hypotheses."

That may well be the only "real difficulty" for scientists, but it isn't the only one for courts. Rodricks is simply conflating two procedures that, in court, are quite distinct. The first decides what evidence is "admissible"; the second gauges "weight." The two inquiries may be linked, and indeed *Daubert*'s references to "fit" suggest that they are. But to suggest that the two inquiries cannot be separated at all is to declare that either the judge (in ruling on "admissibility") or the jury (in assessing "weight") should decide the entire scientific case. That may well be how toxicologists would proceed, but the rules of evidence as fleshed in *Daubert* clearly require something different.

Checklists prepared by research scientists—the Henle-Koch/Evans postulates, or Hill's criteria, or Rodricks's template—obviously do not address legal "admissibility" at all; they address the overall coherence and weight of the evidence from the scientist's perspective. In the legal context, however, a *Daubert* ruling on admissibility must be conducted first; it determines whether a full trial to assess the "weight of the evidence" proffered by different experts will occur at all. Scientists have no need to distinguish between "weight of evidence," on the one hand, and "validity" or "reliability," on the other; pressed to interpret such terms, most scientists would probably answer that they mean pretty much the same thing. In court they don't.

As *Daubert* made clear, a judge ruling on admissibility must consider how each expert's testimony fits into the larger context of the scientific case. Scientific testimony should be fitted, by the party that offers it, into a larger, coherent framework. Testimony that the moon was full is admissible when it bears on the quality of the light at the scene of the crime, and when the rest of the account presented makes the lighting conditions relevant. The same testimony is not relevant, and not admissible, if the witness who claims to have watched the murder had two glass eyes. The scientific fact that glass eyes cannot see renders irrelevant—and therefore inadmissible—scientific testimony about the quality of the light.

The need for fit boils down to the need to place bits and pieces of evidence in the larger context of what is known. Some inconsistency must be tolerated, in light of the lack of perfect theories and the impossibility of perfect knowledge. But discrete assertions of fact or theory that clash too sharply with the totality of the scientific evidence at hand should be excluded, particularly if the expert does not carefully reconcile the discordant evidence with other established knowledge.[22] The connection between the adequacy of a theory and the fit of data may become murky in borderline cases, but many cases are not borderline at all.

And, of course, assertions are sometimes framed in language so loose and indeterminate that they can never be said to fit properly into an exposition of "scientific knowledge." We turn to that issue in the next chapter.

3

Testability and Falsification

Ordinarily, a key question to be answered in determining whether a theory or technique is scientific knowledge that will assist the trier of fact will be whether it can be (and has been) tested. "Scientific methodology today is based on generating hypotheses and testing them to see if they can be falsified; indeed, this methodology is what distinguishes science from other fields of human inquiry." Green, at 645. See also C. Hempel, *Philosophy of Natural Science* 49 (1966) ("[T]he statements constituting a scientific explanation must be capable of empirical test"); K. Popper, *Conjectures and Refutations: The Growth of Scientific Knowledge* 37 (5th ed. 1989) ("[T]he criterion of the scientific status of a theory is its falsifiability, or refutability, or testability") (emphasis deleted).
—*Daubert v. Merrell Dow Pharmaceuticals, Inc.*, 509 U.S. 579, 593 (1993)

The majority opinion in *Daubert* begins with a refractory problem that has occupied the attention of philosophers of science and other scholars for many years: What is a "scientific" proposition? Philosophers and scholars have yet to agree on the answer, and undoubtedly never will. But it is clearly a threshold issue of major importance for the courts. Before judges can consider whether a scientific proposition is "valid" or "reliable," they must determine whether it is even presented in a form that scientists can address.

On this point, the *Daubert* opinion refers only briefly to other authorities. Citing a law-review article by Michael Green,[1] the Court states: "Scientific methodology today is based on generating hypotheses and testing them to see if they can be falsified; indeed, this methodology is what distinguishes science from other fields of human inquiry."[2] The Court follows with a quote from the philosopher Carl Hempel: "[T]he statements constituting a scientific explanation must be capable of empirical test."[3] And then a quote from Karl Popper: "[T]he criterion of the scientific status of a theory is its falsifiability, or refutability, or testability."[4]

Chief Justice Rehnquist (joined by Justice Stevens) reacted tartly to the Popper quote: "I defer to no one in my confidence in federal judges; but I am at a loss to know what is meant when it is said that the scientific status of a theory depends on its 'falsifiability,' and I suspect some of them will be, too."[5]

The Chief Justice did not, apparently, find the help in Green's article, which the majority cited. Green elaborates as follows:

Because of scientists' inductive methods (generalizing or making predictions from empirical observation), David Hume argued that a scientific hypothesis, such as causation, never could be proved conclusively true because there is always the possibility that the observations relied upon were coincidental rather than causal. Hume criticized the inductive, rather than deductive, methodology. From that criticism emerged the idea that while induction never could conclusively prove a proposition, it could falsify one. Thus, based on the framework provided by Karl Popper, knowledge is gained by attempting to disprove or falsify a hypothesis based on empirical investigation. Scientific methodology today is based on generating hypotheses and testing them to see if they can be falsified; indeed, this methodology is what distinguishes science from other fields of human inquiry.[6]

In this view of science, hypotheses are never affirmatively proved, they are only falsified. But a hypothesis that repeatedly withstands attempts to falsify it will become accepted by the scientific community, even if conditionally, as true.

Popper and Falsification

Karl Popper, the man largely responsible for this line of thinking, was one of the preeminent philosophers of the twentieth century. One of his longstanding interests was how to distinguish science from nonscience.

Popper proposed that the defining characteristic of empirical science is that it can be falsified:

I shall certainly admit a system as empirical or scientific only if it is capable of being *tested* by experience. . . . [N]ot the *verifiability* but the *falsifiability* of a system is to be taken as a criterion of demarcation. In other words: I shall not require of a scientific system that it shall be capable of being singled out, once and for all, in a positive sense; but I shall require that its logical form shall be such that it can be singled out, by means of empirical tests, in a negative sense: *it must be possible for an empirical scientific system to be refuted by experience.*[7]

Every 'good' scientific theory is a prohibition: it forbids certain things to happen. The more a theory forbids, the better it is. A theory which is not refutable by any conceivable event is non-scientific. . . . *[T]he criterion of the scientific status of a theory is its falsifiability, or refutability, or testability.*[8]

In his *Conjectures and Refutations*, Popper describes how he arrived at this position in Vienna after the First World War. Deeply frustrated by the debates about Marxism and the psychoanalytic theories of Freud and Adler, he was struck by how easily proponents of these views could find confirmation in everything and refutation in nothing. (See box 3.1.)

Psychoanalysts, for example, could "explain" any clinical observation in terms of their theories, sometimes without even seeing the patient. And "[a] Marxist could not open a newspaper without finding on every page confirming evidence for his interpretation of history; not only in the news, but also in its presentation—which revealed the class bias of the paper— and especially of course in what the paper did not say."[9] By contrast, Einstein's theory of relativity—which was also a matter of great popular interest at the time—made specific predictions about the world, any one of which could demolish the theory if not borne out. Psychoanalysis and Marxism were not falsifiable, Popper concluded, and therefore not science at all. Relativity was.[10]

To be scientific, Popper argued, a theory must make predictions concrete enough to be proved wrong if the claim is not in fact true. The more the theory excludes (at least in principle), the better it is. Thus, Popper's criterion was intended to separate empirical science from other domains of human knowledge. But it also helped to distinguish good science from bad. A theory, even though it may be scientific in its basic thrust, is not a very good theory at all if it is so loosely phrased that it cannot be proved wrong—if it is in fact wrong.

A single, much-publicized example illustrates the point. In 1980 the conservative economist Julian Simon made a wager with Paul Ehrlich, a liberal ecologist well known for his dire predictions that the world is running out of natural resources. If Ehrlich is right, basic commodities of every kind should grow increasingly scarce, and their prices should rise. Simon predicts that commodities will become increasingly abundant as improvements in technology make it possible to extract more resources from the environment. Simon bet Ehrlich that the price of a basket of five metals—any five that Ehrlich cared to choose—would fall between 1980 and 1990. Ehrlich took the bet. Ten years later he lost it, decisively. He sent Simon a check.

Box 3.1

Science: Conjectures and Refutations

Karl R. Popper

source: *Conjectures and Refutations: The Growth of Scientific Knowledge*, fifth edition (Routledge, 1989)

I often formulated my problem as one of distinguishing between a genuinely empirical method and a non-empirical or even a pseudo-empirical method—that is to say, a method which, although it appeals to observation and experiment, nevertheless does not come up to scientific standards. . . .

. . . If observation shows that the predicted effect is definitely absent, then the theory [in question] is simply refuted. The theory is *incompatible with certain possible results of observation*. . . . This is quite different from the situation . . . when it turned out that the theories in question were compatible with the most divergent human behavior, so that it was practically impossible to describe any human behavior that might not be claimed to be a verification of these theories.

(1) It is easy to obtain confirmations, or verifications, for nearly every theory—if we look for confirmations.

(2) Confirmations should count only if they are the result of *risky predictions*; that is to say, if, unenlightened by the theory in question, we should have expected an event which was incompatible with the theory—an event which would have refuted the theory.

(3) Every 'good' scientific theory is a prohibition: it forbids certain things to happen. The more a theory forbids, the better it is.

(4) A theory which is not refutable by any conceivable event is non-scientific. Irrefutability is not a virtue of a theory (as people often think) but a vice.

(5) Every genuine *test* of a theory is an attempt to falsify it, or to refute it. Testability is falsifiability; but there are degrees of testability: some theories are more testable, more exposed to refutation, than others; they take, as it were, greater risks.

(6) Confirming evidence should not count *except when it is the result of a genuine test of the theory*; and this means that it can be presented as a serious but unsuccessful attempt to falsify the theory. (I now speak in such cases of 'corroborating evidence.')

(7) Some genuinely testable theories, when found to be false, are still upheld by their admirers—for example by introducing *ad hoc* some auxiliary assumption, or by re-interpreting the theory *ad hoc* in such a way that it escapes refutation. Such a procedure is always possible, but it rescues the theory from refutation only at the price of destroying, or at least lowering, its scientific status. . . .

One can sum up all this by saying that *the criterion of the scientific status of a theory is its falsifiability, or refutability, or testability.*

> [The following is from footnote 3.]
>
> 'Clinical observations,' like all other observations, are interpretations in the light of theories . . . and for this reason alone they are apt to seem to support those theories in the light of which they were interpreted. But real support can be obtained only from observations undertaken as tests (by 'attempted refutations'); and for this purpose *criteria of refutation* have to he laid down beforehand: it must be agreed which observable situations, if actually observed, mean that the theory is refuted. . . .
>
> . . . [I]f a theory is found to be non-scientific, or 'metaphysical' (as we might say), it is not thereby found to be unimportant, or insignificant, or 'meaningless,' or 'nonsensical.' [footnote omitted] But it cannot claim to be backed by empirical evidence in the scientific sense—although it may easily be, in some genetic sense, the 'result of observation.'

One might question whether economics is a science, and one might debate the relative merits of the two theories. But Simon and Ehrlich had the courage to make testable predictions. This gave each of the theories much greater credibility, at least initially. A decade later, one had been falsified, at least in one instance. We do not, of course, know which theory will prevail in the long run. But the theories are "scientific," in Popper's terms, only to the extent that they make solid predictions formulated concretely enough to be falsified if wrong.

Popper and Hempel: Falsification and Verification

The *Daubert* majority cited a paper by Carl Hempel, a philosopher who has long been identified with logical positivism. That school of philosophy emerged in Vienna during the 1920s, with the "Vienna Circle" consisting of the physicist Moritz Schlick, the philosopher Rudolph Carnap, the mathematician Kurt Gödel, the philosopher Ludwig Wittgenstein, and others. Hempel was associated with the Berlin School, a closely related philosophical group led by Hans Reichenbach.

A reaction against the excesses of nineteenth-century Romanticism, logical positivism was a heterogeneous philosophical movement best known for its efforts to eliminate ideological and metaphysical influences from science and culture, and to develop rigorous standards, based on logic, of scientific validity. Logical positivists held that a statement is meaningful if and only if it can be verified by observation. Statements about God, for example, were said to be unverifiable, and therefore meaningless. Popper's doctrine of "falsifiability" resembles the positivists' criterion of verifiability. But Popper took great pains to distance himself from positivism and to disavow suggestions that he was part of the Vienna Circle.[11]

Hempel is perhaps best known for his work in the logic of confirmation. (See box 3.2.) This body of learning addresses the logical relation between theories and their consequences, and the logical processes by which theories are confirmed through testing their consequences. Some of this formal reasoning is evident in Hempel's selection.

Hempel identifies two characteristics that he requires of a scientific explanation: explanatory relevance and testability. A first, necessary condition for an adequate explanation is met when the explanation "affords good grounds for believing that the phenomenon to be explained did, or does, indeed occur."[12] A second is the requirement that some "empirical finding could possibly bear it out or disconfirm it."[13]

Clearly, Hempel and Popper were talking about different things. Hempel, a logician, was writing about a technical issue: the logical relations between observations and theories. Popper had a broader aim: to explore the uses and limitations of science.

Why Falsification?

Popper has had an influence far beyond the domain of philosophy. His work accounts for the view, often repeated, that scientists should design experiments to falsify hypotheses rather than to "verify" them. This approach may strike many laypeople (and no doubt many scientists too) as unpleasantly negative. We leave aside for the moment Popper's view, which has found little acceptance among philosophers, that falsifiability is the defining characteristic of science. Even within science, an emphasis on falsifying theories can have great benefits, for several reasons.

First, observations that contradict established wisdom are more informative than those that do not. An experiment that merely observes what other scientists have previously observed, or merely "confirms" a theoretical prediction that has been repeatedly tested before, is of little interest. Results that contradict a theory's predictions, or otherwise yield unexpected results, are more illuminating than those that do not.

Box 3.2
Laws and Their Role in Scientific Explanation
Carl Hempel
source: *Philosophy of Natural Science* (Prentice-Hall, 1966)

[S]cience . . . is concerned to develop a conception of the world that has a clear, logical bearing on our experience and is thus capable of objective test. Scientific explanations must, for this reason, meet two systematic requirements, which will be called the requirement of explanatory relevance and the requirement of testability. . . .

. . . [In the] *requirement of explanatory relevance*: the explanatory information adduced affords good grounds for believing that the phenomenon to be explained did, or does, indeed occur. This condition must be met if we are to be entitled to say: "That explains it—the phenomenon in question was indeed to be expected under the circumstances!". . .

To introduce the second basic requirement for scientific explanations, let us consider . . . the conception of gravitational attraction as manifesting a natural tendency akin to love. . . . [T]his conception has no test implications whatever. Hence, no empirical finding could possibly bear it out or disconfirm it. Being thus devoid of empirical content, the conception surely affords no grounds for expecting the characteristic phenomena of gravitational attraction: it lacks objective explanatory power. . . . [This example] illustrate[s] a second condition for scientific explanations, which we will call the *requirement of testability*: the statements constituting a scientific explanation must be capable of empirical test. . . .

What distinguishes genuine laws from accidental generalizations? This intriguing problem has been intensively discussed in recent years. . . .

One telling and suggestive difference . . . is this: a law can, whereas an accidental generalization cannot, serve to support *counterfactual conditionals*, i.e., statements of the form 'If A were (had been) the case, then B would be (would have been) the case', where in fact A is not (has not been) the case. . . . Similarly, a law, in contrast to an accidentally true generalization, can support *subjunctive conditionals*, i.e., sentences of the type 'If A should come to pass, then so would B', where it is left open whether or not A will in fact come to pass. . . .

Closely related to this difference is another one, which is of special interest to us: a law can, whereas an accidental generalization cannot, serve as a basis for an explanation. . . .

Thus, whether a statement of universal form counts as a law will depend in part upon the scientific theories accepted at the time. This is not to say that "empirical generalizations"—statements of universal form that are empirically well confirmed but have no basis in theory—never qualify as laws. . . . The relevance of theory is rather this: a statement of universal form, whether empirically confirmed or as yet untested, will qualify as a law if it is implied by an accepted theory. . . .

Not all scientific explanations are based on laws of strictly universal form. Thus, little Jim's getting the measles might be explained by saying that he caught the disease from his brother, who had a bad case of the measles some days earlier. . . . That connection cannot be expressed by a law of universal form, however; for not every case of exposure to the measles produces contagion. What can be claimed is only that persons exposed to the measles will contract the disease with high probability, i.e., in a high percentage of all cases. General statements of this type, which we shall soon examine more closely, will be called *laws of probabilistic form.* . . .

Scientific hypotheses in the form of statistical probability statements can be, and are, tested by examining the long-run relative frequencies of the outcomes concerned; and the confirmation of such hypotheses is then judged, broadly speaking, in terms of the closeness of the agreement between hypothetical probabilities and observed frequencies. . . .

If probabilistic hypotheses are to be accepted or rejected on the basis of statistical evidence concerning observed frequencies, then appropriate standards . . . will have to determine (a) what deviations of observed frequencies from the probability stated by a hypothesis are to count as grounds for rejecting the hypothesis, and (b) how close an agreement between observed frequencies and hypothetical probability is to be required as a condition for accepting the hypothesis. . . . Broadly speaking, it will depend on the importance that is attached, in the given context, to avoiding two kinds of error. . . . Thus, if the hypothesis concerns the probable effectiveness and safety of a new vaccine, then the decision about its acceptance will have to take into account not only how well the statistical test results accord with the probabilities specified by the hypothesis, but also how serious would be the consequences of accepting the hypothesis and acting on it (e.g. by inoculating children with the vaccine) when in fact it is false, and of rejecting the hypothesis and acting accordingly (e.g. by destroying the vaccine and modifying or discontinuing the process of manufacture) when in fact the hypothesis is true.

More generally, experiments that are designed to find where a theory fails are usually more informative than those that provide easy tests of a theory under conditions where it is likely to succeed. Very commonly, a given observation is consistent with several explanations, not all of which may be evident to the investigator. Experiments that are designed to falsify a theory, if it is wrong, have a better chance of detecting a wrong explanation.

Confirmation Bias

An emphasis on falsifying theories has an additional advantage: it helps to overcome the effects of confirmation bias. Psychologists have found that scientists, like everyone else, tend to settle on a theory quite early; thereafter they tend to look for data to confirm the theory, rather than trying to discredit it. This phenomenon is called *confirmation bias*.[14] Sometimes confirmation bias may lead to egregious miscarriages of justice—when a detective, for example, fails to collect potentially exculpatory evidence about a suspect. Scientists can easily fall into similar traps, collecting easy results that support what is already believed rather than doing hard analysis that might contradict accepted truths.

Confirmation bias is a very clear problem in clinical studies aimed at developing new treatments for diseases. Several hundred clinical papers, for example, describe the use of hyperthermia (heat treatment) for cancer. Most of the reports claim positive benefits of the treatment. But few of the studies had proper controls, which are, in any event, difficult to establish in cancer research. And the studies routinely classified the patients' responses in categories strongly weighted to show "positive" results—even though in most of the studies all the patients had terminal disease with many metastases throughout the body, and most died after the treatment. Thus, if an individual tumor disappeared the tumor had a "complete response," if it shrank there was a "partial response," and any change at all for the better was reported as a "minimal response." The few rigorously controlled studies of hyperthermia as a cancer therapy have disclosed marginal benefits at best.

Confirmation bias should be a matter of great interest and concern to lawyers and judges. For example, lie-detector (polygraph) examiners may start with a hypothesis that they "confirm" by asking just the right questions. Or a mental health professional investigating child abuse may too readily (albeit unwittingly) collaborate with the presumed victim to create memories of abuse that never occurred.[15] The easily made diagnosis of child abuse can be notoriously difficult to falsify, particularly when the victim is an adult and the abuse occurred early in childhood. This has led to several spectacular miscarriages of justice.

Again leaving aside the question whether falsifiability is the defining characteristic of science, it is clear that propositions that are so loosely stated that they cannot be falsified are slippery indeed.

Psychoanalysis may or may not be a science. (Popper thought it was not.) Psychoanalytic theories are far less solid—because they are much harder to falsify—than (for example) the theories of physics. Debates have ranged for generations among different psychoanalytic schools, and between psychoanalysts and physicians, about the causes of mental illness. The warring factions can neither verify their own theories nor disprove those of their opponents to the satisfaction of all parties involved.

Nonfalsifiability is evident in pop psychology. Endless books and articles offer to "explain" the cause of anybody's distress, using popularizations of psychoanalytic theories. People commonly find a ring of truth in such diagnoses, as they often do in Chinese fortune cookies or the astrology columns. But how could they be proved wrong?

The issue of falsifiability has obvious relevance in the courtroom in the insanity defense. Given the financial resources, almost any criminal defendant could locate at least one psychiatrist who would certify that the defendant was insane when committing the crime, particularly if the crime was unusually vicious or bizarre. Prosecutors can invariably locate at least one psychiatrist who will testify equally confidently to the defendant's sanity. Battles between experts like these can never be resolved by still more experts. They teach us more about the state of "psychiatric science" than about the culpability of the defendants. The same cannot be said about physical sciences or engineering; those disciplines make assertions that are usually easier to falsify if wrong and, for that reason, are more reliable.

Naive Falsificationism

For Popper, "falsifiability" is the chief demarcation criterion for science. But, as many philosophers have pointed out, applying this criterion can be so difficult and contentious that its usefulness is very limited. The two main reasons for this are the flexibility of scientific theories and "experimenters' regress."

Scientific theories are malleable. By adjusting parameters and fiddling with assumptions, they can often be made to predict many different things. The astronomical system of Ptolemy, which placed Earth at the center of the universe, could be adapted to fit the observed motions of the planets if one postulated that the planets moved in complex epicycles about the Earth. The Copernican view of the solar system won acceptance in the sixteenth century mainly because it was much simpler. When Michelson and

Morley showed in 1887 that the speed of light was the same in any reference plane, defenders of the old theory simply suggested that the "ether," through which light was said to travel, was being dragged along with the Earth, thus confounding any Earth-based experiment. Who could prove them wrong?[16] This is related to Max Planck's famous dictum that old theories never die, just the scientists who hold them. If scientists have difficulty in falsifying theories, how can falsification be useful in distinguishing science from nonscience?

The interpretation of experimental evidence is subject to another paradox: experimenter's regress. Experiments are designed, and their results interpreted, with the help of theories. Unexpected results can be interpreted to falsify a theory, to arise from some experimental error, or to reflect inadequacy in the experimental design. Some scientists, citing some experiments with otherwise inexplicable results, still argue that "cold fusion" occurs. Skeptics say that the results have conventional explanations, or were wrong. An argument of this kind can go on for long time.

Philosophical Objections

Popper's ideas are appealing and have been enormously influential. They have transformed the way that laypeople and scientists view science, and they are cited with conviction in *Daubert*. But as technical philosophy, Popper's theories have been subjected to sustained examination by other philosophers and found wanting.[17]

One issue is whether Popper's criteria (or other criteria) can demarcate science from other human endeavors—indeed, whether such demarcation is possible at all. As Thomas Gieryn notes in a recent review,[18] some philosophers have argued that there is some essential characteristic that distinguishes science from nonscience, but they have been unable to agree on just what that characteristic is. Popper's falsifiability criterion was one such attempt, but his theory failed in part because of the difficulty of applying the criterion. Others, in particular sociologists of science, insist that the only important distinction between science and nonscience is sociological: science is what scientists do, and attempts by scientists to exclude some intellectual activities from "science" is a form of intellectual turf setting.

Philosophers have objected to Popper's "falsification" criterion on other grounds too. One particularly harsh view was expressed by the philosopher of science David Hull:

Except for operationism, no other philosophical doctrine has been so thoroughly misunderstood or caused more damage in science than falsifiability. . . . [S]cientific laws do not exist in isolation but are organized into theories. In any instance of apparent falsification, too many alternative sources of error are not only possible but plausible. If one could be absolutely sure that a particular observation is veridical and that no modification elsewhere can save a particular hypothesis, then single-minded attention to falsification would be justified. However, in the real world, scientists must balance apparent confirming instances against apparent disconfirmations and make their decisions accordingly.[19]

The theories of Hempel and Popper are problematic for other reasons as well. Logical positivism (the philosophical movement with which Hempel was associated) died in the 1950s because of its intractable philosophical difficulties. The theory is so far out of intellectual fashion that sociologists of science now use "positivist" as a loose epithet to dismiss simplistic views of scientific truth. "Popper," the philosopher of science Ronald Giere recently remarked, "is a minor variant on logical empiricism. . . . [T]he difference [between Popper and Rudolph Carnap, a stalwart of the Vienna Circle] is very small, but Popper exaggerated it."[20] And the philosophy professor Philip Kitcher remarked: "There is a large measure of agreement [among philosophers of science] that the Hempelian approach, which was enormously fruitful in raising all kinds of issues about explanation, is at this stage dead."[21]

Falsificationism and the Practice of Science

Despite Popper's enormous prestige and the lip service that is often paid to his ideas, it is astonishing how little influence he seems to have had on the practice of science. Even a casual reader of the scientific literature will be struck by the strong confirmationist slant in scientific papers. The author of a scientific paper is much more likely to stress how well the data agree with some theory than how decisively they refute some theory. Most scientists, most of the time, still labor to confirm, not to falsify, previously articulated theories. It is, indeed, considered bad manners in science to try too hard to contradict somebody else's theory. And there is obvious reason to suppose that scientists resist publishing results that discredit their own previously published theories.

Some philosophers respond that Popper isn't really supposed to have much practical impact on what scientists do from day to day. Kitcher distinguishes "'nuts-and-bolts' methodological advice about experimental design and statistical analyses of data that is genuinely useful for scientists" from more "grandiose" pronouncements such as Popper's. The latter may be useful as "exhortations to the scientific apprentice," but they are "unneeded (and discarded) by the veteran."[22] (See box 3.3.)

On closer examination, however, there are clear signs of attempts to falsify hypotheses. One need only look at the statistical analyses. The most frequent target is the null hypothesis—the assertion that the treated and untreated groups in an experiment do not differ significantly with respect to some characteristic under scrutiny. Thus, a scientist might report a "statistically significant" difference between a group of animals that took a drug and a control group that did not. Properly understood, this is indeed a falsification of the negative proposition that the drug is biologically inert.

But other studies make no direct attempt to falsify theories, despite what the scientists may consider attempts to test theories. Scientists use theories to design experiments and analyze data, and then interpret the results. This can easily introduce an element of circularity into the process, confusing the relation between observation and theory. For example, a scientist will commonly fit data to an equation derived from a theory, then discuss the physical significance of the values of the fitted parameters using the theory itself for the interpretation. This is hardly a test of the theory. If the theory is grossly inadequate, it will not provide much plausible help in interpreting the data. Even then, the scientist may reason that the theory is correct but cannot be applied to the particular study. Or a scientist may fish around for a theory to use to interpret data already at hand. This process of attempting to lay theory on top of experiment after the fact—post hoc theorizing—is fundamentally different from either verification or falsification as philosophers use those terms. It is also a major source of unreliability in science. Many theories discovered after the fact turn out to be wrong.

Science routinely develops theory after the fact in the hope that it will prove useful in the future. Theorists, in fact, usually can develop an explanation for any recorded observation. The polywater controversy provides

Box 3.3
Believing Where We Cannot Prove
Philip Kitcher
source: *Abusing Science: The Case Against Creationism* (MIT Press, 1982)

Simple distinctions come all too easily. Frequently we open the way for later puzzlement by restricting the options we take to be available. So, for example, in contrasting science and religion, we often operate with a simple pair of categories. On one side there is science, proof, and certainty; on the other, religion, conjecture, and faith. . . .

The idea that evolution is conjecture, faith, or "philosophy" pervades Creationist writings. . . . It is absolutely crucial to their case for equal time for "scientific" Creationism. This ploy has succeeded in winning important adherents to the Creationist cause. As he prepared to defend Arkansas law 590, Attorney General Steven Clark echoed the Creationist judgment. "Evolution," he said, "is just a theory." Similar words have been heard in Congress. . . .

In their attempt to show that evolution is not science, Creationists receive help from the least likely sources. Great scientists sometimes claim that certain facts about the past evolution of organisms are "demonstrated" or "indubitable." . . . But Creationists also can (and do) quote scientists who characterize evolution as "dogma" and contend that there is no conclusive proof of evolutionary theory. . . .

We should reject the Creationists' gambit. Eminent scientists notwithstanding, science is not a body of demonstrated truths. Virtually all of science is an exercise in believing where we cannot prove. Yet, scientific conclusions are not embraced by faith alone. . . .

. . . Conclusive evidence always eludes us. Yet even if we ignore skeptical complaints and imagine that we are sometimes lucky enough to have conclusive reasons for accepting a claim as true, we should not include scientific reasoning among our paradigms of proof. Fallibility is the hallmark of science. . . .

. . . Natural science is not just natural history. It is vastly more ambitious. Science offers us laws that are supposed to hold universally, and it advances claims about things that are beyond our power to observe. . . .

. . . Once we have appreciated the fallibility of natural science and recognized its sources, we can move beyond the simple opposition of proof and faith. Between these extremes lies the vast field of cases in which we believe something on the basis of good—even excellent—but inconclusive evidence.

. . . Even though our present evidence does not *prove* that evolutionary biology—or quantum physics, or plate tectonics, or any other theory—is true, evolutionary biologists will maintain that the present evidence is overwhelmingly in favor of their theory and overwhelmingly against its supposed rivals. . . .

> I have highlighted three characteristics of successful science. *Independent testability* is achieved when it is possible to test auxiliary hypotheses independently of the particular cases for which they are introduced. *Unification* is the result of applying a small family of problem-solving strategies to a broad class of cases. *Fecundity* grows out of incompleteness when a theory opens up new and profitable lines of investigation. . . .
>
> . . . Like Newton's physics in 1800, evolutionary theory today rests on a huge record of successes. In both cases, we find a unified theory whose problem-solving strategies are applied to illuminate a host of diverse phenomena. Both theories offer problem solutions that can be subjected to rigorous independent checks. Both open up new lines of inquiry and have a history of surmounting apparent obstacles. The virtues of successful science are clearly displayed in both.

a memorable illustration: In the early 1960s, Russian scientists claimed to have discovered a new form of water.[23] The discovery was first made by an obscure scientist, Nikolai Fedyakin, but the limelight was soon appropriated by a far more prominent academician: Boris Deryagin. Polywater, the scientists believed, was a new form of water found only in tiny, inaccessible spaces. This discovery was based on experimental observations of certain anomalies in the spectrum of water in tiny capillaries. In 1970 and 1971 experimenters reported that water samples prepared in this way were contaminated; polywater did not in fact exist. By that time, however, two Princeton chemists had already worked out a theory explaining why it did. Their results had been published in prestigious American journals, including *Science* and the *Journal of Colloid and Interface Science*.[24] In many other cases, the outcome of post hoc theorizing is far happier.

Post hoc theorizing is not necessarily wrong, of course. The process is benign and generally useful for science; quite often the theories prove to be useful. But it is too easy to forget, in retrospect, which came first—the observation or the theory—and to incorrectly believe that the one had confirmed the other. Science of this kind can often descend to the level of stock-market punditry, where experts explain with high confidence and precision—though always after the fact—exactly why the market went up or down. All the while, stockbrokers make their money handling other people's investments.

This approach to science, however, often creates difficulties of precisely the kind that Popper addressed. It is easy to fish through the health records of an entire country—Sweden, for example—in search of associations between occupation and disease. According to the statistical test typically employed in such studies, a comparison has one chance in twenty of showing a "statistically significant" difference, even though there may be no real difference between the groups of individuals being compared. Any study that makes enough comparisons between occupational groups and diseases is bound to find many "statistically significant" results, many of which may reflect nothing more than statistical coincidence.

The same phenomenon accounts for the hundreds of "clusters" of cases of disease that are reported in the United States every year. These reports create much public concern, but few result in identification of any public health problem upon follow-up by health authorities. Most, we conclude in retrospect, were just chance occurrences.

Our final example of the dangers of post hoc theorizing is found in the many reports of biological effects of electromagnetic fields. Many of these studies were simply "fishing expeditions" in which an experimenter compared exposed to unexposed animals in search of an effect of exposure. In such a study, the investigator may interpret any differences between the exposed and control groups as an "effect" without bothering to follow up the finding to see whether the phenomenon is real or an artifact. Observations of this kind may be useful for generating hypotheses. Moreover, if an observation is striking enough, it may give some credibility to a hypothesis. But this approach to science is also likely to mislead. The scientific literature contains many reports of biological "effects" of fields that cannot be independently confirmed and may be artifactual. Many of these reports are post hoc theorizing: the investigator never went back to the bench to verify that the "effects" were real.

Because of post hoc theorizing and other unreliable processes of thought, the scientific literature is much less reliable in many respects than nonscientists seem to assume. It is a complicated mixture of descriptions of experiments, reports of data, conclusions that are well supported by data, post hoc theorizing, and conjecture. This is not to say that science cannot approach the truth, or that it does not, in the long term. However, many a discussion in the scientific literature has no stronger basis than stock-market punditry or readings of tea leaves.

Is Creation Science Falsifiable?

In its crudest formulation, Creation Science—the belief that the Earth was created together with all the animal species some 7000 years ago—is surely nonfalsifiable. What if, as some Creationists maintain, the Earth was created 7000 years ago, with all the evidence that evolutionists believe points to a much greater age in place? That is, what if, 7000 years ago, the Creator created dinosaur bones, with just the right mixture of carbon isotopes to appear, from radiocarbon dating, to be millions of years old? This claim may in fact be true. No one has proved it isn't. No one ever could.

But what constitutes falsifiability? Evolutionary theory is so fundamental to large areas of modern biology that few biologists would be able to describe a plausible line of evidence that would make them abandon the theory. More generally, scientific theories do not exist as separate entities; they embody assumptions that derive from other theories. This can lead to endless arguments as to whether an observation has falsified a theory. Radiocarbon dating is based on assumptions about the isotopic composition of matter when it was formed by plants and eaten by dinosaurs. These assumptions may be reasonable to most scientists. But a Creation Scientist might not find them so, and might point out that the "scientific" findings of the great ages of dinosaur bones rest on many other assumptions that make the final conclusion inevitable. Thus, Creation Scientists have argued, Darwinism is as unfalsifiable as Creationism.

Kitcher spent considerable time debunking Creation Science, but he ducked the question of whether it is a science. He simply pointed out that other scientists have repeatedly raised technical objections to Creationism that, if correct, would be absolutely damning to the theory. Creation Scientists have not countered the objections or modified their positions; they have continued to express their ideas in the same ways. Their "epistemic performance is so inflexible," Kitcher noted, "that we either view the cognitive systems in question as poorly designed for the promotion of cognitive goals or suppose that the goals that are being activated are not cognitive at all. . . ."[25] In other words: either Creation Scientists are not interested in science or their science is so lame that it doesn't deserve the label at all. And he let it go at that.

Perhaps Popper's greatest contribution was his articulation of critical rationalism. He insisted that the authority of science comes from the process of testing and falsifying theories, not from God or Aristotle. As the title of Popper's great work suggests, conjectures are the starting point; the subsequent attempts to refute the theory constitute the process that leads to reliable knowledge. Creation Scientists seem little inclined to question their own beliefs. Their psychological stance is totally at odds with Popper's critical rationalism.

The Justices who heard the *Daubert* case are not the only judges to have relied on Popper to help distinguish science from nonscience. In a landmark 1982 ruling, Federal Judge William Overton struck down an Arkansas law that required schools to give equal treatment to Creation Science and evolution. He reasoned, in part, that Creation Science is not science because it is not falsifiable. In Judge Overton's opinion, the "essential characteristics" of science are the following:

(1) It is guided by natural law.
(2) It has to be explanatory by reference to natural law.
(3) It is testable against the empirical world.
(4) Its conclusions are tentative, i.e., are not necessarily the final word.
(5) It is falsifiable.[26]

In the last three of these criteria, the influence of Popper and the logical positivists is very clear.

Many scientists and many philosophers of science applauded Judge Overton's decision in the Arkansas equal-time case. The philosopher of science Larry Laudan, however, criticized Overton's criteria harshly on philosophical grounds, pointing out counterexamples to each criterion. Overton's criteria, wrote Laudan, are "about as remote from well-founded opinion in the philosophy of science as creationism is from respectable geology. It will simply not do for the defenders of science to invoke philosophy of science when it suits them . . . and to dismiss it as 'arcane and remote' when it does not. . . ."[27]

These philosophical disputes do not, of course, negate the usefulness of the *Daubert* criteria as tests of the validity of scientific testimony in the rough and tumble of the courtroom. And Overton's criteria are probably as good a definition of science as one can develop for use in the courtroom. However, the philosophical disputes that underlie them are deep and unresolved, and attempting to demarcate science from nonscience requires one to run across a philosophical minefield.

Science and Trans-Science

Popper was concerned with the criteria for distinguishing empirical science from nonscience. Alvin Weinberg, a prominent health physicist with a long-standing interest in the health effects of ionizing radiation, draws a different distinction between science and "trans-science." The latter, according to Weinberg, concerns questions that are scientific in Popper's sense but are not resolvable in practice. (See box 3.4.)

A simple example of such a question would be the claim that a gasoline additive can improve a car's mileage by a millionth of a mile (about a thirtieth of an inch) per gallon. The claim is scientific in Popper's sense, but it isn't scientific in the world of real engines, real tires, and real roads—in practice, the experimental errors are far larger than the claimed effect.

This example is trivial, but the point behind it is not. The Environmental Protection Agency purports to regulate carcinogens so that the increase in lifetime cancer risk to an exposed person is less than one in a million. But determining how much exposure to the carcinogen would result in such risks is entirely within the domain of trans-science, for it is beyond the capability of science to measure such risks directly. As a result, most federal regulation of environmental pollutants is based on very extended—and commensurately speculative—extrapolation of high-dose animal studies, or of toxicology data obtained from humans in high-dose occupational exposures. There is no feasible way to determine whether EPA policy is effective in regulating the small risks that accrue to humans exposed to the same substances at the much lower levels that are typically found in the environment.

Another trans-scientific question concerns the health effects of low doses of ionizing radiation. At high doses, such radiation demonstrably increases the risk of leukemia and other cancers. Most residents of Hiroshima who survived the initial blast and the next few weeks recovered. Decades later, however, they experienced leukemia at twice the normal rate, and less dramatic increases in other cancer rates. But what are the health risks from exposure to far lower levels of radiation? There is no practical way to find out. We are all bathed in ionizing radiation from natural sources (from outer space, and even from the bricks and stones that make up our houses), and about one-third of us develop some form of cancer at some point in life. In view of this high—and highly variable—background

Box 3.4
Science and Trans-Science
Alvin M. Weinberg
source: *Minerva* 10 (1972): 209–222

Many of the issues which arise in the course of the interaction between science or technology and society . . . hang on the answers to questions which can be asked of science and yet *which cannot be answered by science*. I propose the term *trans-scientific* for these questions since, though they are, epistemologically speaking, questions of fact and can be stated in the language of science, they are unanswerable by science; they transcend science. . . .

[Some questions count as trans-scientific] because, although they could conceivably be answered according to strict scientific canons if enough time and money were spent on them, to do so would be impractical. . . .

. . . [T]here remains a very important class of seemingly social and scientific questions which will always be in the realm of trans-science.

I refer to the behavior of a particular individual. . . . [T]he predictions of social sciences are inevitably less reliable than are those of the physical sciences. . . . [I]t is my impression that there are basic limitations to the predictive powers of the social sciences which derive from the inherent variability and consciousness of the individuals who make up the populations studied by social science. . . .

. . . [A] third class of trans-scientific questions constitutes what I call the axiology of science; these are questions of "scientific value" which include the problem of establishing priorities within science. . . .

Whether the adversary procedure [for debate] is adequate or not seems to me to depend on whether the question at issue is scientific or trans-scientific. If the question is unambiguously scientific, then the procedures of science rather than the procedures of law are required for arriving at the truth. Where the questions raised cannot be answered from existing scientific knowledge or from research which could be carried out reasonably rapidly and without disproportionate expense, then the answers must be trans-scientific and the adversary procedure seems therefore to be the best alternative. . . .

. . . [T]he adversary procedure undoubtedly has considerable merit in forcing scientists to be more honest, to say where science ends and trans-science begins, as well as to help weigh the ethical issues which underlie whatever choices the society makes between technological alternatives. . . .

What are the responsibilities of the scientist in trans-scientific debate? Though the scientist cannot provide definite answers to trans-scientific questions any more than can the lawyer, the politician or a member of the lay public, he does have one crucially important role: to make clear where science ends and trans-science begins. . . .

. . . In a democratic society, the public's right of access to the debate in the sense of being informed about it and participating in it is as great as the

> public demands it to be. Especially where experts disagree, the public has
> little choice but to engage in the debate at an earlier stage than the experts
> themselves find convenient or comfortable.

rate of exposure, there is no practical way to measure comparatively tiny effects. The doubling in the risk of leukemia (one of the less common cancers) is about the smallest increase that can be measured reliably in human populations. Some authorities argue that, at very low exposures, ionizing radiation is actually good for human health.[28] These claims are about as scientific as the more conventional claims on the other side, and they are equally difficult to verify or falsify.

This creates a host of difficult policy issues. Consider radon, an invisible radioactive gas that seeps from the ground and can collect in poorly ventilated homes. At high doses, radon causes lung cancer; this is well established from studies on uranium miners, even though most of them were heavy smokers. The EPA estimates that naturally occurring radon causes 20,000 excess lung cancer deaths every year out of a total of 153,000 deaths from this disease, most of them caused by smoking. This is roughly comparable to the total number of accidental deaths from all causes in American homes every year, and the equivalent of perhaps a hundred jumbo jet accidents a year. If the EPA's numbers are right, radon is one of the most serious environmental health threats in the country.[29] But studies in counties with high radon levels have consistently failed to find any direct evidence of excess deaths from radon. Billions of dollars of remediation expenditures thus ride on a presumed effect that is too small to detect with any scientific and statistical tools currently available. If the health risk exists at all, the victims cannot be identified or even counted reliably.

Trans-science has important implications for risk research, and thus for tort litigation. Epidemiology is a very blunt instrument, with limited ability to detect small effects. And in epidemiology a relative risk of 2 is usually considered a small effect that may be barely identifiable in the data. The reliability of such a finding may be very low, in spite of whatever statistical analysis the investigator presents. But a relative risk of two implies a doubling of risk, which corresponds to the "more likely than not" criterion in civil litigation. Epidemiology becomes very unreliable when looking for effects that are small (compared to the capabilities of the methods) but which are still large enough to be legally significant. The threshold of proof required in tort litigation over toxic substances is close to or even below the boundary between science and trans-science.

The relation between science and trans-science has important implications for the role of the expert witness. Scientists sometimes fail to draw the distinction clearly, and they may issue opinions about essentially unknowable matters as though they were within their areas of expertise. The chemist and professor of science studies Henry Bauer discusses the issue as follows: ". . . trans-scientific questions are posed to scientists, who as a matter of habit give a judgment, an opinion, in the tones of certitude. . . . The specialists are reluctant to admit their own limitations and those of their specialty, particularly since they are not necessarily clear themselves about those limitations." To be "meaningful, informative, useful," public debate must establish "common ground of some sort." Often it may be "no more than an acknowledgment that the question (or some part of it) is indeed trans-scientific and not purely technical." But even consensus of that character "often requires the kind of selfless honesty which a scientist or engineer with a position or status to maintain finds hard to exercise."[30]

This can often lead to serious misunderstandings. Lawyers often want scientist-witnesses to state flatly that there is no risk from a drug. The complete absence of risk is unprovable, and hence the proposition is trans-scientific. At best, scientific study can establish that a risk, if it exists at all, is lower than some stated level. Scientists take this point to be self-evident, but it is much less familiar to many nonscientists. A scientist-witness who waffles at the request to swear under oath that a substance is "safe" (which the scientist interprets to mean "posing zero risk") may be mistaken by the jury as implying that there is evidence for a real hazard. And a scientist who swears that the risk in question is zero is either speaking very loosely or lying.

Falsification in Everyday Medicine

Popper's ideas have important practical applications in medicine, too, even if the average patient does not reflect on the criterion of demarcation when disrobing in the examining room.

The term *differential diagnoses* refers to a systematic process by which a physician attempts to determine which of several possible causes might have led to a patient's symptoms. Handbooks of differential diagnoses contain lists of major symptoms, such as chest pain or sudden weight loss.[31] The books list conditions that may have caused each symptom and criteria for distinguishing among possible causes. In theory, at least, the physician performs the tests needed to rule out competing explanations for the symptoms and then converges on a final diagnosis.[32]

That, in any event, is how it is supposed to work. The clinician and educator John Balla identifies three kinds of diagnoses in the real world. One is the "common sense" diagnosis, where it is "almost impossible to be wrong."[33] Another is the nonfalsifiable ("I say so") diagnosis, typically reserved for common, nonspecific symptoms such as headaches or sore backs. Here, Balla notes, much "depends on the doctor's framework of reference and beliefs."[34] A general practitioner may call a neckache muscle strain or nerve root irritation; an orthopedic surgeon may call the pain degenerative arthritis; a neurologist may call it psychoneurosis; a psychiatrist may call it hysterical conversion reaction. Third, there is the evidential (falsifiable) diagnosis, such as when a tumor is diagnosed on the basis of a biopsy. (Biopsies may not be completely reliable, but they can be repeated and falsified in other ways.[35])

Nonfalsifiable diagnoses are sources of much controversy in the courtroom. Consider, for example, clinical ecology, a fringe medical specialty whose methods are regarded skeptically by mainstream doctors.[36] Some clinical ecologists repeatedly appear as expert witnesses in personal injury suits, offering alarming (and grossly inappropriate) diagnoses such as "chemically induced AIDS" in support of claimants' cases. One syndrome that is often diagnosed by clinical ecologists is multiple chemical sensitivity (MCS), which the doctors believe arises from exposure to trace contaminants in environment. The difficulty, however, is very clear when one examines a list of symptoms that clinical ecologists claim for the syndrome. The symptoms are common and nonspecific, and include the ordinary aches and pains that everybody suffers from time to time as well as symptoms that may appear for many serious diseases. Clinical ecologists have failed to provide criteria that allow a doctor to decide when somebody does not suffer from MCS, which is one of the main reasons why MCS is regarded skeptically by mainstream medicine. This is not to say that no people suffer from nonspecific symptoms due to exposures to low-level pollutants in the environment. But MCS is a nonfalsifiable diagnosis—and often a lucrative one for a doctor. The Chemical Injury Information Network, in White Sulfur Springs, Montana, published a table of nearly 500 symptoms of MCS. A small part of the table lists the following symptoms as related to the genito-urinary system:

persistent mild urge to void
frequency in voiding
urgency, pressure
dysuria (painful or difficult urination)
genital itch
vaginal discharge
yeast infections
PMS
menstrual problems
testicular pain
genital sweating
hot flashes (under 40 years old)
blood in urine
kidney problems
lower back aches

The hundreds of other "symptoms" of MCS in the table are of the same nature—nonspecific and common symptoms which are exhibited by many illnesses (or which may be simply the common aches and pains of ordinary life). In the absence of any diagnostic criteria to tell when a person does not have MCS, this and other similar lists of "symptoms" of MCS are useless. A similar difficulty exists with Gulf War Syndrome, a loose collection of nonspecific complaints that are said to afflict veterans of that conflict.

The problem of nonfalsifiable diagnosis looms large in the ongoing litigation over silicone breast implants. Tens of thousands of women are seeking recompense for injuries allegedly resulting from the use of the implants. In most cases, the alleged injuries consist of vague clusters of symptoms that correspond to no disease that is recognized by mainstream medicine. However, a handful of doctors have developed lucrative practices in diagnosing these ostensible illnesses for purposes of litigation.

The complex medical-legal problem of overprescription of diagnostic tests can also be interpreted in Popperian terms. A physician who is reasonably sure of the cause of a patient's symptoms may prescribe addition-al tests, not to confirm the theory, but to rule out alternative causes of the symptoms. With few exceptions, medical diagnoses are matters of proba-bility. A patient with droopy eyelids is probably just tired but may have myasthenia gravis, a rare and serious neuromuscular disease. Unless the tests prescribed by the physician are dispositive (and in medicine they often are not), some other disease may be to blame. The rarer the patient's dis-ease the more likely that an initial diagnosis will be wrong. Confirmation bias can be fatal to the patient, for it may tempt the physician to overlook an otherwise treatable disease, or to prescribe a dangerous treatment for a disease that the patient does not have.

The physician has to consider legal implications, too. Additional test-ing may not have much chance of benefiting a patient whose symptoms are consistent with a common disease (with high probability) and a rare disease (with small probability). But a doctor may see many thousands of patients over the years and is likely to miss something important sooner or later. Popperian falsification is a strategy employed by physicians to reduce liability.

Is Homeopathy Falsifiable?

The ongoing debate about homeopathy provides a good example of exper-imenter's regress. Homeopathy had its beginnings in 1796 with the German physician Christian Friedrich Hahnemann, though the term itself did not come into use until several decades later. It evolved into a medical system for treating a disease by administering a highly diluted solution of a substance that, in sufficient doses, would produce symptoms similar to those of the disease being treated. The dilutions were so high, in fact, that not a single molecule of the "medicine" would be present in the dose administered to the patient. In the United States, homeopathy had its hey-day in the 1800s, but it had nearly vanished by 1900. Hahnemann University in Philadelphia, founded by homeopathists, is now a conven-tional medical school.

In 1988 homeopathy was suddenly a hot topic again. The prestigious journal *Nature* had published an article in which the biochemist Jacques Benveniste and twelve other authors reported that a solution of an antibody could produce a biological response even though it had been diluted so much as to make it unlikely that even one molecule of the antibody was present.[37] In an accompanying editorial, *Nature* editor John Maddox said that he did not believe the results but had decided to publish the paper anyway. Shortly thereafter, Maddox, accompanied by the magician James Randi (well known for uncovering the secrets of spoon benders) and the scientific fraud buster Walter Stewart, showed up at Benveniste's laboratory to conduct an investigation of his experiment. In a scathing article published in *Nature*,[38] they reported that the study suffered from serious methodological flaws. This unleashed a storm of criticism from other scientists, who thought Maddox had been overaggressive in his attempts to falsify Benveniste's work.

The issue is not closed. Three seemingly well-controlled clinical trials of homeopathy have since reached positive conclusions. The most recent appeared in December 1994 in the prestigious British medical journal *The Lancet*.[39] The study described a randomized double-blind clinical study (the "gold standard" design of clinical trials) of the effectiveness of homeopathic therapy for allergic asthma, against a placebo, in 28 patients. The homeopathic treatment consisted of an allergen, highly diluted and prepared according to homeopathic canon. The patients were followed for four weeks of treatment and four more weeks thereafter. The dilution of the allergen was so high that it was statistically probable that no allergen molecules at all would be present in the solution administered to the patients. Yet according to these three studies, the patients responded to the treatment anyway. What is one to make of these results? At face value, homeopathy is a clear-cut example of pseudo-science. A drug cannot be effective when it is not administered. The authors of these studies ask precisely the right question, however: "Is the reproducibility of evidence in favor of homeopathy proof of its activity or proof of the clinical trial's capacity to produce false-positive results?"[40] Something is going on in these experiments, but is it a persistent subtle error or a real effect of the treatment? Despite a large amount of scientific work, nobody knows for sure, and scientific arguments about such experiments may go on forever. From the perspective of public health, however, the important issue is not whether homeopathy is science in Popper's sense, but which of its claims are well supported by controlled clinical investigation. The answer is: very few.

Is Popper Canon?

In citing two eminent philosophers, the Supreme Court surely did not intend to canonize Popper and Hempel, or to certify their theories in preference to those of competing philosophers. No philosophers were represented before the Court in *Daubert*. The Court is empowered to rule on concrete cases or controversies, not to adjudicate philosophical disputes. Philosophers are not often parties to civil lawsuits. If they were, *Daubert* might well have had a quite different caption: perhaps *Giere, Kitcher, & Co. v. Popper & Hempel et al*. The lawyers for both sides would surely have insisted that theirs was the side that was verifiable, falsifiable, generally accepted, and thoroughly peer reviewed by the philosophical community.

When all is said and done, then, the Supreme Court's citing Popper and Hempel side by side was a legal tip of the hat to two of the most influential philosophers of science. Many scientists have tipped their own hats in those directions too—far more, undoubtedly, than have seriously studied the philosophical work in question.

But legal cases revolve around facts, not epistemology. (More precise, epistemology, the philosophical investigation of how we know "facts," is seldom the issue.) And the goals of the law are judicial, not to achieve "cosmic understanding" (as the *Daubert* Court put it). The objective is to arrive at a reasonably reliable answer in a reasonably short period of time. From that perspective, Popper and Hempel are important not for the details of their philosophical positions, but for their general thrust, and their views are useful. Whatever their deeper philosophical significance, falsifiability and verifiability are useful criteria, if only as rules of thumb. Both help to identify assertions that are so nebulously or imprecisely articulated that they cannot, in practice, engage serious, methodical scientific scrutiny, discourse, or refutation by other scientists.

The Testimony of Shanna Swan

The problem of falsifiability, or verifiability, arises often in tort litigation. In view of the complex and largely unknown processes that cause birth defects or cancer, it is seldom possible to prove that a substance does not cause either of these problems, and claims that one does vary widely in reliability.

Moreover, claims about possible health hazards are easy to state in a way that is so loose as to be virtually impossible to disprove: "Bendectin might possibly cause birth defects." One might support such a claim by sifting through the immense toxicology literature on the drug and picking out bits and pieces of evidence that suggest that the drug might possibly be a human teratogen—without finding any strong evidence that it actually is. Similar arguments (based on the cumulative impression given by weak evidence) are often presented by those who believe that weak electromagnetic fields might possibly cause illness, or that extrasensory perception or flying saucers might possibly exist. The looseness of such claims is related to their unfalsifiability.

Consider, in contrast, a stronger and potentially falsifiable statement: "Bendectin more than doubles the probability of birth defects in children whose mothers used the drug during pregnancy." This claim is falsifiable, and it has been falsified by a mass of toxicological and epidemiological evidence. Because of statistical uncertainties in the data, one might argue that it has not been falsified for certain rare birth defects, although it has not been proved either. How such arguments would play in court involves legal issues, such as standard of proof, that are outside the domain of science.

Daubert involved a proffer of expert testimony framed in a way that clearly was not falsifiable. In her *Daubert* affidavit (box 1.5), Shanna Swan wrote:

Having reviewed the epidemiological studies including, but not limited to Heinonen, Jick, Aselton, Morelock, Cordero, Eskanazi, McCredie, and based upon generally accepted epidemiological techniques and utilizing my education, training and experience it is my opinion that one cannot conclude that there is in fact no statistical association between Bendectin an[d] limb reduction defects. More specifically one cannot draw a conclusion from those studies that Bendectin does not cause limb reduction defects.[41]

From a legal perspective, this two-sentence, 71-word declaration is phrased so artfully that it seems likely to have been drafted by a lawyer rather than a scientist. The first 31 words ("Having reviewed . . . and experience") are all there to meet an arcane legal requirement—to lay a legally sufficient foundation for the conclusion. No scientist writing for other scientists would ever bother to write a phrase like "utilizing my education, training, and experience." The words are purely legalistic: under the rules of evidence, experts—in sharp contrast to all other witnesses—are permitted to base testimony and conclusions on "education, training and experience" rather than on direct observation.

The second and more important legal conceit here appears in the next 40 words ("it is my opinion . . . defects.") Both assertions are phrased as double negatives: "One cannot conclude . . . no association" and "one cannot . . . does not." Again, this phrasing is legally important. From a strictly legal perspective, it is intended to establish quite solidly that there are material facts in dispute. This is a bare minimum that a plaintiff must meet when the opposing side files a motion for summary judgment. Lawyers use words like these to stop a judge from throwing the case out before it even goes to a jury. In this case, the defense experts asserted that there was no credible scientific evidence that Bendectin did cause birth defects. Swan asserted that the evidence at hand did not establish that Bendectin did not cause birth defects. To lawyers focusing singlemindedly on legal form and appearance, that seemed to be enough. The negative-positive asserted by the defendants' experts is flatly contradicted by the negative-negative asserted by Swan. Therefore, they argued to the judge, the case would have to be presented to a jury.

But a "negative-negative" is not science—not, at least, in Popper's terms. Consider again Swan's last sentence: "One cannot draw a conclusion from these studies that Bendectin does not cause limb reduction defects." Swan (or the lawyers who may have drafted her statement) attempts to conceal the inherently nonscientific character of the statement by inserting the words "from these studies." But suppose they had been omitted. Swan would then be attesting: "One cannot draw a conclusion that Bendectin does not cause limb reduction defects." But science never irrevocably proves any negative proposition. No pile of data, no matter how high, can ever prove that Bendectin does not cause limb-reduction defects. Scientific proof involves steadily narrowing the probabilities and steadily tightening the uncertainties. The probabilities can approach 1, the uncertainties can approach 0, but they can never reach it. It is always possible that some small effect is still lurking just over the statistical horizon.

Thus, Swan's statement is not falsifiable. It says nothing of significance about the studies of "Heinonen, Jick, Aselton, Morelock, Cordero, Eskanazi, McCredie," which Swan takes pains to list at the beginning of her declaration; it certainly does not falsify their conclusions. No new set of experiments or tests on Bendectin could ever be designed to falsify Swan's statement. So far as science is concerned, one could insert in the bracketed sections of this sentence any grammatically appropriate sequence of words at all: "More specifically one cannot draw a conclusion from [those studies] that [Bendectin] does not cause [limb-reduction defects]." Any list of studies, any product, any injury can be inserted at the appropriate points here; the statement will remain a truism, and immune to scientific refutation.

A second declaration in Swan's *Daubert* affidavit involves a very similar verbal sleight of hand:

Because limb defects are a rare occurrence, occurring less than one per one thousand live births, many thousands of births would be necessary in a controlled study to reveal even a 100 percent increase. The chances of finding a smaller increase such as a 10 percent or 20 percent would therefore be minuscule. That is one reason why an epidemiologist would not rely only on epidemiology studies in the face of other scientific data to suggest that a drug, such as Bendectin, does not cause birth defects.[42]

Note, to begin with, that the key proposition at the end of the quoted text again revolves around a double negative: An epidemiologist "would not rely . . . to suggest that . . . Bendectin does not cause birth defects." On quick reading, this convoluted sentence appears to assert that scientists should consider both epidemiology and other types of data in deciding whether Bendectin causes birth defects. If that were what the sentence actually said, it would be entirely unproblematic. But here again, Swan has managed to turn what might be an unproblematic proposition inside out, making it unfalsifiable. Scientists never make categorical assertions about the total absence of any risk, which is undemonstrable in any event. There can never be sufficient evidence of zero risk. Nor is that an issue in "toxic tort" litigation. The issue is whether Bendectin probably caused Jason Daubert's birth defects, which is a different thing entirely.

Swan, in her *Daubert* affidavit, takes the leap and concludes, on the basis of unstated arguments from animal toxicology tests, that Bendectin is linked to birth defects. Consider the conclusion of the affidavit: ". . . so there be no question, it is my opinion within a reasonable degree of certainty, based on all of the available data, the Bendectin is associated with birth defects, including limb defects."

In a November 1995 letter to one of our research assistants (reproduced in its entirety in box 3.5), Swan wrote the following:

I never claimed to have shown that Bendectin causes birth defects, and never testified to that. My testimony, almost exclusively given in rebuttal, attempted to show that the studies which the defense relied on were not adequate to establish the safety of Bendectin. I believe it is still not known whether Bendectin is a teratogen, but I also believe that the laboratory and animal studies, as well as some of the epidemiological findings raise significant doubts about safety.

Of course, this statement and the one in the affidavit can be reconciled. Epidemiologists, well aware that association does not prove causation, seldom make strong claims about the causes of associations they uncover. But a layperson, on reading the strongly worded statement Swan submitted in *Daubert*, would surely come away with a far different impression than the one she gave in her subsequent letter.

Daubert Revisited

The Supreme Court remanded the *Daubert* case to the Ninth Circuit Court of Appeals for further proceedings in line with the Supreme Court's opinion. The appellate court's opinion on remand was written by Judge Alex Kozinski. We reproduce it in appendix C. This remand opinion was the last word in the *Daubert* litigation; the Supreme Court denied further review on October 2, 1995.[43]

While not expressly citing Popper, Judge Kozinski echoed some of his thinking. *Daubert*'s statistical experts would only say that "Bendectin could possibly have caused plaintiffs' injuries."[44] Judge Kozinski nailed *Daubert*'s experts precisely because their claims were not "tested or testable." Their assertions had taken the form of "could possibly," not "did probably." They had never quantified the hazard they claimed to have discovered.

After the Supreme Court handed down its *Daubert* opinion, one of the plaintiff's lawyers declared that the ruling "allows the jury to hear all relevant views."[45] This statement about the law was at least concrete enough to be tested and falsified. On remand to the Ninth Circuit, it was. The assertions offered by *Daubert*'s experts would not go to the jury after all.

Box 3.5

November 25, 1995

Dear Ms. Haefner:

Thank you for your letter of November 17th. I never claimed to have shown that Bendectin causes birth defects, and never testified to that. My testimony, almost exclusively given in rebuttal, attempted to show that the studies which the defense relied on were not adequate to establish the safety of Bendectin. I believe it is still not known whether Bendectin is a teratogen, but I also believe that the laboratory and animal studies, as well as some of the epidemiological findings raise significant doubts about safety. Unfortunately, aside from an abstract, I have not published my analyses. This is largely due to the fact that the drug was removed from the market soon after I presented that paper at the annual meeting of the Society for Epidemiological Research. I therefore felt that the public health contribution I could make by further publication was small. In retrospect, in light of legal consequences of failing to publish these results, I should have done so.

Sincerely,

Shanna H. Swan Ph.D.

4

Errors in Science

Additionally, in the case of a particular scientific technique, the court ordinarily should consider the known or potential rate of error, see, *e.g.*, *United States v. Smith*, 869 F.2d 348, 353-354 (CA7 1989) (surveying studies of the error rate of spectrographic voice identification technique), and the existence and maintenance of standards controlling the technique's operation, see *United States v. Williams*, 583 F.2d 1194, 1198 (CA2 1978) (noting professional organization's standard governing spectrographic analysis), cert. denied, 439 U.S. 1117, 59 L. Ed. 2d 77, 99 S. Ct. 1025 (1979).
—*Daubert v. Merrell Dow Pharmaceuticals, Inc.*, 509 U.S. 579, 594 (1993)

The *Daubert* majority pointed to the "known or potential error rate" as a factor to be weighed by trial judges in screening expert testimony. A close examination of potential error rates in proffered scientific testimony is at the very least permitted, and may well be required.

Errors can affect either the reliability of a measurement (i.e., introduce nonreproducible results) or its validity (i.e., lead to incorrect interpretation of the data). A measurement can be reliable (repeatable) but not valid. For example, using a 30-inch "yardstick" one can reliably (i.e., repeatedly) ascertain that a room is "twelve yards wide" even though the true figure is 10 yards. As one text explains, reliability is "the extent to which an experiment, test, or any measuring procedure yields the same results on repeated trials."[1] Validity, in contrast, is the extent to which any measuring instrument measures what it is intended to measure; that is, it "concerns the relation between concept and indicator."[2] As we show below, errors that affect the reproducibility of data are far easier to deal with than those that affect the validity of a study.

Scientists fret about error all the time. They also study it systematically. One of the fundamental problems in science is how to draw valid inferences from data given the inevitable presence of random errors due to the sampling process, or systematic errors due to inadequate experimental design or other factors. This problem occupies many pages in textbooks on epidemiology, the social sciences, business, and other fields. There is a scientific calculus of uncertainty, so to speak. (See box 4.1.)

Asking judges to examine the "known or potential error rate" in a scientific study is a tall order. Science has many tools for estimating and controlling errors, many of them discipline-specific. Scientists are expected to provide some kind of "error analysis" with their results, and most of them do. Standard methods do allow scientists to estimate and report potential errors. But these standards are seldom applied in any consistent manner. And scientists are often overoptimistic about the accuracy of their results.

Taxonomy of Errors

Many scientific treatises explain how to estimate and quantify error. E. Bright Wilson Jr., in his 1952 book *An Introduction to Scientific Research*, emphasizes the need to "know how to estimate the reliability of experimental data and how to convey this information to others."[3] This is also a central challenge for a judge who is trying to screen proffered scientific evidence pursuant to the *Daubert* mandate.

Scientific errors can be classified in several ways. (See box 4.2.) One can distinguish, first, between systematic and random errors.[4] Systematic errors are the same for every measurement, or are functions of the value of the quantity being observed. For example, a defective speedometer in a car may systematically indicate too low a speed. Random errors, in contrast, "average out" in repeated experiments. Rounding figures up or down to the nearest dollar on an income tax return introduces random errors that will normally average out. (The Internal Revenue Service is much more concerned about systematic errors, such as incidental income repeatedly overlooked.)

An authoritative report published by the International Organization for Standardization (ISO) makes a similar distinction. It classifies scientific uncertainty into two types: A and B. Type A uncertainty can be evaluated

Box 4.1
The Interpretation of Epidemiologic Studies

Marcia Angell

source: *New England Journal of Medicine* 323 (1990): 823–825

The *Journal* is receiving a growing number of epidemiologic reports of associations between diseases and possible risk factors. The risk factor in question is often a habit or type of behavior, some element of diet or lifestyle that can presumably be changed. . . .

. . . Each contributing cause may have only a small role. For example, obesity is well established as a risk factor for coronary heart disease, but it is only one of several, none of which can account for the total incidence of this disease. . . .

. . . These are of two principal types: case-control studies and cohort studies. Case-control studies begin with patients who already have the disease in question (case patients) and compare the frequency of past exposure to the risk factor in question with the frequency of exposure in a group without the disease (controls). Cohort studies start before anyone has the disease; they follow people known to be exposed to the possible risk factor and compare the frequency with which the disease in question develops with its frequency in a group not exposed to the risk factor. Either type may demonstrate that a disease or other outcome is more likely in those with a particular exposure. Although such studies usually cannot prove that the exposure is the cause of the disease, they may offer strong support for that hypothesis.

Epidemiologic studies of both types are subject to many biases and therefore present formidable problems in design and execution and even greater problems in interpretation. The chief difficulty is that it is nearly impossible to find groups of people who are alike in every way except for the exposure or disease in question. Usually a number of types of behavior or exposures tend to occur in combination with one another. For example, cigarette smokers are more likely to drink alcohol than are nonsmokers. So when an epidemiologic study shows a link between cigarette smoking and a disease, it is necessary to determine whether the real association is with smoking, drinking (termed a confounding variable in this case), or the combination.

Although there are statistical methods for neutralizing confounding variables, they are not perfect, and they are of no use whatsoever unless the confounding variables are known and measured. For example, epidemiologic studies have shown an association between premature births and lack of prenatal care, but it could be that women who can afford prenatal care are more likely to carry babies to term because such women are, say, better nourished. . . .

When an epidemiologic study shows that an exposure is associated with an outcome, an important question for us is the size of the effect. Does the exposure increase the risk manyfold, twofold, or perhaps by only 20 percent (a relative risk of 1.2)? An important reason for being concerned about the size of the effect is that unknown or inadequately accounted for confounding variables can easily produce artifactual small effects (or mask real ones). It is far less likely that the confounding variables account for large effects. . . .

In addition to being concerned about the size of the effect found in an epidemiologic study, the editors are also concerned about whether the association between the exposure and the outcome is biologically plausible.

by statistical analysis of the data; this kind of uncertainty is random in character. Type B uncertainty requires some other kind of analysis; it is nonrandom.[5] The ISO report calls on scientists to do both a careful statistical analysis of their data and a careful theoretical analysis of their experimental design. The scientist should then report a "combined standard uncertainty" that includes the results of both of these analyses. (See box 4.3.)

Adam Finkel's book *Confronting Uncertainty in Risk Management* presents, from the perspective of risk assessment, a quite different taxonomy of error.[6] Finkel classifies error according to the level at which it occurs in the chain of scientific inference. At the lowest level is "parameter uncertainty": the uncertainty that arises in measuring specific quantities, such as the overall death rate from smoking, that arise from random or systematic errors in data. Parameter uncertainty might arise, for example, in measurements of death rates from smoking if the investigator relied on reports that smokers themselves give about their smoking habits. But Finkel's review also addresses error that can creep into later stages of the scientific process. "Model uncertainty" occurs because of uncertainties in the underlying theory used to interpret the data. Tests of chemical carcinogenicity in one species of animal, for example, are not very good predictors of carcinogenicity in another species. Similarly, studies document a shockingly high incidence of lung cancer in uranium miners, but (as was noted above) most of the miners were also heavy smokers. To separate effects from radiation and tobacco, an investigator must use a theoretical model; this itself may introduce new sources of error. At the highest level is what Finkel calls "decision rule uncertainty"—uncertainty about what measures of remediation will be most effective in countering the threat. Thus, any analysis of "potential error rates" in proffered scientific testimony must address possible errors all along the chain of scientific inference.

Box 4.2
Validity and Threats to Validity

Anthony M. Graziano and Michael L. Raulin

source: *Research Methods: A Process of Inquiry*, second edition (HarperCollins, 1993), pp. 170–182

SOME MAJOR CONFOUNDING VARIABLES

Maturation: . . . [O]bserved changes over time may be due to maturational factors rather than to any effects of the independent variable. . . .

History: During the course of the study many events that are not of interest to the researcher can occur and possibly affect the outcome. . . .

Testing: The effects of repeated *testing* of subjects may be a threat to internal validity because subjects may gain proficiency through repeated practice on the measuring instruments. . . .

Instrumentation: Apparent pre-post changes may be due to changes in the *measuring instrument* over time rather than to the experimental manipulation of the independent variable. This is particularly true when the measuring instrument is a human observer. . . .

Regression to the Mean: . . . [W]henever you select subjects *because* their scores on a measure are extreme (either very high or very low), they will tend to be less extreme on a second testing (i.e., their scores will have regressed toward the mean). . . .

Selection: Confounding due to *selection* can occur when care is not taken to insure that two or more groups being compared are equivalent before the manipulations begin. . . .

Attrition: . . . [C]onfounding due to *attrition* can occur when subjects are lost differentially, such as when there are more dropouts from one group than from another or when subjects with certain characteristics are lost. . . .

Diffusion of Treatment: When subjects in different experimental conditions are in close proximity, such as children in the same classroom, and are able to communicate with each other, earlier subjects may "give away" the procedures to those scheduled later. . . .

Sequencing Effects: . . . For example, if a study includes three conditions and each subject is exposed to all three, their experiences with earlier conditions of the study may affect their responses to later conditions. . . .

. . . [T]here are many ways that subjects, bringing their own expectations and biases, can react in the experimental situation. . . . Thus, the researcher should include controls for these and other possible subject effects to prevent confounding that can reduce the study's validity.

Experimenter Effects also can have significant impact on the outcome of a study. . . . [R]esearchers, too, are human and carry their own potentially biasing expectations and motivations into the study. . . .

. . . [T]he mere fact of finding statistical significance can be quite misleading, and we have to be careful not to conclude that because a finding is statistically significant, it is therefore important or of practical or useful significance.

Box 4.3
Reporting Uncertainty

source: *Guide to the Expression of Uncertainty in Measurement* (International Organization for Standardization, 1993)

7.1 General guidance

7.1.1 In general, as one moves up the measurement hierarchy, more details are required on how a measurement result and its uncertainty were obtained. Nevertheless, at any level of this hierarchy, including commercial and regulatory activities in the marketplace, engineering work in industry, lower-echelon calibration facilities, industrial research and development, academic research, industrial primary standards and calibration laboratories, and the national standards laboratories and the BIPM [Bureau International des Poids et Mesures, a standards organization], all of the information necessary for the reevaluation of the measurement should be available to others who may have need of it. The primary difference is that at the lower levels of the hierarchical chain, more of the necessary information may be made available in the form of published calibration and test system reports, test specifications, calibration and test certificates, instruction manuals, international standards, national standards, and local regulations.

7.1.2 When the details of a measurement, including how the uncertainty of the result was evaluated, are provided by referring to published documents, as is often the case when calibration results are reported on a certificate, it is imperative that these publications be kept up-to-date so that they are consistent with the measurement procedure actually in use.

7.1.3 Numerous measurements are made every day in industry and commerce without any explicit report of uncertainty. However, many are performed with instruments subject to periodic calibration or legal inspection. If the instruments are known to be in conformance with their specifications or with the existing normative documents that apply, the uncertainties of their indications may be inferred from these specifications or from these normative documents.

7.1.4 Although in practice the amount of information necessary to document a measurement result depends on its intended use, the basic principle of what is required remains unchanged: when reporting the result of a measurement and its uncertainty, it is preferable to err on the side of providing too much information rather than too little. For example, one should

a) describe clearly the methods used to calculate the measurement result and its uncertainty from the experimental observations and input data;

b) list all uncertainty components and document fully how they were evaluated;

c) present the data analysis in such a way that each of its important steps can be readily followed and the calculation of the reported result can be independently repeated if necessary;

d) give all corrections and constants used in the analysis and their sources.

A test of the foregoing list is to ask oneself "Have I provided enough information in a sufficiently clear manner that my result can be updated in the future if new information or data become available?"

7.2 Specific guidance [The next two pages provide specific technical information about the reporting of experimental uncertainties.]

Type I and Type II Errors and Level of Significance

One particular type of error closely related to parameter error is of special interest to the law. Science recognizes both false-positive and false-negative errors (type I and type II errors, in commonly used statistical jargon). A false positive is the detection of an effect that is not there (e.g., the incorrect conclusion that a patient has a disease when he or she does not); a false negative is the overlooking of a real effect.

Designing medical tests involves, as a major element, balancing the risks of false positives against the risks of false negatives. There is seldom a sharp line that separates unambiguously positive from unambiguously negative results. Instead, the designer of a test usually has to set a threshold for detection of a "positive" result. The higher the threshold, the more likely it is that a "positive" result is correct—but, at the same time, the more likely it is that the test will miss some real positive cases. If the threshold for detecting a disease is too high, a test may identify victims of the disease with few false alarms (that is, with a low rate of false positives.) But, by the same token, the test may overlook many real victims of the disease (that is, it may have a high rate of false negatives).

The designer of a test has to choose the parameters carefully, depending on how the test is to be used and what consequences may result from either false positives or false negatives. Either kind of error can cause real harm. For example, an incorrect diagnosis of breast cancer can cause serious emotional stress; a false negative may be fatal. If the condition being screened for is uncommon (e.g., HIV infection in the general population) the test has to have an exceedingly low rate of false positives, or it will yield many false indications of infection for every real case it detects. But pushing the risk of false positives down may result in a test that misses a relatively large fraction of infected individuals. If the condition is more common (e.g., HIV infection in urban gay men), the test designer may accept a higher rate of false positives so as to push down the risks of false negatives.

Thus, when specifying the "accuracy" of a test, one needs to consider the rates of both false positives and false negatives. The accuracy of a test is usually defined as the frequency with which the test will produce positive results when given known positive samples; the specificity is the proportion of negative results for a group of known negative samples. We shall return to the issue of accuracy of detection as it relates to scientific testimony in chapter 5.

Statistical Significance and Confidence Intervals

Another source of uncertainty is sampling error, which is inevitable when an investigator studies a small sample and extrapolates the data to a much larger population—as when a pollster interviews a few hundred potential voters, measures the sample mean (the stated preferences of the voters), and then estimates the population mean (the results of the election). Sampling error casts a shadow of uncertainty over any study that attempts to describe entire populations on the basis of studies of sample groups.

Sampling error and a related issue, statistical significance, are sources of great confusion when epidemiologic evidence is presented in court. A typical epidemiological study compares different groups of people (exposed vs. unexposed subjects, for example) in search of a difference in the incidence of an illness between groups. The results of such a study pertain to the sample—e.g., 100 middle-aged American males, rather than all middle-aged Americans. A difference in sample means may not indicate any real difference between the populations (a difference in population means). Because of sampling errors, the difference between the groups of subjects may be only a statistical fluke. Careful pollsters and scientists qualify their results with some indication of the sampling uncertainties.

The statistical uncertainties due to sampling error are chiefly determined by the size of the sample. When one is searching for small effects (such as a possible association between lung cancer and passive smoking, or between lung cancer and radon in the home), this calls for large studies with correspondingly small sampling errors. Larger effects (e.g., lung cancer in smokers) can be detected reliably with much smaller studies. (Whether other, nonrandom errors are significant is a different matter entirely.)

Scientists use several methods to estimate and report sampling error. One common method is to report confidence intervals—"error bars" about the results of a study, within which the correct results for the entire population will lie with a given probability. If a hypothetical epidemiologist reports an odds ratio of 2 with 95 percent confidence intervals from 0.5 to 8, he or she means that the ratio of the number of exposed individuals with a disease to those without the disease, divided by the ratio of nonexposed individuals with the disease to those without (i.e., the odds ratio) for the people in the study, was 2. A similar ratio, if calculated on the basis of the entire population, would fall between 0.5 and 8 with a probability of 95 percent. The exposure may have led to an eightfold increase in risk, or to no effect, or even to a modest protective effect. In statistical jargon, this increase in odds ratio above 1 is "not statistically significant," and few scientists would accept the reported difference as indicating a real effect. In other words, there is an unacceptably high probability that the "effect" is a result of random sampling errors.

Scientists constantly argue over the criteria for rejecting the null hypothesis (i.e., for concluding that there is a real difference between the groups being compared). Most scientists require that the difference between control and exposed groups in a study be "statistically significant" at the $p = 0.05$ level. This means that there is a probability of less than 5 percent—according to the statistical tests used—that the investigators would have recorded a difference as large in the sample if the populations from which the groups were drawn were the same with respect to the properties being compared. A difference that is statistically significant has a low probability of being a statistical fluke: the two populations being compared probably are different.

As with medical tests, deciding whether a difference is statistically significant requires that the investigator choose an arbitrary threshold above which differences between the two groups are considered too large to be due to chance. A difference that is statistically significant is likely to represent a real effect—but how likely it is depends on the threshold one chooses for the test. Increasing the threshold (raising p from 0.05 to 0.10, for example) makes it less likely that one will overlook a real effect, but at the same time makes it more likely that one will find a nonexistent difference (i.e., incorrectly reject the null hypothesis). All this refers to random sampling errors only; nonrandom errors may also be present, but they cannot be estimated by statistical tests.

These issues are difficult for many scientists to understand, and they open the door to much confusion in court. Relative risk (the ratio of the incidence of disease in an exposed population to that in an unexposed population) describes the strength of association between exposure and disease. The confidence interval is a measure of the uncertainty in estimating that strength.

Some tort lawyers, backed by some scientists, have demanded that statistical tests be based on a confidence level of 0.50. This reflects a serious misunderstanding of statistics. Choosing a confidence level of 0.50 would lead to a very high rate of false positive results—a tort lawyer's dream. For their own part, many scientists would rather miss a small effect than falsely identify an effect that is not present. For that reason, perhaps, scientists generally prefer a smaller p value, typically 0.05. Some epidemiologists prefer to use a p value of 0.10, on the grounds that public health is better served by increasing the chances of reporting a real effect, even though this also increases the chances of a false alarm.

The decision to accept or reject a hypothesis on the basis of statistical considerations requires judgment which, to a lay observer, may be obscured by the apparent precision of the analysis. The statement that a difference between two groups is statistically significant presupposes a sharp line between what is "statistically significant" and what is "not significant." "Statistical significance" as used in this context has nothing to do with the layperson's use of "significance" to mean importance. And where the line lies is not a scientific matter at all. Perhaps more serious, pronouncing that a difference is statistically significant does not describe the magnitude of the effect or the uncertainties in the measurement.

In an attempt to increase the objectivity of scientific reports, some scientists have suggested moving away from discussions of "level of significance" toward more sophisticated approaches, based on confidence intervals, that characterize the data but allow the users of the data to make their own decisions about its precision. The epidemiologist Kenneth Rothman notes that "the use of confidence intervals . . . yields a remarkable improvement in clarity of interpretation for everyone and

Box 4.4
The Lower Courts' Focus on Significance Testing Is Based on the
Inaccurate Assumption That "Statistical Significance" Is Required in
Order to Draw Inferences from Epidemiological Information

brief amicus curiae of Professors Kenneth Rothman, Noel Weiss, James Robins,
Raymond Neutra, and Steven Stellman in support of petitioners, *Daubert v. Merrell
Dow Pharmaceuticals, Inc.*, Dkt. No. 92-102 (U.S. Dec. 11, 1992) (citations omitted)

The notion that only when data demonstrate "statistical significance" do
epidemiologists draw inferences about observed associations between suspected risk factors and medical conditions is mistaken. Significance testing
is nothing more than a statistical technique that attempts to evaluate what
is called "chance" as a possible explanation for a set of observations, and
classify the observations "significant" or "not significant" based on the likelihood of observing them if there were no relationship between the suspected cause and effect. Testing for significance, however, is often mistaken for
a *sine qua non* of scientific inference.

It is crucial that this Court understand the distinction between these two
separate and distinct processes. Scientific inference is the practice of evaluating theories. As such, it is a thoughtful process, requiring thoughtful evaluations of possible explanations for what is being observed. Significance
testing, on the other hand, is merely a statistical tool that is frequently, but
inappropriately, utilized in the process of developing inferences.

. . . Significance testing serves, however, merely as a tool for epidemiologists to achieve their scientific objectives. Indeed, the term "statistical significance" could be expunged from the lexicon of the epidemiologist with
no loss; accordingly it should not be allowed to assume an importance or
role in law beyond its use as an epidemiological tool. When used to evaluate the association between exposure and disease, the concept of statistical
significance is often misleading and never descriptive of the magnitude of
effect or the precision of measurement. Nonetheless, a factfinder who is told
that a body of data is not "statistically significant" is made to believe that
the data has no value. Unfortunately, the seemingly talismanic phrase "statistically significant" creates a misleading aura of infallibility totally out of
relation to its actual value. . . .

Significance testing . . . places too high a value on a "yes-no" answer
to an oversimplified question: Is the probability that the observed association could appear by chance, even if there is no actual relationship, low
enough to justify rejection of chance as the explanation of the observed
association? . . .

A better approach to evaluating the error in scientific measurement is the
use of "confidence intervals." A confidence interval is a range of possible
values for a parameter that is consistent with the observed data within specified limits. The process of calculating a confidence interval within the chosen limits is know as "interval estimation." . . .

Without expressing a position on the ultimate issue of the toxicity of Bendectin, it is obvious to us that no "massive weight" or sense of consensus can flow from the observation that a number of studies have been published involving Bendectin and that the authors of those studies did not infer a "statistically significant association." To give weight to the failure of epidemiological studies to meet strict "statistical significant" standards—to use such studies to close the door on further inquiry—is not good science. . . . [I]t is both bad science and bad policy. . . .

The analysis employed by the lower courts forecloses the use of valid inferences that may be drawn from the combination of many studies, even when none of the studies standing alone would justify such inferences.

Empirical research quite often yields data that suggest an association between a suspected risk factor and a medical condition, but with too small a data set to proclaim confidently that the observed association is real, and not merely the result of random factors. . . .

This commonsense observation is not novel or controversial, yet the opinion of the appellate court forecloses analysis based on it. To the extent that the lower courts' opinion bars expert opinions not based on published conclusions, that opinion removes relevant information from the legal decision maker. . . .

Thus, to the extent that the opinion of the appellate court would bar consideration of the cumulative effect of many studies, even when none of them individually is "statistically significant," it should be rejected on the basis that such a conclusion is scientifically inappropriate.

prevents overt misinterpretation by unwary readers or investigators."[7] In box 4.4 we present an excerpt from an amicus brief filed by Rothman and other epidemiologists that echoes this view of significance testing, and in box 4.5 we present a rejoinder by Feinstein.

Meta-Analysis

One way to reduce sampling error is to increase the size of the sample. Meta-analysis is one technique for combining the results of individual studies in an attempt to identify small effects that can be hidden in them. In effect, the technique averages the results of the studies. Meta-analysis is routinely used by investigators to help identify subtle adverse effects of drugs, for example. Meta-analysis has played an important role in debates about risk of lung cancer from passive smoking, in which individual studies failed to detect a link but a meta-analysis of the data suggested (at least to the Environmental Protection Agency) that a link existed.

Box 4.5
Special Problems in Aggregation of Data

brief amicus curiae of Professor Alvan R. Feinstein in support of respondent, *Daubert v. Merrell Dow Pharmaceuticals*, No. 92-102 (U.S. Jan. 19, 1993)

... What is important to understand ... is that both significance testing and confidence intervals are tools for evaluating the stability of the numbers being examined. In urging that significance testing be scientifically expunged and "removed from the inappropriate legal pedestal," Rothman, et al. completely ignore the necessity that the data used for drawing inferences be numerically stable, and that specific statistical standards must be established to demonstrate that stability. . . .

... Rothman, et al. are apparently urging that the occasionally excessive rigidity of P values be replaced by the anarchy of unrestricted confidence intervals. . . .

Rothman, et al. suggest that their position on numerical stability is supported by "a large community of respected epidemiologists." ... If so, I suspect that the epidemiologists do not really understand precisely what is implied in Rothman, et al.'s recommendations. I feel certain that most members of the "community" of scientists would reject the numerical anarchy that is being proposed. They would insist that standards of intellectual discipline be honored, that standards of numerical stability be maintained, and that evidence not be accepted if it fails to meet the standards of numerical stability. The standards can be established either via P values or circumscribed confidence intervals (or even with some new "fragility" techniques that are beyond the scope of this discussion). The standards should be appropriately flexible, but they must exist if science is to preserve its tradition of intellectual discipline and high quality research.

I can think of no better way to allow "junk science" into both the published literature and the courtroom than to remove the constraints that demand numerical stability for data. If researchers can choose confidence intervals in an *ad hoc* manner, without justifying their selection of appropriate boundary values according to accepted scientific standards, the result will be confidence games, not confidence intervals.

Meta-analysis became an issue in the Bendectin litigation. Numerous studies individually failed to find a statistically significant association between the use of the drug and birth defects; the plaintiffs' expert witnesses argued that an association existed. One witness, the aforementioned Alan Done, summarized numerous Bendectin studies in an attempt to uncover an effect, but he explicitly denied using meta-analysis. (In fact, it appears, he did not use any statistically valid method of analysis at all—see the last section of this chapter.) In contrast, several meta-analyses of the Bendectin data published in the scientific literature failed to find any effects.

Meta-analysis, though useful, is hardly capable of overcoming many fundamental limitations of epidemiology. As Feinstein points out in his *Daubert* amicus brief, the studies whose results are averaged may vary greatly in quality and design, and meta-analysis can easily lead to "apples and oranges" comparisons whose real uncertainties are obscured by the apparent precision of the results. Moreover, the individual studies will have nonrandom errors that may or may not cancel out in the averaging of the data. In short: If the data are weak, statistically massaging them doesn't much improve the chance of drawing a reliable inference. In this as in other areas in science, it is always difficult to measure reliably signals that are buried in noise. Fancy statistics can be a powerful tool, but they can also lead to an illusion of precision that is entirely misleading.

Quantifying and Reporting Scientific Error

A judge attempting to assess an expert's proffered testimony might well begin by considering how carefully the expert has documented potential errors in methods or data. Wilson's *Introduction to Scientific Research* and the ISO standards might be used by judges as benchmarks.

In practice, few scientific reports would meet the ISO's or Wilson's standards, and judges should bear this too in mind. In normal scientific work, scientists are expected to provide some kind of "error analysis," but just what kind is usually left up to the individual scientist to decide. Research that is federally regulated (for example, drug or toxicology testing) must meet relevant standards (e.g., Good Laboratory Practices in toxicology testing)—but these standards are directed more toward maintaining the integrity of data than toward ensuring thorough analysis of potential errors in them.

Error analysis in scientific reports varies greatly in thoroughness and in approach. Error assessment in science is governed by few standards. The ISO standards are voluntary; they are not enforced in any deliberate way, and they probably are unfamiliar to most scientists in any event. Scientists disregard them with impunity. Few scientists conduct the exhaustive error analysis that the ISO recommends, and few scientific papers are written in a way that would meet the ISO norms. Scientific findings that are expected or uncontroversial, or those that agree with a scientist's pet theory, typically receive far less thorough analysis of potential errors than unexpected or controversial results.

However, the obligation of scientists to carry out an investigation of the potential errors in their work is still very clear. A scientist's failure or unwillingness to directly confront potential errors in his or her own work is almost conclusive proof, in and of itself, that the work is flawed. As John Ziman points out, "a properly phrased scientific communication should never be a categorical assertion, but should always convey the author's assessment of the credibility of his own claims." (See box 4.6.)

Cautionary Tales

A surprisingly large fraction of scientific reports are wrong. Scientists, like other people, are frequently overconfident in their work. The much-praised reliability of science occurs only in the long term; in the short term, science is as flawed, as error-prone, and as subject to manipulations and intellectual passions as any other human activity. (See boxes 4.7 and 4.8.)

Pathological science was first described in a cynical but amusing 1953 lecture in which the chemist Irving Langmuir recounted the histories of several great discoveries that eventually turned out not to be real. (The physicist Richard Feynman described an even more pathological "cargo cult science"—see boxes 4.9 and 4.10.) "Pathological science," according to Langmuir, typically begins when a scientist thinks that he or she has discovered a new effect that is barely detectable in the noise, becomes personally committed to the "discovery," and sets aside the good scientist's normal skepticism. The "discovery" generates much enthusiasm, at first, until the bubble bursts. Though it came long after Langmuir's day, cold fusion is one recent and notorious example. It is fair to say that similar incidents occur frequently in science but remain hidden from public view because of the relative obscurity of the controversies. Cold fusion differed only in its greater public visibility.

Box 4.6
Signal or Noise?

John M. Ziman

source: *Reliable Knowledge: An Exploration of the Grounds for Belief in Science* (Cambridge University Press, 1978), pp. 64–70 (citations omitted)

It is a commonplace of elementary scientific method that every experimental result is subject to some degree of uncertainty. . . . The logic of the empirical is made three-valued by *experimental error*. . . . A properly phrased scientific communication should never be a categorical assertion, but should always convey the author's assessment of the credibility of his own claims. . . .

. . . The aim of the research is to produce a publishable scientific result, of adequate plausibility, not complete proof. . . .

In the physical sciences, experimental uncertainties can take on an active role. . . . In very sensitive instruments the unavoidable uncertainties and errors of observation are magnified into an apparently autonomous random disturbance, impishly impeding the honest search for truth.

The techniques used to separate the desired signal from the noise are very important in highly instrumented science, and cannot be ignored in any assessment of the ultimate reliability of scientific knowledge. . . .

But these techniques may not be so efficient when we look for a signal that may not be there at all, or whose basic characteristics can only be guessed. . . .

In the physical sciences, we can often reduce the level of background noise by improvements in our apparatus. But the intrinsic variability of biological organisms and social institutions is usually quite incorrigible, and the design of a deliberately causal experiment runs into ethical or political obstacles—or ends up by killing the goose that laid the golden eggs. In desperation we invent refined techniques of statistical analysis to separate the 'signal' from the 'noise', but the uncertainties of strict causality may turn out to be irreducible. . . .

The point to be emphasized is that the information exchanged between scientific observers, and eventually transmitted to the archive as consensual elements of public knowledge does not include every pointer reading of every physical instrument, nor the answers given to every sociological questionnaire. . . . It is the task of the individual observer to minimize, but not to underrate, the noise content of his data, for it will be the goal of the scientific community to select the correct signals from the background rubbish, and to give them out, stripped of all apparent uncertainty, as reliable knowledge and the scientific truth.

Box 4.7
A Fistful of Fallacies I

Petr Skrabanek and James McCormick

source: *Follies and Fallacies in Medicine* (Prometheus Books, 1990) (citations omitted)

The fallacy of authority is believing things to be true because of the authoritative source of the information. It must be true because I read it in the paper, saw it on television, the surgeon said so, the *Lancet* published it. . . .

[The Fallacy of "Everybody Says So"] . . . In the current medical textbooks, two specialty monographs, and also in a standard pharmacopoeia, it is said that phenytoin, a drug commonly used to control fits, can cause red urine if the urine is acid. B. M. Derby and J. W. Ward traced this myth to a reference in a pharmacy journal. After telephoning the author they were given the exact source of his reference, which when checked turned out to be without foundation. . . .

[The Fallacy of the Golden Mean] . . . Scientific truth is established on the basis of irrefutable evidence, not upon the majority opinion. . . .

[The Fallacy of Obfuscation] . . . In medical writing, we should strive for clarity. . . . Verbiage may hide manipulation of data. . . .

[The Fallacy of Covert Bias] It is relatively easy by careful reading of most scientific articles to discover the direction in which the authors would wish to see the results of a study going, and thus to be alerted to the possibility that the results were pushed in that direction. . . .

[The "Gold Effect" Fallacy] . . . At the beginning a few people arrive at a state of near belief in some idea. A meeting is held to discuss the pros and cons of the idea. More people favoring the idea than those disinterested will be present. A representative committee will be nominated to prepare a collective volume to propagate and foster interest in the idea. The totality of resulting articles based on the idea will appear to show an increasing consensus. A specialized journal will be launched. Only orthodox or near orthodox articles will pass the referees and the editor.

Incidents of pathological science have much in common with popular delusions such as stock market bubbles or the frenzy for speculation in tulips that developed in Holland in the seventeenth century. Incidents of pathological science differ from such popular delusions only in the level of specialization. Anyone can speculate in tulip bulbs, but the number of scientists who are equipped to do experiments on cold fusion (for example) is very small. Because of the self-correcting nature of science, incidents of pathological science are undoubtedly much shorter lived than many popular delusions. If the "discoveries" appear to be at all important, many

Box 4.8
When Does Intellectual Passion Become Conflict of Interest?
Eliot Marshall
source: *Science*, July 31, 1992: 620–624

Financial conflicts of interest are very much in the news in science, particularly in the cutting edge fields of biology that border on biotechnology. As the financial stakes grow, the confusion is likely to grow as well, until the scientific community settles on rules and procedures for dealing with conflicts between research and profit. . . . But in talking with researchers about potential financial conflicts, *Science* heard one refrain over and over again: that money problems are simple compared to the intellectual conflicts of interest that scientists have always had to deal with.

What did those researchers mean by intellectual conflicts of interest? They were referring to the fact that, although science is often thought of as a dispassionate pursuit of facts, in reality it is much more than that. Scientists are, after all, human beings. They often begin their work with a hypothesis and become deeply invested in it, long before peers regard it as credible. Along the way to proving a thesis, therefore, scientists must be sustained by something that approaches faith. And, as paleontologist-essayist-historian Stephen Jay Gould says, it is a "pervasive fact of human existence as social beings" that we find it extraordinarily difficult to step outside our own convictions and see them through the eyes of a detached observer.

Every researcher relies on personal intuition to some extent, so the important question is: When does a scientist's enthusiasm for an idea cross the line that separates passion from obsession? It doesn't take a sociologist to recognize the extreme cases. Working scientists can and do readily identify peers whom they regard as having become advocates, no longer capable of reading evidence in an evenhanded way. But sometimes those advocates are right. And in these rare cases, science is advanced by the determined, committed, even the obsessed individual, not by the doubting peers. . . .

. . . [A]lmost every researcher . . . talked to on this subject acknowledged that intellectual conflicts of interest—or potential conflicts—are pervasive. The key difference among scientists, they said, is not between those who have conflicts and those who do not, but in how the potential conflicts are handled—whether the researcher has the detachment required to be the severest critic of his or her own work.

All researchers tend to "mythologize" their research, says Boston University's philosopher of anthropology, Misia Landau. And this isn't necessarily bad, she adds, because it takes self-confidence to push ahead. Landau thinks "the most inspired work gets done in light of some hypothesis" that serves as a "guiding paradigm." Yet scientists must also be ready to drop a cherished idea the moment better information comes along. It's important, she says, to "practice a certain self-reflection."

In the absence of that self-reflection, an advocate becomes so deeply invested that it's almost impossible to let go, even in the face of contrary evidence. "Any theory can be patched, by ad hoc addition of assumptions to fit with existing data," writes psychologist Anthony Greenwald of the University of Washington in Seattle, who has analyzed problems scientists have in developing good research strategies. The goal is to "disconfirm" an idea, Greenwald writes, not confirm it. Otherwise, the scientist risks becoming "ego-involved" in the idea and "may be willing to persevere indefinitely," despite negative results.

scientists will soon enter the picture, and nondiscoveries will quickly vanish. This may not happen, easily, however, if strong forces from outside science come into play. Trofim Denisovich Lysenko kept his crackpot theories of genetics alive for years with the help of his patron, Josef Stalin.

There is an element of schadenfreude in Langmuir's lecture, a bit like the pleasure one may feel upon reading about the disastrous losses of "expert traders" in the stock market. But Langmuir's lecture had a serious purpose. The characteristics of pathological science he lists are not prescriptions for good scientific reasoning; they are warning signs to help steer careful scientists away from trouble. The difficulty, as always, lies in recognizing a speculative bubble (in either the scientific or financial world) for what it is before it bursts. Charles MacKay's 1841 book *Extraordinary Popular Delusions and the Madness of Crowds* (reprinted in 1980 by Harmony Books) did not stop many other financial bubbles from inflating and then bursting in the century and a half after its publication. Langmuir's lecture did not prevent the cold-fusion episode from unfolding decades later. The true believers were, for the most part, reputable scientists who got carried away with an exciting, beautiful, but incorrect theory.

Langmuir's description of pathological science has important implications for the courtroom. Most obvious, science has its speculative bubbles and its true believers in unlikely theories. At the very inception of a case of pathological science, Langmuir points out, there are often as many supporters as skeptics of the theory. It takes time for the balance of scientific opinion to shift decisively. Many (even most) of the original believers see the errors of their ways and abandon the theory. Other scientists gradually make up their minds and reject the fallacious claim. But any scientific cause, no matter how hopeless it might appear, will find some reputable scientists who will continue to back it. Such true believers may end their days as peripatetic and well-paid expert witnesses.

Box 4.9
Symptoms of Sick Science
Irving Langmuir

source: "Pathological Science," *Physics Today*, October 1989: 36–48 (transcribed and edited by R. N. Hall) (emphasis added)

The Davis-Barnes experiment and the N rays and the mitogenetic rays all have things in common. These are cases where there is no dishonesty involved but where people are tricked into false results by a lack of understanding about what human beings can do to themselves in the way of being led astray by subjective effects, wishful thinking or threshold interactions. These are examples of pathological science. These are things that attracted a great deal of attention. Usually hundreds of papers have been published on them. Sometimes they have lasted for 15 or 20 years and then they gradually have died away. Now here are the characteristic rules:

The maximum effect that is observed is produced by a causative agent of barely detectable intensity. For example, you might think that if one onion root would affect another due to ultraviolet light then by putting on an ultraviolet source of light you could get it to work better. Oh no! *Oh no!* It had to be just the amount of intensity that's given off by an onion root. Ten onion roots wouldn't do any better than one and it didn't make any difference about the distance of the source. . . . We know why it had to be of low intensity: so that you could fool yourself so easily. Otherwise, it wouldn't work. . . .

Another characteristic thing about them all is that *these observations are near the threshold of visibility of the eyes.* Any other sense, I suppose, would work as well. Or *many measurements are necessary—many measurements— because of the very low statistical significance of the results.* . . . Statistical measurements of a very small effect. . . were thought to be significant if you took large numbers. Now the trouble with that is this. [Most people have a habit, when taking] measurements of low significance, [of finding] a means of rejecting data. They are right at the threshold value and there are many reasons why [they] can discard data. . . .

There are claims of great accuracy. Barnes was going to get the Rydberg constant more accurately than the spectroscopists could. Great sensitivity or great specificity . . . .

Fantastic theories contrary to experience. In the Bohr theory, the whole idea of an electron being captured by an alpha particle when the alpha particles aren't there, just because the waves are there, [isn't] a very sensible theory.

Criticisms are met by ad hoc excuses thought up on the spur of the moment. They always had an answer—always.

The ratio of the supporters to the critics rises up somewhere near 50% and then falls gradually to oblivion. The critics couldn't reproduce the effects. Only the supporters could do that. In the end, nothing was salvaged. Why should there be? There isn't anything there. There never was. That's characteristic of the effect.

Box 4.10
Cargo Cult Science
Richard P. Feynman

source: *Surely You're Joking, Mr. Feynman!* (Bantam Books, 1985)

In the South Seas there is a cargo cult of people. During the war they saw airplanes land with lots of good materials, and they want the same thing to happen now. So they've arranged to make things like runways, to put fires along the sides of the runways, to make a wooden hut for a man to sit in, with two wooden pieces on his head like headphones and bars of bamboo sticking out like antennas—he's the controller—and they wait for the airplanes to land. They're doing everything right. The form is perfect. It looks exactly the way it looked before. But it doesn't work. No airplanes land. So I call these things cargo cult science, because they follow all the apparent precepts and forms of scientific investigation, but they're missing something essential, because the planes don't land.

Now it behooves me, of course, to tell you what they're missing. But it would be just about as difficult to explain to the South Sea Islanders how they have to arrange things so that they get some wealth in their system. It is not something simple like telling them how to improve the shapes of the earphones. But there is *one* feature I notice that is generally missing in cargo cult science. That is the idea that we all hope you have learned in studying science in school—we never explicitly say what this *is*, but just hope that you catch on by all the examples of scientific investigation. It is interesting, therefore, to bring it out now and speak of it explicitly. It's a kind of scientific integrity, a principle of scientific thought that corresponds to a kind of utter honesty—a kind of leaning over backwards. For example, if you're doing an experiment, you should report everything that you think might make it invalid—not only what you think is right about it: other causes that could possibly explain your results; and things you thought of that you've eliminated by some other experiment, and how they worked—to make sure the other fellow can tell they have been eliminated.

. . . There is also a more subtle problem. When you have put a lot of ideas together to make an elaborate theory, you want to make sure, when explaining what it fits, that those things it fits are not just the things that gave you the idea for the theory; but that the finished theory makes something else come out right, in addition. . . . If you've made up your mind to test a theory, or you want to explain some idea, you should always decide to publish it whichever way it comes out. If we only publish results of a certain kind, we can make the argument look good.

At a deeper level, Langmuir's lecture points to the difficulty science has in identifying small effects. Most of the incidents of pathological science have occurred only because the phenomena were small, at the very edge of detectability. But many phenomena of interest in the courtroom—such as the purported teratogenic effects of Bendectin—are also at the edge of detectability(if they exist at all). And for subtle hazards the "edge of detectability" often corresponds to a doubling of risk, which coincides roughly with the "more likely than not" criterion of civil litigation.

It is astonishing how unreliable the scientific literature is, at least in the short term. One authority notes the literature contains many reports of biological "effects" of electromagnetic fields that are nonreproducible and presumably wrong.[8] (See box 4.11.) The epidemiology literature contains many reports of associations between exposure and disease that are not confirmed upon further examination. The supposed link between coffee and pancreatic cancer is one. This link was reported by an eminent Harvard epidemiologist, then "un-reported" a few years later.[9] In all these cases, the scientists tried their best to detect small effects in noisy data. They were wrong.

Scientific errors do not usually excite scientists (except when they are caught making them). And few scientists profess any enthusiasm for "doing something about" pathological science. Most scientists would simply shrug their shoulders and say that error is an inescapable part of taking intellectual risks. Science that takes few risks (for example, painstaking animal screening studies in toxicology) may be useful, but to most scientists it would be dull and hardly worth reading.

The errors that Langmuir documents are outside the range of normal science. But even within normal science, errors are commonplace. Indeed, most of the measurements of certain well-defined physical constants (such as the speed of light) made over a period of many years differ from the currently accepted values.[10] For example, many scientists have measured the speed of light. Today we have a very accurate figure at hand, so we can look back and see how well scientists estimated their own errors in the past. The results, discussed in box 4.12, are instructive. As the studies continued, the reported values gradually converged toward the now-accepted value. But the errors in the individual studies were clearly not random. For years at a time, results of successive studies were either too low or too high.

Box 4.11
Phantom Effects from Small Errors

As box 4.12 shows, scientists often have difficulties in estimating the reliability of their measurements. But the consequences of this difficulty can vary greatly. A small error in the measurement of a physical quantity, such as the velocity of light, might not lead to serious qualitative errors. But a small error, when searching for a small effect, may lead to major error: the identification of an "effect" that is not really there.

Studies of the biological effects of electromagnetic fields show this problem very clearly. Exposing an animal to strong fields will lead to obvious effects: it takes no great science to identify changes in a rat when it is placed in a microwave oven. But effects, if any exist, from fields at typical environmental levels are subtle and difficult to detect in the face of a great deal of biological variability.

E. L. Carstensen gave some idea of the magnitude of the problem in his 1987 book *The Biological Effects of Transmission Line Fields*, which listed 239 reported biological effects of 50–60-hertz electric fields, at field strengths ranging from near the dielectric breakdown strength of air to as low as 0.04 volts per meter. A smaller number of effects were reported from power-frequency magnetic fields, some in the range of Earth's magnetic field or lower. About a quarter of these effects were later confirmed by other investigators and are presumably real. (The confirmed effects generally were reported at high field levels and involve obvious phenomena such as shock and corona.) But a large fraction of these reported effects from electric fields (about a third) could not be confirmed by other investigators and presumably are artifacts. The remainder of the reported effects were (as of the time of Carstensen's review) not followed up to the point where they could be judged to be either confirmed or negated. Fifty effects have been claimed from exposure to 50–60-Hz magnetic fields, of which barely a tenth have been independently confirmed.

The history of the supposed effects of microwave energy on the blood-brain barrier illustrates the problem. The blood-brain barrier is a physiologically and anatomically complex system in vertebrates that protects sensitive brain tissues from ordinary variations in the composition of the blood, while allowing transport of nutrients into the brain. The first report that exposure to microwave fields was associated with a change in the barrier permeability appeared in a Russian journal in 1972. The issue came to life in 1975 when an American investigator reported that exposure to microwave energy (at levels far below the accepted microwave exposure standards of the time) caused the leakage of fluorescent dye from blood into the brain of rats. In the following decade at least 15 groups worked on the problem, using progressively better controlled and more sensitive techniques. The effect went away except at high exposure levels that raised the temperature of the brain to 42–43 degrees Celsius. One of the investigators who

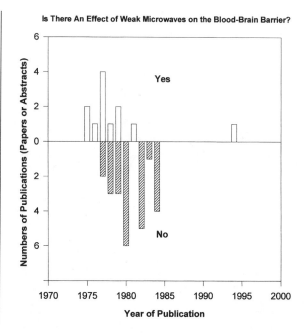

Is There An Effect of Weak Microwaves on the Blood-Brain Barrier?

first reported an "effect" of microwave exposure at levels below 100 watts per square meter later reported a study—employing an improved technique with 200 times the sensitivity of his earlier measurements—that found no changes in the permeability of the blood-brain barrier over the range of power levels employed, 0–400 W/m^2. The figure in this box shows the number of reports of an "effect" or of "no effect" of microwaves at levels below accepted safety standards during this time period. The science converged, and by the mid 1980s most investigators agreed that no effect could be detected at low exposure levels. But it took a decade for this agreement to be reached, and some scientists would undoubtedly still maintain that an effect was present nevertheless.

The wheel turns: in 1994 a Swedish group reported that amplitude-modulated microwaves can affect the blood-brain barrier of rats, apparently by a mechanism different from simple heating. What happened? Detecting small changes in the blood-brain barrier is beset with many technical problems. The few studies that claimed large effects from small exposures to microwave energy were weak, and their results could not be confirmed by later studies. Nobody disputes that gross heating of the brain will disrupt the barrier, and some of the studies that reported effects from low-level microwaves might have actually have reported thermally induced changes. The results of the 1994 Swedish study remain unexplained and, for the moment, unconfirmed.

The scientists, it appears, designed or conducted their experiments to produce results that did not depart too sharply from what the experimenters expected to find—which is to say, values reported by other scientists of the day. If the original estimates of the standard errors in the studies were correct, two-thirds of the reported values should fall within what the original investigator estimated to be one "standard error" of what we now know to be the accurate value. But there are many more outlying values with far larger errors than would be expected if the original estimates of potential errors were accurate. The investigators, in many cases, underestimated the errors in their studies, sometimes by large amounts.

If physics—the hardest and most precise of the hard sciences—can give rise to systematic mistakes like these, what about softer sciences such as epidemiology and economics? Alexander Shlyakhter examined past predictions about population and energy consumption and found that many turned out to be wrong by amounts that exceeded the uncertainties the forecasters provided at the time.[11] Again, the scientists badly underestimated the uncertainties in their studies. According to Shlyakhter, scientists typically report uncertainties in their predictions that are, on the average, too small by factors ranging from 2 to 10 (depending on the field). In other words, the predictions often missed the mark by amounts that far exceeded the original estimates of their uncertainty. Scientists working in the "precise" physical sciences were typically more accurate in estimating the uncertainties in their predictions than those working in the social sciences. Nobody, it seems, is very reliable in estimating true uncertainties in his or her predictions. These errors are not pathological in any sense. It is not easy to probe the unknown very precisely; it is even more difficult to estimate at the time how imprecise one's probing really is. Schlyakhter offers a simple prescription to compensate for this overconfidence: increase the "uncertainties" that an investigator reports by a factor ranging from 2 to 10, depending on the past track record of the field. In effect, the investigator's data are far less precise than he or she reports. Judges would be well advised to similarly discount estimates of potential errors presented by scientists or other experts in court.

The most benign interpretation of the seemingly universal tendency of experts to underestimate their errors is their failure to account for all of the potential errors. For example: When presenting results of DNA tests in

Box 4.12
Measurement of Errors: Larger than the Experts Think

Measurements of the speed of light (*c*) show clearly both the characteristic overconfidence of scientists and the ability of science to converge on correct answers. The accompanying figure (from M. Henrion and B. Fischhoff, Assessing uncertainty in physical constants, *American Journal of Physics* 54 (1986): 791–797) shows 21 values of *c* reported in the twentieth century.

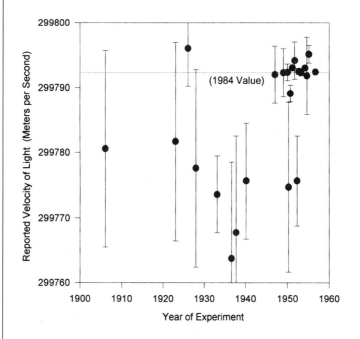

The error bars in the figure show the standard error, either as quoted by the investigators or as estimated by Henrion and Fischhoff. They represent the confidence intervals for the measurements. If the measurements were normally distributed about the mean (correct) value, about a third of the values would miss the correct (currently accepted) value by an amount that exceeds the standard error. In fact, eight of the 21 reported measurements miss the mark by amounts that exceed their standard errors—about as expected.

However, not all is well. The distribution of the errors shows that many investigators badly underestimated their errors. Henrion and Fischhoff pointed out that only 2 percent of the results should miss the mark by an amount that exceeds the 98 percent confidence interval (2.33 times the standard error). But, out of 27 measurements of *c* made over the period 1875–1958, three missed the mark by this much. If the original estimates of the standard errors were correct, the number of measurements that were so far off should have been less than one. Henrion and Fischhoff show that similar problems are found in the measurements of many other physical constants.

The figure also shows that the reported values did converge. Particularly since 1950, measurements of c have become progressively more precise (with smaller error bars) and more accurate (closer to the correct value). However, close examination of the data since 1950 shows that many investigators still underestimated their errors. The measurements had become more precise (with smaller error bars), but the error bars were still too small. Optimism is eternal.

court, experts typically stress the very small probability (one in billions) that the DNA recovered from the scene of the crime would match that of an individual randomly chosen from the population. By this measure, the probability of a false positive result—of incorrectly determining that the defendant was the source of the DNA found at the crime scene—is vanishingly small.[12] These very small error rates have contributed to the perception that DNA testing is infallible. But these numbers reflect only population genetics, not the analytical procedures that laboratories employ. One study, in which blood and semen samples were supplied to testing laboratories, showed false-positive detection rates (i.e., rates of incorrect matches) that ranged from about one per hundred to one per thousand tests.[13] These error rates, associated with analysis of samples, are so vastly greater than the false-positive detection rates calculated on the basis of population genetics that the latter are virtually irrelevant to the real world of courtrooms and evidence. Errors in collecting and handling the evidence will increase error rates further.

Finally, one must also keep in mind that the worst errors often come from how science is used rather than from how science is performed. As William Havender and Aaron Wildavsky have pointed out, efforts to mitigate hazards correctly identified by science may in fact end up aggravating problems rather than mitigating them. (See box 4.13.)

Fraud and Data Torturing

Beyond honest error, of course, lies the possibility of either reckless or deliberate misrepresentation. In 1830 the mathematician Charles Babbage identified several kinds of fraud and data manipulation.[14] His distinctions remain useful today:

Trimming "consists of clipping off little bits here and there from those observations which differ most in excess from the mean, and in sticking them on to those which are too small. . . ."

Cooking is "an art of various forms, the object of which is to give to ordinary observations the appearance and character of those of the highest degree of accuracy. . . . One of its numerous processes is to make multitudes of observations, and out of these to select those only which agree, or very nearly agree. If a hundred observations are made, the cook must be very unlucky if he cannot pick out fifteen or twenty which will do for serving up."

A *forger* is "one who, wishing to acquire a reputation for science, records observations which he has never made. . . . Fortunately instances of the occurrence of forging are rare."

Deliberate manipulation of scientific data is, of course, unethical—and in many instances it is illegal. Gross fraud seems to be quite rare in science. But all scientists throw out data that are clearly erroneous, and scientists commonly repeat experiments until they get what they are looking for. The line between this honorable and necessary practice and "cooking" or "trimming" is by no means precise.

Such abuses are subtler and harder to detect than plagiarism and other forms of gross fraud; they are also more common. "The big problems are not with FFP [fabrication, falsification, plagiarism], but with other aspects of how scientists go about their jobs," said the statistician John Bailar. "I'm thinking of violations of high standards: not telling readers everything they need to know to evaluate a piece of work fairly. For example, repeating an experiment until you get the 'right' result and only reporting that is misconduct. [Conducting] 20 statistical tests until one is significant and only reporting that is misconduct. . . . None of these things fall under FFP, but they have become so widespread that they are a substantially greater threat to progress than relatively infrequent occurrences of FFP."[15]

In a 1993 article in the prestigious *New England Journal of Medicine*, the epidemiologist James Mills provides a different perspective on the same phenomenon.[16] (See box 4.14.) "Data torturing," as defined by Mills, is manipulation of data or post hoc interpretation of a study to reveal interesting features. The rubric covers a range of practices that fall within the broad gray zone between ethical and unethical scientific practices. The common thread is an investigator's tendency to focus on "interesting" aspects of data, and often to arrange results to highlight some features, while downplaying or disregarding others. For example, if the investigators

Box 4.13
Why Less Is More: A Taxonomy of Error
William R. Havender and Aaron Wildavsky
source: *Searching for Safety*, ed. A. Wildavsky (Transaction Books, 1988) (emphases added)

[V]irtually no attention has been paid to the many ways in which the direct effort to reduce identified risks can perversely, bring about a net increase in those same or other risks. Numerous examples of this paradox—less risk is more—can be cited. . . . We propose six categories of such errors:

Ignoring opportunity benefits [i.e., overlooking those existing risks that will continue unabated by the choice to delay the introduction of new technology that could reduce them]
Decisions to delay introducing new technologies may be motivated by a fear of new dangers associated with the innovation. But all too frequently, opportunities to reduce existing risks through innovation are merely ignored, and are never properly brought into the balancing of risks and benefits.

A classic instance of opportunity benefits foregone is "drug lag." Here, in the wake of the thalidomide tragedy, FDA required new drugs be proved "safe" before they could be marketed, a step that has added several years to the approval process of a new drug. While delay does reduce the chance of another thalidomide kind of episode . . . at the same time it raises risks of another sort, namely, the prolonged illnesses and unnecessary deaths that result from the delayed introduction of new and improved drugs, especially those that after prolonged testing in fact turn out to be safe and efficacious. . . .

Ignoring the "safety" risks associated with a proposed remedy
When a substance is in use, we learn a lot although, needless to say, not everything) about it. . . . Even if it has adverse effects, there is no point in abandoning it unless we are prepared to do without, or know of something better. . . .

Ignoring large existing benefits while concentrating on small existing risks
Many times the remedy is worse than the disease. Safety precautions may lower small risks while increasing more major risks. . . .

Ignoring the effects of economic costs on safety
[The] FDA's requirement for testing to establish the efficacy and safety of new drugs does not result only in delaying introduction of new drugs; it also increases substantially the costs of getting new drugs registered. Higher costs mean that it has become increasingly uneconomical to develop drugs for which the potential market is small. . . .

> *Ignoring the inevitable tradeoff between Type I (errors of commission) and*
> *Type II (errors of omission)*
> There is a kind of irreducible statistical uncertainty that limits how safe we
> can become, namely, the complementary relationship between Type I and
> Type II errors. An error of commission (Type I) is one that falsely raises an
> alarm when no hazard exists, and an error of omission (Type II) is one that
> falsely ignores a hazard that is in fact real. . . .
>
> *Ignoring risk displacement*
> The Clean Air Act mandated uniform maximal pollution standards across
> the country, specifically ruling out exemptions from the national standards
> for the localities immediately adjacent to power plants. These "hot spots"
> were the prime source of such pollutants. The solution? Disperse pollutants
> over a wide area by smokestacks a thousand or more feet in height. Dispersal
> did succeed in bringing local pollution levels into compliance with the man-
> date—but only by causing the offending substances to be wafted away by
> the prevailing winds to come down elsewhere, perhaps in the form of acid
> rain. . . .

in an epidemiological study perform 20 different comparisons when analyzing their data, one comparison will probably show a difference that is
"statistically significant" at the 5 percent level through chance alone. If
the investigators report the single "statistically significant" difference and
not the results of the 19 nonsignificant comparisons, they will give the
reader a very misleading impression of the overall significance of the study.

Data torturing may not cross the boundary into scientific fraud, but it
leads directly away from scientific objectivity. A doctor who focuses on
the patients who are cured by a treatment, and who loses track of those
who failed to respond, will end up publishing an overoptimistic assessment
of the treatment. That may deter others from exploring or using more
effective alternatives. Patients may be seriously harmed as a result. The
failure to follow up all patients who received a treatment is one of the most
common failures in research on "alternative medicine." A statistician who
sifts through health records and reports the few "statistically significant"
findings, but not the many comparisons conducted that revealed no "statistically significant" differences, is committing the same error. Casino slot
machines foster this kind of error deliberately: the bells ring only when
someone wins.

Box 4.14
Data Torturing
James L. Mills
source: *New England Journal of Medicine* 329 (1993): 1196–1199

There are two major types of data torturing. In the first, which I term "opportunistic" data torturing, the perpetrator simply pores over the data until a "significant" association is found between variables and then devises a biologically plausible hypothesis to fit the association. The second, or "Procrustean," type of data torturing is performed by deciding on the hypothesis to be proved and making the data fit the hypothesis (Procrustes, a robber in Greek mythology, made all his victims fit the length of his bed by stretching or cutting off their legs). . . .

One slightly fictionalized example of opportunistic data torturing is a study of parents' occupational exposures as a risk factor for birth defects in their offspring. Seven major categories of occupational exposure were identified. When no significant relation between these categories and birth defects was found for either the mothers or the fathers (14 comparisons), the categories were split into 64 separate occupations for the mothers and 80 separate occupations for the fathers. Not surprisingly, the authors then found "significant" associations with birth defects. Although the authors mentioned that some positive results could have occurred by chance, the differences were treated as real. The probability that all their "significant" findings were real? Three in 10,000.

. . . When this type of data torturing is done well, it may be impossible for readers to tell that the positive association did not spring from an a priori hypothesis.

Procrustean data torturing, or manipulating the data so that they prove the desired hypothesis, requires selective reporting. It can take several forms. First, exposure may be redefined in a way that strengthens the association. One study of adverse effects of oral contraceptives on the outcome of pregnancy defined exposure as presumed use within 600 days before a delivery or miscarriage; the choice of an inappropriately extended period to define exposure produced a positive result by including women not actually exposed during pregnancy. Second, study subjects whose experiences do not support the hypothesis may be dropped. For example, the report on a cancer-therapy trial might include outcomes only for subjects who survive more than three months, on the grounds that earlier deaths were inevitable and unrelated to the experimental therapy. In fact, these deaths could have resulted from toxic effects of the agent being tested. Third, disease outcomes may be lumped together, split, or dropped altogether to produce the desired results. In the cancer trial, for instance, the investigators' original intention might have been to look at differences in survival according to six-month intervals. But if no significant differences were found, the data could be reanalyzed according to

longer or shorter time intervals until a significant difference was found. . . .
Finally, normal ranges for laboratory results may be altered (although this
must be done with care when common tests are reported). . . .

Procrustean data torturing is more difficult to carry out than opportunistic data torturing, but its results are often more believable if one starts
with a popular hypothesis. It is also more destructive, because it may produce results that are seen as definitive proof of the hypothesis, whereas
opportunistic data torturing is often viewed as only hypothesis generation.

Such abuses can be very hard to detect. Referees of a scientific paper
can examine data that appear in the paper but cannot examine data that
have been omitted. Data manipulation compromises the reliability of a scientific paper in ways that cannot be judged on the basis of error bars or
other formal ways of describing uncertainty.

All this means that individual reports of new effects, even in peer-
reviewed papers, are likely to be very unreliable. There are simply too
many ways in which error can be introduced into scientific research, too
strong motivations for individual scientists to slant their interpretations of
data, and inadequate mechanisms in science to detect such problems.
Reliability in science develops when other scientists pick up the trail and
independently investigate phenomena and test theories. In short:
Reliability in science is a collective phenomenon that can be judged only
partly by examining "error bars" or other measures of scientific uncertainty. We will return to this in chapter 5.

Prescriptive Standards to Reduce Error

In the United States, standards for toxicology and drug studies are developed and enforced on science (that is, on scientists) by the Food and Drug
Administration, the Environmental Protection Agency, and other agencies.
Other countries have similar rules. These standards maintain "good cognitive design" (Philip Kitcher's phrase)—they help to ensure that the data
on which regulatory decisions are based are as reliable as possible. They
define generally accepted scientific practice in the areas in which they
apply. Perhaps more important, these standards are aimed at preventing
the kinds of data manipulation discussed above.

The most widely used of these guidelines are Good Laboratory Practices (GLP) and Good Clinical Practices (GCP). These rules are designed to ensure integrity of data and traceability. They require extensive documentation of the experimental protocol, extensive quality-control measures, and the use of independent auditors to make sure that the study is done according to plan. GLP and GCP are prescriptive rules with real teeth: regulatory agencies have the privilege of examining the raw data on which a report was based, and regulators have arrest privileges. Regulatory agencies would surely deny the pre-market-approval application of a pharmaceutical or chemical company that submitted toxicological data from studies not done under GLP. Some investigators have attempted to develop analogous guidelines for epidemiological studies.[17]

Other organizations set prescriptive standards for the conduct of scientific research and testing. In particular, AOAC International (formerly the Association of Official Analytical Chemists), an association of chemists working in the public and private sectors, periodically issues descriptions of approved methods for analyzing substances at various levels of reliability. This process, which is based on extensive peer review and inter-laboratory collaborative studies, defines techniques and methods for analysis that are accepted within the scientific community as standards of good practice.

GLP, GCP, AOAC standards, and other such guidelines are probably as close as one can come to "gold standards" for quality control in scientific research or scientific testing. These prescriptions deal with the process of gathering scientific evidence and are much closer to questions of evidentiary reliability than the rules of thumb for scientific inference discussed elsewhere in this book. To the extent that they enforce standardized experimental methods and standardized methods of collecting and reporting data, they are effective in reducing "data dredging," "data torturing," "cargo cult science," "pathological science," and other abuses.

Data Torturing and Advocacy

Professional advocates may find it difficult to condemn data dredging, for data dredging is the essence of good advocacy. Nobody expects both sides in a legal dispute to present fair and complete assessments of all the data, as would be required for an objective scientific analysis. Whatever his or her goals may be in the laboratory, a scientist, when employed as an expert in a lawsuit, is being used for purposes of advocacy. The employers don't want a fair and accurate assessment of the science; they want an assessment strong enough to withstand challenge and win the case. The expert witness may thus be under a great deal of pressure to dredge data, and may even be a willing or an eager accomplice.

In their roles in legal proceedings, scientists and physicians can have both the desire to serve as advocates and the means to do it effectively. In dealing with a patient covered by workers' compensation, a physician may be tempted to manipulate the diagnosis so as to assist the patient financially rather than medically. As the physician and legal consultant Daniel Voiss points out, "the relationship between patient and doctor, in the worker compensation system or in personal injury, is a triangular relationship, not an exclusive, dual relationship; it is public, not private."[18] This same advocacy role is also played by scientists. (See boxes 4.15 and 4.16.) "Toxic tort" litigation often turns on scientific evidence for small effects—i.e., reported effects that are comparable to the statistical and other uncertainties in the data. In sifting through such data, an expert can drastically skew results by simple choices of which data to include and how to weigh them. Omitting even a few data points in a meta-analysis may raise the relative risk from 1.5 to 2—a small change in light of typical uncertainties in this kind of research, but a significant one from a legal perspective.

The expert witness may thus be under a great deal of pressure to dredge data. If data dredging is a problem in the normal practice of science, where the tendency to advocate is simply part of a scientist's mission to report something interesting, then data dredging is certain to be a prominent feature of expert testimony in the courtroom. The circumstances of a trial call for a selective interpretation of data, post hoc, and by their very nature encourage a lack of objectivity on the part of the expert. The legal system expects litigants to dredge their data, but that practice corrodes scientific objectivity and rewards grossly erroneous conclusions by scientists in court.

Box 4.15
Occupational Injury: Fact, Fantasy, or Fraud?

Daniel V. Voiss

source: *Neurologic Clinics* 13 (1995): 431–446 (citations omitted)

Neurologists are frequently confronted with presumed occupational conditions . . . not the least of which is Chronic Pain Syndrome (CPS). . . [which] may designate any body site as the focus for verbal complaints of pain in the absence of objective medical findings. These patients require sophisticated individual neurological, psychiatric, and psychological assessments which are rarely undertaken. . . .

The concept of occupational injury essentially began in the late nineteenth century with the introduction of the worker compensation system in Europe. . . . Over time, however, the definition of what constituted an injury was eroded and expanded to include a host of ill-defined "injuries" . . . . Descriptive terms were medicalized as diagnoses, even in the absence of any defined pathology. . . . The propensity for human beings to engage the psychological mechanisms of externalization and projection would simply not be dismissed by the legal edict, "no-fault"; the target changed, but not the bullet. If a neuromuscular condition could not qualify as an occupational injury, it could eventually be redefined as an occupational disease. . . .

. . . The doctor and the patient may be constrained from too much fantasy by the diagnostic realities of an injury with positive findings on radiograph, such as an identified fracture. . . . These are objective findings that may be correlated with verbal complaints. . . .

. . . The causative relationship between a work activity and an ill-defined and undiagnosed complaint, however, is ambiguous at best. . . .

The relationship between the doctor and the patient depends upon negotiation of a mutually-acceptable diagnosis. . . . The relationship between patient and doctor, however, in the worker compensation system or in personal injury, is a triangular relationship. It is not an exclusive, dual relationship and a public, not a private one. . . . Unfortunately, the patient and physician relationship can be undermined by the presence of a third party, even health insurance. Thus, the most important element in medical care, the omnipotence of the physician and the magic and sense of safety, trust and support in the doctor and patient relationship, is threatened. . . .

The common wisdom and most legal jurisdictions define an injury as a sudden and tangible incident of a traumatic nature which produces a relatively immediate result and occurs from without, and such physical conditions as may result from that incident. . . . Controversy generally revolves around physical conditions that may result from that incident. . . . The conditions that are attributed to that injury, beyond the immediate effects, are rarely clear because the adaptive use of such an event offers limitless possibilities for a patient to resort to externalization of personal difficulties; to invoke the creativity of the [brain]. . . .

The determination of fact, fantasy, or fraud in a particular clinical case is primarily the responsibility of the attending physician. Yet, in my experience . . . the attending physician has relied primarily upon the necessarily unreliable subjective complaints of the patient, and minimal, if any, objective data as a basis for his or her conclusions in these disputed cases. . . . .

. . . In a triangular relationship, however, such as one encounters in worker compensation and particularly cases of disputed personal or occupational injury, the attending physician usually becomes as much of an advocate as his patient's attorney. He or she promotes unsubstantiated beliefs about the causality of subjective complaints. The fantasy, not the facts is determinative. . . .

. . . In essence, this confusion devolves to a primary failure on our part as clinicians; the failure to differentiate fact from fantasy.

The Bendectin Testimony of Alan Done

Alan Done, a former FDA toxicologist now self-employed as a consultant in pharmacology and pediatrics, appeared in numerous Bendectin cases as an expert for the plaintiffs, where he summarized epidemiologic studies related to Bendectin and birth defects. His performance in *DeLuca v. Merrell Dow*[19] illustrates the importance of critical review of proffered testimony.

In *Deluca*, Done submitted an affidavit stating his conclusions that Bendectin was linked with birth defects. In a second affidavit, the aforementioned Shanna Swan (also serving as an expert witness for the plaintiff in this case) stated that it was her "professional opinion that the methodology relied on by Dr. Done in preparing [an exhibit that was part of that] affidavit is sound and acceptable from both a statistical and epidemiological point of view."[20]

Done's affidavit included a figure (shown here as figure 4.1) purporting to summarize the results of 106 findings from more than 30 previous Bendectin studies. The overwhelming impression from this figure is that Bendectin increases the risk of birth defects. In his initial deposition, Done had not provided enough information to allow the defense to conduct a critical review of his methods or even to identify the studies that he referenced. After Done provided a table identifying the studies summarized in the figure, experts for the defense uncovered dozens of errors in his analysis, ranging from simple typographical errors, arithmetic mistakes,[21] and misrepresentations[22] to serious methodological deficiencies.[23] When questioned, Shanna Swan was unable to confirm or even explain numerous aspects of Done's analysis.[24]

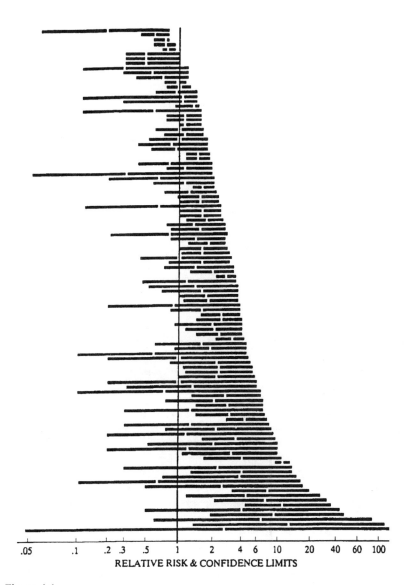

.05   .1   .2 .3   .5   1   2   4   6   10   20   40   60   100
RELATIVE RISK & CONFIDENCE LIMITS

Figure 4.1
From Alan Done's affidavit in *Deluca v. Merrell Dow*, a summary of Bendectin data as interpreted by Done. The relative risk for birth defects determined from each study is indicated by the small broken area at the middle of each horizontal bar. The bars indicate the "confidence intervals" (corresponding to unspecified *p* values). The data are arranged according to the upper confidence limit. The lowest bar indicates a study that reported a relative risk of approximately 2.5, with confidence limits between 0.05 and approximately 180. The figure suggests a consistent pattern of increased risks (relative risks above 1).

Box 4.16
The Borderland between Neurology and History: Conversion Reactions
Edward Shorter
source: *Neurologic Clinics of North America*, special issue on Malingering and Conversion Reactions, ed. M. Weintraub (1994)

The pitfalls of misdiagnosis and mismanagement of pseudoneurological patients in the past demonstrate the validity of the proposition that . . . "[y]ou should never try to do neurology without some kind of historical backup." . . .

In the last decade of the twentieth century . . . a long-term shift of symptoms from the motor side of the nervous system to the sensory side is now completing itself. As for attribution, the media's predominance as a source of medical information (and the corresponding loss of medical authority) means that patients tend to attribute non-specific collections of aches and pains to what they have most recently seen on television. . . . [I]n daily practice the neurologist is now confronted with legions of somatizing patients whose symptoms are characteristic of no organic disease but who cling resolutely to a fixed illness attribution. . . .

. . . It is for example striking to note in the chronicles of saints' lives how often miracle cures were reported for hysterical seizure disorders, or pseudoepilepsy. . . . [I]t is reasonable to assume that Guillaume Guyat, and thousands of similar sufferers, had pseudoepilepsy, a common psychosomatic complaint in an era that believed illness to be caused by demonic possession, and that prayer had the power of cure.

During the nineteenth century the frequency of pseudoepilepsy dropped off greatly, and by the end of the twentieth century hysterical seizure disorders have almost reached the status of curiosities. . . .

A second example of a long-term shift in presentation is hysterical paralysis. Although relatively uncommon before 1800, during the nineteenth century functional muscle paresis and paralysis became widespread. . . . Functional paralysis as a motor symptom was uncommon before the nineteenth century, and after the First World War it too, like pseudoseizures, became a clinical curiosity.

In the history of changing symptoms what characterizes the twentieth century is the predominance of sensory symptoms: chronic pain and chronic fatigue in particular. . . .

. . . By the end of the twentieth century chronic pain and chronic fatigue would become the characteristic complaints of postmodern patients suffering conversion reactions, such once-popular symptoms as pseudoepilepsy and hysterical paralysis long forgotten among middle-class urban-dwellers. . . .

. . . Pseudoneurological illness, which the patient believes to be organic in nature and which the physician often interprets as the result of the patient's distinctive personal history and development, obeys larger rules that are dictated by larger forces, particularly cultural notions of what constitutes "valid" organic disease. What the patient brings to the doctor is therefore very much historically determined. . . . [P]hysician advocacy is essential in launching an epidemic of non-disease, and in chronic fatigue syndrome and fibrositis as well one notes a small claque of physician-advocates, often quoted by the media and lionized by patient support-groups. . . .

[Chronic Fatigue Syndrome] was just the edge of the wedge. Its wide acceptance by the public, despite the absence of mainline scientific support, established the notion that "new diseases are being discovered every day," and that the media, not the medical profession, is the ultimate arbiter of what constitutes a "real" disease.

In his summary judgment opinion for the defendants, Judge Garrett Brown Jr. wrote:

Defense experts, Drs. Monson, Wright and Lamm, have itemized numerous errors made by Dr. Done in the calculation of the "data sets" he included on his chart [figure 4.1]. . . . The defense experts as well as Dr. Swan testified that the precise method used by Dr. Done in making some of his calculations was a mystery and was not in conformance with any known methodology. . . . Dr. Done presented percentage numbers of studies that are compatible with an increased risk of birth defects, but failed to inform the reader that the same studies were also compatible with a decreased risk of birth defects. . . . Although the Jick '80 draft, Plaintiffs' Ex. 20, contained at least four data sets, Dr. Done, with no explanation, ignored the one most favorable to a lack of association. . . .[25] [See box 4.17.]

Gross errors like these have little to do with the subtler scientific errors discussed earlier in this chapter, and the criticisms of Done's "science" have nothing at all to do with the sociological criticisms of science described in chapter 7. However, they illustrate just how far the torturing of data can be pushed.

Box 4.17
DeLuca v. Merrell Dow Pharmaceuticals, Inc., 791 F. Supp. 1042 (1992)
(Garrett E. Brown, Jr., J.) (citations omitted)

In his affidavit, Dr. Done stated the bases for his conclusion that Bendectin caused the congenital limb defect suffered by Amy DeLuca were his "knowledge of the properties of Bendectin, the compatibility of the timing of Bendectin exposure in this case with the particular defect, the fact that the defect is of the type for which there is substantial evidence of Bendectin causation, the absence of another more likely cause in this case, evidence of teratogenicity of Bendectin from animal teratogenicity and in-vitro mechanistic studies, and the ample evidence of human teratogenicity of Bendectin from the epidemiologic studies analyzed. . . . With the exception of epidemiologic studies, Dr. Done provided no supporting data or explanations for the other bases upon which he relied. . . .

Although Dr. Brenholz testified that she has no direct evidence that smoking or Mrs. DeLuca's prior abortion were in any way related to Amy's birth defects . . . the standardized texts and literature consulted by Dr. Brenholz in her practice list smoking as a possible teratogen and abortion as a subject of debate. . . . In his testimony, Dr. Done failed to address either as another more likely cause of Amy's birth defects, did not consider any other cause, and did not explain his reasoning for ruling out any other cause. . . .

Although the calculation of a relative risk is a simple arithmetic calculation . . . the defense experts as well as plaintiff's co-expert, Dr. Swan, testified that the precise method used by Dr. Done in making some of his calculations was a mystery and was not in conformance with any known methodology. Drs. Monson, Wright, Lamm and Swan, all qualified epidemiologists, in many cases could not replicate Dr. Done's calculations. . . . Accordingly, this Court is uncertain as to the precise technique or methodology employed by Dr. Done in making his calculations which he included on his chart, and thus, I conclude that his methodology is indeed novel. This factor weighs against admissibility. . . .

Dr. Done has not identified any specialized literature endorsing his particular methodology, nor has his methodology been endorsed by other experts. Accordingly, there is no likelihood that Dr. Done's methodology or technique has been exposed to critical scientific scrutiny. . . .

Dr. Done primarily relies upon the field of epidemiology in formulating his opinion. It is undisputed that Dr. Done has had no formal training in a degree program in epidemiology. . . . It is further undisputed that Dr. Done does not have a Bachelor or Doctorate degree in epidemiology nor has he undertaken any fellowship in epidemiology. . . .

Dr. Done has presented no evidence that his methodology has been put to any non-judicial use. . . .

Although Dr. Done's inclusion and exclusion of certain data may be nothing more than a matter for the experts to battle, when viewed in light of the numerous errors in calculation of that data and selectivity biases, this Court concludes that Dr. Done's testimony would serve to confuse and mislead a jury. . . .

Dr. Done purports to have taken the numbers he entered in the boxes on his chart [figure 4.1] from either the underlying studies themselves, or, in the articles where no calculations were made, from his own calculations. In many cases, as previously noted, this is simply not true. Dr. Done frequently used numbers of his own, even where calculations were available. Often, his "re-calculations" were wrong and could not be replicated by plaintiff's other expert, Dr. Swan, or the defense experts. . . .

. . . Dr. Done specifically relied upon several types of data experts in the field would not use in forming their opinions. . . .

. . . Dr. Done has thus used data upon which no epidemiologist would rely.

5

Reliability

[T]he trial judge must ensure that any and all scientific testimony or evidence admitted is not only relevant, but reliable. . . . [T]he requirement that an expert's testimony pertain to "scientific knowledge" establishes a standard of evidentiary reliability.

—*Daubert v. Merrell Dow Pharmaceuticals, Inc.*, 509 U.S. 579, 589–590 (1993) (footnote omitted)

Much of the *Daubert* majority opinion deals with what the Supreme Court views as the hallmarks of "reliable" science. The *Oxford English Dictionary* defines "reliability" as "the quality of being reliable," which it in turn defines as "that may be relied upon; in which reliance or confidence may be put; trustworthy, safe, sure." This lay usage of the term fits comfortably with the overall thrust of *Daubert* and undoubtedly conveys exactly what the Court intended.

As a term of art in science and statistics, *reliability* refers to the reproducibility of data. A reliable test can be repeated under identical circumstances and yield the same results. The results may be consistently wrong, but that is an issue of validity, not reliability. The first (lay) definition is broader than the second but is clearly related to it. A test that is not reliable in the statistician's sense is not reliable in the lay sense either. But the two meanings are not equivalent. The Scholastic Aptitude Test may be reliable in the statistical sense (a student who takes the test repeatedly will receive similar scores), but it may not be a trustworthy measure of scholastic aptitude.

The issue of reliability of scientific evidence arises in stark form in the interpretation of medical tests—for example, screening tests for HIV infection or tuberculosis in food workers. Such tests are very good at identifying infected individuals. More precise, their true-positive detection rate is very high—that is, an infected person would, with very high probability, be identified as such by the test. But their false-positive detection rate (the frequency with which the test will falsely identify individuals as positive if applied to a group of individuals known to be negative) is significant too. There are many circumstances in which the results of such tests are very unreliable in the lay sense of the term. Thus, one issue related to reliability (in the lay sense) is whether a medical diagnosis is correct.

Conjecture

Another issue is whether a theory is correct. The *Daubert* majority used the word "conjecture" to help define "reliability" by its opposite. Federal Rule of Evidence Rule 702, the Court noted, requires that an expert's testimony contain scientific "knowledge." "[T]he word 'knowledge' connotes more than subjective belief or unsupported speculation," the *Daubert* majority reasoned.[1] At the end of its opinion the Court added:

The scientific project is advanced by broad and wide-ranging consideration of a multitude of hypotheses, for those that are incorrect will eventually be shown to be so, and that in itself is an advance. Conjectures that are probably wrong are of little use, however, in the project of reaching a quick, final, and binding legal judgment—often of great consequence—about a particular set of events in the past.[2]

"Conjecture," the *Oxford English Dictionary* explains, derives from the Latin *conjectura*, "a throwing or casting together, a conclusion derived from comparison of facts, an inference, conclusion, guess, etc." It cites as examples "interpretation of signs or omens; interpretation of dreams; divining; a conclusion as to coming events drawn from signs or omens; a forecast, a prognostication." Few scientists would admit basing an opinion on dreams, signs, or omens; however, conjectures are often the starting point, the first stage in the discovery of reliable science.

In 1865 the chemist August Kekulé described a vision he had had, in his study at the University of Bonn, of the structure of benzene—six carbon atoms arranged in a ring:

I was sitting writing at my textbook, but the work did not progress; my thoughts were elsewhere. I turned my chair to the fire, and dozed. Again the atoms were gamboling before my eyes. This time the smaller groups kept modestly in the background. My mental eye, rendered more acute by repeated visions of this kind, could now distinguish larger structures of manifold conformations; long rows, sometimes more closely fitted together; all twisting and turning in snake-like motion. But look! What was that? One of the snakes had seized hold of its own tail, and the form whirled mockingly before my eyes. As if by a flash of lightning I woke. . . . I spent the rest of the night working out the consequences of the hypothesis. Let us learn to dream, gentlemen, and then perhaps we shall learn the truth.[3]

Truths do sometimes emerge from dreams. Kekulé's insight was indeed one of the most important discoveries in the history of chemistry. It is equally clear, however, that many other vivid, compelling "dreams" or conjectures turn out to be wrong. History records countless instances of reputable scientists' having flashes of inspiration that turn out to lead nowhere.

Conjectures aren't unreliable only when they are radically new. Even the most mundane of scientific claims is, in its initial stages, conjectural and thus highly unreliable. "A scientific discovery at birth," the chemist John Charles Polanyi remarked recently, "is at best 10 percent pebble [fact] and 90 percent shimmer [illusion]. For a discovery to be 100 percent pebble, evidence would have to exist that admits no doubt. That concept does not sit well with either the legal or the scientific professions."[4]

"Conjectures," then, may subsequently be affirmed—they may, in other words, be "valid." But they lack sufficient foundation to be termed "reliable." For that reason, they fail *Daubert*'s reliability requirement.

A Statistical Perspective

At some level of abstraction, all science is probabilistic, whether it involves a medical diagnosis, an eyewitness identification, or a DNA "fingerprint." No observation, test, or study is ever infallible. So the question always lurks in the background: How likely is it that this was the time the test or observation failed? The answer to that question, stated in terms of probability, lies in the statistician's way of quantifying reliability.

First, reliability must be quantified in terms of two simpler and more familiar terms: sensitivity and specificity.[5] The *sensitivity* of a test is the probability of detecting (say) infection if the test is applied to a group of individuals who are known to be infected.[6] The *specificity* of a test is the probability that the test, when applied to a group of people who are known not to be infected, will indicate no infection.

One measure of reliability (in the broader, lay sense of the term) is the predictive value of the test: the probability that a person who tests positive really is positive. The reliability of a test (for HIV infection, say) depends, as one might expect, on the quality of the test itself—its sensitivity and its specificity. But—contrary to ordinary intuition—the reliability of a test also depends on the prevalence of the infection among the population tested. Statisticians call the prevalence of infection in the population the *base rate*. This can lead to a seemingly paradoxical situation in which a test may be highly accurate but its results—because of an unfavorable base rate—may be very unreliable (that is, very likely to be wrong).

Richard Wilson, a professor of physics and an expert on risk assessment, provides a simple illustration to show why.[7] A child who reports "I saw a dog running down Fifth Avenue" is quite believable. Accepting as reliable "I saw a lion running down Fifth Avenue" requires additional information: Were the Ringling Brothers in town, and did their truck crash? "I saw a stegosaurus running down Fifth Avenue" is never reliable, even when Steven Spielberg is in town. The reliability of each report depends not only on the child's veracity and eyesight but also on knowledge that has nothing to do with the child at all—knowledge about how frequently dogs, lions, and stegosauruses run down city streets. In other words, the first statement is more probable than the second and third statements, because the general frequency with which dogs run down streets is larger than the frequency with which lions and stegosauruses run down streets. This is true even for a witness whose accuracy, as measured in terms of sensitivity and specificity, is held constant across all three statements.

Bayes' theorem states the dog/stegosaurus lesson more formally. Thomas Bayes, an eighteenth-century Scottish minister and mathematician, was the first to set forth a mathematical theorem for combining information about observational accuracy with information about base rates to assess the overall reliability of a claim or an observation. Bayes' "Essay Towards Solving a Problem in the Doctrine of Chances" (published in 1763, two years after his death) demonstrated mathematically how the reliability of a hypothesis based on a new piece of evidence depends on

Table 5.1

	Infection present	Infection absent
Tests positive	*A* individuals (true positives)	*B* individuals (false positives)
Tests negative	*C* individuals (false negatives)	*D* individuals (true negatives)

the probability that the hypothesis is correct, before the new evidence becomes available (the so-called prior probability) (e.g., how likely it is that a stegosaurus would in fact walk down Fifth Avenue),

the probability that the evidence would have been observed given that the hypothesis is true (e.g., how likely it is that the boy's eyes would see a stegosaurus if one really did walk down Fifth Avenue),

and

the probability that the evidence would have been observed given that the hypothesis is false (e.g., how likely it is that the boy's eyes would have incorrectly seen a nonexistent stegosaurus).

Bayes' theorem tells us how to combine information about sensitivity, specificity, and base rates to arrive at an overall measure of the test, called *predictive value*, that accords with the lay meaning of reliability. Thus, a test that has a high predictive value is likely to identify individuals correctly; it is trustworthy. Predictive value clearly depends on both the qualities of the test itself (sensitivity and specificity) and the base rate. The predictive value is the ratio of true positives (individuals who test positive and who really are infected, for example) to the total number of people who test positive, whether correctly or incorrectly.

These relations can be summarized as in table 5.1. Here the sensitivity of the test is the ratio of the number of true positives to the total number of infected individuals: $A/(A + C)$. The specificity of the test is the ratio of the number of true negatives to the total number of noninfected individuals: $D/(B + D)$. The predictive value of the test is the ratio of the number of true positives to the total number of people who test positive: $A/(A + B)$.

Bayes' Theorem in the Real World

To anyone but a statistician, all this may seem very abstract. But Bayes' theorem, in fact, has enormous practical importance.

Table 5.2

	HIV-infected	Not infected
Tests positive	1325 individuals (true positives)	7648 individuals (false positives)
Tests negative	23 individuals (false negatives)	3,816,372 (true negatives)

For example, tests used to screen groups of apparently healthy people for uncommon ailments can be both highly accurate (highly sensitive and specific) and highly unreliable—the latter for reasons that have nothing to do with the quality of the test but have to do with an unfavorable base rate. The screening test for HIV (the enzyme immunoassay test) is astonishingly good—far better than most other medical tests. It has a sensitivity of 98 percent and specificity of 99.8 percent. Yet a person drawn at random from the general population who tests positive for HIV is in all probability not infected.[8] Why? The base rate of HIV infection in the general American population is very low—roughly one person in 3,000 has the infection. The numbers, based on the work cited in note 8, are as shown in table 5.2. The sensitivity of the test is 1,325/1,348 = 98.3 percent. The specificity of the test is 3,816,372/3,824,020 = 99.8 percent. The predictive value of the test is 1,325/8,973 = 14.8 percent (based on a total assumed population of 3,825,368 individuals and an assumed prevalence of 0.035 percent). This simple analysis shows that a person drawn at random from the general population who tests positive has only a 15 percent probability of being infected. Six out of every seven people who test positive will not be infected. Applied in this way—to people drawn at random from the general population—the test is both very accurate and very unreliable. Applied to people who are inherently at higher risk of being infected—intravenous drug users, for example—the test becomes much more reliable.

Statistical reasoning of this kind applies to "tests" and observations of all kinds, not just medical ones. The following example is based on one that is often presented in the psychology literature: Mrs. Smith witnesses an accident involving a taxi. Her eyesight has been rigorously tested; the tests establish that she can identify the color of a taxi correctly 80 percent of the time. (In other words, she says "yellow" 80 percent of the times in which the taxi really is yellow and 20 percent of the times when it is some other color.) She testifies in court: "I saw the taxi. It was yellow." How

Table 5.3

	Taxi was yellow	Taxi was not yellow
Mrs. Smith says yellow	64 taxis (true positives)	4 taxis (false positives)
Mrs. Smith says not yellow	16 taxis (false negatives)	16 taxis (true negatives)

likely is it that she's right? The correct answer will almost never be "80 percent of the time." (See boxes 5.1 and 5.2.)

If 80 percent of the taxicabs in the city are yellow, the "It was yellow" report will be correct 94 percent of the time. Assuming that Mrs. Smith has an 80 percent chance of either correctly identifying a yellow taxi as yellow or correctly identifying a not-yellow taxi as not yellow, and that 80 percent of the taxis in the city are yellow, we find for a hypothetical group of 100 reports by Mrs. Smith the results shown in table 5.3. The report "it was yellow" will be correct 64 out of 68 times (94 percent). Combining good (80 percent) eyesight with a high background probability (80 percent) that a taxi is yellow pushes the probabilities higher still—much higher than one might suppose from considering eyesight alone. If every taxi in the city is yellow, Mrs. Smith's "yellow taxi" call will be right 100 percent of the time, even if Mrs. Smith is certifiably blind. But the numbers can go sour very fast. Suppose Mrs. Smith has the same 80 percent vision but she makes an "orange taxi" call. If 80 percent of the taxis in the city are in fact yellow, and 20 percent are orange, Mrs. Smith's call will be wrong exactly half the time[9] (not just 20 percent of the time, as her vision alone would suggest). If Mrs. Smith has 20 percent vision and "sees an orange taxi" in a city where only 20 percent of the taxis are in fact orange, she will be wrong 94 percent of the time.

There are only two "simple" cases in which the numbers in this example would track our ordinary intuitions. Both of these cases involve perfection—either perfect eyes, or a world in which all taxis are yellow. With perfect eyes, or perfectly uniform colors, every "yellow taxi" report is utterly reliable (no matter how bad the eyes). But neither case has anything to do with the real world.

This tells us something legally important about the reliability of tests: Tests that purport to identify things that are common to begin with are likely to yield correct results—whatever their inherent quality, they are reliable because external circumstances make them so. Thus, if a test shows that an

Box 5.1
Inevitable Illusions: How Mistakes of Reason Rule Our Minds
Massimo Piattelli-Palmarini
source: *Inevitable Illusions: How Mistakes of Reason Rule Our Minds* (Wiley, 1994)

We are . . . all easy prey to various "cognitive illusions": that is, to the illusion of knowing. These are errors we commit without knowing that we do so, in good faith and errors that we often defend with vehemence, thus making our power of reasoning subservient to our illusions. . . .

[W]hen judgments about what is 'typical' come into play, even when they're based on the slightest of evidence, we completely lose sight of any objective probability. . . .

[This tendency leads to something called] neglect of base rates. . . . [S]pontaneous shallow judgments based on cliches (i.e. typicality) *do* win over estimates of base rates. . . . [C]linicians and jurors still do fall prey to the neglect of base rates. . . .

. . . My purpose is to give the reader an intuitive notion of this law, and to show how Bayes' law for all it simplicity can free us from the tunnel of native probabilistic reasoning. . . .

. . . An intuition that is correct at the absolute level of 100 percent is *no longer* correct in cases that lie 'close' to that 100 percent limit. . . .

. . . *it is vital to emphasize that probabilistic correlations are not "like" a somewhat less certain certainty.* Such correlations can be treated rationally only by Bayes' law.

The Seven Deadly Sins [perils that support our illusion of knowing]:

Overconfidence   The results obtained [from tests] show a widespead tendancy to overconfidence.

Magical Thinking   [A] statistical correlation is not a near certainty or a slightly less "certain" certainty. [With regard to Popper's falsifiability criterion,] [w]e are naturally and spontaneously verifiers rather than falsifiers or debunkers.

Predictability in Hindsight   [W]ith hindsight we all honestly think we could have predicted what happened, as long as we know, or think we know, that it actually did happen.

Anchoring   Another classic experiment consists in asking a subject, for instance, how many African nations there are in the United Nations. Before asking him tht question, however, one turns the wheel of fortune in full view of the subject, stopping it on some number between 1 and 100. . . . The number of African states will be anchored to the number turned up by the wheel of fortune. . . .

Ease of Representation   The easier it is to imagine an event or a situation, and the more the occurrence impresses us emotionally, the more likely we are to think of it as also objectively frequent. Things that seem "odd" to us are usually anything but. Curious "coincidences" turn out to be perfectly ordinary.

Probability Blindness   Any probabilistic intuition by anyone not specifically tutored in probability calculus has a greater than 50 percent chance of being wrong.

Reconsideration under Suitable Scripts [the most deadly sin]   Offering a "plausible" sequence of events that are causally linked one to another has the effect of immediately raising our estimate of probability. . . . [T]he probability of an entire chain (or the last link) being true is *always and without exception less probable than the probability of the least probable link in the chain.*

individual suffered from chickenpox during childhood, she probably did; we don't have to know anything at all about the test to assert that it is quite "reliable." In a case like this, it hardly matters how good your "scientific eyesight" happens to be. If you consult a psychic or a soothsayer you will do nearly as well.

The opposite case is equally important. Tests, even quite good ones, will yield unreliable results—far less reliable than intuition suggests—if used to screen for rare events. Tests that purport to diagnose childhood exposure to sexual molesters are likely to be highly unreliable (at least, if child molestation is a lot less common than chickenpox). If abuses of this kind are as rare as HIV infection, tests purporting to uncover those abuses will be unreliable even if they are as sensitive and specific as the HIV enzyme immunoassay test. If child abuse is relatively rare, and if tests for it are a lot less sensitive and less specific than tests for HIV (as they almost certainly are), then tests purporting to uncover child abuse in previously unrecollecting adults will be so grotesquely unreliable as to be utterly worthless. (Many incidents of child abuse leave evidence that is appallingly obvious, and the reliability of such observations is hardly open to question.) In both the case of HIV and that of child abuse, the unreliability of the results of the test arises from the low incidence of the condition.

The base-rate problem has been the downfall of medical entrepreneurs who invested resources in developing screening tests for uncommon diseases without realizing that the tests must have impossibly low false-positive detection rates if they are to yield useful results. This is why some medical groups oppose HIV screening for the general population and others recommend against routine mammograms for young women who are asymptomatic for breast cancer. Some experts oppose random testing for drugs in the workplace for similar reasons. Other examples of illusions based on probability are described in boxes 5.1 and 5.2.

Box 5.2
Conditional Probability, Blackjack, and Drug Testing
John Allen Paulos
source: *Innumeracy: Mathematical Illiteracy and Its Consequences* (Vintage, 1988)

One needn't be a believer in any of the standard pseudosciences to make faulty claims and invalid inferences. Many mundane mistakes in reasoning can be traced to a shaky grasp of the notion of conditional probability. . . .

. . . Imagine a man with three cards. One is black on both sides, one red on both sides, and one black on one side and red on the other. He drops the cards into a hat and asks you to pick one, but only to look at one side; let's assume it's red. The man notes that the card you picked couldn't possibly be the card that was black on both sides, and therefore it must be one of the other two cards-the red-red card or the red-black card. He offers to bet you even money that it is the red-red card. Is this a fair bet?

At first glance, it seems so. There are two cards it could be; he's betting on one, and you're betting on the other. But the rub is that there are two ways he can win and only one way you can win. The visible side of the card you picked could be the red side of the red-black card, in which case you win, or it could be one side of the red-red card, in which case he wins, or it could be the other side of the red-red card, in which case he also wins. His chances of winning are thus 2/3. The conditional probability of the card being red-red given that it's not black-black is 1/2, but that's not the situation here. We know more than just that the card is not black-black; we also know a red side is showing. . . .

An interesting elaboration on the concept of conditional probability is known as Bayes' theorem, first proved by Thomas Bayes in the eighteenth century. It's the basis for the following rather unexpected result, which has important implications for drug or AIDS testing.

Assume that there is a test for cancer which is 98 percent accurate; i.e., if someone has cancer, the test will be positive 98 percent of the time, and if one doesn't have it, the test will be negative 98 percent of the time. Assume further that .5 percent—one out of two hundred people—actually have cancer. Now imagine that you've taken the test and that your doctor somberly informs you that you've tested positive. The question is: How depressed should you be? The surprising answer is that you should be cautiously optimistic. To find out why, let's look at the conditional probability of your having cancer, given that you've tested positive.

Imagine that 10,000 tests for cancer are administered. Of these, how many are positive? On the average, 50 of these 10,000 people (.5 percent of 10,000) will have cancer, and so, since 98 percent of them will test positive, we will have 49 positive tests. Of the 9,950 cancerless people, 2 percent of them will test positive, for a total of 199 positive tests (.02 × 9,950 = 199). Thus, of the total of 248 positive tests (199 + 49 = 248), most (199) are false positives, and so the conditional probability of having cancer given that one tests positive is only 49/248, or about 20 percent! (This relatively low percentage is to be contrasted with the conditional probability that one tests positive, given that one has cancer, which by assumption is 98 percent.)

Applications of Bayes' theorem to particular problems such as HIV testing are interesting in their own right, but the larger lesson that they teach is even more important: One cannot separate judgments about the reliability of basing conclusions on certain evidence from judgments about the inherent likelihood of the proposition that the evidence purports to confirm. Statisticians understand this "base-rate" problem very well. After *Daubert*, judges must grasp it too. This is absolutely fundamental to the evaluation of the reliability of a claim based on an observation or a test of any kind.

Bayes' Theorem as a Model for Scientific Decision Making

Recent years have seen the development of an important line of research—broadly called "behavioral decision theory"—that sheds a great deal of light on scientific decision making. Decision theory explores the logical and cognitive processes that ordinary people use to make decisions on the basis of uncertain data. The research was pioneered by the psychologists Amos Tversky and Daniel Kahneman, the social scientist Paul Slovic, and others. A related line of work in the philosophy of science is based on an extension of Bayes' theorem to the scientific decision process itself (and far from the narrow range of applicability of the theorem). In their book *Scientific Reasoning*, Colin Howson and Peter Urbach provide an extensive (and comparatively nontechnical) introduction to the philosophical implications of Bayes' theorem.[10]

This new line of research is less concerned with identifying the correctness of a theory than with determining the degree of belief (more precise, the personal probability) that an individual would accord it. A personal probability of 50 percent means that a person would accept a bet with even odds that a theory is correct. Philosophers who hold this view argue that such personal probabilities are about as close as one can get to measuring the truth of a theory.

The process goes more or less like this: When a scientific question first arises, a scientist will list all the possible hypotheses and arbitrarily assign probabilities to each one. As more evidence comes in, each scientist changes his or her personal probabilities for each hypothesis and assigns new values, which are called *posterior probabilities*. Eventually, scientists (individually and in the aggregate) converge on some final sets of values. In Bayesian statistics, this final probability that is assigned to each hypothesis is independent of the probabilities (*prior probabilities* in Bayesian jargon) that one initially assigned to the various hypotheses. Thus, in a hypothetical example, scientists might arrive at final probabilities of 80 percent that a substance causes cancer in humans at some stated level of exposure and 20 percent that it does not. This is as close to the "truth" about the possible carcinogenic properties of the substance as science can get.

This view recognizes that knowledgeable scientists may hold quite different views about a particular issue at different times; their views evolve with the weight of the evidence at hand. At the very beginning, individual scientists will make quite different guesses, based on little evidence, as to how likely it is that a hypothesis is correct. Eventually, after a lot of evidence has accumulated, most scientists will assign similar probabilities to the hypothesis, at least in theory. It is at this stage that the weight of the evidence is extensive, and the knowledge can be said to be quite reliable. In Bayesian terms: Prior probabilities (that is, initial guesses) play smaller and smaller roles as new evidence accumulates.

Investigators have proposed this as a normative model as well, to describe how scientific decisions should be made. The psychologist Jonathan Baron[11] and the philosopher Philip Kitcher[12] both suggest that scientists should make their decisions using a Bayesian strategy. Advocates of this Bayesian approach maintain that the element of subjectivity in the theory is, in the words of Howson and Urbach, "minimal . . . and exactly right."[13]

Science has many examples where personal probabilities have converged. Virtually all scientists agree that smoking causes lung cancer, for example. With the morning sickness drug Bendectin, personal probabilities have converged in the other direction. The fears that the drug caused birth defects were raised by case reports in the medical literature of individual mothers who had used it and then given birth to children with birth defects. Single-case observations of this sort carry little weight in demonstrating a hazard of the drug, for a variety of medical and statistical reasons. There may be an effect or there may not; one cannot know until other users of the product have been examined. Thus, after reading original case reports, one scientist might initially have assigned a probability of 90 percent to the hypothesis that Bendectin causes birth defects. Another scientist might have assigned a probability of 1 percent to the same hypothesis. So long as they were based on single-case reports, both judgments were unreliable, because neither was based on a significant body of evidence; no such body of evidence yet existed. Later, however, a substantial number of excellent epidemiological studies were conducted. These studies found no links between Bendectin and birth defects. By now, most scientists would assign a very low probability to the hypothesis that Bendectin causes birth defects. In its review of the issue, the Food and Drug Administration agreed.

Consider, as another example, how the Bayesian perspective evolved in connection with asbestos. Suppose we are back in the 1950s, and a first study suggests that workplace exposure to asbestos causes 80 percent of all cases of mesothelioma. There is not much other evidence at hand, so we do not know (at this stage) whether most mesotheliomas are caused by occupational asbestos or by other factors. This means that we don't yet have any real way of gauging the overall reliability of this first study. If most mesotheliomas are in fact caused by asbestos (the consensus on which science will eventually converge in the 1970s), then this first study will be judged, in retrospect, as almost certainly very reliable indeed. By 1970, we will be able to look back and accept the 1950s work even if the investigators who conducted it were generally sloppy and inept. (If all mesotheliomas are in fact caused by asbestos, it does not matter how sloppy and inept; their conclusion that some group of mesotheliomas probably were caused by asbestos cannot be anything but correct.) Over time—between 1950 and 1970—other studies will be conducted by other observers. If these studies confirm a unique and strong association between asbestos and mesotheliomas (as in fact they did), our confidence in the reliability of the original study will grow steadily. If these later studies find no such association, our confidence will shrink. The results of all the studies together will eventually establish the trustworthy "background" rates that we need. Only from that collective body of evidence can we ultimately gauge the reliability of an individual test, study, or diagnosis, whenever it was conducted.

The Bayesian framework of analysis thus leads us to a fundamental insight about the scientific process as a whole. In our taxi example, we gauged the reliability of a single observation ("Mrs. Smith saw a yellow taxi") using one piece of information about the quality of Mrs. Smith's eyes and a second about the fraction of taxis in the city that are yellow. But where did that second piece of information come from? We were able to assess the reliability of Mrs. Smith's individual observation only because we presumed we had a more reliable set (or collection) of eyes somewhere there in the background, counting every taxi in town and giving us the "real" overall breakdown of yellow and orange taxis (the Bureau of Motor Vehicles, perhaps).

Bayesian theory has obvious application to the identification of teratogens, carcinogens, and other risky (or, in other contexts, beneficial) substances. In a "toxic tort" case, for example, "structure-function" analysis—a line of chemical evidence presented in some Bendectin suits—is a test (but not a very good one) by which to determine if Bendectin is a human teratogen. As with any other test, analysis of the reliability of this test (more precisely, its predictive value) requires information on its selectivity and specificity. It also requires knowledge of the base rates of occurrence of teratogens—how many chemicals, randomly pulled off the shelves, are human teratogens. Absent such information, the likelihood that a substance identified by a test is a teratogen simply cannot be judged. In legal terminology, structure-function tests are "not dispositive." The plaintiffs' experts in the Bendectin cases, as far as we can tell, had little to say about these crucial issues. Without a careful analysis of these questions, the advice of a soothsayer would be just as reliable.

This is not to say that "structure-function" analysis is useless. Regulatory agencies use analysis of just this kind as a first step in risk assessment, to help identify chemicals that are promising candidates for more accurate animal tests. But information that is reliable enough to suggest potentially fruitful avenues of research will often not be reliable enough to buttress (or undermine) larger conclusions about what that research might reveal. And, in either case, reliability must be gauged properly, with meticulous attention to background rates and to the sensitivity and selectivity of the tests.

Similar considerations apply to the screening of potential drugs for the treatment of disease. Until recently, the National Cancer Institute screened potential drugs using rodents with artificially induced tumors; a drug that reduced the size of an animal's tumor might be considered as a promising candidate for human use. However, such tests are unreliable for identifying drugs that are useful for treating cancer in humans: many drugs that produce favorable responses in rodents have no such effects when used in humans. The National Cancer Institute stopped using these screening tests and replaced them with tests using human cell lines, which were followed by more reliable animal tests. (See box 5.3.)

Consider what this learning implies for the reliability of evidence offered in the Bendectin case or in similar litigation. If there is a strong statistical association between exposure to the drug and birth defects, the issue of causation is moot from a legal viewpoint (unless there is a strong reason to doubt the epidemiology) and from a scientific perspective.

But suppose a scientist tried to argue—on the basis of structure-function analysis, or in vitro (cellular) tests, or high-dose animal tests—that the drug caused birth defects in humans, but the epidemiological evidence was negative or even weakly positive (relative risk above 1 but below 2).

The first question required in an appropriate analysis is "How reliable is the 'eyesight'?" If a chemical causes birth defects in rabbits, can one conclude that it will cause birth defects in humans too? The answer often happens to be "no"—interspecies extrapolations of this kind are known to be quite unreliable. What fraction of chemicals implicated by "structure analysis" actually cause birth defects in humans? The answer happens to be "very few"—chemicals with quite similar structures commonly have very different biological effects. Strong results from standardized teratogen assays using animals would be a valid reason for concern, nevertheless—but Bendectin is not a strong animal teratogen. (Most tests, in fact, do not show that it is a teratogen at all.)

A second key question—routinely overlooked by nonexperts—pertains to base rates. Suppose Bendectin did cause birth defects. If so, what fraction of birth defects would it cause? If we are trying to find out whether Bendectin did cause one specific birth defect, we need to gauge the reliability of our answer by having at hand information about the fraction of birth defects in general that are caused by Bendectin.

To begin with, we can ask the testifying expert whether he or she claims that the test shows that the relative risks of human birth defects associated with the drug are very high—say, that it causes a tenfold increase in the

Box 5.3
Screening and Preclinical Testing of Potential Anticancer Drugs

source: Office of Technology Assessment, U.S. Congress, Federal and State Regulation of Unconventional Treatments and Evaluating Unconventional Cancer Treatments, in Unconventional Cancer Treatments (September 1990) (OTA-H-405) (citations omitted)

Until recently, the most common type of primary screening test for botanical products (and other substances) involved the use of tumor-bearing rodents—mice or rats with tumors that arose and were maintained in inbred strains. . . .

. . . Agents that tested positive in these tests were generally tested further in animal systems before being considered for human trials. . . .

Animal tumor tests can generate information about a new agent's biological properties. . . . The usefulness of such data depends on the degree to which they predict corresponding effects in human beings. The information gained from animal tumor tests can be used to select agents for clinical testing in human beings.

The limitations of animal tumor tests are well known. Their results do not necessarily correlate with results in human patients with cancer, although the degree of correlation varies with the type of test and the type of human cancer. There are many examples in which the response in an animal tumor system failed to predict a similar response in humans, in addition to examples in which animal results correlated closely with clinical responses. One way around this problem has been to use a variety of different tests to study each new agent. In general, the greater the number of animal tumor systems that show antitumor responses to a drug, the greater the chances that the drug will be active in humans. Activity in only one or two animal systems tends to correlate with little chance of activity in humans.

In 1985, [the National Cancer Institute] discontinued the use of animal tumor systems for routine, primary screening testing, in part because of these problems. In their place, a test system of human tumor cell lines grown in culture is currently being set up for initial screening of possible antitumor agents. The new system focuses on identifying substances that may be active in specific tumor types. Substances that test positive in this new system would then be tested in human tumor-bearing athymic (nude) mice, and then in other whole animal systems for toxicology testing as a final step before use in human subjects.

risk to humans. In that case the effect would be very obvious in epidemiological studies, and the issue of causation would be moot from both the legal and the scientific point of view. (Such high relative risks are certainly ruled out by the epidemiological evidence regarding birth defects and Bendectin.)

Suppose, however, that the expert concedes that he is making a 10 percent call—that the drug is associated with a relative risk of 1.1. Such a result might well be consistent with the available epidemiological data regarding Bendectin. Then we are forced to ask how the witness knew that this particular birth defect in that particular child was caused by the drug. We are thrust back to the other end of the curve and to the lethal pairing: (1) a weak test (e.g., structure-function analysis) (2) purporting to diagnose the cause of inherently low-probability events (birth defects caused by Bendectin, in a world where at least 90 percent of birth defects in children of Bendectin users have non-Bendectin causes). This kind of call is inherently very unreliable. Indeed, it will almost never be correct. No matter how careful and cautious the expert, the statistics are just too powerfully against him. He will have to claim extraordinarily acute vision (90 percent accuracy) in order for the specific observation to be correct with even 50 percent probability.

With "toxic tort" evidence, the odds against reliability pile up higher and higher. It is not just that rabbit tests are poor predictors of birth defects in humans; tests of a weak teratogen conducted in a small group of rabbits are poor predictors of birth defects in rabbits. If a test employs too few animals or if it was poorly done for other reasons (as was true of some of the animal studies cited in the Bendectin litigation), it will be outrageously weak as a forensic test for the cause of a birth defect in a human child.

Bayesian statistics (or base-rate problems) have many implications for the law, apart from establishing causation in "toxic tort" suits. The evaluation of the reliability of evidence requires careful and simultaneous consideration of *two* factors. The first is the accuracy (sensitivity and selectivity) of the test. The second is the base rate of the thing being tested—the frequency of "positive" individuals in the population at large. In an excellent law-review article, Michael Saks and Jonathan Koehler point out that the sensitivity and selectivity of few forensic tests have been established.[14] One exception is "DNA fingerprinting," but this has only recently been studied under real-world conditions.[15] With many other tests, we lack even basic information about accuracy and reliability when applied to mixed populations.[16] Saks and Koehler suggest that this may be because so many forensic tests were developed in an environment far removed from the rigors of normal scientific and medical practice.

This is not to say that a proper statistical analysis of such tests is always easy, least of all in the context of a real trial. The predictive values of widely used animal and cellular tests for identifying human carcinogens and teratogens are poorly established, and usually only approximate and qualitative information is available about such issues. And many other conceptual problems arise. There is reasonable agreement, for example, about rates of HIV infection in the American population as a whole. But what are the rates among white gay males in small Midwestern towns? To calculate a "base rate" one must first choose an appropriate reference population, and that may be difficult. For similar reasons, legal decisions cannot be reduced to mathematical formulas. Statistics do, however, make explicit the kinds of information needed to evaluate the reliability of a scientific test, and to point out where unstated assumptions may be hidden in an expert's conclusions.

The general, qualitative insights that emerge from Bayesian analysis are as follows:

• We cannot gauge the "reliability" of any single observation—such as "this child's birth defect was caused by her mother's use of Bendectin"— without considering prior knowledge. The prior knowledge can be a strong observed association between use of the drug and birth defects—a high relative risk. Absent such evidence, an argument based on animal or other tests can be highly reliable when the accuracy is great (as when the test used by Dr. X is perfectly accurate and yields no false positive results) or when the background statistics make them so (for example, Bendectin is such a strong teratogen that any other cause—if the mother took the drug—is inherently unlikely).

• In an argument based on animal or other indirect evidence, the precise numbers depend critically on the false-positive and false-negative rates of the test and the background statistics (the base rate). When tests are highly accurate in identifying human teratogens and background statistics are favorable (most substances are teratogens), the results of a test can be very reliable indeed. But if the background statistics are unfavorable (few substances are teratogens), results of the individual tests can be unreliable.

Either kind of unfavorable odds can poison the well completely. Even terrifically good eyes (95 percent) are very unreliable when they report chartreuse (1 percent) taxis. It takes both good tests and favorable background statistics to make an observation or an inference reliable. In a world with few proven human teratogens, correct identification of human teratogens using an indirect test of low reliability is therefore quite rare. For that same reason, initial diagnoses of rare diseases are often incorrect (see chapter 2).
• The process of assessing reliability of a test requires far more than a statistical analysis of the particular data in question. It requires observations about the results of the test when applied to many other substances.

One solution to the base-rate problem is to use a better test. But in most cases there is no set of inherently superior and more trustworthy eyes at hand. In the "yellow taxi" example we have only Mrs. Smith, Mrs. Jones, and a dozen (or a hundred) others, each reporting his or her own individual observations from a different point of view. We cannot gauge the reliability of any single observation without accurate information on the larger, collective figure. If we know only that Mrs. Smith's eyes are 80 percent accurate and that she claims to have seen a yellow taxi, we have no way of knowing how likely that claim is to be true. If yellow taxis are in fact common (i.e., if Jones, Brown, White, et al. all see them often), then Mrs. Jones's claim is probably true. But if almost all taxis are orange (i.e., if Jones, Brown, White, et al. all report orange taxis often, and yellow ones rarely if ever), then Mrs. Smith's claim is almost certainly false—even if her eyes are 95 percent accurate!

This would seem to make the inquiry completely circular. We can't gauge the reliability of Mrs. Smith's individual observation until we have accumulated the results of observations from Jones, White, and many others. But how can we accumulate many independent observations if we can't decide whether to trust even one? It turns out, however, that the process is not circular. It normally converges if we simply weigh each individual observation according to how closely it conforms with others made before. We weigh Mrs. Smith's report of a yellow taxi heavily if it is one of many such reports, and lightly if most reports say orange. Over time, then, the numbers can and do converge as observations accumulate and patterns emerge.

This process is never that simple, however. Even in science, a strict Bayesian model is not a very accurate description of the way science actually works. This is due in part to practical necessity. Scientists have to cut corners and throw out some hypotheses early in the game. As Kitcher points out, "there are convergence theorems about the long run—but . . . we want to achieve correct beliefs in the span of human lifetimes."[17] Judges have to "achieve correct beliefs" in much shorter times than that.

Perhaps more significant to the law, the Bayesian process often fails to converge in practice. Scientists always have a range of opinions about an issue. Controversies related to low-level environmental agents and their impact on health take a long time to converge, and some never do. The issue of power-line fields and childhood cancer has raged for nearly 20 years, with science neither able to identify a hazard clearly nor to prove that none exists. Scientists remain divided in their estimates as to whether any hazard exists at all, while at the same time admitting freely that the evidence so far does not demonstrate that weak electromagnetic fields are hazardous.

Finally, the data and analysis that are needed to establish the sensitivity and selectivity of most animal or cellular tests for human teratogens or carcinogens either don't exist or are very unreliable. A few standardized animal tests have been validated well enough that informed guesses can be made by scientists about their predictive value for human risks, but in many cases important legal or regulatory decisions must be made from evidence of uncertain reliability.

Bayesian Fallacies in the Real World

It is especially important for judges to understand the above concepts, and to apply them in assessing reliability, because laypeople rarely do.[18]

Legal scholars have long debated[19] whether juries should be permitted to hear (and make inferences from) "base-rates" statistics,[20] and have often concluded that they shouldn't—in large part for legal reasons not related to evidentiary reliability. But base rate and other statistical issues are important nonetheless. Studies show that ordinary people easily fall into logical traps, particularly when asked to solve problems that involve statistical reasoning. Massimo Piattelli-Palmarini's recent book *Inevitable Illusions* offers a good description of these fallacies for nonscientists.[21]

Numerous psychological tests confirm that people routinely misapprehend the importance of base rates, even in easy cases. In one famous study,

Kahneman and Tversky gave test subjects descriptions of various individuals in a group.[22] The subject was told that 70 percent of the members of this group are lawyers and 30 percent are engineers. But each description included suggestive items like "good communication skills" or "likes to work with numbers." The test subject then labeled each individual a lawyer or an engineer. Invariably, the subjects chose labels that reflected the accepted stereotype: good talkers must be lawyers, good number crunchers must be engineers. And these categorizations did not change even when the investigator flipped the 70-30 mix of lawyers and engineers. In other words: People often ignore the most important, quantitative, and reliable piece of information they have at hand. A sure strategy for "passing" the aforementioned test—with a very respectable score of 70 percent—would be to label every individual in the group a lawyer, however good his or her number skills may be. The descriptive clues are much less reliable than the simple quantitative one. They rely on the subjective, human-centered, nonquantitative, and unreliable factoids ("communicates well") far more than they should. They disregard the objective background numbers.[23] If judges don't force the issue of statistical reliability into the pre-trial process of screening expert testimony, juries are very unlikely to handle the testimony correctly in the trial that follows.

The Reliability of Negative Evidence

As was discussed in chapter 3, science cannot prove negative propositions; it can only prove the falsity of positive ones. Science cannot, for example, prove that Bendectin does not cause birth defects; the most scientists can do is search for evidence that it does cause them. In the United States, federal law explicitly requires drug companies to prove the "safety" of new drugs and medical devices, but the Food and Drug Administration does not in practice require industry to accomplish this impossible negative-proving task. The FDA insists, instead, that the companies conduct a reasonable number of clinical and animal studies to show the effectiveness of the drug (which can be proved) and to rule out (or at least fail to detect) major adverse effects. After enough fruitless searching for things they cannot find, scientists and regulators may conclude (provisionally) that the drug is safe.

But negative epidemiological studies do not prove that a substance poses no risk; they prove only that the study has been unable to identify any risk that might be present. One of the most basic fallacies in science is to confuse a lack of evidence of an effect with evidence for no effect. Because of sampling errors, epidemiological studies are limited in their power to detect small increases in risk; even a large study may be unable to detect less than a doubling of risk. Thus, an environmental pollutant might cause many cases of illness in a population, yet the increase in incidence of the disease may be too small to be detected. This is the problem of "trans-science," discussed in chapter 3 with reference to the measurement of lung cancer risks from radon.

There is, as a result, endless controversy in risk assessment about substances that are unequivocally causes of cancer in highly exposed animals but for which human epidemiological data are either negative or mixed. PCBs, dioxin, trichloroethylene, and (at low exposure levels) asbestos and radon owe their notoriety largely to animal studies or epidemiological studies involving high exposures. But epidemiological studies of humans exposed at typical environmental levels are mixed and (taken as a whole) negative.[24] In their book *In Search of Safety*, John Graham et al. describe enduring controversies over the possible human carcinogenicity of benzene and formaldehyde—substances that are clearly toxic at high levels of exposure but whose risks at low exposures are simply too small to measure reliably.[25] After each negative study, the questions remain: Was there truly no effect? Or was there a weak effect that the study was not powerful enough to detect? Or was a real effect masked by a deficiency in the design of the study, such as confounding or misclassifying the exposure? After each weak positive study, the question of study validity arises.

There are two ways to deal with these problems. One is to wait and see how the scientific evidence develops. Later studies, with better designs and more careful dosimetry, may uncover what earlier studies missed. At some point, the claim that a mass of negative epidemiological evidence has overlooked a significant effect because of inadequate study design loses credibility. As of this writing (1996), more than a hundred epidemiological studies have examined a possible relation between exposure to electromagnetic fields and cancer. None has clearly identified a large effect, although many are "positive" in reporting small associations; however, the evidence points in many directions and is, on the whole, inconclusive.

Unless a future study uncovers a group of people who were unequivocally exposed to high levels of electromagnetic fields and who unequivocally suffered high incidence of disease, the issue will die—not because any scientist has proved that no risk exists, but because the line of investigation has led nowhere. This is how Bendectin research ended: faced with a large body of solidly negative results, funding agencies and scientists gave up. And, faced with an equally large body of lawsuits, the industry stopped manufacturing the product.

The second approach in assessing the reliability of negative studies is to consider other lines of evidence, such as animal studies. Perhaps a theory will emerge that lends credibility to the hypothesis that there is "something there" after all. Epidemiological studies linking passive smoke and lung cancer show increases in risk that are—at best—at the very edge of detectabilty. These results are still taken seriously by many scientists and by the U.S. Environmental Protection Agency, however, because there is a strong association between active smoking and the disease, and because animal studies unequivocally confirm that tobacco smoke is a strong carcinogen.

But how should this evidence be weighed? In "toxic tort" cases, courts have generally insisted on epidemiological data showing that the relative risk exceeds 2, particularly when the only other available evidence is animal toxicology data with questionable applicability to humans. This approach is reasonable in view of the standard of proof in civil litigation: that the plaintiff more likely than not was injured by the exposure. Animal studies, particularly those with questionable relevance to humans, carry relatively little weight. This may change in the future, when advances in molecular biology may allow scientists to identify "biomarkers" in the human body that are good indicators of increased risk from exposures to potentially hazardous substances,[26] and a scientifically strong case for causation might be developed in the absence of direct epidemiological evidence.

Curiously, regulatory agencies typically place greater weight on animal studies than on epidemiological studies when setting exposure standards for toxic substances.[27] Animal studies are better controlled, and for that reason they are less susceptible to challenge in court. The reason for this difference has less to do with science than with the different legal constraints in these different fields.

The statement that science cannot prove a negative becomes, at some point in a line of investigations of a potentially toxic substance, a mere platitude. In some philosophical sense, the statement is always true. But in a practical sense, after enough study, society can reasonably conclude that it is very unlikely that new evidence will be forthcoming that will warrant placing a chemical or a drug on the very short list of proven human teratogens (for example) under realistic exposure conditions. The teratogenicity of accepted human teratogens—alcohol, Thalidomide, and so on—is confirmed by strong animal and epidemiological evidence. Nothing of the sort ever developed with respect to Bendectin, a scattering of weak positive results in disputed studies notwithstanding. Under these circumstances, we are entitled to bend the philosophical rules a bit and say that Bendectin does not cause birth defects.

Conclusion

The difference between conjecture and supportable inference—the difference between "might have caused" and "probably did cause"—is fundamentally one of probabilities. And the reliability of scientific tests used to draw such inferences is also a matter of probabilities.

The issue, ultimately, is a scientific and philosophical one: What evidence is needed to "prove" a theory about an empirical issue? Lines must still be drawn. A partial truth, a factoid, or a building block presented as if it were a complete proof is very likely to be misleading and confusing. If a mathematician claimed to have proved Fermat's last theorem but offered only half of a very complicated proof, the half might be quite correct so far as it went yet would still be no proof at all. If the theorem happened to be an issue in a civil trial (as it could be in a case involving software or a computer algorithm), the "proof" in question would properly be excluded—not because it was wrong, but because it was incomplete. Half a proof is not a whole, but a jury might have a lot of trouble telling the difference if a mathematician were to present the first half and then announce "F.L.T., Q.E.D."

In matters of health and disease, one never has a "proof"; one always has something less: evidence that would lead a rational individual to accord greater or lesser credence to a theory. The line of reasoning can be tested, and the reliability of the tests can and should be examined.

In view of experimenter's regress (chapter 3), potential errors in data (chapter 4), and different views among scientists themselves about the reliability of different lines of evidence, these issues will never be resolved, particularly when the effects being discussed are small. Moreover, legal disputes often arise about issues that are scientifically unresolved. "[F]orms of guidance are needed," Sheila Jasanoff has argued, that are "more realistically attuned to the indeterminacy of scientific knowledge in the actual contexts of litigation, and mindful of the institutionalized strengths and weaknesses of judicial dispute resolution."[28] Bayesian analyses can give important insights into these questions.

In the end, the use of the term "reliability" in *Daubert* raises the crucial question "Reliable enough for what?" To sentence a criminal to death? To enjoin the discharge of a pollutant into a river? Or to put to a jury vote a scientific question that bears on the compensation of someone who claims injury, the financial health and future operation of one defendant, and a larger profession or industry that practices medicine, manufactures drugs, produces chemicals, or builds cellular phones?

The meaning of *Daubert*'s reliability inquiry ultimately revolves around a second question: Just how reliable do courts want their own judgments to be? In formulating the answer, one must keep in mind that the Federal Rules of Evidence do not distinguish one legal context from another. The standard of reliability, whatever it is, will be the same for criminal and civil cases, the same for injunctive cases (simply ordering a party to do or not to do something), and cases in which monetary compensation is sought.

One way or another, trial judges must screen expert evidence and make the binary choice whether to admit or reject it. They must use guidelines that are qualitative and in some measure subjective. Perfect decision rules do not exist. However, imperfect decision rules exist, and they can be applied methodically, in a reasonably neutral and objective manner, to enhance the overall reliability of legal judgments.

6

Scientific Validity

Proposed testimony must be supported by appropriate validation—i.e., "good grounds," based on what is known. . . . In a case involving scientific evidence, *evidentiary reliability* will be based upon *scientific validity*.
—*Daubert v. Merrell Dow Pharmaceuticals, Inc.*, 509 U.S. 579, 590–591 & n.9

The most convenient (and no doubt the most reliable) synopsis of the *Daubert* holding appears in Chief Justice Rehnquist's dissent. (Had the Chief Justice somehow misapprehended the majority's emphasis, the misunderstanding would have been corrected, and votes changed accordingly, long before either *Daubert* opinion saw the light of day.) The Chief Justice summarized the majority views that he himself could not accept:

[T]he Court concludes that reliability and relevancy are the touchstones of the admissibility of expert testimony. . . . It stresses that the subject of the expert's testimony must be "scientific . . . knowledge," and points out that "scientific" "implies a grounding in the methods and procedures of science," and that the word "knowledge" "connotes more than subjective belief or unsupported speculation." From this it concludes that "scientific knowledge" must be "derived by the scientific method." Proposed testimony, we are told, must be supported by "appropriate validation." Indeed . . . the Court decides that "[i]n a case involving scientific evidence, *evidentiary reliability* will be based upon *scientific validity*."[1]

The Chief Justice chose not to dwell on the textually curious arrangement of key words in the majority opinion. The final (and crucial) sentence quoted by the Chief Justice comes from a footnote in the majority opinion. Footnote material is usually of secondary importance, but italics are not used lightly in Supreme Court opinions.[2]

In its italicized reference to "scientific validity," this footnote contains what may be the most important language of the opinion.[3] References to "scientific validity" also reappear at numerous other points in the majority opinion. The majority concluded the main section of its opinion by reiterating that the "overarching subject" of the Rule 702 inquiry is "the scientific validity—and thus the evidentiary relevance and reliability—of the principles that underlie a proposed submission."[4]

Popper on Judging Science

The *Oxford English Dictionary* offers several definitions of "validity." The first involves "legal authority, force, or strength." The second is broader, reflecting its lay usage: "The quality of being well-founded on fact, or established on sound principles, and thoroughly applicable to the case or circumstances; soundness and strength (of argument, proof, authority, etc.)."

In discussing the solidity of science, Karl Popper offered a similar perspective, based on the same metaphor of "foundation." "Science does not rest upon solid bedrock." Instead, science rises above "a swamp," like a "building erected on piles." There is no "natural or 'given' base." "[I]f we stop driving the piles deeper, it is not because we have reached firm ground. We simply stop when we are satisfied that the piles are firm enough to carry the structure, at least for the time being."[5] Popper thus put little faith in any categorical statements about validity of science. Moreover, he (along with most other philosophers of science) denied the existence of any simple "scientific method" of the kind presented to many students in their introduction to science.[6]

In Popper's view, judging the soundness of a scientific theory is not a simple, one-step process. It is a process of repeated testing. It is the ongoing search for failure, or—in Popper's terms—"falsification." Strength (or reliability, or validity) is what gradually emerges from repeated unsuccessful attempts to falsify. Popper lists various positive ways in which a theory can be judged:

(1) by comparing the conclusions that can be deduced from the theory among themselves, to see whether they are internally consistent

(2) by investigating the logical form of the theory, to determine "whether it has the character of an empirical or scientific theory, or whether it is, for example, tautological"

(3) by comparing the theory with other theories, "with the aim of determining whether the theory would constitute a scientific advance should it survive our various tests"

(4) by "testing of the theory by way of empirical applications of the conclusions which can be derived from it."[7]

These criteria are cumulative; the more exhaustive the testing, the more confidence we can have in a theory's strength.

Popper's checklist offers a good summary of how scientists evaluate other scientists' theories. It also has strong parallels with the *Daubert* criteria.

The first of Popper's criteria, logical consistency, though not expressly mentioned in *Daubert*, is a predicate for any inquiry of this kind, whether conducted by Karl Popper or a federal judge. As we discuss later in this chapter, a theory must be logically coherent if any further examination is to be possible. Logical consistency is the first requirement of scientific validity; without it there can be no validity.

Popper's second criterion, which addresses how a proposition is framed, points back to our discussion of "falsifiability" in chapter 3. Popper regarded falsifiability as the defining character of empirical propositions, but here we can set aside that controversial philosophical point. How a proposition is framed says much about how solid or slippery it really is. This is as true in science as it is in ordinary discourse. Whether they come from children, politicians, judges, or scientists, plain, definite, and straightforward statements are more likely to be strong and sound than verbal circumlocutions, simply because plain lies and errors are so much easier to detect and knock down.

Popper's third criterion is one of novelty. If a claim or a theory doesn't assert something new or different about the world, it will be of little interest to scientists. Also, there will be little reason for scientists to scrutinize or challenge it independently. Only scientific advances attract attempts to falsify or verify. This leads to Popper's fourth criterion: verification. This, too, touches on validity. A theory whose predictions conflict with observations cannot be called valid.

Thus, in Popper's view, the testing of a scientific claim has no final stopping point. Stopping points are determined, instead, by the how the theory is to be used, and that may include strictly practical and social considerations. When a theory can be labeled "strong enough" depends largely on what it is to be used for. Newton's laws work exceedingly well for the ordinary world of buildings and airplanes. They serve admirably for virtually all engineering tasks, from space flight to the design of mechanical watches. But Newtonian mechanics was overthrown twice during the twentieth century, in two independent revolutions in science: relativity and quantum mechanics. Both theories are more valid than Newtonian mechanics, because they describe the behavior of physical systems under ordinary conditions and also in ranges of size (atomic and subatomic dimensions) and speed (close to the speed of light) where Newtonian mechanics fail. For most purposes Newton's laws remain adequate, however. No physicist—and certainly no engineer—would use quantum mechanics to design a bridge. Most scientists would still consider Newton's laws valid because they are logically consistent, and within their range of validity they are highly successful in predicting observations. They are not valid when applied on either an atomic or a cosmic scale, however. The logical consistency is still there, but the laws don't predict what scientists actually observe.

Determining the validity of a theory is not the same as establishing its truth. Moreover, the connection between science and truth is as philosophically contentious an issue as the nature of science itself. Popper's checklist—like similar ones developed by other philosophers—has a lesser aim: testing the strength of a theory. Such testing is akin to "testing the pilings," in Popper's metaphor. Whether one makes use of a theory or not depends on the circumstances. How much weight is to be placed on the pilings? How bad will it be if the platform on the pilings should fall? Theories that are logically consistent and that agree with observations are valid, for the time being, until some scientist proves them wrong.

There is nothing esoteric or abstract in this point of view or in Popper's criteria. Scientists test a claim by subjecting it to the same skeptical questioning that any intelligent layperson would apply to any factual claim about the world. Judges can exercise their duty under *Daubert* in similar fashion, and they are directed by *Daubert* to do so. The subject matter may be highly technical or esoteric, but the *Daubert* analysis need not be. Scientific theories that are logically inconsistent, or that sharply conflict with already established scientific principles, fail the test of validity in both the scientific sense and the ordinary dictionary sense of the word.

Logical Validity

We have described validity as a composite of two characteristics: logical consistency and agreement of a theory with experiment. But the word "validity" has narrower meanings too: it is used as a term of art in both science and philosophy. The *Oxford Companion to Philosophy* defines "validity" as "most commonly attributed to . . . deductive arguments, which are such that if the premises are true the conclusions must be true . . . or to propositions that . . . are true under any alternative interpretation of the non-logical words."[8] (In contrast to the few words devoted to this definition of "validity," the *Oxford Companion* devotes a full page to "truth" and has nothing at all to say about "reliability.") In this narrow sense, validity is uncomplicated; an argument is valid if it is logically consistent and if it parses.

This test of validity can also be applied to less formal arguments. Arguments built on non sequiturs, ad hominem attacks, appeals to ignorance, begging the question, and special pleading all lack validity at the basic level of logic. A scientific argument that is based on non sequiturs or whose logic does not parse is invalid on its face and would be rejected by scientists if its proponent could not quickly remedy the problem; for the same reason, it must fail *Daubert*'s validity requirement.

A large literature describes invalid forms of reasoning engaged in by both scientists and nonscientists.[9] The epidemiologists and public health experts Petr Skrabanek and James McCormick have described several of these fallacies as they relate to the misinterpretation of medical claims (box 6.1), and the astronomer Carl Sagan has presented a list of criteria for "baloney detection" (box 6.2). Such kits, Sagan reports, are given to scientists in their training. But they are simple and universal precepts for clear thinking which show again that valid scientific reasoning is not different from reasoning in nonscientific fields.

The list of potential errors in reasoning is long. In his book *Thinking and Deciding*, Jonathan Baron enumerates 46 different errors in reasoning categorized by psychologists.[10] Most of these errors are related to the handling of statistical data. The human mind is poorly designed for probabilistic reasoning, and logical errors easily creep into well-intentioned arguments. Scientists are not noticeably better than nonscientists at making off-the-cuff

---

Box 6.1
A Fistful of Fallacies II

Petr Skrabanek and James McCormick

source: *Follies and Fallacies in Medicine* (Prometheus, 1990)

Strictly speaking we can never prove causality from an association, however perfect such an association may appear. . . . In Dublin, the density of television aerials was strongly associated with birth rate and infant mortality, not because television was lethal to infants but because the density of aerials reflected poor housing, overcrowding, and poverty. . . .

[Collateral or Indirect Correlation]   . . . [I]n a debate on an Irish Family Planning Bill, a number of prominent doctors publicly maintained that making condoms freely available would cause an upsurge of promiscuity and venereal disease. Their conviction that there was a causal relationship was based upon an indirect association. . . .

[Necessary and Sufficient Cause]   Even if an association between A and B is causal, it still does not follow that every A will be followed by B. In other words, a necessary cause is not always a sufficient cause. . . .

[Noncausal Time Correlation]   Among the most common fallacious associations that occur in epidemiology are those that depend upon a time correlation. Any two independent variables that change linearly over time will show a perfect correlation. . . .

[The Ecological Fallacy]   The ecological fallacy stems from transferring relationships that occur in populations to individuals. . . .

[The Faggot Fallacy]   . . . The faggot fallacy is a belief that multiple pieces of evidence, each independently being suspect or weak, provide strong evidence when bundled together. . . .

[The Weight-of-Evidence Fallacy]   . . . Weighing evidence in this context is about the accumulation of all evidence that confirms belief on one side of the scales, and showing that its quantity and bulk are greater than the counter-evidence that can be placed upon the other side. . . .

[The Bellman's Fallacy]   In Lewis Carroll's "The Hunting of the Snark" the Bellman says: "What I tell you three times is true." This is a degenerate form of the faggot fallacy. . . .

[The Fallacy of Risk]   The fallacy of risk stems from a failure to distinguish between relative and absolute risks. . . . The relative risk, although an important index of the strength of an association between a putative risk marker and a disease, has no bearing on the probability that an individual will acquire that disease. . . .

[The Fallacy of Inappropriate Extrapolation]   . . . There is much expert debate about the nature of the relationship between low-level radiation and undesirable effects, in particular whether the relationship is linear or nonlinear and whether there is a threshold below which no effect occurs. . . .

[The New-Syndrome Fallacy]   Medical literature is full of articles reporting a small number of patients, usually one, who suffer from two uncommon and hitherto unrelated conditions that are now declared to establish a new "syndrome," with the tacit hope that it will become eponymously known by the describer's name. . . .

[The Fallacy of Insignificant Significance]   Clinicians reading medical literature are tempted to equate statistical significance with clinical importance. . . . If large numbers of patients are required to show benefit from a treatment, it is certain that the treatment is marginal and it is probable that it is of no practical importance. . . .

. . . When the groups are large, differences in terms of *relative risk* may often be statistically significant but of no importance in terms of an alteration in *absolute risk*. Small differences in large studies should also be regarded with suspicion because of the many sorts of bias that may afflict such studies. On the other hand, large differences in small studies run the risk of being disregarded if the differences are not statistically significant. This is technically known as a Type 2 error.

[The Fallacy of Post-hoc Statistics]   . . . Differences that are discovered by accident then become the verification of an ad-hoc hypothesis that was the result of the observation. This is fallacious because it confuses pre- and post-test probabilities.

[The Fallacy of "Positive" Results]   The fallacy of "positive" results is . . . finding a significant difference between groups due to sampling variation, when in fact there is no real difference between the populations studied. . . .

[Error of the Third Degree]   . . . Statistical significance has become the yardstick by which treatments and many other things are evaluated, yet relatively few physicians are statistically sophisticated. As a result the use of an inappropriate statistical method may demonstrate difference where none exists. . . .

[The 'Hush, Hush' Fallacy]   . . . Since the consequences of medical error may have dramatic results, there is a strong tendency to deny them: the good physician does not make mistakes.

calls about what facts logically imply, particularly when asked to make judgments based on statistical reasoning.[11] (See box 6.3.)

Validity in Science

"Validity" is also a term of art in science, where it is sometimes further delimited by adjectives such as "construct" or "face." This creates difficulties in offering a precise definition. The epidemiologist Alvan Feinstein maintains that "'validity' has so many connotations . . . that its specificity of meaning has been lost."[12] Most meanings, however, relate to the

Box 6.2
Baloney Detection

Carl Sagan

source: *The Demon-Haunted World: Science as a Candle in the Dark* (Random House, 1995) (footnote omitted)

In science we may start with experimental results, data, observations, measurements, "facts." We invent, if we can, a rich array of possible explanations and systematically confront each explanation with the facts. In the course of their training, scientists are equipped with a baloney detection kit. The kit is brought out as a matter of course whenever new ideas are offered for consideration. If the new idea survives examination by the tools in our kit, we grant it warm, although tentative, acceptance. If you're so inclined, if you don't want to buy baloney even when it's reassuring to do so, there are precautions that can be taken; there's a tried-and-true, consumer-tested method.

What's in the kit? Tools for skeptical thinking.

What skeptical thinking boils down to is the means to construct, and to understand, a reasoned argument and—especially important—to recognize a fallacious or fraudulent argument. . . .

Among the tools:

• Wherever possible there must be independent confirmation of the "facts."
• Encourage substantive debate on the evidence by knowledgeable proponents of all points of view.
• Arguments from authority carry little weight. . . .
• Spin more than one hypothesis. . . . What survives, the hypothesis that resists disproof in this Darwinian selection among "multiple working hypotheses," has a much better chance of being the right answer than if you had simply run with the first idea that caught your fancy.
• Try not to get overly attached to a hypothesis just because it's yours. . . .
• Quantify. If whatever it is you're explaining has some measure, some numerical quantity attached to it, you'll be much better able to discriminate among competing hypotheses. What is vague and qualitative is open to many explanations. . . .
• If there's a chain of argument, *every* link in the chain must work (including the premise)—not just most of them.
• Occam's Razor. This convenient rule-of-thumb urges us when faced with two hypotheses that explain the data *equally well* to choose the simpler.
• Always ask whether the hypothesis can be, at least in principle, falsified. Propositions that are untestable, unfalsifiable are not worth much.

Box 6.3
Seeing What We Expect to See: The Biased Evaluation of Ambiguous and Inconsistent Data

Thomas Gilovich

source: *How We Know What Isn't So: The Fallibility of Human Reason in Everyday Life* (Free Press, 1991)

[O]ur expectations can often be confirmed by any of a set of "multiple endpoints" after the fact, some of which we would not be willing to accept as criteria for success beforehand. . . .

The problem of multiple endpoints is most severe when the subject under investigation is inherently fuzzy and hard to define. For instance, suppose someone claims that day care during infancy hinders "personal adjustment" in later life. Well, what is "personal adjustment" and how does one measure it? . . . It is at times such as these, when the meaning of the phenomenon under investigation is unclear, that our preconceptions have their greatest effect. . . .

An interesting analogue . . . is what could be called the problem of "variable windows." The essence of a number of beliefs is that certain events tend to happen within some (unspecified) period of time. The belief that things "happen in threes" is a perfect example: Many people believe that events like plane crashes, serial-killing sprees, or birth announcements tend to occur in triplets. It is almost certainly the case, however, that these beliefs are mere superstitions that stem from the tendency to allow the occurrence of the third event in the triplet to *define* the period of time that constitutes their "happening together." . . .

. . . Certain beliefs or suppositions imply a similarity between two entities: A child should look like his or her parents, identical twins should behave alike, or a personality description ought to resemble the person it describes. However, if the two entities are sufficiently complex, then mapping one onto the other will almost certainly produce a number of points of over-lap, and the expectation will appear to be confirmed. . . .

. . . Some [asymmetries] derive from their relation to broader theories that we hold. Popular superstition informs us that the period of the full moon is an unusually dangerous time of the month. Consequently, any homicide, suicide, or accident during that time will command our attention and be linked to the full moon—*even if we do not believe in the superstition.* Similar events during other periods of the month will be thought of exclusively as what they are, and not as tragedies that happened in the *absence* of a full moon. . . .

. . . Perhaps the most common determinant of whether an event is one-sided is the base-rate frequency of the different possible outcomes. When certain outcomes occur frequently enough, they become part of our experiential background and go unnoticed. Departures from normality, in contrast, can generate surprise and draw attention. The unexpected can sometimes be unusually memorable.

> . . . Sadly, people who are diagnosed as having certain forms of cancer rarely recover. An instance in which someone does recover, therefore, is rather noteworthy, particularly if the person did anything unconventional to try to effect a cure (such as visiting a faith healer or travelling to Mexico for Laetrile therapy).

connection between a theory or results of a particular study and the empirical world. "Validity," one well-known text explains, "applies to the overall acceptance of study results (whether conclusions are justified based on design and interpretation) or in the case of external validity (whether results can be generalized to settings and subjects outside those described in the study)."[13]

Validity as a term of art in science depends on considerations that are external to the technique or theory itself. One introductory social science textbook explains that "any measuring device is valid if it does what it is intended to do. An indicator of some abstract concept is valid to the extent that it measures what it purports to measure . . . validity concerns the crucial relationship between concept and indicator. . . . One does not assess the validity of an indicator but rather the use to which it is being put."[14]

In this scientific sense, validity is not a binary yes-or-no quality, as it is when the validity of a mathematical proof is in question. Here validity depends instead on the concordance between the theory by which one interprets data and how the inferences drawn from the data are going to be used. A bathroom scale, for example, provides a valid measure of a person's weight. It would not normally be accepted as providing a valid measure of a person's waist size. Weight and waist size can be roughly correlated, however, and weight can be used as a surrogate measure of waist size. Similar correlations are used to infer all sorts of things about the sizes and shapes of dinosaurs, complete examples of which are not available for weighing. Surrogate measures of this sort are used quite often in science when direct measures are not available. But when a simple and accurate instrument like a scale is feasible, it would earn the badge of validity in preference to other less accurate, more speculative alternatives. However, the accuracy of the instrument is also important in defining its validity for its intended use: a bathroom scale is not a valid instrument for use as a postal scale.

A more socially important example is the use of IQ tests to measure intelligence. The validity of such tests is very hard to ascertain, in no small part because intelligence itself is not well defined and because the needs for information about intelligence are diverse. An IQ test might be valid enough to identify an individual child in need of special help; it is almost certainly not valid enough to support any sweeping conclusions about race and intelligence. Stephen Jay Gould describes how intelligence tests were used early in the twentieth century to "prove" that there was a large proportion of "mental defectives" among immigrants from Eastern and Southern Europe.[15] The tests included questions on topical subjects, such as American baseball players. Not surprisingly, they identified a high rate of mental deficiency. These tests were probably quite valid if their purpose was to justify legislation that would exclude from American soil non-English-speaking immigrants deficient in their knowledge of American culture, but as measures of innate intelligence they were clearly lacking.[16]

Validity in Statistical Inference

The validity of statistical inference has emerged as a well-defined issue in the use of statistical tests. Many scientific fields rely heavily on statistical inference: clinical medicine, epidemiology, social sciences, education. The available data in these fields are rarely so clear cut as to compel a single, indubitable conclusion by casual inspection of the experimental results. In these fields, therefore, scientific claims are routinely based on statistical analysis. Professional journals require that major conclusions be supported by adequate statistical analyses of data.

In a typical study, a medical scientist might compare the outcomes of two groups of people: patients who were treated with a drug and untreated controls. Using an appropriate statistical test, the scientist attempts to determine whether the treatment worked.[17] Perhaps 50 percent of treated patients, but only 40 percent of untreated patients, recovered. Does this difference confirm the efficacy of the drug? Or, to put the question another way, how likely is it that future patients will benefit from the same treatment? Using a formal statistical test, the investigator tries to determine the probability that the observed difference between groups of treated and untreated patients is a real effect. The validity of such statistical inferences depends on the suitability of the test for the given purposes. That depends, in turn, on the assumptions that underlie the test. Choosing an appropriate test requires an adequate knowledge of statistics, which many scientists simply lack.

Scientists universally acknowledge the central role of statistics in their profession, yet a great number of scientific papers present conclusions based on statistical analyses that are not valid. Many—by some accounts, most—of the papers published in even the most prestigious medical journals contain serious errors in their statistical analyses.

An audit published in the July 1988 *British Journal of Surgery* reported that 39 percent of the articles surveyed contained serious statistical errors that would have been sufficient to justify rejection of the paper.[18] One review of 28 such assessments concluded: ". . . the findings reported . . . suggest that the average [medical] practitioner will find relatively few journal articles that are scientifically sound in terms of reporting usable data and providing even moderately strong support for their inferences. . . . The mere fact that research reports are published, even in the most prestigious journals, is no guarantee of their quality."[19] The statistician John Yancey elaborates: "It is important to understand that the data analysis errors identified by just about every review of the medical literature are not trivial misunderstandings important only to those of us who teach statistics. . . . Most of the errors are of the magnitude of claiming to have scientific evidence that one surgical procedure is superior to another when no such valid scientific data are presented."[20]

The errors that concern Yancey and the other statisticians quoted above result from improper use of statistical tests; they are, at bottom, errors in logic. They have little to do with the differences in scientific judgment that concern sociologists of science, and they seldom reflect any intent to deceive. These errors do not necessarily lead to incorrect results, of course. Even a Ouija board can sometimes give correct answers. But, Yancey notes, "if a surgeon based a clinical decision upon the output from a Ouija board, because he sincerely thought it to be a scientific instrument, his conclusion would still be scientifically invalid, professionally incompetent, and ethically wrong."[21] In box 6.4 we present Yancey's ten rules for reading clinical research reports, abstracted from his article in the *American Journal of Surgery*.

Box 6.4
Ten Rules for Reading Clinical Research Reports
John M. Yancey
source: *American Journal of Surgery* 159 (1990): 533–538

Since it is reasonably clear that all clinical researchers are about as likely to start analyzing their data according to the rigorous rules of science as it is that all advertisements in clinical journals are going to do likewise in presenting their wares, the typical consumer of both the advertisements and the articles might benefit from the following rules for the proper understanding of research data published in contemporary clinical journals.

Rule I: *Be skeptical.* As noted earlier, the odds are good that the authors have arrived at invalid conclusions. This does not mean their conclusions are wrong, but it does mean that their conclusions may not have the scientific validity attributed to them by their authors. . . .

Rule II: *Look for the data.* Once upon a time, clinical researchers said, "Here is a detailed description of what we did and here is what happened and this is what we think it all means; but since we have reported our data, you are free to draw your own conclusions." Contemporary journal authors are more likely to say, "Here is a description of what we did, here are our statistical analyses, and this is what all that mumbo jumbo means; trust us." But the readers' only consult with nature is via the data reported in the article. Everything else is a consult with authority. That is not science. . . .

Rule III: *Differentiate between descriptive and inferential statistics.* I believe the single most serious error made by clinical researchers is the failure to understand the fundamental difference between statistical indices that summarize the data collected by the study and those that attempt to answer questions about data that have not been collected, and likely never will be collected.

Statistics such as means and standard deviations describe the data in hand; hence, they are called descriptive statistics. Tools that generate p values allow one to make inferences about the population of data from which the present study is but one random sample; hence, they an called inferential statistics. . . .

Rule IV: *Question the validity of all descriptive statistics.* It has been said that a fellow with one leg frozen in ice and the other leg in boiling water is comfortable, on average. . . .

Rule V: *Question the validity of all inferential statistics.* Almost every review of the medical literature has found that many researchers are wrong about what inferential statistics actually index. . . .

Rule VI: *Be wary of correlation and regression analyses.* The great majority of clinical studies I have examined over the past 30 years involving correlation and/or regression analysis have been seriously flawed. The worst mistake is accepting the authors' implicit suggestion that an individual clinician may safely use the regression equation to make predictions for individual patients. Sometimes equations or graphs are given for 95% confidence intervals, but these usually are misinterpreted to be confidence intervals for individual predictions rather than correctly understood to be estimates of population means, which, more often than not, are of no use to clinicians. . . .

Rule VII: *Identify the population sampled.* . . . In almost all instances, the statistics used are about what would happen if the present study were to be repeated over and over. They say nothing about what would happen if even slight changes were to be made in either treatments or patient populations. . . .

Rule VIII: *Identify the type of study.* Only truly randomized, tightly controlled, prospective studies provide even an opportunity for strong cause-and-effect statements. Often there are very good reasons why such a study cannot be done, but that has no effect upon the logic that says that in the absence of true random assignment and rigid control of the treatment groups, any differences in outcome might be a function of differences in the groups other than the treatment difference. . . .

Rule IX: *Look for indices of probable magnitude-of-treatment effects.* The great majority of the inferential statistical tools employed by 1987–1988 *Journal* authors were estimates of *directional* differences in population means or population proportions. Few articles provided estimates of the probable *magnitude* of these differences. . . .

Rule X: *Draw your own conclusions.* The primary difference between science and other methods of finding the truth is that science consults nature while other methods consult authority. Your only consult with nature in a research article is the section that presents the raw data. Everything else is some authority telling you what the truth of the matter is.

Validity in the Design of Epidemiological and Clinical Studies

Epidemiology is "the branch of applied statistics that studies the determinates and correlates of human disease."[22] Epidemiology is an observational (rather than experimental) science, and it is therefore more subject to ambiguity in interpretation than an exact science such as physics. In experimental science, an investigator is free to repeat an experiment, adjusting parameters, and controlling for other variables that may be significant. Epidemiologists have no such luxury. Nor do most researchers who conduct clinical studies about the efficacy of treatment, though these studies are often easier to control than epidemiological studies on diverse populations.

Epidemiological studies search for statistical associations between exposure and disease. It is a canon of science that association never proves causation. Owing to the complexity of the human population, there are many opportunities for spurious associations to infect results. Moreover, no epidemiological study can be wholly free of flaws that might invalidate its results. One can always question whether a statistical association reported by a study is due to a real cause-effect relation or whether it is merely an artifact of sampling or inadequate methodology. Hill's criteria, discussed in chapter 2, represent one attempt to formulate decision rules to answer this question.

The problem, for the law, is compounded by the fact that epidemiological reports in the scientific and the lay literature vary tremendously in quality. "Junk epidemiology," such as *New Yorker* reports of disease clusters,[23] occupy one extreme. These reports often create great public anxiety; however, when followed up by health authorities, few of them ever culminate in a finding of a real public health problem, whatever may have been the afflictions of the individuals involved. Most of these reports are based on post hoc rather than controlled observations. The disease clusters are usually products of pure chance: people living near each other becoming ill for independent reasons, with no causal link between the cases. Reports of clusters of disease, of which the health authorities receive hundreds every year, are so unreliable in their interpretation as to be virtually worthless to those interested in protecting public health. Much the same is true of the popular literature on alternative medicine—a field that relies heavily on testimonials about new treatments from satisfied patients. The same description applies to many "clinical studies" reported by purveyors of quack nostrums. The individuals involved in alternative medicine or quack nostrums are rarely willing or able to carry out well-designed studies. (See box 6.5.)

At the other pole are professionally conducted epidemiological studies that are well designed for their intended purposes. Typically they are large

Box 6.5
Federal and State Regulation of Unconventional Treatments
source: Unconventional Cancer Treatments (Report OTA-H-405, Office of Technology Assessment, U.S. Congress, September 1990)

[The gap between the scientific data that constitutes valid evidence of safety and efficacy for regulatory purposes and the data provided by advocates of unconventional cancer treatments is very great. This selection from a report of the Office of Technology Assessment suggests ways in which existing data from unconventional cancer treatments might be evaluated to identify treatments that might be promising candidates for further testing. —K. Foster and P. Huber]

There is no question that existing unconventional treatments *could* be treated like new treatments in the conventional pipeline, tested in the laboratory, in animals, and then in humans. But that is highly unlikely to happen, since most unconventional practitioners have not recognized the need for such testing, and the government would not undertake such an effort without a reason to believe the treatment might be effective. The operative question becomes, then, can the experience of patients taking these treatments be used in any way to determine whether they *might* be effective, and worth evaluating further, and also whether they pose particular dangers for patients? . . .

Efficacy: "Best Case Reviews"

One way to determine whether a treatment has antitumor effects is to test it in a phase II trial. Given a treatment that has been used by hundreds or thousands of patients, however, is there another way of efficiently generating some, at least preliminary, information before a prospective trial is contemplated? . . . [The] "best case" approach, with modifications, could be used more prominently in determining which might deserve further investigation. . . .

The objective of the best case review is to produce evidence of tumor shrinkage (or, in particular cancers, other accepted objective measures of lessening disease) in a group of selected patients (either current or former), with evidence documenting that the patients had the particular unconventional treatment under study and, as far as possible, that they did not have any other treatments during that time period.

The basic elements of each case in a best case review would be: 1) documented diagnosis by an appropriate licensed professional, including pathology reports and microscope slides of the tumor; 2) history of prior treatments; 3) length of time between the most recent treatment and the treatment under evaluation; 4) x-ray studies from before and after the treatment under evaluation was administered; and 5) a statement from the physician and the patient saying that no other treatments were administered at the same time as the particular treatment under evaluation.

These elements require a significant amount of documentation. Clearly, many patients who benefit from cancer treatment—mainstream or unconventional—could not be included in a best case review, because their records would not be sufficient to meet these demands. However, an adequate and convincing review could be based on as few as 10 or 20 successful cases. If a treatment is even moderately successful and has been used for many years, that number meeting the criteria should be available. Such a review will require time, patience, perseverance, resources, and the cooperation of professionals in the mainstream community, such as pathologists, oncologists, and specialists in nuclear medicine, which may seem a steep climb for an unconventional clinic to undertake. . . .

CAPITALIZING ON THE EXPERIENCE OF TREATED PATIENTS: SAFETY

Just as described above for assessing efficacy, there are some informative and some not very informative ways of using patient experience to assess the safety of treatments. . . .

In cases where unconventional practitioners or clinics keep detailed patient records, it would theoretically be possible to examine them for adverse side-effects that might be related to the treatment. The practitioners themselves might also be good sources of this information, if they noted particular patterns of unintended effects. Such a means of detection is not unlike the way newly discovered adverse drug effects are reported to the FDA, at least for rarer effects that would not necessarily be detected in formal premarketing clinical trials. OTA found no reports of systematic records-based studies of adverse effects by unconventional practitioners, however, and it is probably not realistic to expect many, if any, to undertake these studies.

Another possible approach to gathering information on adverse effects in past (and possibly current) patients is by examining medical reports from physicians and hospitals who have seen patients after they leave unconventional treatment or who are seeing them concurrent with the unconventional treatment. Results of laboratory tests not generally carried out at unconventional clinics (e.g., liver function, kidney function, cardiac tests), descriptions of clinical symptoms, and autopsy reports for patients who have died are available in some cases. This type of investigation is most likely to be undertaken by mainstream groups concerned with unknown adverse consequences of unconventional treatments. Given that it is not the type of study in which the unconventional community is likely to participate, locating patients and confirming information about their unconventional treatment may be a difficult exercise.

affairs, costing a million dollars or more. Also at this pole are more modest studies that uncover effects strong enough for even small studies to detect reliably. Some of these results are quickly accepted by the medical community, despite weaknesses in the designs of the studies. The first major epidemiological study that linked smoking and lung cancer, by Richard Doll and Austin Bradford Hill,[24] is widely cited as a landmark in epidemiology, yet it is not difficult to spot a serious error in its design: the investigators compared lung cancer victims in hospitals to other patients suffering from other lung diseases, some of which are also caused by smoking. Had the tobacco-cancer effect not been so strong, the Doll-Hill study might have missed the association between smoking and lung cancer. This flaw, if anything, increased the confidence of other scientists in its results, since it would tend to weaken any association.

Junk testimonials and the Doll-Hill study represent the two poles of epidemiology. The reliability of most studies falls in between. Some—such as the studies linking occupational exposures to benzene and leukemia—become widely accepted by scientists and the regulatory community, even though some scientists continue to challenge their validity. Other studies never gain wide acceptance, because the statistical associations are weak and because the results are seriously compromised by potential design flaws; they fail to convince most scientists of their validity.

For example, although hundreds of studies report associations between exposure to electromagnetic fields and cancer, no causal link is widely accepted by scientists or regulators—in part because many of the studies have poor assessments of exposure, and in part because the results are weak and inconsistent. Repeated reviews of the literature on electromagnetic fields and cancer by expert panels of scientists have failed to find credible evidence that the fields cause disease. Many experts and expert groups (including the American Physical Society) therefore conclude that these fields have no public-health significance at all[25]; other experts still recommend a policy of "prudent avoidance" as a hedge against the possibility that an effect is present.[26]

Studies linking dioxin or PCBs to cancer fall into the same broad middle range of epidemiology. The chemicals cause cancer in animals at high doses, but the human epidemiological evidence involves low exposures. The risks the studies claim to detect are close to the lower limits of what the statistics can detect from the available data. Individually, the studies suffer from deficiencies in design that cast doubt on their validity. Results of different studies are, in many respects, weak and inconsistent. The studies raise important questions about risk but provide no convincing proof of its existence. Many of the legal controversies described in our earlier book, *Phantom Risk*, turn on different interpretations of this literature.

Scientists themselves often disagree about just how to weigh a body of scientific evidence. Just how differently epidemiologists can view the findings of other respected members of their own profession is strikingly illustrated by an ongoing debate that pits the prominent epidemiologist Alvan Feinstein against other distinguished members of his own profession. Feinstein's blunt commentaries point out methodological and conceptual problems that, in his view, negate the validity of many epidemiological studies. His adversaries reply that Feinstein's standards of inference are too strict, and that flawed studies should be taken seriously if they suggest the possibility of a public health problem.[27] They argue that "physicians and policy makers should consider both the costs and benefits of actions, bearing in mind the uncertainties in causal inference and the impossibility of perfect decision rules."[28] (See boxes 6.6–6.8.)

All in all, clinical and epidemiological studies face so many potential threats to their validity that even carefully conducted studies may culminate in unreliable interpretations. Assessing the validity of an epidemiological or a clinical study requires careful analysis of its design. If the results are to be valid, unless the effect is so strong as to be indisputable (as in the case of smoking and lung cancer), the study must be very painstakingly designed; often it must be quite large too. Studies by amateur scientists (e.g., news reporters or concerned citizens), and even preliminary studies by professional scientists, are likely to be very unreliable.

The Knowledge Filter

In the popular imagination, science is a solid edifice of established fact. In this image, scientists are like patient bricklayers, each adding one small solid piece at a time to an already solid structure. In this view, the validity of science is hardly an issue—if it's "science," it's valid.

Science does not work that way at all. As we have repeatedly noted, the scientific literature is a vast collection of individual contributions, highly

Box 6.6
Scientific Standards in Epidemiologic Studies of the Menace of Daily Life
Alvan R. Feinstein
source: *Science*, December 2, 1988: 1257–1263

Of the three menacing relationships under discussion here, the first was reported about 14 years ago. Three retrospective case control studies . . . published in the same issue of the same journal, all found a positive association between breast cancer and reserpine, a medication that was then widely prescribed for treating hypertension. . . .

The second menacing relationship was reported in a case-control study in 1981, when the risk of pancreatic cancer was estimated to be about 2.5 times as high in people who drank coffee as in those who did not. . . .

The third "menace" was found as an association between alcohol and breast cancer in two convenience-cohort studies, reported in the same issue of the same journal in 1987. . . .

All of these highly publicized accusations of "menace" came from research that had been approved by the "peer review" of authoritative experts. The peer review process, however, provides assurance only that an act of research complies with accepted methods in a field of investigation. The process provides no assurance about the methods themselves, particularly if the reviewing experts also establish and maintain the very methods that they are asked to approve.

[Requirements for a valid epidemiological study:]

1) *A stipulated research hypothesis.* To plan an experimental trial, the investigator identifies the cause-effect comparison that will be tested as the research hypothesis. . . .

Thus, all three of the menacing relationships were not from previously stipulated research hypotheses, but from statistically significant results in computerized multiple explorations.

2) *A well-specified cohort.* In randomized trials, the cohort under study is well specified by examinations done before the exposure (or nonexposure) begins, and in subsequent follow-up to see whether the selected outcome event has occurred. . . .

The basic scientific principle of a well-specified cohort was not maintained in any of the studies under discussion.

3) *High-quality data* . . . [I]n both the convenience cohort and the case-control studies, the investigators often sought "false positive" errors by trying to confirm reported diagnoses of the target disease, but seldom checked for the vital counterpart error of "false negative" diagnoses.

4) *Analysis of attributable actions.*   An ideal experimental design should allow an observed agent to be held responsible for the outcomes that follow it, but few human agents are received in isolation, and many are maintained in an erratic manner with frequent changes in schedule. . . .

None of the three case-control studies of the reserpine–breast cancer relation specified the amount of reserpine required for "exposure," and none reported documentary data for a dose-duration-response relation. . . .

5) *Avoidance of detection bias. . .*   [D]etection bias was not considered in the basic plans for any of the cited studies.

---

variable in quality. Some papers are brilliant, others are junk. Most scientific papers, once published, are never cited and are quickly forgotten. The scientific literature is full of inaccurate data, conjectures that turn out to be incorrect, and theories that lead nowhere. Many studies are like fishing expeditions: the scientist tries something to see what happens, planning an experiment on a conjecture or on no theory at all.

Yet, at the same time, science, and technology based on science, are very trustworthy indeed. Vaccines and jet engines really do work. If science were not valid in some overall sense, no sane person would ever step onto an airplane.

How can the whole be so much sounder and stronger than its original inputs and its constituent parts? The paradox is easily resolved. Reliable scientific knowledge, like reliable technology, develops over time. Data and theories are kept, modified, or discarded as the totality of knowledge accumulates. Given time, scientists and engineers develop a good sense of what works and learn to avoid what does not. Reliability is a collective attribute of the whole body of learning, which contains many bits and pieces of unreliable evidence.

This process is clearest with applied technology: A Boeing 727 can be trusted to fly because similar airplanes have been in use for many years. Each crash, tragic though it is, helps makes the remaining planes more airworthy, because causes are identified and corrective measures are implemented.[29] The 727 is built with technology that—at this point in time—is familiar, well understood, and thoroughly reliable. A new military jet, built with the very latest technology and designed to perform at the outer limits of what is technologically feasible, is much more likely to fail.

Box 6.7

Scientific Standards of Criticism: A Reaction to "Scientific Standards in Epidemiologic Studies of the Menace of Daily Life," by A. R. Feinstein

David A. Savitz, Sander Greenland, Paul D. Stolley, and Jennifer L. Kelsey

source: *Epidemiology* 1 (1990): 78–82 (notes omitted)

Feinstein has promoted a misleading view of epidemiology by presenting well-known limitations of observational research as if they were generally unrecognized, by emphasizing only those study limitations that would negate causal associations, and by failing to distinguish important from unimportant biases. . . .

We perceive several false assumptions underlying Feinstein's position, especially in his recent article in *Science*:

Premise 1: Failure to Adhere to Scientific (Experimental) Standards Generally Leads to False-Positive Association

. . . Feinstein consistently overlooks the fact that the net impact of all methodologic deficiencies will often be to spuriously dilute measures of effect.

Premise 2: Epidemiologists Are Complacent About Their Deficient Methods

. . . Feinstein has failed to revise his position in light of changes in the field.

Premise 3: Epidemiologists (and the Media and the Public) Overinterpret Positive Associations, and Propose Policy or Behavioral Modifications Based on Insufficient Evidence

. . . No less than other scientists, epidemiologists seek to conduct scientifically valid research and provide an objective, complete accounting of methods and results. . . .

Although Feinstein's most important errors concern judgment and interpretation, there are numerous technical inaccuracies. . . .

1. *Misclassification always results in overestimation of association*:   . . . What Feinstein fails to note is the impact of such errors: If the errors are independent and nondifferential with respect to disease status, the average bias across exposure categories is toward the null. . . .

2. *Measures of disease occurrence are interchangeable*:   . . . Feinstein's criticism is, however, based on a completely erroneous calculation. . . . Elsewhere, he confuses "prevalence at death" with "annual incidence" of endometrial cancer to draw erroneous inferences about detection bias.

3. *Absence of a dose-response gradient precludes causality*:   Although a clear monotonic gradient can support causality if the gradient is predicted by

a biologic theory, a biologic effect need not follow a monotonic dose-response curve across all exposure levels; for example, there may be a threshold or ceiling effect. . . .

In addition to technical errors, Feinstein makes a number of dubious assertions, such as:

1. *Contradictory results are symptomatic of poor methods*: Feinstein portrays epidemiology as "unscientific" because of the frequency of contradictory results. First, contradictory results do not indicate poor methods are common, at least as reflected by the controversies in far more advanced scientific disciplines. . . .

2. *Anticipations of the study designers affect study results in ways not explained by the actual conduct and analysis of the study*: . . . Exploiting existing data to address previously unanticipated research questions has the virtue of time and cost efficiency, and would generally avert subtle bias in the data collection process owing to anticipation of the study hypothesis.

Science is, thus, heterogeneous. It consists of a growing margin—"proto-science," "frontier science," or something of that sort—that is interesting but often wrong. Its core is much less controversial (because it is familiar) but very reliable. There is a wide gray area in between. The high regard for science in the popular imagination undoubtedly arises from the fact that ordinary textbook science is usually true. But much of the science that the layperson encounters in the mass media, or perhaps in court, doesn't come from the textbooks. It is, at best, frontier science—the scientific equivalent of an experimental aircraft that may or may not someday be robust enough to fly.

The chemist and professor of science studies Henry Bauer describes science as a "knowledge filter."[30] (See box 6.9.) In his model, the growing margins of science (where most scientists work, or at least try to) constitute "frontier" science; the established core constitutes "textbook" science. As time goes on, scientific ideas are constantly filtered and refined, and—if they withstand the give-and-take among scientists and become adopted by the scientific community—eventually come to be regarded by scientists and others as sound.

The "knowledge filter" operates by means of a complicated set of positive and negative criteria, applied by individuals but accumulating through a collective process. There is no simple threshold test that admits a discrete piece of scientific knowledge into the body of science as "valid." Popper's

---

Box 6.8
Reprise and Lyrics for Another Chorus
Alvan R. Feinstein
source: *Epidemiology* 2 (1991): 72–76

Savitz and Kelsey state discreetly that "compliance (with the principles) is not universal." I would contend that it is often nonexistent. I shall cite two prime examples.

. . . Detection bias continues unabated as one of the major scientific lesions in epidemiologic methods today. . . .

. . . [A]scertainment bias is not just frequently ignored; it is often explicitly incorporated into the research. . . .

. . . Savitz and Kelsey may have confused the distinctions among disease, etiology, and exposure when they called the diagnostic tests "biologic markets of exposure." . . .

As long as many chronic-disease epidemiologists continue to claim a special right to operate outside the realm of ordinary, customary scientific principles for basic evidence and inference, complaints will continue to occur about the scientific quality of the operations.

---

checklist, summarized at the beginning of this chapter, identifies the kinds of tests that scientists typically apply when examining one another's work.

The negative criteria are the easiest to grasp. Scientific papers that are badly flawed usually are rejected by journals. If published, they are ignored in embarrassed silence by other scientists. Theories that are not reconcilable with well-established facts and with established theories likewise die on the vine.[31] The positive criterion that counts most is usefulness, either to scientists in their work or for practical applications. Another is fruitfulness in helping to identify and solve important new questions—what the philosopher Philip Kitcher calls "fecundicity."

The test of time is the ultimate test of data and theories. The proposition that Bendectin causes birth defects is probably wrong in light of the toxicology of known human teratogens, but it cannot be dismissed on theoretical grounds alone. The proposition has not been supported by the vast majority of published studies, despite one or two isolated exceptions. The proposition failed because there never were enough supporting data to keep even a scientific (as distinct from a legal) controversy alive, let alone

Box 6.9
How Science Really Works
Henry H. Bauer
source: *Scientific Literacy and the Myth of the Scientific Method* (University of Illinois Press, 1994)

Research, or frontier science, is by no means a disciplined, homogeneous activity in which all the participants agree with one another about most things. Very far from it. Scientific research is a medley of all sorts of attempts to gain new knowledge, in every way that human ingenuity can conceive—by cutting corners; by doing "quick-and-dirty" experiments, not just carefully systematic ones; by following hunches or "just playing around," as well as by trying carefully thought-out things. After all, research is done by people who differ from one another in all the usual sorts of ways: in having noble or ignoble motives, great or little energy, many or few ideas, and so on.

The inchoate ferment that research scientists produce cannot become part of the accepted canon of science until it has been published; but getting published means convincing editors and referees that something about the work is sound and useful. And so, once again, individual frailties or imperfections must run the gauntlet of communal scrutiny, with the result that much of the error, bias, and dishonesty that exists within the ferment of frontier science does not enter the scientific literature. . . .

. . . Only what has stood some test of time, as interesting and useful and not obviously wrong, becomes incorporated into the secondary literature of review articles, monographs, and graduate-level textbooks; and this then represents something like the prevailing consensus in the various research communities. It is pretty reliable stuff, mostly. But it is known in detail only to people who work actively in that particular field or in closely related ones.

The scientific knowledge that has widest currency is that contained in undergraduate textbooks, and there is an appreciable time-lag between something making its way into reviews or monographs and finding its way into textbooks. . . .

Overall, then, the raw stuff of frontier science has those characteristics of uncertainty, subjectivity, and lack of discipline that one should surely expect whenever human beings try to do what has never been done before. But after successive filterings through the institutions that science has evolved over the centuries, what remains easily gives the appearance of being objective and true. In point of fact, what remains is (relatively) impersonal rather than strictly objective, and it is hugely reliable and trustworthy rather than warranted true for all time; but in practice one rarely or never notices the difference—nor does that usually matter. John Ziman has ventured the guess that, in physics, textbook science may be about 90 percent right, whereas the primary literature is probably 90 percent wrong.

to classify the drug among the few established human teratogens. Propositions like this one survive as viable scientific theories only if they muster enough data, or present enough new insights, to excite the interest—and then gain the acceptance—of scientists and funding agencies. The alleged links between Bendectin and birth defects never did.

In this case, the knowledge filter acts through the positive criterion of the usefulness of a theory or a result to protect public health. One problem for the law, however, is that material rejected by the filter remains in print. Scientific results that are strong enough to be published in good peer-reviewed journals may not stand the test of time; but, though they are not read or cited by scientists,[32] they remain in the literature. Lawyers who go dredging can and do find them.[33]

Bauer's procedural view of the scientific process describes how science works, at least most of the time. It does not say how scientists come to accept or reject theories in practice; it supplies no descriptive models for scientific decision making. Nor does it tell us how they should decide—it offers no normative prescriptions, and the knowledge filter certainly has nothing to do with establishing the ultimate truth of a theory. A filtering process does not describe what goes into the filter at one end, or what comes out at the other; it describes, instead, an ongoing process of refinement and testing—a process that in the long run produces an improved product. The knowledge filter does for science what a curator does for art. The difference is that the criteria for preservation in science are not (in the main) aesthetic; they are epistemic and cognitive. Ultimately, they are based on the usefulness of the product.

Daubert's "validity" mandate requires judges to serve as knowledge filters too. Whether or not they are wholly comfortable with the role, judges must make a preliminary call as to whether or not the facts, theories, and conclusions attested to by an expert witness are reliable and valid—sound and strong enough to justify presentation in court. One surrogate measure is the extent to which the ideas have passed through the knowledge filter of science.

7

Peer Review and the Scientific Community

"[G]eneral acceptance" can yet have a bearing on the inquiry. A "reliability assessment does not require, although it does permit, explicit identification of a relevant scientific community and an express determination of a particular degree of acceptance within that community." . . . Widespread acceptance can be an important factor in ruling particular evidence admissible, and "a known technique that has been able to attract only minimal support within the community". . . may properly be viewed with skepticism.
—*Daubert v. Merrell Dow Pharmaceuticals, Inc.*, 509 U.S. 579, 594 (1993) (quoting *United States v. Downing*, 753 F.2d 1224, 1238 (9th Cir. 1985))

In chapter 3 we addressed Popper's "falsifiability" standard and the need to frame scientific propositions in terms concrete enough to be challenged. As we noted there, Popper's perspective is philosophical, and his claim that "falsifiability" is the defining characteristic of science has been vigorously disputed by other philosophers. But Popper's views have important practical implications, nonetheless. By stating a proposition in terms clear and definite enough to be falsified, he invites other scientists to go ahead and falsify it if they can.

In *Daubert* the Supreme Court grasped this. Immediately before citing Popper, the majority wrote: "Ordinarily, a key question to be answered in determining whether a theory or technique is scientific knowledge that will assist the trier of fact will be whether it can be (and has been) tested."[1] The "has been" follows naturally, from the "can be." Propositions that can be tested will be, if they are at all important.

They will usually be tested by someone else. As Popper constantly pointed out, reliable knowledge develops through independent attempts at testing and refutation and, more generally, through repeated use. As we discussed in chapter 3, the original proponent of an idea is rarely its best critic. Individuals quickly get wedded to their own ideas and grow too fond of them. A broader community is needed to supply skepticism. (See box 7.1.)

Box 7.1
Reliable Knowledge
Paul Kurtz

source: *The New Skepticism: Inquiry and Reliable Knowledge* (Prometheus Books, 1992)

Is it possible to have reliable knowledge? Or is that which we claim to know reducible simply to illusion and self-deception? When Pyrrhonist skeptics analyze the basis of knowledge, they claim that it dissipates into sheer human presumption. Knowledge is like a house of cards, they say; by disturbing the foundations, the entire edifice topples. All knowledge, they conclude, is uncertain, untrustworthy, vacuous. There are *no* standards for judging truth, they insist; for all criteria collapse into human subjectivity.

Now I submit that although knowledge is relational, it need not be subjective. For there are effective criteria for judging claims to truth, and these are used throughout life. Knowledge is not about a fixed realm of essences; it does not give us ultimate truth; nor can it be understood entirely independent of the processes of investigation and discovery. As we have seen, knowledge is a product of a behavioral process of active inquiry. . . .

To say that one has knowledge means that what one knows is true; and truth implies some knowledge about obdurate realities independent of the knower's wishes and desires. A useful distinction thus can be made between belief and knowledge. We may believe something to be true; but our beliefs may be false; and if so, they are not equivalent to knowledge. We may think that we have knowledge, but if our beliefs are false we are laboring under misapprehensions or harboring misconceptions. . . Thus knowledge refers only to those items of a person's or a community's beliefs that have been found to be justified by adequate grounds. A true belief is equivalent to knowledge when the claim made on its behalf is supported by evidence and reasons. . . .

Many people may be convinced of their beliefs, but these beliefs may turn out to be false. I may believe that "Grandma's chicken soup will cure a common cold." Only careful testing will confirm or disconfirm that. If it does turn out to be the case, then I have a piece of information that is a part of the body of knowledge, and I could affirm that I know it for a fact because I can confirm its effectiveness empirically. . . . Yet people may cling to their beliefs tenaciously, cherish and venerate them, especially in religion and metaphysics, even though they are patently false. . . .

C. S. Peirce properly pointed out that we fix beliefs, at least in science, in a community of inquirers and not in a lone, inner solipsistic self. We share common experiences by means of trans-subjective standards of measurement and we develop independent criteria of verification. We often can get intersubjective agreement because the objective facts under experimental observation enable us to resolve the issue. Whether water boils at 100 degrees Centigrade and freezes at 0 degrees Centigrade can easily be resolved by establishing test conditions for the claim. Anyone who understands what we're talking about can enter into a public process of confirmation.

It is important here to focus on the concept of a claim. For in the world of social transactions, individuals often make claims and are asked to justify them. Thus we may assert that something is the case and that it should be acknowledged as true. . . . Here the burden of proof is placed upon the claimant to show why others should accept the belief as true. . . .

Knowledge, at least ideally, is true belief intersubjectively corroborated by reference to objective factors observed, examined, and tested. . . . A meaningful knowledge claim may be mistaken; but at least in principle it can be disconfirmed. . . .

. . . The sciences employ various techniques to discover probable causes: from the simplest statistical studies, where a method of isolation and variation is used to isolate causal correlations, to the more complex introduction of theoretical constructs to explain data. . . . The hypotheses introduced are not unique or isolated, but connected in some way to other hypotheses. Each hypothesis is tested by reference to experimental data—to a firsthand, secondhand, or thirdhand meter-reading, for example—in a controlled laboratory setting. But any one hypothesis should bear some kind of logical relationship to others that have been similarly postulated and tested. . . .

Thus, "submission to the scrutiny of the scientific community is a component of 'good science,'" the *Daubert* majority wrote, "in part because it increases the likelihood that substantive flaws in methodology will be detected."[2] Thus, publication (or the failure to publish) in a peer-reviewed journal is "a relevant, though not dispositive, consideration in assessing the scientific validity of a particular technique or methodology on which an opinion is premised."[3]

Not every scientific claim or methodology will undergo meticulous scrutiny by many independent scientists. As the *Daubert* majority acknowledged, some propositions "are too particular, too new, or of too limited interest to be published."[4] Ordinarily, neither a doctor's diagnosis and opinion about the cause of a patient's illness nor an engineer's analysis of why a bridge collapsed is subjected to peer review.

A subtle but legally important distinction between a scientist who is proposing a new theory and a physician who proposes a diagnosis of a new patient bears on the issue of peer review. As we noted in chapter 1, *Daubert* addressed "scientific knowledge," not "technical, or other specialized knowledge." A physician or an engineer who testifies about a particular patient or bridge will be talking, at least in part, about particular retrospective diagnoses or analyses. The admissibility of such testimony will be gauged under other criteria. But the same doctor or engineer may also, and at the same time, rely on general principles, methods, and insights. These are based on scientific knowledge, and the testifying expert will attest to their validity, either implicitly or explicitly. The original *Frye* case (discussed further in chapter 9) involved a lie-detector test. The indications the test gave as to the veracity of a particular individual were not, of course, issues of "scientific knowledge." The general reliability of lie detectors was. Opinions about "scientific knowledge" are subject to *Daubert*, even when they merely support much more specific, particularized testimony by a doctor or an engineer. This is particularly applicable to criteria for diagnosing illnesses, and even to the definition of an illness.

The Process of Peer Review

Peer review is an integral part of what Bauer calls the "knowledge filter" of science, as routine a matter among scientists as cross-examination is among trial lawyers. Indeed, science borrowed the term "peer" from the law. The *Oxford English Dictionary* offers as its first definition of "peer" the original, legal one: "An equal in civil standing or rank; one's equal before the law."

Peer review of a manuscript by a journal is the first formal step in the "knowledge filter" of science. Journal editors use peer review to determine whether a paper is suitable for publication. Papers are screened for obvious methodological problems with the study, adequate citations to previous work, compliance with the stylistic requirements of the journal, and so on. (See box 7.2.) This review filters out at least the most glaringly deficient contributions. Peer review serves many other functions as well. For example, granting agencies use peer review to select the best proposals for funding, and personnel committees use it to evaluate a candidate for promotion or hiring.

Box 7.3 contains excerpts from a paper by the physicist John Ziman, cited by the *Daubert* majority.[5] In earlier writings, Ziman had defined science as the search for a consensus among competent researchers: science "is never one individual . . . . It is a group of individuals, dividing their labor but continuously and jealously checking each other's contributions."[6]

Box 7.2
Rule 702 of the Federal Rules of Evidence Embodies a Requirement That Expert Opinions That Lack a Legitimate Scientific or Medical Basis Are Not Admissable

brief of the American Medical Association et al. as amici curiae in Support of Respondent (amici: American Medical Association, American Medical Association/ Specialty Society Medical Liability Project, American Academy of Allergy and Immunology, American Academy of Dermatology, American Academy of Family Physicians, American Academy of Neurology, American Academy of Orthopaedic Surgeons, American Academy of Pain Medicine, American Association of Neurological Surgeons, American College of Obstetricians and Gynecologists, American College of Pain Medicine, American College of Physicians, American College of Radiology, American Society of Anesthesiologists, American Society of Plastic and Reconstructive Surgeons, American Urological Association, and College of American Pathologists

source: *Daubert v. Merrell Dow Pharmaceuticals, Inc.*, Dkt. No. 92-102 (U.S. Jan. 19, 1993)

[T]here is a fundamental and widely accepted distinction between opinions that are based upon scientific knowledge and those that are not: An opinion is only based upon scientific knowledge if it is developed in accordance with the scientific method. Those are the only opinions that Rule 702 permits to be presented to the jury.

Scientific knowledge is the body of knowledge that has been developed through application of the scientific method. This method involves empirical testing of a hypothesis. . . .

In addition to proceeding from a scientific framework, the development of scientific knowledge requires that testing be conducted, and scientific evidence be developed, in accordance with techniques that science has determined over time to provide reliable and replicable data. . . . [T]he validity of any scientific theory depends entirely on a reviewable empirical foundation. . . . Absent some accessible (usually published) deduction from a body of empirical evidence, a theory cannot be considered scientific. . . .

. . . [S]cientific method depends significantly upon the peer review process. It requires the scientist to devise methods of data collection that are replicable and to explain precisely how the scientist performed the experiment. Peer reviewers then can analyze the methods and identify potential flaws in the techniques, in the data, or in the statistical methods employed. Research that satisfies the rigors of peer review thus provides assurances that the 'knowledge' derived from that research is 'scientific.'. . .

. . . The mere fact that research has not been subjected to peer review does not render unscientific that which otherwise conforms to scientific standards. Nonetheless, peer review usually assures that knowledgeable experts in the field have already read a paper with critical eyes, and thus it can play an important role in the court's Rule 702 determination. . . .

Peer review cannot assure the ultimate validity of an article's conclusions. . . . Peer review, however, is a significant indicator that an article is 'scientific,' because reviewers are well-positioned to identify conceptual departures from the scientific method. . . .

Moreover, it is implicit within the scientific method's requirement of reproducibility that results will in fact be reproduced and confirmed by other scientists. Peer review and publication further that process, which makes it more likely that fraud or other shortcomings will be detected. . . . Thus, publication in a peer-reviewed journal should constitute significant evidence that the research adhered to "scientific" standards, as Rule 702 requires. The absence of peer review, particularly in circumstances in which the theory is novel or contrary to the weight of the scientific research, is a strong indication that the testimony lacks a scientific foundation.

This "jealous checking" requires a full written report of a scientific investigation. Abstracts, conference proceedings, and other nonrefereed publications characteristically omit information needed to evaluate the study: an analysis of errors, or even a careful description of just what the investigators did. Complete written papers, published in archival journals, form the core of science. Seminars can provide an opportunity for a scientist to present early results, but they provide no adequate opportunity for close, detailed examination of the work by others. The first forum in which "jealous checking" of a new scientific contribution typically occurs when an author writes up the results of a study and submits it to a journal.

Any discussion of peer review is complicated by the diversity of the scientific literature. The best-known scientific journals, and the ones most widely read by American scientists, are *Science* and *Nature*. They offer a mix of reporting, commentary, and original (usually brief) research papers selected as much for newsworthiness as for scientific quality. There are thousands of other scientific journals, ranging from flagship publications of major scientific societies to obscure journals that are independently produced. Most of these journals, including many prestigious ones, cater to specialized audiences; they may have circulations of only a few hundred or a few thousand. Most depend on unsolicited manuscripts for their content. Editorial content is controlled mostly by a volunteer editor (typically, an active scientist), perhaps assisted by a handful of associate editors (also scientists) whose chief function is to screen the manuscripts for publication. Publishing scientific journals is a cottage industry with many independent enterprises. Most scientific journals are modestly profitable,

Box 7.3
The World of Science

John M. Ziman

source: *Reliable Knowledge and Exploration of the Grounds for Belief in Science* (Cambridge University Press, 1978), pp. 124–157

The intellectual authority of science . . . resides in the processes by which scientific knowledge is created and accredited. The sources of its reliability are not simply that it is expressed in unambiguous language and is capable of experimental verification; they are to be found in the historical processes of its growth, and in the social relationships of those who brought it into being. . . .

. . . The network of scientists is not merely an extended observational apparatus; it is an instrument which analyses and selects for preservation only those messages that receive overwhelming consensual support. . . . Drawn towards the unattainable goal of a complete consensus, scientific knowledge evolves by critical selection. . . .

. . . In order that science may retain its reliability and credibility, each scientist is expected to exercise critical vigilance over his own work and the claims of his contemporaries. . . .

. . . Even a complete consensus is seldom publicly determined or proclaimed, the best we may expect is an answer that is said to be the 'almost unanimous opinion of the experts', backed by what they would describe as 'the overwhelming weight of the evidence'. . . .

. . . The first announcement of a discovery is always an exciting moment in science; yet until the provocative, unexpected message has been to some extent 'processed' by the social instrument of the scientific community it can neither be ignored nor taken as a basis for action, and thus lies outside the dimensions of scientific belief and doubt. . . .

. . . What can be deceptive is the degree of credibility that the experts themselves assign to particular scientific propositions. Scientific knowledge is too vast in quantity, and is amassed and assessed too haphazardly, for anyone to have a sound perception of the relative status of all the little pieces of information that go to make a scientific discipline. . . .

Nor is it obvious that the contents of the scientific archives would be improved if all new knowledge had to be approved by, so to speak, juries of lay persons previously unacquainted with the complexities of the issues involved. . . . [I]t is not clear that public debate resolves the underlying intellectual issues. The serious critic inevitably begins to acquire some of the expert knowledge of an 'insider', and becomes an adjoint member of the scientific community rather than a genuinely independent assessor. . . .

. . . [The] manner in which ["mad scientist" claims] are handled may have considerable influence on the public 'image' of science, and under pathological political conditions may be highly relevant to our theme. . . .

The fact is, of course, that almost all such earnest [layman] endeavor, whether in the form of a handwritten letter, or as a handsomely printed

> volume under the imprint of a major publisher, is quite worthless. . . . Yet the professional scientist, in all the panoply of his learning, must remain alert to the possibility that the strange communication from an official of the Swiss Patent Office comes from another A. Einstein. . . .
>
> . . . [P]arascientism has roots in the human psyche, and a role in human culture and social organization, closer to those of revealed religion than of natural philosophy. . . .
>
> But parascientism is a dangerous disorder for the experienced scientist, tending to lower his skeptical guard, and often bringing out an extraordinary capacity for credulity and self-deception.

earning tidy sums from page charges to authors and subscription fees. There are far more journals than would be warranted by the number of truly important papers. For a scientist, it is a seller's market.

Some feel for the selectivity of journals is given by the statistics recently published on the Internet by the *Annals of Biomedical Engineering*, probably a fairly typical journal in terms of how readily it accepts or rejects submitted papers. (See box 7.4.) Of the 171 papers the journal received in 1995, nearly one-third were rejected following initial peer review. A few were accepted immediately. As of early 1996, the rest were still working their way through one or more cycles of revision, possibly with additional review. In short, perhaps half of the papers submitted to this journal are published eventually, sometimes after extensive revision. *Science* and *Nature* accept a far smaller fraction of the submitted manuscripts.

Although most journal editors are experts in the general field covered by their publication, they typically have neither time nor specialized expertise to review carefully (or even to read) every manuscript that they receive. They rely instead on two to five outside reviewers of each manuscript. Journals typically give their referees guidelines or checklists around which to organize their reviews. Some guidelines consist of an open-ended invitation to review the paper according to broad and diverse criteria. Others provide detailed checklists, inviting comment on strictly editorial considerations as well as technical issues (such as statistical analyses or data) that bear directly on the scientific validity of the paper. The reviews vary widely in quality and depth. Some are simply notes scribbled by the referee on a form; others are searching examinations of the study. Boxes 7.5 and 7.6 include excerpts from reviewer guidelines used by a major journal in biophysics and a journal devoted to clinical research on pain.

Box 7.4
Current Status of Manuscripts Submitted, as of January 31, 1996
source: *Annals of Biomedical Engineering*

	Number of mss.	Percentage of submissions
Under first review	17	9.9
In first revision	32	18.7
Under second review	13	7.6
In second revision	3	1.8
Under third review	4	2.3
In third revision	1	0.6
Accepted—with editor	5	2.9
Accepted—in press	16	9.4
Published	19	11.1
Rejected	54	31.6
Inactive—6 months	6	3.5
Withdrawn	1	0.6
Total	171	100.0

Average time until first review returned to editorial office: 29.9 days
Average time until response to authors sent (first submission): 60.5 days
Average time until revised manuscript resubmitted: 71.2 days
Average time until second review returned to editorial office: 25.9 days
Average time until response to authors sent (2nd submission): 45.0 days
Average time until second revised manuscript resubmitted: 38.4 days

The peer-review process is quite efficient at screening out papers that are too speculative or where there are serious errors in the design of the study or in the analysis of data. There are, however, limits to what peer review can accomplish, even when diligently conducted. A paper will probably be rejected if serious deficiencies in the design of the study are apparent from the final write-up. But an artfully written paper can conceal major deficiencies in the study it reports. There is no way for the reviewer to determine independently how much the data may have been manipulated or selected. Scientific papers present boiled-down data rather than the raw materials, much as a Gallup poll presents overall statistics rather than individual questionnaires. The reviewer rarely asks for the original data in the

Box 7.5
Journal Editors' Instructions to Referees
source: a major journal of biophysics

[The referee is provided with two forms for his/her review. One, entitled "Confidential Report to the Editor," has the following checklist. —KF and PH]

1. DOES THIS PAPER ADVANCE THE FIELD?   What is the problem that it addresses, and is it a significant problem? Do the authors state the problem and the conclusion of the paper clearly?
2. IS THIS PAPER CORRECT?   Does the data support the conclusion? Have the authors done the proper controls? Do the authors properly cite and represent important previous work?
3. IS THIS PAPER WELL WRITTEN?   Do grammatical or stylistic lapses obscure the meaning or distract from the messages? Are parts of the paper too long or too terse? Are there unnecessary or hard-to-understand figures or tables?

[This list is followed by a blank area captioned "Comments to the Author(s)." A second sheet, also entitled "Confidential Report to the Editor," has the following checklist.]
Please check the category that best describes this manuscript.

1. One of the best papers that I have read recently in its field. Certainly publish, (after minor revision if suggested on accompanying form).
2. A solid paper that advances its field. Worthy of publication, (after minor revision if suggested on accompanying form).
3. Little or nothing wrong with this paper, but it mainly confirms existing knowledge and makes no significant contribution to its field. Do not publish in [this journal].
4. Needs major revision or clarification. Until this is done, I cannot determine its suitability for publication.
5. So weak that even if the authors were to correct its flaws it could not reach category 1 or 2. The authors should not submit a revised manuscript.
6. Deals with a topic or uses an approach that is not suitable for [this journal].
7. If the paper does not fit into one of these categories, please explain and comment on suitability for publication.

[This page has a large white space captioned "Other comments that should not be seen by the authors."]

Box 7.6
Guidelines for Reviewers
source: a journal of clinical pain research

1) The unpublished manuscript is a privileged document. Please protect it from any form of exploitation. Reviewers are expected not to cite a manuscript or refer to the work it describes before it has been published, and to refrain from using the information it contains for the advancement of their own research.

2) A reviewer should consciously adopt an unbiased and constructive attitude towards the manuscript under review. The reviewer should be the author's ally, with the aim of promoting effective and accurate scientific communication, act as a catalyst and facilitate publication.

3) If you believe that you cannot review a particular manuscript impartially, please return the manuscript immediately to the editor with an explanation.

4) Reviews should be completed within two weeks of receipt. If you know that you cannot finish the review within the time specified, please telephone the editorial office to determine what action should be taken.

5) A reviewer must not discuss a paper with its author.

6) Please do not make any specific statement about the acceptability of the paper in your comments for the author. Advise the editor of your recommendations on the form provided for that purpose.

7) In your review, please consider the aspects of the manuscript as listed on the rating sheet:

Originality of the material

Validity of the experimental design

Validity of the data and statistics

Importance of the information

Relevance of discussion

Validity of conclusions

Clarity of writing

Clinical relevance

Appropriateness of figures and tables

Adequacy of references

Appropriate length

Requirement for statistical consultation

Desirability of editorial comment

8) In comments intended for the author, criticism should be presented objectively, dispassionately, and constructively and abrasive remarks must be avoided.

9) Suggested revisions should be indicated as such, and not expressed as conditions for acceptance. On the form provided, please distinguish between revisions considered essential and those judged merely desirable.

10) Your criticisms, arguments, and suggestions concerning the paper will be most useful to the editor if they are carefully documented and numbered.

11) You are not required to correct deficiencies of style or mistakes in spelling or grammar, but any help you can offer to the editor in this regard will be appreciated.

12) Please feel free to write comments, make corrections or alterations on the manuscript itself. If you do so, please return the MS to the editor.

13) Please type all your comments on both the rating sheet and comments to authors sheets.

14) A reviewer's recommendations are gratefully received by the editor, but since editorial decisions are usually based on evaluations derived from several sources, a reviewer should not expect the editor to honor every recommendation. You will be asked to indicate whether you wish to review the revision.

study and seldom repeats the author's calculations or statistical analyses. In the vast majority of cases, there is no motivation. Time constraints are also severe: a busy scientist may receive one or more papers a week to review, and the need to keep the paperwork moving seriously limits the "jealous checking" of most papers reviewed.

In the regulatory arena the review process is typically far more careful and systematic. Regulators require that documents submitted to them contain far more detail than is typically found in papers submitted to professional journals. For example, EPA regulations require chemical manufacturers to submit file cabinets full of toxicology data and analysis for each new pesticide, and the FDA requires drug manufacturers to submit huge amounts of data. These agencies require studies to be conducted under Good Laboratory Practices or Good Clinical Practices—standards far more rigorous than those commonly used in university research. The data are carefully scrutinized by panels of scientists and statisticians, which will reject an application that has irregularities in the documentation. (Unlike journal editors, federal investigators can file criminal charges against scientists who misrepresent their data.) Moreover, clinical data on the safety and efficacy of drugs, and toxicology data on chemicals, are often published only in extensive reports submitted to regulatory agencies, not in peer-reviewed journal articles. In subsequent litigation, these administrative reports—not peer-reviewed journals—may provide parties with the solidest available data.

Scientists' Perspectives on Peer Review

Boxes 7.7 and 7.8 survey some of the views that scientists themselves have expressed about the peer-review process. In box 7.7 the biochemist David Horrobin describes the purposes of peer review in science and the need for editors of journals to strike an appropriate balance between quality control and encouragement of innovation[7]; in box 7.8 a former editor of *Technology Review*, Jonathan Schlefer, discusses the overall reliability of peer review.[8]

Scientists generally agree on the importance of peer review as a quality-control mechanism and on the importance of publication in peer-reviewed journals. They also are aware of peer review's limitations as a mechanism for ensuring the reliability of published scientific work. Both views were eloquently stated by the epidemiologist Alvan Feinstein in his amicus brief in *Daubert*:

[S]erious scientists know that their work does not become scientific information until it is published. If they believe the work is worthwhile but unappreciated by a set of reviewers at a particular journal, the authors will try elsewhere (perhaps after making some improvements or other changes suggested by the reviewers). Thus, if the work is rejected by Journal A, the authors try Journal B. If Journal B says "no," they try Journal C. They may go on to many more journals, but eventually they get the work published. If the work is worthwhile, somewhere in the scientific "establishment", the authors will find an editor and/or reviewer who will appreciate—or at least tolerate—it. . . .

[R]esponsible scientists will almost always decline to rely upon work that has not been published. The absence of publication means that the author has not had the intellectual discipline and self-respect, and enough "confidence" in the work itself, to get it published. Of course, a great deal of valuable information can be involved in the "informal exchanges" of meetings, conversations, letters, or even gossip among scientists. If the information is serious and valuable, however, it becomes expressed more formally in the true "currency" of scientific exchange: publication. An author or investigator who is unable or unwilling to get his work accepted in the fundamental primary "court" of scientific publication should surely not expect to get it accepted secondarily in a court of law.[9]

Box 7.7
The Philosophical Basis of Peer Review and the Suppression of Innovation
David F. Horrobin
source: *Journal of the American Medical Association* 213 (1990): 1438–1441

The question I will address is the fundamental one: what is peer review for? . . .

Explicit in many articles on peer review, and implicit in most, is the concept that the purpose of peer review is quality control. This is an unsatisfactory answer to the question I have posed. Quality control is one means of achieving an end, but it is not the end itself. . . . The purpose of peer review should be nothing less than to facilitate the introduction into medicine of improvements in curing, relieving, and comforting. . . .

. . . The public ultimately provides money for medical research for one purpose only—to generate improvements in patient care. . . . If improved medical care is not delivered, support for medical research—and hence for medical journals—will dwindle and atrophy.

. . . So long as an important disease problem remains unsolved, there is likely to be support for a broadly based and relatively unfocused research effort. But researchers should not be under the illusion that this situation would continue if tomorrow there emerged dramatically effective solutions to major scourges such as cancer or acquired immunodeficiency syndrome. Much of the support would disappear rapidly. . . .

And if we are to deliver results, quality control can be only one side of the editorial equation. The other must be the nourishment and encouragement of high innovation. There I think we have a problem. In all that is said and written about peer review, quality control appears overwhelmingly important and the encouragement of innovation receives little attention. That is a recipe for failure.

. . . I think we must take seriously the possibility that we have traded innovation for quality control, not only in medical publishing but throughout medical science. . . .

The history of many innovations, both in medicine and in other areas of endeavor, indicates that the innovators are often erratic, unsystematic, and difficult to deal with. The quality controllers often regard the work as of poor quality and not worth publishing or noting. The only problem is that the quality controllers, while exquisite in their crossing of t's and dotting of i's, rarely discover anything that matters. The improvement in research quality over the past years is not all gain if it has occurred at the expense of innovation.

I believe that the great majority of editorial decisions are fair. The quality controllers are right to congratulate themselves that the frequency of error is low. But unfortunately, from the point of view of innovation, that is irrelevant. . . . Peer review must therefore be judged by how it handles those rare articles that genuinely offer the possibility of new approaches that might eventually lead to improvements in curing, caring, and comforting. . . .

. . . While antagonism to innovation during the peer review process may not be the norm, it is far from being exceptional.

Box 7.8
Truth, Beauty, and Peer Review
Jonathan Schlefer
source: *Technology Review*, October 1990

Peer review is widely seen as the modern touchstone of truth. Scientists are roundly drubbed if they bypass it and "go public" with their research. Science writers count on it as the test for what to report on.

Peer review is doubtless useful to help evaluate articles for journals on a particular discipline and as one mechanism, albeit fallible, to allocate grants. But our society often wants to see peer review as a mechanical certification of truth for which no one has to take responsibility. No such mechanism is conceivable.

The first limitation of peer review is that nobody can say quite what it is. Journal editors give manuscripts to a panel of scholars who remain anonymous. Some journals publish only articles that receive a majority of votes, but articles rejected by one peer-reviewed journal are often published by another: this touchstone is wobbly. Reporting on an American Medical Association conference on peer review in June 1989, Lawrence K. Altman of the *New York Times* noted that journal editors may reject articles that the panel praises or accept articles it criticizes. No one knows how often this happens because journals do not report their policies.

. . . In practice, scientists regard journal articles skeptically, as statements in an ongoing debate. Time and replication of experiments are the real mechanisms science relies on to weed out error.

A more pernicious danger is that peer review may reject important work, particularly for research funds. As Charles W. McCutchen, a physicist at the National Institutes of Health, has put it, peers on the panel reviewing a grant applicant "profit by his success in drawing money into their collective field, and by his failure to do revolutionary research that would lower their own ranking in the profession. It is in their interest to approve expensive, pedestrian proposals." He cites the case of Donald Glaser's research on the bubble chamber, an apparatus to display nuclear reactions for which he ultimately won the Nobel Prize in physics. The National Science Foundation and other agencies considered it "too speculative" to fund, but fortunately the University of Michigan scrounged up $750 to support his work. . . .

We don't eschew expert advice: we may well ask informal opinions on unusual articles from knowledgeable people, often at MIT. But there can be no peer review of articles that inextricably blend fact and opinion. We have even had informal readers refuse to comment on manuscripts on the grounds that they don't want to become "silent coauthors." So we scratch our heads, discuss manuscripts, and make the best decision we can.

Then begins the editing process, an intellectual exploration involving countless further decisions to help authors clarify their thinking as well as their writing. Even if the original had been peer reviewed, the final result would not be. Editing ends at 6:00 in the evening of the day the final page proofs go to the printer with titles, blurbs, and captions. That's a frightening moment.

If the article is truly foolish, I can expect a barrage of letters, and time will likely set the matter straight. If we made the opposite mistake, failing to publish important new thinking, I can rest assured that I will never be blamed, except perhaps by one author. But that is the worst mistake possible.

Scientists, it should be emphasized, regard peer review as a simple fact of life, and are comfortable playing the alternating roles of examiner and examinee. In the role of referee they are providing *pro bono* service to a journal in which they themselves are likely to publish.

Outside the role as referee, a scientist's "jealous checking" of a submitted manuscript or a newly published paper is impelled by the exigencies of craft, not by any imperative to purify science. (Most scientists would emphatically disavow wanting to purify science, in any event.) Scientists are more interested in the early opportunity to learn of new ideas, data, and insights. There may also be an element of professional rivalry: peer review of unpublished manuscripts or grant applications provides an opportunity to keep tabs on the competition.

Peer Review and Professional Reputation

Defenders of the legal process often argue that scientific views receive much more thorough scrutiny in a legal trial than they ever do in a professional journal. Up to a point, this is quite true. An affidavit by Alan Done receives far closer scrutiny in adversary litigation than a paper by Done would typically receive from reviewers when submitted to some obscure but nevertheless peer-reviewed scientific journal. (See last section of chapter 4 above.)

But this argument overlooks a second important function of publication and peer review: these are the key instruments by which a scientist establishes and maintains a professional reputation. Publishing rubbish in an archival journal entails a high cost: It will be there, within easy reach of scientific peers, forever after. It will be open to scrutiny not just by one or two other opposing experts, but by every other scientist who cares to visit a scientific library. A scientist cannot easily overcome a reputation for producing shoddy goods. In this respect, courtroom proceedings are far less demanding. Few scientists other than those actually involved in *Daubert* or *DeLuca* will ever see or read the affidavits filed by the experts in those cases. The reputational costs of signing a scientifically incompetent affidavit are far lower than the costs of signing a scientifically incompetent journal article. Affidavits rarely get much public notice, and most of them vanish even from legal view once a case is over.

Some scientific and medical societies have come to recognize that their public credibility can be undermined by egregiously deficient legal testimony from some of their members. Several societies' journals have begun to publish expert testimony offered in litigation, and have subjected it to peer review after the fact, with or without the acquiescence of the testifying expert. Many lawyers react angrily to these proposals; they accuse scientific societies of attempting to intimidate dissenters, discourage expert testimony, or chill the legal process. But this kind of open disclosure is a very effective means of ensuring that scientists act responsibly when presenting their views in public forums. Scientists have both the right and the responsibility to scrutinize their colleagues' work wherever it may be publicized—in professional journals, on the labels of patent drugs, or from the witness stand in court. By the same token, a scientist who makes important scientific pronouncements in a public forum but objects when they are made available to scientific peers simply lacks integrity.

Peer Review as "Knowledge Filter"

Peer review effectively filters out studies that are egregiously flawed, studies whose designs reveal glaring and irremediable deficiencies, and manuscripts that include too slanted an interpretation of the data or that are too badly written to be useful. Thus, it dramatically raises the average quality of the papers in a journal by excluding the garbage.

Peer review also encourages authors to moderate their claims. In response to actual or anticipated criticism by peer-review referees, authors lace their manuscripts with caveats and qualifications. In contrast, the system of lawyer-led question and answer hardly encourages the kind of caveats and qualifications that referees usually insist on in the interpretation of the results of a study.

Peer review does not, however, certify "scientific knowledge," still less "scientific truth." Some sociologists might argue that peer review is a mechanism the scientific community uses to legitimize its own pronouncements, but that is a different matter entirely. Its goal is not to provide a "*Good Housekeeping* seal of approval," as an amicus brief in *Daubert* unfairly accused a lower court of assuming (box 7.9), but rather to ensure a threshold level of reliability for published scientific reports (box 7.10).

As we noted in chapter 6, many results published in good journals are incorrect, peer review notwithstanding. All peer review certifies is that an article was read critically by at least one knowledgeable person who found it acceptable for publication. Peer review is somewhat analogous to an independent audit by an accounting firm. It provides no guarantee against subtle or well-hidden irregularities in the books, still less any assurance of future growth, profitability, or even financial survival. It does provide a threshold level of assurance that the scientific books have been maintained in a way that at least one or two independent scientists consider proper, or at least acceptable. The main difference, however, is that the scientific "auditors" have no access to the original data, nor is there a simple list of generally accepted accounting standards.

Even if reviewers had the time and inclination to check every paper very critically, and in exhaustive detail, there are good reasons why they should not. Scientists try to advance knowledge, to raise new and interesting ideas, and to suggest new possibilities—goals that would not be furthered by excessively skeptical peer review. The rigorous quality-control mechanisms that govern some scientific research (such as Good Laboratory Practices) were imposed on science by outside forces (the regulatory system, in the case of GLP). Such standards are unpopular among scientists, because they greatly increase the cost and difficulty of doing research. Unlike regulators, editors often accept a paper describing an obviously preliminary or even obviously flawed study if the work promises to be important or usefully provocative and controversial. Thus, the goals of science make it undesirable to strive for too high a level of reliability in published papers, and encourage a little creative noise in the system.

Box 7.9
The Ninth Circuit's Elevation of Publication in Peer-Reviewed Journals to the *Sine Qua Non* of Admissible "Good Science" Is Insupportable
source: Brief Amici Curiae of Physicians, Scientists, and Historians of Science in Support of Petitioners, *Daubert v. Merrell Dow Pharmaceuticals, Inc.*, Dkt. No. 92-102 (U.S. Dec. 2, 1992) (amici: Ronald Bayer, Stephen Jay Gould, Gerald Holton, Peter F. Infante, Philip Landrigan, Everett Mendelsohn, Robert Morris, Herbert Needleman, Dorothy Nelkin, William Nicholson, Kathleen Joy Propert, David Rosner) (citations omitted)

The Ninth Circuit's test for whether scientific research meets its admissibility standards of "general acceptance" and "consensus" ultimately boils down to a requirement that the study or research on which a scientist would base her opinion have been published in a peer-reviewed journal. But the appearance of a study in a peer-reviewed journal does not necessarily mean that the study is generally accepted or even sound. Conversely, the fact that a study has not been published in a peer-reviewed journal does not mean that the study and any opinion based thereon are unreliable and would be of no help in resolving a question of fact.

The peer review process that precedes publication in many scientific journals is valuable, to be sure, but the Ninth Circuit is confused about the purpose and limits of that process. Peer review is a vital editorial tool whose "main functions," in the words of Dr. Arnold S. Relman, then editor-in-chief of the *New England Journal of Medicine*, are "to improve the quality of what is published" and "to help editors decide what they want to publish in their journals." . . . The Ninth Circuit has made a fetish of publication, even though peer review takes place in many fora within the scientific community other than journals: peer review of papers submitted for presentation at conferences and meetings; review of grant applications; review of advisory committees. But "the peer review process is 'not meant to determine ultimate truth or falsity.'" . . .

Whether a particular scientist's research has been published in a peer-reviewed journal may be relevant to how much weight the study is accorded by other scientists or by a government decision-maker, be it a civil jury or a regulatory agency. But the Ninth Circuit has made peer review into something it never claimed to be: a talisman of truth. . . . For medical experts routinely rely on the unpublished (and sometimes even unwritten) observations and opinions of other experts in diagnosing, treating, and determining the cause of disease, just as research scientists rely on the as-yet unpublished work of their colleagues.

Moreover, federal regulations expressly authorize federal regulatory agencies to rely on unpublished scientific research in determining health hazards and in crafting safety standards to protect the public. . . .

The Ninth Circuit has set a daunting task for federal judges by mandating that they apply a vague "general acceptance" standard to screen the testimony of all qualified scientific experts before admitting their testimony to a jury. It therefore comes as no surprise that the court below seized upon what it apparently took to be a quick and easy "Good Housekeeping Seal of Approval" for the scientific community—publication in a peer-reviewed journal. . . .

For these reasons, the existence of a large body of peer-reviewed publications favoring one side or the other does not stop, or even seriously deter, parties from litigating scientific disputes. Some peer-reviewed articles can usually be found to support the other side, no matter how tenuous its case may be. The lengthy legal controversies surrounding Bendectin and the Ortho vaginal spermicide stemmed largely from case reports in prestigious peer-reviewed journals describing birth defects in babies born to women who used the products or (in the case of Bendectin) other products containing components of them. A lawsuit involving trichloroethylene-tainted well water in Woburn, Massachusetts, turned on a report—published in a peer-reviewed journal by well-credentialed Harvard epidemiologists—of an unexpectedly high number of childhood leukemia cases in that area.[10] This finding was never explained, and the increase in childhood cancer persisted for years after the study was released. The controversial part was the attempt to link the health problems to minute traces of trichloroethylene in the water; other epidemiologists disputed the claimed link and argued that it was not consistent with toxicologic considerations.[11]

Which "Peers"?

A scientific "jury" can be stacked like any other. Journal editors are famously able to steer papers to reviewers whom they know to be particularly critical or lenient. As experts having broad knowledge about particular fields, they can also steer papers away from (or into) the political storms that embroil all of science. The process of peer review is easily manipulated by an editor, though usually for entirely benign reasons.

In science, as in other fields, the advice one receives depends critically on who one asks and on how the questions are phrased. In late 1994, for example, the Harvard Center for Risk Analysis took an informal poll of its advisory committee on the risks of electromagnetic fields. The committee had been formed at the behest of the communications industry to review

Box 7.10
Good Science, the Minimum Standard of Credibility for Any Research, Requires Peer Review and Publication
Brief of *New England Journal of Medicine, Journal of the American Medical Association,* and *Annals of Internal Medicine* as Amici Curiae in Support of Respondent, *Daubert v. Merrell Dow Pharmaceuticals, Inc.,* Dkt. No. 92-102 (U.S. Jan. 19, 1993) (citations omitted)

[Peer review] focuses on the methodology, analysis and results recited in an article in an attempt to weed out error (e.g., from observer bias, improper statistical analysis, insensitive methods, carelessness and failure to recognize and control for confounding variables) and to assure that the text of an article is complete so that readers may judge the work for themselves. . . .

. . . Unlike the biases inherent in litigation—which may skew an expert's opinion or results to benefit one party over another—good science is not primarily concerned with what the results may turn out to be, but rather with the accuracy and reliability of the experimental methodology and data by which they are reached. . . .

. . . [Peer review] and publication does not end the scientific inquiry. Indeed, the mere act of publication frequently provokes scientific critique of the article by readers, who often submit Letters to the Editor commenting on the strengths or weaknesses of the work and its implications. . . .

Because [peer review] does not, and cannot, inquire into whether the authors actually did what they report, the reviewers cannot assure the readers of the truth of the ultimate conclusion contained in an article. . . .

. . . [Peer review] does not guarantee that results are error free. . . .

The goal of publication and [peer review], as part of good science, is to prevent premature reliance on certain propositions by the scientific community before the supporting evidence has been reviewed by a panel of expert peers and published for all to see; the goal of the rules of evidence, as part of due process, is to prevent premature reliance on certain propositions by a fact finder before it has been found probative, relevant and reliable. Neither guarantees the accuracy of the information or assesses its weight in finding the truth. But both establish a threshold level of reliability. In either situation it would be imprudent to rely upon a proposition before, at a minimum, it has been passed upon for plausibility.

The only mechanism available to assess the credibility of a scientific opinion crucial to the question of liability, independent of the biases of litigation, is to confirm that the opinion was reached by good science, e.g., based upon published evidence that has been [peer reviewed], and then subject to replication and verification. Accordingly, were this Court to repudiate [peer review]—an action which Amici strongly oppose—there would be no objective standard for a court to apply in evaluating the credibility of a scientific opinion. [Peer review] and publication of scientific data and conclusions, simply put, are the only available non-biased checks on scientific opinion available to the courts and should, therefore, be employed to the extent feasible.

research on potential health effects of cellular telephones; its members were respected scientists from a variety of scientific and engineering fields, all expert in the subject. The poll asked the committee members to indicate what they judged to be the probability that some link might be found between electromagnetic fields and cancer. The members judged that the probability was between 20 and 60 percent.

But other expert panels (some of which included members of the Harvard committee) have repeatedly surveyed the literature and found no evidence linking electromagnetic fields and cancer. In early 1995 the board of directors of the American Physical Society approved, nearly unanimously, a resolution that the issue was baseless. At least in part, the inconsistency with the Harvard poll reflects the self-selected nature of the groups being polled. Scientists who had spent their careers working in the field know more about the subject, but they also had strong vested interests in keeping the field alive. Most physicists, in contrast, have no such interest. And the physicists have generally been very skeptical of claims of health effects of electromagnetic fields, because they discern no apparent mechanism for such an effect. In addition, the two groups considered different questions. The physicists examined existing evidence related to electromagnetic fields and cancer. The scientists surveyed in the Harvard poll were asked, in effect, about the likelihood that such a link might be uncovered at some time in the future.

The views of "the scientific community" thus depend on who is polled and on how the questions are framed. Some argue that this negates the possibility of any valid expression of scientific consensus. The sociologist and lawyer Sheila Jasanoff, for example, maintains that "the law's view of what constitutes the 'mainstream' position in science may be an artifact of the legal system's limited and highly contingent ability to interrogate the scientific community."[12] (See box 7.11.)

Reports of Consensus Groups

Jasanoff may be right about any poll an individual judge might attempt to conduct on a controversial issue. But the American scientific community has formal procedures for preparing "consensus reports," through such mainstream groups as the National Academy of Sciences. Expert consensus

Box 7.11
What Judges Should Know about the Sociology of Science
Sheila Jasanoff
source: *Judicature* 77 (1993): 77–82 (citations omitted)

The most significant insight that has emerged from sociological studies of science in the past 15 years is the view that science is *socially constructed.* . . . "[F]acts" are produced by human agency through the institutions and processes of science, and hence they invariably contain a social component. . . .

. . . From a sociological viewpoint, scientific claims are never absolutely true but are always *contingent* on such factors as the experimental or interpretive conventions that have been agreed to within relevant a scientific communities. . . .

. . . [S]cience as we know it often takes the form of written texts or *inscriptions*, such as a curve on graph paper, a scattering of dots on photographic film, or an x-ray picture that looks like a supermarket bar code. . . . The inscription is a substitute for reality. . . .

. . . For sociologists of science, *deconstruction* means nothing more arcane than the pulling apart of socially constructed facts during a controversy. . . . The adversarial structure of litigation is particularly conducive to the deconstruction of scientific facts, since it provides parties both the incentive (winning the lawsuit) and the formal means (cross-examination) for bringing out the contingencies in their opponents' arguments.

. . . When scientists wish to contradict each other's findings (as routinely happens in legal proceedings), the indeterminacy of experimentation provides a natural pathway of attack: Were the instruments properly calibrated? Were background conditions stably maintained? Was the experiment adequately controlled? Were the resulting inscriptions correctly interpreted? Was there a valid statistical analysis of the data? . . .

. . . Effective boundary drawing insulates scientific work from unexpected and possibly ill-motivated challenge by inadequately credentialed critics. . . .

Daubert did well to recognize that "peer review" should not be adopted as a blanket prerequisite for admissibility, replacing Frye's even less workable criterion of "general acceptance." . . .

. . . When judges exclude expert testimony, appoint their own expert witnesses, or render summary judgments, they inescapably give up the role of dispassionate observer to become participants in a particular construction . . . of scientific facts. They help shape an image of reality that is colored in part by their own preferences and prejudices about how the world should work. Such power need not always be held in check, but it should be sparingly exercised. Otherwise, one risks substituting the expert authority of the black robe and the bench for that of the white lab coat—an outcome that poorly serves the cause of justice, or of science.

groups, including diverse specialists with different viewpoints, are convened by various government and nongovernment agencies. The reports of these groups indicate a consensus of informed scientific opinion. They effectively map out the broad areas of agreement on scientific issues, and specify as clearly as possible the range of opinions that are held by competent scientists. Sometimes minority reports by dissenting members are included.

For example, the National Research Council (a part of the National Academy of Sciences) has a long and distinguished record of providing independent analysis and advice about scientific issues. Consensus groups of the National Institutes of Health serve a similar function for clinical medicine. The Food and Drug Administration study group that examined the safety of Bendectin was another consensus group. The viewpoints of such groups vary, and they almost always recommend more research. But they can be counted on to provide responsible discussions of the issue at hand—much more so than witnesses in court. Any expert witness who disagrees with the reports of such consensus groups should bear a heavy burden of clarifying the nature of and the reasons for the disagreement.

The great care that consensus groups take in reviewing reports stands in sharp contrast to the often haphazard review process of scientific journals. Box 7.12 outlines the peer-review process of the National Council on Radiation Protection and Measurements, a respected independent organization that deals with health and safety issues related to radiation. This extensive peer review ensures that any report adopted by NCRP is as accurate as possible, and reflects a consensus of experts in the field of the report. Such reports carry far more weight in regulatory and other decision making processes than articles by individual scientists, and represent the best scientific opinion that is currently available about an issue. This level of care is not, however, uniformly followed by other organizations.[13]

Crackpots

If "consensus group" is a label for the core of the "scientific community," "crackpot" is a label for those outside the periphery. By choice, or by the judgment of scientists, crackpots operate entirely outside the bounds of science. (See boxes 7.13 and 7.14.)

Box 7.12
Peer Review by National Council on Radiation Protection and Measurements
source: The NCRP—Structure and Operations (National Council on Radiation Protection and Measurements, 1995)

Review of Draft Reports

Critical Reviewers. A draft report being prepared by a NCRP committee undergoes essentially continuous review by the committee, but the NCRP also employs a rather elaborate review process that only begins when the committee has finished its drafting work. When the committee has produced what is deemed to be the penultimate draft, that is, the draft that is expected to require only one more review by the committee to complete the work, this draft is sent not only to the committee members for the final review, but also to four to eight Council members who have been selected to serve as critical reviewers for the report. . . . They are not asked to approve or disapprove of the report. . . but rather, are expected to proffer suggestions and advice on how the draft report might be improved prior to submission to the full Council membership.

When the comments of all of the critical reviewers and any resulting from the review by the committee members are collected, they are made available to the committee, considered and any needed modifications are made. . . . The goal should be recognition of the fact that the critical reviewer's comments have been carefully considered.

Council Review. With the critical review process completed, the draft report, as modified on the basis of the comments generated during the critical review process, is sent to the full Council (75 members) for review. . . . The draft is also sent to honorary members and to those organizations that have collaborating status or have entered into a special liaison relationship with the NCRP. . . . It may also be sent, as a draft, to other interested and informed individuals and organizations both here and abroad, with requests for comments. . . .

The comments resulting from the review are collected (responses from more than 50 Council members can be expected) and the process of examination and modification by the committee begins again. . . .

Usually, dealing with extensive comments or disapprovals is a process of education in which the committee is made aware of the broad perspective embraced by the Council members and the member, in turn, becomes cognizant of the detailed specifics recognized as important by the committee. . . .

Box 7.13
In the Name of Science
Martin Gardner
source: *Fads and Fallacies in the Name of Science* (Dover, 1957)

There are five ways in which the sincere pseudo-scientist's paranoid tendencies are likely to be exhibited.

(1) He considers himself a genius.
(2) He regards his colleagues, without exception, as ignorant blockheads. Everyone is out of step except himself. . . .
(3) He believes himself unjustly persecuted and discriminated against. . . .
(4) He has strong compulsions to focus his attacks on the greatest scientists and the best-established theories. . . .
(5) He often has a tendency to write in a complex jargon, in many cases making use of terms and phrases he himself has coined. . . .

. . . If the present trend continues, we can expect a wide variety of these men, with theories yet unimaginable, to put in their appearance in the years immediately ahead. . . . [I]t will be well for ourselves and for society if we are on our guard against them.

As defined by its own members, the scientific community consists of individuals with similar education and credentials. Most scientists in a field, even those who strongly disagree with one another on specific issues, ordinarily accept the same basic paradigms. But now and again an individual gains notoriety by challenging truly fundamental beliefs. Scientists respond in much the same way as ordinary people do, with both rational argument and name calling. "Crackpot" is an epithet reserved for one whose views are well outside "serious" science.

One striking example how a scientist views "crackpots" appears in a paper by Fred Gruenberger. (See box 7.15.) Gruenberger's paper appeared in the prestigious journal *Science* toward the end of a period of heated discussions among scientists about the planetary theories of Immanuel Velikovsky. In his best-selling book *Worlds in Collision*, Velikovsky postulated that Earth had suffered great cataclysms within recorded human history, all caused by wanderings of the planet Venus. Most scientists dismissed this as nonsense, the work of a crackpot. But Velikovsky's theories gained wide and respectful attention in the lay press.

Box 7.14
Lessons

John R. Huizenga

source: *Cold Fusion: The Scientific Fiasco of the Century* (Oxford University Press, 1993) (citations omitted)

Scientific research does not flourish in isolation. Instead, in order to succeed, the scientific process usually takes place within a broad social and historical arena where researchers exchange their ideas and observations. . . . Failure to communicate suppresses the free and open debate by which scholars teach one another. . . .

The whole cold fusion saga is a striking illustration of what happens when science is done in isolation. Fleischmann and Pons' claim of having observed nuclear fusion at room temperature lacked credibility from the beginning because not only were their results contrary to all understanding of nuclear reactions, their reported neutron data were artifacts. . . .

As novices in nuclear physics, Fleischmann and Pons fell into several traps that might have been avoided had they consulted experts in nuclear physics. For example, it has been clearly shown that they lacked the equipment and expertise to assay their cells for the production of fusion products. . . .

Outsiders have the advantage in terms of the public's perception of their research accomplishments in an unfamiliar field. This was especially true in fusion research where the experts had spent billions of dollars with no payoff in sight for controlled fusion energy. . . .

Scientists and journalists often have different points of view about what is newsworthy. Scientists usually publish in peer-reviewed journals and strive to fit their discoveries into the larger framework of information in their special discipline, emphasizing the continuity and cumulative nature of science. Interesting contributions to science are usually those that advance the field as a whole in steady small steps, although on rare occasions major advances occur like the recent discovery of high-temperature superconductivity. On the other hand journalists tend to focus on striking single events that are often dramatic or even controversial, such as cold fusion. Journalists also tend to emphasize personalities and personality conflicts. . . .

The whole cold fusion fiasco serves to illustrate how the scientific process works. However, seldom do far-out claims receive the amount of national and international attention given to cold fusion. Scientists are real people and errors and mistakes do occur in science. These are usually detected either in early discussions of ones research with colleagues or in the peer-review process. . . .

The scientific process is self-corrective. This unique attribute sets science apart from most other activities. . . . The significant characteristic of the scientific method, however, is that in the end it can be relied upon to sort out the valid experimental results from background noise and error. . . .

The University of Utah's handling of cold fusion is a striking illustration of what happens when scientists circumvent the normal peer-review process, when scientists use the press as a conduit to disseminate information about a claimed discovery in an unrealistic and overly optimistic tone, when scientists require too many miracles to account for their results, when research is done in isolation by scientists who are outside their field of expertise, when data are published by private communication rather than by those responsible, when administrators use potential royalties to force premature publication and when university administrators lobby for large federal funds before the science is confirmed. Cold fusion is an example of bad science where the normal rules and procedures of the scientific process were violated. One can only be amazed by the number of scientists who reported confirmation of cold fusion by press conference, only to follow later with a retraction or at least a confession of irreproducibility. Reproducibility is the essence of science. It has taken upwards of some fifty to one hundred million dollars of research time and resources to show that there is no convincing evidence for room-temperature fusion. Much of this effort would not have been necessary had normal scientific procedures been followed. The idea of producing energy from room-temperature fusion is destined to join N rays and polywater as another example of a scientific aberration.

In the ensuing public debate, a few scientists made fools of themselves by their authoritative and unsupportable assertions. Some astronomers rejected Velikovsky's theories out of hand, while admitting that they had not read his book.[14] The debate had the positive effect of compelling scientists to reexamine their knowledge claims. It also prompted a wave of discussions among scientists about crackpot science.

Gruenberger proposes a "scale of crackpots" that superficially resembles Irving Langmuir's checklist for "pathological science" (box 4.10). But there is an important difference: Langmuir's criteria apply to the substance of "scientific" claims; Gruenberger's apply in large part to individuals who make them. Gruenberger's criteria have a strong ad hominem component, which is largely absent in Langmuir's discussion. His criteria are clearly designed to identify people who are beyond the pale.

In *Beyond Velikovsky*, a searching critique of Velikovsky's theories and their reception by other scientists, Henry Bauer comments on Gruenberger's scale. The scale "does not lead to the certain identification of cranks." It addresses how an individual operates, "not, what really interests us, whether or not the ideas may be valid." Moreover there is "no overall score above which one can place 'scientists' and below which we have 'cranks.'" Finally, "one is dealing not with two classes of people—

Box 7.15
A Measure for Crackpots
Fred J. Gruenberger
source: *Science* 145 (1964): 1413–1415

What follows . . . is a checklist of some significant items that are thought to be among the main attributes of the scientist (or, in some cases, the crackpot). . . .

1) *Public verifiability—12 points.*   The scientist says "I did thus and so and observed its effect; you are free to repeat my steps." The crackpot often says, "This is revealed truth; sorry, but I and my followers are the only ones who can obtain these results." . . .

2) *Predictability—12 points.*   To what extent can the technique or "science" being advocated be applied to the future? When a man can predict, and the predictions turn out to be true (as in the case of Einstein) a great deal has been gained toward credibility. . . .

3) *Controlled experiments—13 points.*   . . . The scientist seeks to devise controlled experiments if he can (the astronomer, for example, rarely can). The crackpot, on the other hand, often seeks to avoid controlled experiments, or, if some are performed, he may invent marvelous excuses to explain why they did not bear out his theories.

4) *Occam's razor—5 points.*   This is the principle which says that, of two possible explanations for the same phenomenon, scientists prefer the simpler—that is, the one requiring the fewest hypotheses. It is not a stringent test, but it is a point to consider. . . .

5) *Fruitfulness—10 points.*   The argument here is that the more scientific a subject is the more it tends to lead to "fruitful" results. *Fruitful* here means the ability to suggest new ideas—new approaches and new tests—rather than practical or material results. . . .

6) *Authority—10 points.*   Weight of authority tells, among scientists; it is equivalent to building up credit. . . .

7) *Ability to communicate—8 points.*   Most scientists soon discipline themselves in accepted methods of communication with their colleagues, their cohorts, and the public. The crackpot scorns accepted channels (he is even apt to deride those who "knuckle under" to accepted practices). . . .

8) *Humility—5 points.*   This is a minor point, perhaps, but we expect a scientist to tend toward humbleness, and we tend to honor him accordingly. . . .

9) *Open-mindedness—5 points.*   . . . In general . . . the scientists tends to use such phrases as "It appears that," "It would seem plausible," and the like. . . .

10) *Fulton non sequitur—5 points.*   . . . The true crackpot can frequently be spotted on this test alone. He proceeds with an argument like this: "They laughed at Fulton. He was right. They're laughing at me. *Therefore*, I must be an equal genius." . . .

11) *Paranoia—5 points.* . . . It is the lack of paranoia characteristics that is on the 5-point end of the scale. Again, the crackpot can be spotted on this test alone. . . .

12) *Dollar complex—5 points.* . . . [T]he crackpot almost always is overly impressed with the value of his discoveries. . . .

13) *Statistics compulsion—5 points.* It seems to be a characteristic of crackpot literature (perhaps because a little knowledge is a dangerous thing and the crackpot has as little as anyone) that statistics are not only used but continuously explained.

scientists and cranks—but with human beings, whose attributes on any such metric will fall on a continuum."[15]

Paul Feyerabend, an iconoclastic philosopher of science, offers a different perspective on the distinction between a crackpot and normal scientist. Feyerabend avoids the ad hominen character of Gruenberger's approach and makes no attempt to set sharp boundaries. A crackpot is distinguished, Feyerabend maintains, not by the content of his or her theory, but by the failure to subject it to the criticisms of other scholars, and to deal responsibly with any objections:

The crank usually is content with defending the point of view in its original, undeveloped, metaphysical form, and he is not at all prepared to test its usefulness in all those cases which seem to favor the opponent, or even to admit that there exists a problem. It is this further investigation, the detail of it, the knowledge of the difficulties, of the general state of knowledge, the recognition of objections which distinguishes the "respectable thinker" from the crank. The original content of his theory does not.[16]

The defense of the failure of scientists to deal seriously with Velikovsky presented by the chemist and philosopher of science Michael Polanyi is more sophisticated than Gruenberger's. "Only plausible ideas are taken up, discussed and tested by scientists," he writes. The "assessment of plausibility is based on a broad exercise of intuition guided by many subtle indications." A shared, tacit understanding is essential for science to function day to day, Polanyi reasons. "Journals are bombarded with contributions offering fundamental discoveries in physics, chemistry, biology or medicine most of which are nonsensical. Science cannot survive unless it can keep out such contributions." But, Polanyi acknowledges, the tacit criteria shared by scientists are "altogether undemonstrable." They develop through common education and long experience, which laypeople do not share. "Laymen normally accept the teachings of science not because they share its conceptions of reality, but because they submit to the authority of science. Hence, if they ever venture seriously to dissent from scientific opinion, a regular argument may not prove feasible. It will almost certainly prove impracticable when the question at issue is whether a certain set of evidence [for scientific theories] is to be taken seriously or not."[17] In other words, according to Polanyi, scientists reject implausible theories on the basis of tacit criteria, without taking the time to develop point-by-point rebuttals. This makes sense from the viewpoint of the scientists themselves, who have to focus their energies on productive lines of research. Few physicists, for example, would spend much time arguing with nonphysicists about theories that dispute relativity. The same holds for most biologists when it comes to engaging Creationists. Prominent physicists who have reportedly hired assistants to debunk claims of perpetual-motion machines, or to refute refutations of Einstein's theories of relativity, may fairly be considered closed-minded about those issues. But this does not mean, as some sociologists might suggest, that those who believe in relativity and those who don't are on equally firm epistemic grounds. Nor does it mean that the differences between them are purely sociological.

Dismissing a "crackpot" without dealing seriously with his or her views may be philosophically reprehensible, but it is also quite understandable and usually justifiable in retrospect. Thomas Kuhn points out that science periodically undergoes scientific revolutions in which new paradigms arise.[18] The new paradigm is not commensurate with the conventionally accepted paradigm it replaces. It might, unfairly, be dismissed by scientists as the work of crackpots. But most incipient scientific revolutions fail because they prove not to be fruitful at all. A "crackpot" with a strange theory might eventually be vindicated—but it is far more likely that the theory will fail, and the skepticism of mainstream scientists will, in retrospect, appear well justified. Debates between mainstream biologists and Creationists have gone on for a century. The pragmatic decision to ignore Creationists makes much sense for a modern biologist more interested in phenotypes than in theology.

Relativists may dispute the distinction between "crackpot science" and "normal science." They may argue that "crackpots" are just pursuing their own scientific revolutions, developing alternative paradigms that are (in the Kuhnian sense) incommensurate with those of mainstream science but perhaps no less valid. Along similar lines, the psychologist R. D. Laing claimed that schizophrenia is a "sane response to an insane world."[19] But in the real world, and most particularly in the legal arena, labels still matter. Judges will still commit "dangerous schizophrenics" to secure institutions, while leaving the rest of us to roam free. For practical, legal purposes, what matters is, on one hand, the civil liberties of the schizophrenic, and, on the other hand, the possibility that the schizophrenic will engage in self-destructive or violent behavior. The law must make a binary judgment to commit some people to institutions and not others. Diagnostic boundaries between schizophrenia and other mental illnesses are surely useful, as are those between sufficiently and insufficiently reliable science.

But criteria such as those in boxes 7.13 and 7.15 are not "reliable" for identifying "reliable" science. Gruenberger's criteria can help identify patterns of behavior that often culminate in unreliable scientific claims, but they are not useful in public discourse: a scientist who publicly dismisses a "crackpot" without examining the underlying beliefs (as many scientists did with Velikovsky) is dogmatic and arrogant. Gruenberger's criteria are therefore of limited practical use to a federal judge who is trying to enforce the Rules of Evidence.

Much more problematic is Polanyi's "tacit component" of scientific judgment, which implies an unbreachable mental gulf between scientists and others. If scientists really can't justify their arguments to nonscientists without relying on something that cannot be articulated at all, then all policy makers (and scientists) are in trouble.

Perhaps the most benign interpretation of Polanyi's concept of tacit criteria is that it refers to the unstated assumptions, terms of art, and assumed paradigms that underlie all professional discourse among lawyers and scientists alike. These assumptions are not insurmountable barriers, but they do make communication difficult. *Daubert* presumes that scientific knowledge can be presented in ways that nonscientist judges can weigh against standards of reliability and validity. It can be.

Science and Sociology

Many sociologists of science would attach labels of their own to Gruenberger's and Polanyi's views. Scientists, the sociologists argue, engage in "boundary setting." They demarcate and defend turf, like a dog urinating. The "relevant scientific community" referred to in *Daubert* is, a sociologist might argue, nothing more or less than a social entity.

In recent years, a new academic movement has crystallized around such views. It operates under the broad rubric of "science and technology studies" (STS).[20] The adherents of this movement make much of the fact that science is practiced by people who are never "objective" or value-neutral. "The authority of scientific claims derives," says Sheila Jasanoff, "not directly, from the representation of physical reality, but indirectly, from the certification of claims through a multitude of informal, often invisible, negotiations among members of relevant disciplines."[21] "Scientific evidence, however good, does not wear its human meaning or its policy implications on its sleeve," writes the ethicist David Callahan, not himself a member of the STS community. "Interpretation is unavoidable. The necessity for interpretation inevitably opens the door to obfuscation as much as to truth and clarity."[22]

The STS movement is, in part, a reaction against logical positivism. The STS professors Brian Martin and Evelleen Richards decry the "positivist approach" that assumes that there are "no social factors intervening between nature and scientific truth."[23] Jasanoff urges judges not to appoint their own experts, for doing so is to imply that some views are more neutral or objective than others and to surrender the judge's "role of dispassionate observer."[24] (See box 7.16.) The movement is heavily influenced by postmodernism: it espouses relativism rather than realism, and it is very concerned with the politics of knowledge. Some leaders of the movement have espoused goals that are frankly political, such as to "enfranchise the technically ignorant public and to both empower and inform them."[25]

To put the STS movement's views in perspective, compare them with the views of the physicist Sheldon Glashow, which undoubtedly reflect those of most physical scientists:

Box 7.16
Intuitive Toxicology: Expert and Lay Judgments of Chemical Risks
Nancy Kraus, Torbjorn Malmfors, and Paul Slovic
source: *Risk Analysis* 12 (1992): 215–232 (citations omitted)

Human beings have always been intuitive toxicologists, relying on their senses of sight, taste, and smell to detect harmful or unsafe food, water, and air. As we have come to recognize that our senses are not adequate to assess the dangers inherent in exposure to a chemical substance, we have created the sciences of toxicology and risk assessment to perform this function. Yet despite this great effort to overcome the limitations of intuitive toxicology, it has become evident that even our best scientific methods still depend heavily on extrapolations and judgments in order to infer human health risks from animal data. Many observers have acknowledged the inherent subjectivity in the assessment of chemical risks and have indicated a need to examine the subjective or intuitive elements of expert and lay risk judgments. We have begun such an examination by surveying members of the Society of Toxicology and the lay public about basic toxicological concepts, assumptions, and interpretations. Our results demonstrate large differences between toxicologists and laypeople, as well as differences between toxicologists working in industry, academia, and government. . . .

Among the most important findings in this study was the great divergence of opinion among the toxicologists themselves about fundamental issues in risk assessment and, in particular, the high percentage of toxicologists who doubted the validity of the animal and bacterial studies that form the backbone of their science. These results provide a quantitative description of the criticisms and disagreements that are clearly evident in statements of individual scientists and in detailed case studies of specific chemical controversies. These results also clash with the messages given the public. . . .

These results place the problems of risk communication in a new light. Our risk management processes are open and adversarial—we battle in courtrooms and community halls, in view of the media, with experts on each side of the issue attacking the other's credibility, models, and data. The young science of risk assessment is too fragile, too indirect, to prevail in an adversarial atmosphere. . . . [T]he public is well aware of the limitations of expertise in risk assessment. Risk assessment, though invaluable to regulators in the design of management strategies, is not at all convincing to the public. Perhaps this should not surprise us, given the many criticisms of risk assessment in the literature. Our survey indicates that these criticisms are not a minority view. The affiliation bias we and others have observed is a natural outgrowth of the scientific ambiguity—but a disturbing one nonetheless. It feeds the public sense of distrust.

Several other findings were noteworthy: (a) the public's tendency to attribute causality to a temporal association between pesticide use and birth defects; (b) the strong negative attitudes of the public toward chemicals and their risks; (c) the relatively favorable perceptions of prescription drugs; (d) the finding that 30% of the public respondents did not agree that a 1 in 10,000,000 lifetime risk of cancer from exposure to a chemical was too small to worry about. . . .

. . . Being contaminated clearly has an all-or-none quality to it—like being alive, or pregnant. . . .

We [scientists] believe that the world is knowable, that there are simple rules governing the behavior of matter and the evolution of the universe. We affirm that there are eternal, objective, extrahistorical, socially neutral, external and universal truths and that the assemblage of these truths is what we call physical science. Natural laws can be discovered that are universal, invariable, inviolate, genderless and verifiable. They may be found by men or by women or by mixed collaborations of any obscene proportions. Any intelligent alien anywhere would have come upon the same logical system as we have to explain the structure of protons and the nature of supernovae.[26]

These two sets of views are not necessarily contradictory, since they pertain to different things (acquisition of knowledge about fundamental properties of the universe on the one hand; the social use of scientific knowledge on the other). The sociologists' "external" viewpoint does offer some valuable insights into how science operates. Professional disagreements between psychoanalysts and psychiatrists (and within their respective fields), for example, plainly involve a good measure of turf protecting. And these disputes can affect the care of patients, sometimes in serious ways (as when a psychoanalyst tries to treat a patient who is really suffering from an organic brain disease which is best treated by drugs). They may also profoundly shape courtroom testimony.

There is, moreover, abundant and well-documented evidence—much of it generated by scientists not associated with the STS movement—that scientists frequently disagree on fundamental paradigms of their fields, and that these differences are correlated with sociological factors.

For example, the sociologist Paul Slovic and his colleagues have studied "intuitive toxicology"—the opinions of scientists and laypeople about the risks of chemicals and ways to measure those risks (box 7.16).[27] Professional toxicologists have very different views about the risks of chemicals than laypersons; for example, they are generally less concerned about the risks (or nonrisks) of exposure to tiny amounts of chemical pollutants.

Perhaps more surprising, toxicologists disagree sharply among themselves about the basic paradigms of their field. As Kraus, Malmfors, and Slovic (note 27) show, industrial toxicologists are much more sanguine about the risks of chemicals, and put more faith in the usefulness of high-dose animal testing, than their counterparts in academia. Although Slovic (a prolific and influential researcher in risk perception) is apparently not cited in the 800-page *Handbook of Science and Technology Studies*, his studies provide clear illustrations of sociological variables that are related to the opinions of scientists.

It is also beyond dispute that technologies (including medicine) have important social dimensions, and that it is difficult to separate their "objective" scientific aspects from their social functions. The psychiatrist Thomas Szasz points out that medical diagnoses are often driven by social or legal considerations; indeed, the very definition and classification of disease reflects social as well as scientific views. (See box 7.17.) Many other examples of the importance of social factors in the definition and diagnosis of disease can be found.

Thus, no one can disagree that scientists and physicians respond to social influences—scientists have marshaled some of the best available evidence that they do. Nor does anyone seriously believe that the issue is whether scientists can be classified as "objective scientists" (on one hand) or as "junk scientists," "pathological scientists," "nonscientists," or "crackpots" (on the other). The real challenge is how to judge the reliability of scientific knowledge, given the very human character of the individuals who offer it in legal proceedings.

Popper (who was influenced by logical positivism but who was not a card-carrying member of the movement) strongly criticized sociologists of science—especially the Marxist ones aligned with the Frankfurt School[28]—but he strongly emphasized the importance of social aspects of science. The objectivity of science, Popper believed, "is not based on an impartial state of mind in the scientists, but merely on the fact of the public and competitive character of the scientific enterprise and thus on certain social aspects

Box 7.17
Mental Illness Is Still a Myth
Thomas Szasz
source: *Society*, May 1, 1994: 34–39

Diseases are demonstrable anatomical or physiological lesions, that may occur naturally or be caused by human agents. Although diseases may not be recognized or understood, they "exist." People have hypertension and malaria, regardless of whether or not they know it or physicians diagnose it.

Diagnoses are disease names. Because diagnoses are social constructs, they vary from time to time, and from culture to culture. Focal infections, masturbatory insanity, and homosexuality were diagnoses in the past; now they are considered to be diagnostic errors of normal behaviors. In France, physicians diagnose "liver crises"; in Germany, "low blood pressure"; in the United States, "nicotine dependence."

These considerations raise the question: Why do we make diagnoses? There are several reasons: 1) Scientific—to identify the organs or tissues affected and perhaps the cause of the illness; 2) Professional—to enlarge the scope, and thus the power and prestige, of a state-protected medical monopoly and the income of its practitioners; 3) Legal—to justify state-sanctioned coercive interventions outside of the criminal justice system; 4) Political-economic—to justify enacting and enforcing measures aimed at promoting public health and providing funds for research and treatment on projects classified as medical; 5) Personal—to enlist the support of public opinion, the media, and the legal system for bestowing special privileges (and impose special hardships) on persons diagnosed as (mentally) ill.

It is no coincidence that most psychiatric diagnoses are twentieth-century inventions. The aim of the classic, nineteenth-century model of diagnosis was to identify bodily lesions (diseases) and their material causes (etiology). The term "pneumococcal pneumonia," for example, identifies the organ affected, the lungs, and the cause of the illness, infection with the pneumococcus. Pneumococcal pneumonia is an example of a pathology-driven diagnosis.

Diagnoses driven by other motives—such as the desire to coerce the patient or to secure government funding for the treatment of the illness—generate different diagnostic constructions and lead to different conceptions of disease. Today, even diagnoses of (what used to be) strictly medical diseases are no longer principally pathology-driven. Because of third-party funding of hospital costs and physicians' fees, even the diagnoses of persons suffering from *bona fide* illnesses—for example, asthma or arthritis—are distorted by economic considerations. Final diagnoses on the discharge summaries of hospitalized patients are often no longer made by physicians, but by bureaucrats skilled in the ways of Medicare, Medicaid, and private health insurance reimbursement—based partly on what ails the patient, and partly on which medical terms for his ailment and treatment ensure the most generous reimbursement for the services rendered.

As for psychiatry, it ought to be clear that, except for the diagnoses of neurological diseases (treated by neurologists), no psychiatric diagnosis is, or can be, pathology-driven. Instead, all such diagnoses are driven by non-medical, that is, economic, personal, legal, political, or social considerations and incentives. Hence, psychiatric diagnoses point neither to anatomical or physiological lesions, nor to disease-causative agents, but allude to human behaviors and human problems. These problems include not only the plight of the denominated patient, but also the dilemmas with which the patient, relatives, and the psychiatrist must cope and which each tries to exploit.

of it."[29] His complaint, rather, was that the writings of sociologists (at least, those of the aforementioned Marxists) were pompous and trivial.[30]

The sociologists do provide some new insight by viewing science from a lofty, "external" perch. But by doing so, they study only *people*. They never engage in a struggle over the content of their ideas. Analogously, anthropologists studying African tribal practices describe female genital mutilation; they express no moral judgments about the practice. Some insist that moral judgment by outsiders is wholly inappropriate; the morality of such practices can be judged only within and by the culture in which they occur.

This same Olympian perspective may sometimes serve beneficent political purposes. It leads to the assertion that Christians and Muslims are both OK, only different; or that astronomers and astrologers are both OK, only different. Both assertions are reasonable and even useful if the political objective is to discourage people from planting bombs. But it is equally easy to cite false equalities that do much harm. A person with treatable cancer can be killed by a failure to distinguish the medicine of doctors at the Mayo Clinic from the medicine of Laetrile clinics in Mexico.

The "external" attitude easily slides into a pernicious relativism which asserts that all knowledge claims are OK, that the only difference among them is in the character or the social circumstances of the individuals who express them. (See box 7.18.) That is clearly false. The epistemic strengths of astronomy (which is a science) and astrology (which began as one but no longer is) are quite different, and judging their epistemic strengths is not a sociological but a scientific issue. A scientist who dismisses astrology as bunk is not just protecting turf, although that may be going on as well. Advocates for alternative medicine often present sociological reasons

Box 7.18
Transgressing the Boundaries
Alan D. Sokal

source: Transgressing the boundaries: Toward a transformative hermeneutics of quantum gravity, *Social Text* 14 (1996): 217–252 (citations omitted)

There are many natural scientists, and especially physicists, who continue to reject the notion that the disciplines concerned with social and cultural criticism can have anything to contribute . . . to their research. . . . Rather, they cling to the dogma imposed by the long post-Enlightenment hegemony over the Western intellectual outlook, which can be summarized briefly as follows: that there exists an external world, whose properties are independent of any individual human being and indeed of humanity as a whole; that these properties are encoded in "eternal" physical laws; and that human beings can obtain reliable, albeit imperfect and tentative, knowledge of these laws by hewing to the "objective" procedures and epistemological strictures prescribed by the (so-called) scientific method.

But deep conceptual shifts within twentieth-century science have undermined this Cartesian-Newtonian metaphysics. . . . It has thus become increasingly apparent that physical "reality," no less than social "reality," is at bottom a social and linguistic construct; that scientific "knowledge," far from being objective, reflects and encodes the dominant ideologies and power relations of the culture that produced it; that the truth claims of science are inherently theory-laden and self-referential; and consequently, that the discourse of the scientific community, for all its undeniable value, cannot assert a privileged epistemological status with respect to counterhegemonic narratives emanating from dissident or marginalized communities. . . .

Here my aim is to carry these deep analyses one step further, by taking account of recent developments in quantum gravity. . . . In quantum gravity, as we shall see, the space-time manifold ceases to exist as an objective physical reality; geometry becomes relational and contextual; and the foundational conceptual categories of prior science—among them, existence itself—become problematized and relativized. . . .

General relativity is so weird that some of its consequences—deduced by impeccable mathematics, and increasingly confirmed by astrophysical observation—read like science fiction. . . .

Thus, general relativity forces upon us radically new and counterintuitive notions of space, time and causality; so it is not surprising that it has had a profound impact not only on the natural sciences but also on philosophy, literary criticism, and the human sciences. . . .

In mathematical terms, Derrida's observation relates to the invariance of the Einstein field equation $G_{\mu\nu} = 8\pi G T_{\mu\nu}$ under nonlinear space-time diffeomorphisms (self-mappings of the space-time manifold that are infinitely differentiable but not necessarily analytic). The key point is that this invariance group "acts transitively": this means that any space-time point, if it exist, at all, can be transformed into any other. In this way the infinite-dimensional invariance group erodes the distinction between observer and observed; the π of Euclid and the G of Newton, formerly thought to be constant and universal, are now perceived in their ineluctable historicity; and the putative observer becomes fatally de-centered, disconnected from any epistemic link to a space-time point that can no longer be defined by geometry alone.

However, this interpretation, while adequate within classical general relativity, becomes incomplete within the emerging postmodern view of quantum gravity. When even the gravitational field—geometry incarnate—becomes a noncommuting (and hence nonlinear) operator, how can the classical interpretation of $G_{\mu\nu}$ as a geometric entity be sustained? Now not only the observer, but the very concept of geometry, becomes relational and contextual. . . .

. . . [T]he postmodern sciences deconstruct and transcend the Cartesian metaphysical distinctions between humankind and Nature, observer and observed, Subject and Object. Already quantum mechanics, earlier in this century, shattered the ingenuous Newtonian faith in an objective, prelinguistic world of material objects "out there." . . . Just as quantum mechanics informs us that the position and momentum of a particle are brought into being only by the act of observation, so quantum gravity informs us that space and time themselves are contextual, their meaning defined only relative to the mode of observation. . . .

. . . [P]ostmodern science provides a powerful refutation of the authoritarianism and elitism inherent in traditional science, as well as an empirical basis for a democratic approach to scientific work. . . . [H]ow can a self-perpetuating secular priesthood of credentialed "scientists" purport to maintain a monopoly on the production of scientific knowledge? . . .

In addition to redefining the content of science, it is imperative to restructure and redefine the institutional loci in which scientific labor takes place—universities, government labs, and corporations—and reframe the reward system that pushes scientists to become, often against their own better instincts, the hired guns of capitalists and the military.

why mainstream doctors dismiss their science. But that does not mean that they can treat acute appendicitis equally well. The obvious fact that scientists are people does not prove that reliable knowledge is impossible. It proves only that the process is fraught with peril. So too, one might add, is the process of publishing postmodern critiques of science. (See boxes 7.18 and 7.19.)

The perils notwithstanding, specific scientific findings and claims can still be critically evaluated. Sheldon Glashow may or may not be right in

Box 7.19
A Physicist Experiments with Cultural Studies
Alan Sokal
source: *Lingua Franca*, May–June 1996, pp. 62–64

[T]o test the prevailing intellectual standards, I decided to try a modest (though admittedly uncontrolled) experiment: Would a leading North American journal of cultural studies . . . publish an article liberally salted with nonsense if (a) it sounded good and (b) it flattered the editors' ideological preconceptions?

The answer, unfortunately, is yes. . . .

What's going on here? Could the editors really not have realized that my article was written as a parody?. . .

Throughout the article, I employ scientific and mathematical concepts in ways that few scientists or mathematicians could possibly take seriously. . . .

. . . I intentionally wrote the article so that any competent physicist or mathematician (or undergraduate physics or math major) would realize that it is a spoof. Evidently, the editors of *Social Text* felt comfortable publishing an article on quantum physics without bothering to consult anyone knowledgeable in the subject. . . .

It's understandable that the editors of *Social Text* were unable to evaluate critically the technical aspects of my article (which is exactly why they should have consulted a scientist). What's more surprising is how readily they accepted my implication that the search for truth in science must be subordinated to a political agenda, and how oblivious they were to the article's overall illogic.

Why did I do it? While my method was satirical, my motivation is utterly serious. What concerns me is the proliferation, not just of nonsense and sloppy thinking per se, but of a particular kind of nonsense and sloppy thinking: one that denies the existence of objective realities, or (when challenged) admits their existence but downplays their practical relevance. . . .

Social Text's acceptance of my article exemplifies the intellectual arrogance of Theory—postmodernist *literary* theory, that is—carried to its logical extreme. No wonder they didn't bother to consult a physicist. If all is discourse and "text," then knowledge of the real world is superfluous; even physics becomes just another branch of cultural studies. If, moreover, all is rhetoric and language games, then internal logical consistency is superfluous too: a patina of theoretical sophistication serves equally well. Incomprehensibility becomes a virtue; allusions, metaphors, and puns substitute for evidence and logic. My own article is, if anything, an extremely modest example of this well-established genre. . . .

The results of my little experiment demonstrate, at the very least, that some fashionable sectors of the American academic Left have been getting intellectually lazy. The editors of *Social Text* liked my article because they liked its conclusion: that "the content and methodology of postmodern science provide powerful intellectual support for the progressive political project." They apparently felt no need to analyze the quality of the evidence, the cogency of the arguments, or even the relevance of the arguments to the purported conclusion.

. . . My article is a theoretical essay based entirely on publicly available sources, all of which I have meticulously footnoted. All works cited are real, and all quotations are rigorously accurate; none are invented. . . . The editors' duty as scholars is to judge the validity and interest of ideas, without regard for their provenance. (That is why many scholarly journals practice blind refereeing.). . . .

. . . I offered the *Social Text* editors an opportunity to demonstrate their intellectual rigor. Did they meet the test? I don't think so.

I say this not in glee but in sadness. . . . Why should the right wing be allowed to monopolize the intellectual high ground?

And why should self-indulgent nonsense—whatever its professed political orientation—be lauded as the height of scholarly achievement?

his view that science can uncover absolute truth about the universe, if only because the relation of scientific theory to underlying reality will forever be controversial among philosophers. But even if Glashow's philosophy of knowledge is naive, one can still evaluate his scientific theories for internal consistency, agreement with other well-established physical theories, agreement with experimental evidence, and so on. Judging Glashow's physics is a matter of science, not sociology or cultural studies.

The danger, in court, is that the "external" viewpoint of sociologists of science can lead to a decision not to make any judgments about science, on the (false) ground that knowledge claims are equally (un)reliable. As construed by the Supreme Court in *Daubert*, the Federal Rules of Evidence reject that view. *Daubert* requires judges to evaluate the scientific validity of proffered testimony. Sociology aside, the screening of testimony on the basis of the criteria outlined in *Daubert* is not a matter of labeling scientists or naming the intellectual tribes to which they belong.

The Scientific Community and Bendectin

As we noted in chapter 1, the science of Bendectin evolved in tandem with the litigation. Bendectin's possible risks were more in doubt in the 1970s, when the first Bendectin cases were filed, than now, when the last of them are finally being decided. At the same time, it must also be noted that, while the weight of the Bendectin evidence has increased, its overall implication has not changed. There was no serious debate in the scientific literature of the 1970s as to whether Bendectin caused birth defects, and there is none today.

Some critics suggest that there is no way to separate the science of Bendectin from the litigation, since all of the science is done in a context of litigation. However, this clearly is not true. Several Bendectin studies— in particular, the animal toxicology studies by William McBride[31]—were conducted specifically for purposes of litigation. McBride administered massive doses of the drug to marmosets and (not surprisingly) reported signs of reproductive toxicity. But dozens of other studies were conducted by investigators who had no apparent connection to Bendectin litigation, and the results of these studies were overwhelmingly negative. (See box 1.4.)

Robert Brent, a specialist in reproductive toxicity and an occasional witness for the defense in Bendectin suits, makes a further point:

Most of the defense experts have performed investigations or published their opinions in the scientific literature. Only two of the plaintiff's experts have published their views on Bendectin. None of the plaintiff's experts have published an analysis, review, or research paper that indicated that Bendectin was a human teratogen. . . . McBride's . . . research was judged to be fraudulent. . . . Although one may not expect a high level of scientific scholarship or rigorous adherence to the scientific method from lawyers, jurors, news commentators, or the public, one should expect scholarship from scientists who enter the courtroom to provide their expertise to the judge and jurors. Bendectin litigation could not have proceeded without the participation of scientists who failed in their role as objective experts during the Bendectin litigation. There is a formidable inertia and fearfulness among the leaders of organized biomedicine to solve this problem.[32]

8

Prejudicing, Confusing, or Misleading the Jury

Throughout, a judge assessing a proffer of expert scientific testimony under Rule 702 should also be mindful of other applicable rules. . . . Rule 403 permits the exclusion of relevant evidence "if its probative value is substantially outweighed by the danger of unfair prejudice, confusion of the issues, or misleading the jury. . . ." Judge Weinstein has explained: "Expert evidence can be both powerful and quite misleading because of the difficulty in evaluating it. Because of this risk, the judge in weighing possible prejudice against probative force under Rule 403 of the present rules exercises more control over experts than over lay witnesses." Weinstein, 138 F.R.D., at 632.

—*Daubert v. Merrell Dow Pharmaceuticals, Inc.*, 509 U.S. 579, 595 (1993)

Rule 403 of the Federal Rules of Evidence permits a trial judge to exclude evidence of any kind "if its probative value is substantially outweighed by the danger of unfair prejudice, confusion of the issues, or misleading the jury." While construing only Rule 702 in *Daubert*, the Court did point out that Rule 403 provides separate grounds for excluding testimony. The Court's opinion followed with a quote from Judge Jack Weinstein noting that expert evidence "can be both powerful and quite misleading because of the difficulty in evaluating it" and that a federal trial judge applying the rule "exercises more control over experts than over lay witnesses."[1] Judge Alex Kozinski likewise cited this evidentiary rule in the *Daubert* remand and emphasized its independent importance: "Federal judges must . . . exclude proffered scientific evidence under Rules 702 and 403 unless they are convinced that it speaks clearly and directly to an issue in dispute in the case, and that it will not mislead the jury."[2]

How easy is it to prejudice, confuse, or mislead laypersons on scientific issues? The question interests not only judges and lawyers; sociologists, psychologists, and scientists have studied the matter for many years.

Box 8.1
The Abuse of Language and Logic in Epidemiology
James S. McCormick
source: *Perspectives in Biology and Medicine*, winter 1992: 186–188 (citations omitted)

A glance at some of the journals currently on my desk provides examples of the abuses of language and logic that, when reported more widely, contribute to the devaluation of health information.

Perhaps the commonest abuse surrounds the concept of risk markers or risk factors. The abstract from a paper entitled "Is baldness a risk factor for coronary heart disease? A review of the literature," states, "Overall, the data reviewed suggest that a small risk of coronary heart disease *due* to baldness may exist. . . ." Nothing of the kind! The data reviewed, incidentally in a sophisticated manner, suggest that there may be a small independent *association* between baldness and subsequent coronary disease.

The abstract that accompanies "A meta-analysis of physical activity in the prevention of coronary heart disease" concludes, "The authors also find that methodologically stronger studies tend to show a larger *benefit* of physical activity than less well-designed studies." Nothing of the kind! The data reviewed show some evidence of an *association* between physical activity and a reduced risk of subsequent coronary disease.

In the same issue of the *American Journal of Epidemiology*, there is a paper entitled "Caffeine and the risk of hip fracture: the Framingham study." . . . The authors report that "Overall, intake of greater than two cups of coffee per day (four cups of tea) *increased* the risk of fracture." Nothing of the kind! Fortunately they went on to point out that "Since caffeine use may be associated with other behaviours that are, themselves, risk factors for fracture, the association may be indirect." . . .

These are examples of the abuse of language that endangers reason and logical conclusion. My last example is from a paper entitled "Opiate addiction in adult offspring through possible imprinting after obstetric treatment." In this study, the drugs given to mothers within 10 hours of the birth of those who subsequently became known opiate addicts were compared with the drugs given to mothers at the time of birth of the presumably nonaddicted siblings. At the end of the study, they were able to demonstrate a trend that suggested that the opiate addicts had had a greater exposure to transplacental opiates and barbiturates than their nonaddicted siblings. The hypothesis was that this early potential "imprinting" was related to subsequent addiction. . . . But their conclusion was as follows: "The results are compatible with the imprinting hypothesis. *Therefore*, for obstetric pain relief methods are preferable that do not permit substantial passage of drugs through the placenta." No way, *therefore*!

In most parts of our society . . . the a priori risk of opiate addiction is extremely small, so that even if the use of opiates in intranatal care had a major effect, the addition to the absolute risk would remain extremely small and for all practical purposes negligible. . . .

This communication was predictably headlined in the newspapers, and there is reason to fear that some mothers will, as a result, either refuse or be denied adequate analgesia during labor.

. . . The dangers are obvious and do the public health a great disservice. We should take more care.

This problem is entirely distinct from the ones discussed elsewhere in this book. Juries may not usually be shown photographs of a post-mortem examination of a murder victim, even though the pictures themselves are perfectly faithful reproductions of what the pathologist actually saw. Such pictures are "reliable," but many judges conclude that they prove too little, and inflame too much, to be admissible. In the *Daubert* context, Rule 403 does not concern the unreliability of scientific evidence. It concerns the tendency of laypeople to accept scientific-sounding words and ideas as reliable, because they are unwilling or unable to examine them critically. It concerns what Judge Richard Posner has called "the deceitful potential of scientific rhetoric."[3]

Sophistry

The Greek sophists were itinerants who taught rhetoric and other subjects for a fee. They emphasized the art of persuasion—clearly an important skill for ordinary citizens of the time who had to argue their own cases in court. Many sophists believed that truth and morality were essentially matters of opinion. "Sophistry" came to connote the artful merger of fact and opinion, conducted to persuade rather than to reveal the truth.

Scientists are well equipped to engage in sophistry when they choose to. They are not trained in rhetoric, but they often have even more effective verbal tools at their disposal. As Judge Posner writes: "Scientists seek to bolster their authority by affectations of mathematical rigor, by use of intimidating jargon, by suppressing doubts, and by concealing the personal, judgmental factor in the evaluation of experimental, statistical, or observational results."[4]

It is also possible to mislead nonscientists by means of scientific-sounding arguments that, when examined closely, are seen to be fallacious. For

Box 8.2
Something Out of Nothing: The Misperception and Misrepresentation of Random Data

Thomas Gilovich

source: *How We Know What Isn't So: The Fallibility of Human Reason in Everyday Life* (Free Press, 1991) (citations omitted)

We are predisposed to see order, pattern, and meaning in the world, and we find randomness, chaos, and meaninglessness unsatisfying. Human nature abhors a lack of predictability and the absence of meaning. As a consequence, we tend to "see" order where there is none, and we spot meaningful patterns where only the vagaries of chance are operating. . . .

We do not "want" to see a man in the moon. We do not profit from the illusion. We just see it.

The tendency to impute order to ambiguous stimuli is simply built into the cognitive machinery we use to apprehend the world. . . . The predisposition to detect patterns and make connections is what leads to discovery and advance. The problem, however, is that the tendency is so strong and so automatic that we sometimes detect coherence even when it does not exist. . . .

. . . The predisposition to impose order can be so automatic and so unchecked that we often end up believing in the existence of phenomena that just aren't there. . . .

Many of the beliefs we hold are about *relationships* between two variables. . . .

. . . Consider someone trying to determine whether cloud seeding produces rain. An instance in which cloud seeding is followed by rain is clearly relevant to the issue in question—it registers as an unambiguous success for cloud seeding. In contrast, an instance in which it rains in the absence of cloud seeding is only indirectly relevant—it is neither a success nor a failure. Rather, it represents a consequence of *not* seeding that serves only as part of a baseline against which the effectiveness of seeding can be evaluated. Additional cognitive steps are necessary to put this information to use.

Non-confirmatory information can also be harder to deal with because it is usually framed negatively (e.g., it rained when we did not seed), and we sometimes have trouble conceptualizing negative assertions. Compare, for example, how much easier it is to comprehend the statement "All Greeks are mortals" than "All non-mortals are non-Greeks." Thus, one would expect confirmatory information to be particularly influential whenever the disconfirmations are framed as negations. The research literature strongly supports this prediction. . . . As Francis Bacon noted long ago, "It is the peculiar and perpetual error of the human understanding to be more moved and excited by affirmatives than negatives."

. . . By placing too much emphasis on positive instances, people will occasionally "detect" relationships that are not there. For many of the real-world phenomena that are of greatest interest, one is sure to encounter many positive instances even when there is no relationship at all between the two variables. Although there is surely no validity to the common belief that we are more likely to need something once we have thrown it away, examples of acute longing for a discarded possession may be easy to come by. By letting necessary evidence "slip by" as sufficient evidence, people establish an insufficient threshold of what constitutes adequate support for a belief, and they run the risk of believing things that are not true.

nonscientists, one of the most familiar errors involves post hoc, ergo propter hoc deduction. A woman who used a cellular telephone develops brain cancer; the report is publicized on national television, and the stock value of Motorola (a leading manufacturer of cellular phones) plummets. Another person exposed to traces of a chemical develops cancer: the chemical therefore caused the disease. This reasoning is obviously fallacious, but it can be powerfully persuasive nonetheless. The medical literature contains many case reports of bad things that have happened to people who have taken drugs or been exposed to chemicals. It is easy to recognize these reports for what they are: anecdotes that carry very little weight beyond raising an alert about a possible link that may merit systematic investigation by way of a controlled study. Such anecdotes remain, nonetheless, the stock in trade of the tabloid press, and even the legitimate media. Readers clearly find them interesting, and perhaps persuasive. Case reports of illness in women with the silicone breast implants helped fuel a rising tide of public anxiety. But the controlled studies that followed found no statistically significant excess of disease.[5]

Another common rhetorical device involves the misuse of statistics. At worst, this becomes a cynical attempt to manipulate the audience. Laypeople have trouble understanding statistical arguments, and this makes them easy targets for those willing to manipulate statistical data in support of whatever position they wish to advance. Quite apart from the other factors discussed in *Daubert* and elsewhere in this book, a judge has an obligation to exclude testimony of this kind under Rule 403, because the probative value is greatly outweighed by the danger of misleading lay jurors.

Judge Weinstein took this approach in the Agent Orange litigation when reviewing testimony claiming to find a causal link between the veterans' illnesses and exposure to the herbicide.[6] The most prominent of the plaintiffs' witnesses was Samuel Epstein, whose testimony boiled down to this:

Box 8.3
Resemblance, Correlation, and Pseudoscience
Paul Thagard

source: *Science, Pseudo-Science and Society*, ed. M. P. Hanen et al. (published for Calgary Institute for the Humanities by Wilfrid Laurier University Press, 1980) (citations omitted)

I want to argue that there is a fundamental distinction between two kinds of reasoning, which I call resemblance thinking and correlation thinking. Resemblance thinking infers that two things or events are causally related from the fact that they are *similar* to each other; in contrast, correlation thinking infers that two things or events are causally related from the fact that they are *correlated* with each other. . . . I consider whether that distinction provides the basis for the distinction between pseudoscience and science. It turns out that the distinctions do not completely mesh: I argue that the use of resemblance-thinking is sufficient but not necessary for branding as pseudoscientific such disciplines as astrology. . . .

. . . [Resemblance thinking] is a method which is very natural for human beings in general. . . . Suppose people are asked to judge the career of the following individual: "Steve is very shy and withdrawn, invariably helpful, but with little interest in people or in the world of reality. A meek and tidy soul, he has a need for order and structure, and a passion for detail." Research shows that people judge the probability that Steve is, for example, a librarian by considering how similar Steve is to their stereotype of a librarian. Serious errors of judgment result from neglecting such factors as the percentage of librarians in the total population, a factor which Bayes' theorem requires us to introduce in the form of a prior probability. . . .

Let us now turn to the question of pseudoscience and what differentiates it from science. . . . Because the use of resemblance thinking is so integral to astrology, it is tempting to suggest that resemblance thinking is a central feature of all pseudoscience. . . . However, the resemblance/correlation distinction does not mesh so neatly with the pseudoscience/science distinction.

. . .[N]ot all pseudoscience uses resemblance thinking. . . .

The deans of modern pseudoscience, Immanuel Velikovsky and Erich von Däniken, both use a very rough sort of correlation thinking in support of their peculiar theories. . . .

More problematically, we can look for uses of resemblance thinking which are not pseudoscientific. . . . Literary interpretation, art appreciation, and the history of philosophy all in part involve the detection of similarities and the comparison of symbols. . . .

It . . . appears that the use of resemblance thinking is a sufficient but not a necessary condition for pseudoscience. . . . 1. Sciences: using correlation thinking. . . . 2. Pseudosciences: (a)using resemblance thinking. . . . (b) using inadequate correlation thinking. . . . 3. Nonsciences: using neither resemblance nor correlation thinking, but dealing with non-causal matters such as textual interpretation or with normative issues, including ethics and aesthetics. . . .

In sum, resemblance thinking is attribution of causal relations on the basis of similarities. . . . The use of resemblance thinking is sufficient to render a discipline pseudoscientific, but pseudosciences can also be founded on incomplete or spurious correlation thinking. In the latter case, we must use a more general demarcation criterion. . . .

(1) The plaintiffs had been exposed to Agent Orange. (2) There was a "causal relationship . . . between exposure to Agent Orange and a wide range of multi-system and multi-organ effects." (3) The plaintiffs' medical conditions were therefore "much more likely than not caused by exposure to Agent Orange."[7] But Judge Weinstein ruled that this testimony could not go to a jury. Epstein's own book, *The Politics of Cancer*,[8] had emphasized the manifold environmental causes of cancer. The testimony Epstein offered failed to consider that the plaintiffs' diseases might have been caused by other factors.

One can engage in sophistry on either side of the aisle; a skilled sophist can appear to debunk valid science as readily as he can appear to validate scientific bunk. In *Thinking and Deciding*, the psychologist Jonathan Baron points out that "there are dangers in stressing the detection of fallacious arguments, as opposed to the construction of positions that are carefully thought through." The dangers are all too familiar in the legal community. The most obvious is the new breed of sophist—"skeptical and even cynical, able to 'shoot down' any position, to show that it is imperfect without asking whether it might still be best, despite its imperfections, and without asking how it might be improved." As Baron points out, a good "critical thinker" is not simply "one who can criticize other people's arguments." At worst, the sophist-skeptics use "their knowledge of fallacies as a way of defending their own beliefs and policies against any kind of challenge." Baron labels thinking of this kind as "actively close-minded."[9]

A variant of this form of sophistry involves attacks on science that is, in fact, reasonably sound. Virtually every scientific study is prone to error of some kind, and every investigator has some sort of bias, however mild or suppressed. One can usually identify a potential bias in almost any epidemiologic study—for example, by pointing out that the study did not control for a variable as carefully as it might have. It is difficult to analyze a

Box 8.4
Simple Statistical Mistakes
John Allen Paulos

source: *Innumeracy: Mathematical Illiteracy and Its Consequences* (Vintage Books, 1988)

Hypothesis testing and estimates of confidence, regression analysis, and correlation—though all are liable to misinterpretation, the most common sorts of statistical solecisms involve nothing more complicated than fractions and percentages. This [box] contains a few typical illustrations.

That one out of eleven women will develop breast cancer is a much cited statistic. The figure is misleading, however, in that it applies only to an imaginary sample of women all of whom live to age eighty-five and whose incidence of contracting breast cancer at any given age is the present incidence rate for that age. Only a minority of women live to age eighty-five, and incidence rates are changing and are much higher for older women. . . .

A man is downtown, he's mugged, and he claims the mugger was a black man. However, when the scene is reenacted many times under comparable lighting conditions by a court investigating the case, the victim correctly identifies the race of the assailant only about 80 percent of the time. What is the probability his assailant was indeed black?

Many people will of course say that the probability is 80 percent, but the correct answer, given certain reasonable assumptions, is considerably lower. Our assumptions are that approximately 90 percent of the population is white and only 10 percent black, that the downtown area in question typifies this racial composition, that neither race is more likely to mug people, and that the victim is equally likely to make misidentifications in both directions, black for white and white for black. Given these premises, in a hundred muggings occurring under similar circumstances, the victim will on average identify twenty-six of the muggers as black—80 percent of the ten who actually were black, or eight, plus 20 percent of the ninety who were white, or eighteen, for a total of twenty-six. Thus, since only eight of the twenty-six identified as black were black, the probability that the victim actually was mugged by a black given that he said he was is only . . . approximately 31 percent!

The calculation is similar to the one on false positive results in drug testing, and, like it, demonstrates that misinterpreting fractions can be a matter of life and death.

Another example involves the spate of articles a few years ago about the purported link between teenage suicide and the game of "Dungeons and Dragons." The idea was that teenagers became obsessed with the game, somehow lost contact with reality, and ended up killing themselves. The evidence cited was that twenty-eight teenagers who often played the game had committed suicide.

This seems a fairly arresting statistic until two more facts are taken into account. First, the game sold millions of copies, and there are estimates that up to 3 million teenagers played it. Second, in that age group the annual suicide rate is approximately 12 per 100,000. These two facts together suggest that the number of teenage "Dungeons and Dragons" players who could be expected to commit suicide is about 360 (12×30)! I don't mean to deny that the game was a causal factor in some of these suicides, but merely to put the matter in perspective.

report of a completed study so as to draw firm conclusions about the significance of potential errors. Usually the only recourse is to conduct more studies, refining their designs as one proceeds. Often, however, the original conclusions will end up being confirmed, not refuted. Scientific studies invariably contain errors and incorporate biases, but most of them are benign. It can be all too easy to make trivial flaws in a scientific study or investigation appear to be devastatingly large.

Scientism

At the opposite extreme, people are encouraged to assume that anything labeled "science" must be completely objective, correct, and value free. Trading on the reputation of science is a well-practiced form of sophistry. Ads for patent medicines used to feature pictures of doctors touting the nostrums. No doubt, some graduates of legitimate medical schools did honestly believe in the efficacy of what they endorsed. Some of the nostrums may in fact have been effective. But advertising of this form carries the clear risk of conveying the strong but false impression that an entire medical community or scientific discipline stands behind the one representative depicted in the advertisement.

A physician or a scientist on the witness stand may mislead a jury in precisely the same way. The witness is formally qualified as an "expert," and is permitted to testify on matters that an ordinary witness would not be allowed to discuss. Although there are specific legal reasons for this, the laypeople on the jury are likely to get the impression that the witness represents scientific truth (or, at least, speaks with the authority of science). Even if it is very clear that the scientist speaks as an individual, many laypeople will be disinclined or unable to question his or her views.

Whatever mistakes laypersons may make in this regard might be dispelled by competition in the marketplace, or by cross-examination and the presentation of opposing experts in court. The misleading effect of a doctor's picture on a jar of snake oil may be neutralized by other pictures of other doctors on other bottles of medicine or by a broader scientific literature that debunks the nostrum. Misleading testimony by a doctor can be countered by devastating cross-examination by an opposing attorney. But it is also possible that baffled buyers or jurors will simply accept the scientist as an authoritative source, even when a nostrum is worthless or a scientist's testimony is flawed.

The difficulty that laypeople often have in questioning a scientist's statements can cut both ways. Sheila Jasanoff has pointed out that judges often identify professionally with physicians, since both are members of a high-status profession that requires the mastery of a specialized and highly academic body of knowledge. Judges, she argues, may allow a physician to present ethically problematic opinions as science without challenge. "Judges are swayed by their perceptions of what science is and who is a scientist when they certify an expert's credibility."[10]

In any event, it is clear that expressions of unsubstantiated or value-laden opinions in scientific or pseudoscientific terms can mislead the unwary. The essence of the error, here, is conflating the particularized views of an individual who has the credentials of a scientist with general, objective, scientific truth. Deferring to an expert in value-laden judgments that go beyond objective and verifiable matter of fact is one manifestation of scientism.

Sophistry in Numbers

Posner's comment (cited above) that "scientists seek to bolster their authority by affectations of mathematical rigor" echoes a criticism that is occasionally leveled by sociologists of science. "[Quantitative] decision rules are more likely to support a bid for power by outsiders or the effort of insiders to fend off powerful challenges," Theodore Porter writes in his book *Trust in Numbers*.[11] However, such sociological insights (either by Posner or, in more sophisticated form, by Porter) have nothing to do with the truth of an argument. Lawyers, too, may use all sorts of mumbo-jumbo in describing the state of the law, but even impenetrable or pompous prose may describe the state of the law quite correctly.

By the same token, numbers sometimes paint accurate pictures and sometimes don't. Many lay complaints about a scientist's affectations of mathematical rigor may reflect the observer's difficulties with numbers rather than any problems inherent in the mathematical analysis. As we pointed out in chapter 6, much of science relies on statistical inference, which has to be analyzed by means of appropriate quantitative tests. Even the proffered testimony of Alan Done and Shanna Swan refers, directly or indirectly, to quantitative statistical analyses. The problem in these cases was not affectation of mathematical rigor; it was deficient logic or unsubstantiated opinion.

Many scientists emphasize quantitative methods not because numbers are inherently scientific but because quantitative concepts are essential to any understanding of, or careful reasoning about, statistical phenomena. Number-free observations about risk and safety are very likely to mislead. The issue is never whether substances are "toxic"; it is how much exposure is how likely to cause harm. Any rigorous evaluation of questions about health and disease requires quantitative discussion. Laypeople must either come to grips with that plain fact or abandon any responsible attempt to grapple with the issues.

The *Daubert* Testimony of Swan

Expert witnesses have many subtle ways, many of them perhaps unconscious, of inviting juries to engage in unscientific reasoning. The Supreme Court acknowledged that Shanna Swan has respectable professional credentials,[12] yet what she wrote in affidavits submitted in *Daubert* and in other Bendectin cases illustrates some of the difficulties that prompted this book.

Swan's testimony can be approached from several different perspectives, including that of falsifiability and that of the expression of inappropriate personal opinion in a form that a lay jury might easily confuse with legitimate expert testimony. Consider the following statement made by Swan in one of her affidavits:

Box 8.5

Examination of Dr. Shanna Swan in *Sekou Ely et al. v. Richardson-Merrill*

source: *Sekou Ely, et al. v. Richardson-Merrell, Inc.*, No. 83-3504 (D.D.C. July 8, 1987), at 3598, 3658–3659, 3662

Q. What are the chances of the best one then, the Jick study, finding 100 percent increase [a doubling]?

A. 17—about 17 percent, 17.6.

Q. Would it be [an] accepted practice by epidemiologists to rely upon a study or even four studies, none of which had a power greater than 17 percent to detect 100 percent increase to decide that a drug is safe and could not cause birth defects?

A. No. . . .

Q. . . . Based on the various studies that we talked [about], Heinonen, Jick, Aselton, Morelock, Cordero, Eskenazi, McCredie, can you as an epidemiologist, can epidemiologists generally and reasonably draw conclusions based on those studies, first of all, that there is no association between Bendectin and limb reduction defects?

A. Absolutely not.

Q. Can they draw a conclusion from those studies that Bendectin does not cause limb reduction defects? . . .

A. No, they cannot. . . .

Q. . . . Can an epidemiologist, in your opinion, based on the studies and the sales charts, conclude that Bendectin in not associated with limb reduction defects? . . .

A. No, you cannot.

Q. Same question, then, based on the same studies, can you conclude that, as an epidemiologist, that Bendectin does not cause limb reduction defects when one looks at the sales charts in those various studies we have talked about?

A. No, you cannot. . . .

Q. Based on Heinonen, Jick, Aselton, Morelock, Cordero, Eskenazi, McCredie articles that we have talked about, do you have an opinion within a reasonable degree of epidemiological certainty as to whether or not Bendectin is associated with limb reduction defects?

A. I do.

Q. What is that opinion?

A. It is my opinion that it more probably than not does increase the risk of limb reduction defects.

In analyzing the various epidemiology studies, one quickly can see that the studies either have insufficient numbers, inappropriate control groups, inappropriate pooling of malformations, misclassification of exposure or confounders.[13]

The first problem with this statement is small but also telling: all epidemiological studies can be said to "have insufficient numbers." This phrase simply begs the question "Sufficient for what?" Since she is a witness for the plaintiffs, Swan's implied answer would seem to be "Sufficient to prove that Bendectin does not cause birth defects." If that is what Swan meant, her statement was technically correct, but at the same time it was trivial and likely to mislead. No amount of data can ever prove a strictly negative assertion about risk. Scientists also have "insufficient" numbers to prove that Bendectin does not cause tornadoes.

If, on the other hand, Swan means that the data are too sparse to exclude a doubling of the risk of limb-reduction defects, her statement may be technically correct. As the FDA panel pointed out, the data on Bendectin, extensive though they are, are not sufficient to exclude relative risks as "small" as 2 for rare birth defects. But Swan didn't make that specific a statement. If she had, it could have been examined, and perhaps refuted, by analyzing the existing studies or by conducting new ones.

Reading between the lines, one can perhaps infer that Swan is saying something quite different. She is intimating that the key scientific studies cited by the defense are not valid and not reliable—they are, to the contrary, rife with errors, or at best inconclusive. At first glance this seems to fit very well with the issues discussed in chapter 4 and emphasized by the *Daubert* majority. Under *Daubert*, expert testimony may be admitted only if "valid," "reliable," and based on studies whose error rates that are acceptably low. Swan implies that the defendants' evidence does not meet these thresholds.

But interpreted this way, Swan's statement is not a scientific statement—it is a legal conclusion. *Daubert* doesn't require experts (or even permit them) to declare their own work to be reliable, valid, and not excessively prone to error—that is what the judge is to decide. Legally speaking, Swan is simply reversing the burden of proof. She declares that she is not persuaded that the evidence on the other side is solid. Well then, suppose it isn't. Suppose, indeed, that the other side offers no evidence at all. Swan could then make her own statement even stronger: she could then declare that no epidemiology studies at all support . . . support what? Swan supplies no explicit answer. But the whole logic of what she writes is that it is somehow up to the defendant to prove that Bendectin is safe.

This proposition is not scientifically correct or incorrect; it is not a scientific proposition at all. As a matter of law, however, the proposition is simply wrong. The burden of proof in a civil case is on the plaintiff, not the defendant. In the complete absence of any "valid," "reliable," or "error-free" evidence about Bendectin, the plaintiff loses.[14]

The most generous possible reading of Swan's statement is that none of the evidence at hand is very good, and that neither Swan nor any other scientist really knows whether Bendectin increases the risk of the rare birth defect that Jason Daubert suffered. A systematic poll might indeed establish scientifically that 95 percent of scientists agree that they 'just don't know' whether Bendectin doubles the risk of limb reduction birth defects, yet this scientifically valid poll could not properly be admitted in the *Daubert* trial.

Why couldn't it? Two related legal reasons, both of them subtle, compel that conclusion. The first concerns legal relevance. The overall state of scientific knowledge or ignorance is not on trial in a Bendectin case. Plaintiffs cannot lawfully win or lose depending only on whether scientists in any field—Bendectin included—are very sure of themselves or very unsure. The key issue in this case is what they know; only secondarily does it matter how well they know it.

To caricature the point: Suppose Shanna Swan (or, alternatively, an expert for the defendants) had asserted that most astrologers just don't know whether Bendectin doubles the risk for limb reduction defects. This statement is undoubtedly true, but it would not be relevant—and would therefore not be admissible—in a trial about birth defects and Bendectin. (It might be admissible in a trial in which an astrologer was being prosecuted for fraud, or the unlicensed practice of medicine.) Replacing "astrologers" with "epidemiologists" does not make the statement any more relevant to the trial, so long as the statement is couched purely in terms of ignorance. Ignorance is never relevant in a trial, and therefore never admissible—least of all when it is affirmed by an "expert" who is supposed to testify exclusively about "scientific knowledge." Unadorned statements about ignorance are inadmissible because they are irrelevant. They don't tend to prove one side of the case or the other. Legally speaking, they are just superfluous fluff.

Such statements also present a second, much graver problem: the problem of prejudicing and confusing the jury. Legally speaking, they are highly prejudicial because they are likely to lead jurors into an erroneous chain of reasoning. A somber scientist, credentialed, serious, and reflective, is presented to the jury as an "expert." She then declares, in all solemnity, "We just don't know if Bendectin causes birth defects." Other scientists know what to make of such a statement: nothing. One could equally well say "We just don't know if Bendectin prevents birth defects." When placed carefully in the context of things that are known, statements about ignorance help delineate an important boundary. But out of that context, statements about ignorance assert nothing at all.

The average nonscientist juror, however, can easily be seduced by statements like these into a whole chain of logical error. Bendectin is consumed during pregnancy—which we all know is a risky time. We all know that other notorious products consumed during pregnancy—Thalidomide in particular—cause birth defects. Jason Daubert has a birth defect. His mother took Bendectin. The other side has not proved that the drug does not cause birth defects. It all fits—Bendectin is to blame.

But it does not all fit, of course. The expert would surely not be permitted to say all this on the stand; reasoning of this form is hugely prone to error and is neither reliable nor valid in any sensible meaning of those words. If the expert's statement that "we just don't know" somehow fails to kick off this chain of thought in the minds of jurors, no harm is done, but no good either—the jurors then simply dismiss it out of hand, as scientists would. But if the expert does manage to induce this kind of thinking, the entire effect of admitting the "scientific" expert has been to induce fallacious reasoning. The expert is trying to get the jury to think what the expert would not be permitted to say.

In the *Daubert* remand, Judge Kozinski cut through Swan's verbal fog very quickly. Swan and other plaintiff experts were "unprepared to testify that Bendectin caused plaintiffs' injuries; they were willing to testify only that Bendectin is 'capable of causing' birth defects."[15] The plaintiffs' lawyers had, in turn, argued to the court that "these scientists use the words 'capable of causing' meaning that it does cause. This is an ambiguity of language. . . . If something is capable of causing damage in humans, it does."[16] This compact little passage in Judge Kozinski's opinion sharply highlights just how quickly science can get dilapidated in legal proceedings. To begin with, there are many things "capable" of causing injury that don't do so (at least, not often enough to matter. All scientists would agree that a massive asteroid colliding with Earth is capable of destroying mankind. But no one would say that asteroids colliding with the earth do destroy mankind. It might happen, but it hasn't yet. (Dinosaurs are another story.) The scientific step from "capable of" to "does" or "did" or "probably will" is a serious one. Taking it requires a much deeper discussion of probabilities, frequencies, and so forth.

Consider the second statement "X-rays are capable of causing birth defects." This statement is certainly true, but it is also very vague. It is by no means equivalent to saying that x-rays did cause birth defects in any specific individual. Getting to "did" requires a much more detailed study of intensities and areas of exposure. Dental x-rays of the upper jaw, conducted on patients shielded in lead gowns, almost certainly don't cause birth defects, at least not with any significant probability.

It will not suffice simply to edit the original statement to read "Thoracic x-rays conducted during pregnancy are capable of causing birth defects." That still leaves unanswered the key questions of frequency, level, and area of exposure. Some scientific theories hold that any exposure—even a "single hit" by an energetic photon—may knock an electron out of place in a key strand of DNA and thus lead, eventually, to cancer. The assertion is scientifically plausible. But whether this ever happens, or how likely it is to happen, is a fundamentally different question than whether it is capable of happening or whether it could happen.

The *Daubert* lawyers' attempt to translate "capable of" into "does" highlights a further, grave problem in presenting expert testimony of this form to a lay jury. The plaintiffs' lawyers hoped and expected that a jury, hearing "capable of," would make the logical leap to "does." And from "does," they would conclude "did." The whole idea was to invite the jury to reason "Bendectin is capable of causing birth defects, therefore it does, and therefore it did cause the birth defect suffered by Jason Daubert." But no respectable scientist would ever accept such a simple-minded and logically insufficient line of reasoning. The only possible value of the expert's assertion, in other words, was to entice jurors to engage in a pseudoscientific kind of reasoning that no serious expert would ever explicitly endorse.

An unadorned declaration that something is capable of causing something else does not even pass Popper's condition of falsifiability. Suppose one replaces "x-rays" with "the darker phases of the moon." The resulting statement is almost certainly false, but how can it be disproved? Compile a database of 1 million pregnancies and their outcomes, and then align the data on lunar cycles: there is no correlation whatsoever. But perhaps some weaker influence is still lurking just over the statistical horizon—one that will be revealed only by studying 2 million pregnancies. Or a billion. Or a trillion. The astrologer can always retreat into the refuge of smaller effects that will be revealed only by larger studies.

Can a "capable of causing" assertion ever be rephrased in terms that pass scientific muster? Not until "capable of" gives way to numbers. The statement that dark phases of the moon (or that using Bendectin as prescribed) double(s) the risk of limb defects is quite easily falsified, at least in statistical terms. With a million pregnancies in a database, one can establish (and for Bendectin the data do establish) to a reasonable degree of probability that the statement is false. Again, there is no absolute certainty—it is always possible that the people compiling the data have been very unlucky and, by pure accident, have stumbled upon a million unusually fortunate women who somehow dodged the bullet of lunar cycles or Bendectin exposure, or that the scientists made some error in their survey and overlooked victims of the drug. But as the database grows, and more studies are done, the statistical confidence gets progressively more solid. One can assert with steadily rising confidence that the original claim was false.

Expert statements phrased in "capable of" language cause difficulty where scientific standards meet up with the legal ones. The assertion "Use of Bendectin as prescribed increases the risk of limb defects" is scientifically sufficient (though probably wrong), but it is not legally sufficient. This is obvious if one recasts the statement as one about the risk of damaging a child's limb in a car accident. Driving a child around in a Toyota undoubtedly increases, by some small but quantifiable degree, the child's risk of injury. One can easily frame that proposition in scientifically rigorous terms. But that alone is hardly enough to get a claim to a jury in a civil lawsuit. In a case against Toyota, the Dauberts wouldn't be able to get to a jury simply by proving that (a) Jason Daubert's mother had driven Jason around in a Toyota after he was born and (b) Jason suffered an injury of some kind to his arm. A plaintiff has to assert that some defect in the car caused the injury.

Such an assertion can be built on purely statistical evidence. But if it is, the statistical links have to be strong—at least a doubling of the risk. Why double? Because the plaintiff's burden is to show that the defendant was "more probably than not" responsible. In a strictly statistical case, that burden is met only when one can assert that most of the injuries derive from the one targeted causal agent. Judge Kozinski focused directly on this point in the *Daubert* remand opinion:

[W]hat plaintiffs must prove is not that Bendectin causes some birth defects, but that it caused *their* birth defects. To show this, plaintiffs' experts would have had to testify either that Bendectin actually caused plaintiffs' injuries (which they could not say) or that Bendectin more than doubled the likelihood of limb reduction birth defects (which they did not say).[17]

9

Conclusion

Just when a scientific principle or discovery crosses the line between the experimental and demonstrable stages is difficult to define. Somewhere in this twilight zone the evidential force of the principle must be recognized, and while courts will go a long way in admitting expert testimony deduced from a well-recognized scientific principle or discovery, the thing from which the deduction is made must be sufficiently established to have gained general acceptance in the particular field in which it belongs.

—*Frye v. United States*, 293 F. 1013, 1014 (D.C. Cir. 1923)

That the *Frye* test was displaced by the Rules of Evidence does not mean, however, that the Rules themselves place no limits on the admissibility of purportedly scientific evidence. Nor is the trial judge disabled from screening such evidence. To the contrary, under the Rules the trial judge must ensure that any and all scientific testimony or evidence admitted is not only relevant, but reliable. . . . The subject of an expert's testimony must be 'scientific . . . knowledge.'

—*Daubert v. Merrell Dow Pharmaceuticals, Inc.*, 509 U.S. 579, 589, 590 (1993) (footnotes omitted)

Frye was a criminal case. The defendant was accused of murdering a doctor. He had confessed, then recanted. At trial he offered a weak alibi and sought to introduce evidence that he had passed a "systolic blood pressure deception test"—a primitive precursor of the "lie detector" polygraph. The trial court rejected this evidence. In affirming that ruling, the District of Columbia Circuit Court of Appeals articulated the "general acceptance" rule to govern the admission of expert testimony in federal courts.[1] James Alphonso Frye served 18 years in prison. The "*Frye* rule" was applied by federal courts for more than 50 years and is still enforced by many state courts.

In any discussion of what the rules of evidence should be, it is useful to keep the facts of *Frye* in mind. Rules of evidence apply in criminal cases as well as in civil ones, and they apply equally to prosecutors and defendants. Rules that are "liberal" for civil plaintiffs in "toxic tort" cases will be "liberal" for prosecutors in capital murder cases too. Rules that may seem to tilt things in a socially desirable direction in today's case may tilt the opposite way in tomorrow's. (See box 9.1.)

In drawing lines between expert testimony that is good enough to be used in court and expert testimony that isn't, the best rule is to try not to tilt in one direction or another. The criteria set forth in *Daubert* address directly the issue of reliability of evidence, and are similar to criteria that scientists might apply. Viewed in that light, the *Daubert* majority opinion was a good one. At first, lawyers on both sides of the debate applauded it. In the Ninth Circuit on remand, however, the defendants prevailed. The Ninth Circuit excluded the testimony proffered by the plaintiffs. With no admissible expert evidence to back their claims, the *Daubert* plaintiffs could proceed no further. The case was dismissed. *Frye* would have yielded the same result. Indeed, it already had: the Ninth Circuit had applied *Frye* in its first review of the *Daubert* case to exclude the expert testimony proffered by the plaintiffs. The Supreme Court's ruling in *Daubert* compelled the appellate court to write a new opinion. In the end, however, it did not compel the trial judge to admit the "scientific" evidence proffered by the *Daubert* plaintiffs.

Frye and *Daubert*

When all is said and done, a great number of judges applying the new terms will end up making calls very similar to those they would have made under *Frye*. How is this possible, if *Daubert* rejected the substance of *Frye*? As we noted in chapter 1, the simple answer is that it didn't. The Supreme Court correctly recognized that the 1975 Federal Rules of Evidence did not expressly incorporate *Frye*. A new phrase—"scientific knowledge"—had replaced "general acceptance." But that narrow conclusion did not define what "scientific knowledge" means. Nor did it determine the extent to which "scientific knowledge" and "general acceptance" overlap. Are *Frye* and *Daubert* really much different from one another in practice? The question is of more than abstract legal interest. Civil suits about Bendectin or breast implants, and criminal prosecutions of murder or civil rights

---

Box 9.1
Witch Hunts: On the Social Psychology of Risk
William C. Clark

source: Witches, floods, and wonder drugs: Historical perspectives on risk management, in *Societal Risk Assessment: How Safe Is Safe Enough?* ed. R. Schwing and W. Albers (Plenum, 1980) (citations omitted)

For several centuries spanning the Renaissance and Reformation, societal risk assessment meant witch hunting. Contemporary accounts record wheat inexplicably rotting in the fields, sheep dying of unknown causes, vineyards smitten with unseasonable frost; human disease and impotence on the rise. In other words, a litany of life's sorrows not very different from those which concern us today.

The institutionalized expertise of that earlier time resided with the Church. Then, as now, the experts were called upon to provide explanation of the unknown and to mitigate its undesirable consequences. Rather than seek particular sources of particular evils, rather than acknowledge their own limitations and ignorance, these experts assigned the generic name of "witchcraft" to the phenomenology of the unknown. Having a name, they proceeded to found a new professional interest dedicated to its investigation and control.

As the true magnitude of the witch problem became more apparent, the Church enlisted the Inquisition, an applied institution specifically designed to address pressing social concerns. The Inquisition became the growth industry of the day, offering exciting work, rapid advancement, and wide recognition to its professional and technical workers. Its creative and energetic efforts to create a witch-free world unearthed dangers in the most unlikely places: the rates of witch identification, assessment and evaluation soared. By the dawn of the Enlightenment, witches had been virtually eliminated from Europe and North America. Crop failures, disease, and general misfortune had not. And more than half a million people had been burned at the stake, largely "for crimes they committed in someone else's dreams." . . .

. . . In 1610, after a century of witch hunting, the exceptional Inquisitor Alonso Salazar y Frias carried out an extensive analysis of witch burnings at Logrono, Navarre. He showed that most of the original accusations had been false, that torture had created witches where none existed, and that there was not a single case of actual witchcraft to show for all the preaching, hunting, and burning which had been carried out in the name of the Church. He did not rule on whether witches existed. He did order that the Spanish Inquisition no longer use torture under any circumstances, and that accusations no longer be considered unless supported by independent evidence. The number of witches brought to trial declined precipitously.

In modern terms, Frias had instituted a grand jury condition between accusation and trial. Further, he had introduced rules of evidence which recognized the perverse and essentially meaningless forms which unstructured "facts" could take.

violations, can be brought in either state or federal court. But only federal courts are bound by *Daubert*; state courts frame their own rules of evidence, and a good number still follow *Frye*. Even federal judges have to decide how much to continue relying on the *Frye* jurisprudence in particular cases. If *Frye* courts unanimously excluded polygraph evidence, can *Daubert* courts continue doing so without conducting new inquiries?

Bert Black, Francisco Ayala, and Carol Saffran-Brinks, in their review of *Daubert*, argue that the two criteria are far apart. *Frye*, they reason, employs "general acceptance" as a surrogate for "evaluating whether scientific claims are really scientific." They conclude that "viewed as a first effort to state the principle that scientific evidence should conform to the standards and practices of science, general acceptance is a reasonable rule," but that "trying to apply it as a substitute for real understanding [of the scientific issues] is futile" since "the bottom line is the need for lawyers to understand science when they offer it into evidence and for judges to understand science before they rule on its admissibility" and "courts that want to dig into the details of an expert's reasoning and the validity of his or her testimony can do so with or without *Frye*."[2] The thrust of *Daubert*, Black et al. state, is that judges and lawyers directly examine the validity of an expert's testimony.

But how different will that inquiry be in actual legal practice under *Daubert* than under *Frye*? This is not a philosophical question; philosophy deals in abstractions and requires no immediate resolution of very practical questions (such as whether to admit Shanna Swan's testimony into court). Nor is this a scientific question; scientists have their own, different, much more informal procedures and heuristics for deciding what to listen to. The concrete question for judges and lawyers is how much more or less is required to get an expert's statements about "scientific knowledge" admitted into federal court than would have been required under *Frye*.

Only time will tell how different the two standards really are in practice. But, as we have discussed, both refer to the criteria that scientists use to grade the quality, reliability, and overall validity of claims purporting to reflect scientific knowledge. In *Frye* the reference was indirect, by means of the surrogate label "general acceptance." In *Daubert*, the reference was direct and explicit. We would be hard pressed to imagine testimony that would be rejected by a judge conscientiously applying *Frye* but accepted by the same judge conscientiously applying *Daubert*.

"General Criteria"

As we have acknowledged throughout this book, no precise boundaries separate scientific knowledge from other spheres of wisdom or ignorance.[3] At the highest level of abstraction, philosophers reject all ready-made criteria of "scientificity" that purport to delineate science from nonscience.[4] Changing the vocabulary to focus on words like "reliability" or "validity" doesn't resolve things. These words have different meanings in lay and scientific contexts, and a range of meanings within science itself. Loose and rhetorically charged terms such as "good science" and "good scientist" invite equally rhetorical rejoinders.[5]

But none of this means that the line-drawing exercise can or should be abandoned. In any event, it won't be abandoned in federal courts. The Federal Rules of Evidence, as construed by the Supreme Court in *Daubert*, firmly require judges to make such judgments. One line definitely does exist: some expert scientific testimony will be admitted into court; some won't be. The views of the experts presented by the plaintiffs in *Daubert* itself ultimately weren't.

Daubert set out what the Court called "general criteria," and these at least help organize a judge's thinking about what to admit and what to exclude. When all is said and done, the *Daubert* criteria are similar to those that most intelligent laypeople would apply in deciding whether or not to accept any empirical claim about the world. Although they address science, the *Daubert* criteria are not themselves scientific. And they are, of course, applied to resolve disputes in legal arenas, not scientific ones. Although some scientists and some physicians urge that scientific debates and medical disputes be resolved by "science courts" or "blue ribbon" juries, this won't happen and probably shouldn't.

Lists of factors never provide very precise guidance, however, and many scientists have put forward lists that differ in varying degrees from that of *Daubert*. Philip Kitcher and Michael Polanyi have proposed checklists that differ significantly from that of *Daubert*.[6] (See table 9.1.) Joseph Rodricks has offered another checklist for weighing toxicologic evidence, Robert

Table 9.1

Kitcher	Polanyi	*Daubert*
Independent testability (ability "to test auxiliary hypotheses independently of the particular cases for which they are introduced")	Exactitude [i.e., precision and accuracy of the data]	Whether the theory or technique in question can be (and has been) tested
Unification ("the result of applying a small family of problem-solving strategies to a broad class of cases")	Systematic importance [to science]	Peer review and publication
	Intrinsic interest of subject matter	Known or potential error rate
Fecundity ("when a theory opens up new and profitable lines of investigation")		Existence and maintenance of standards controlling the operation of a technique
		Whether a technique has attracted widespread acceptance within a relevant scientific community

Koch another for disease etiology, Irving Langmuir yet another for pathological science, and Austin Bradford Hill yet another for epidemiology.[7] Weigh-the-factors checklists never provide precise guidance for judges, scientists, or anyone else; however, checklists do initiate and guide an important process of evaluation of knowledge, and emphasize its depth and seriousness.

These checklists serve a second function—an exclusionary one. The legal scholar Sheila Jasanoff has complained that calls for "good science" can mask attempts to cloak morally difficult judgments under the false guise of objectivity. According to Jasanoff, the need is to judge the "adequacy of knowledge . . . against the purposes for which knowledge was needed."[8] The *Daubert* criteria are well designed for precisely this purpose.

Social purposes are, of course, implicit in law's rules of evidence. Such rules are created and applied to organize a process in which society decides whether to execute murderers, or whether to transfer assets from chemical companies to women with breast implants. But, at the same time, social purposes are conspicuously absent from every single one of the "good science" checklists summarized in table 9.1.

More important still, social purposes do not appear in the checklist set forth by the Supreme Court in *Daubert*. The *Daubert* criteria do not distinguish between evidence offered by a civil plaintiff in a birth-defect case evidence offered by a criminal defendant in a capital murder trial. They do not distinguish between evidence offered to protect the public from toxic chemicals and evidence bearing on the efficacy of drugs used in lethal-injection executions. As the Supreme Court emphasized in *Daubert*, a judge's inquiry into scientific "validity," "relevance," and "reliability" must focus "solely on principles and methodology, not on the conclusions that they generate."[9] We will return to this fundamental point at the end of this chapter.

"Fit"

We began our discussion, as the Supreme Court did, with the broad issue of "relevance" or "fit." Can a test, a study, a calculation, or an observation be related, by a credible theory, to the issue at hand? A fact may be reliable and accurate, yet the inferences that it suggests may still be confusing, misleading, or plain wrong. It may be true that Jupiter was aligned with Mars; however, that fact is almost never relevant to whether a driver born under the astrological sign Scorpio behaved negligently when entering an intersection. Used out of context or viewed from the wrong perspective, true facts can be used to imply false conclusions.

As we noted in chapter 2, Rule 702 of the Federal Rules of Evidence requires expert testimony to "assist the trier of fact . . . to determine a fact in issue." This complements the general requirement of Rule 402: that all testimony, expert or lay, must be "relevant" to be admissible. This "helpfulness" requirement, the *Daubert* Court stated, "requires a valid scientific connection to the pertinent inquiry as a precondition to admissibility."[10]

But, as we inquired in chapter 2, how can one decide what does or doesn't fit? How can one assemble many different pieces of scientific evidence into a solved puzzle that presents an acceptably clear and understandable picture?

Regulators have developed elaborate criteria and guidelines for identifying what kinds of evidence to consider in assessing both the risks and the benefits of exposure to drugs, chemicals, radiation, and so forth. But there is often no very good theory that relates a given observation (e.g., some feature of chemical structure) to a particular health effect of interest. Assessing fit with this kind of evidence is much harder than assessing the relevance of astrology (the easy example offered by the *Daubert* majority). Raw observations themselves have no meaning; it is the theory that determines fit, and *Daubert*'s emphasis on fit implies that judges should pay close attention to the theory and not just to the observation.

As we concluded in chapter 2, the question of fit often ends up turning on how much other evidence there is and on how consistently the totality of the evidence at hand supports a theory for what is going on. These additional factors lend support to the theory that determines the fit. The better we understand the precise cause(s) of a disease, the less we tend to argue about fit. Discordant bits and pieces of evidence that do not fit in an otherwise coherent and overwhelming mass of evidence are, in practice, simply disregarded by risk assessors. But when there is no coherent theory, and no overwhelming mass of data, there is no discordant evidence, either, nor any possibility of fit.

In effect, the inquiry about fit requires judges to survey all the scientific evidence that bears on the proposition in dispute. "Fit" acquires meaning only in a broader context. Therefore, a judge ruling on admissibility has no choice but to consider how each expert's testimony fits into the larger context of the scientific case. Fit boils down to placing bits and pieces of evidence in the larger context of what is known. Discrete assertions of fact or theory that clash too sharply with the totality of the scientific evidence at hand must be excluded—particularly if the expert does not carefully reconcile the discordant evidence with other established knowledge.

Testability and Falsifiability

A "scientific proposition," the *Daubert* Court indicated, must be phrased in a way that can be falsified by other scientists if it is wrong. The majority cited Hempel and Popper. In dissent, Chief Justice Rehnquist insisted that he was "at a loss to know what is meant when it is said that the scientific status of a theory depends on its 'falsifiability.'"[11]

As we noted in chapter 3, the *Daubert* dissenters are not alone in this regard. The philosophical views of Popper and Hempel are quite distinct— and both of their views are vigorously disputed by other philosophers and sociologists of science. By citing both, the Supreme Court majority simply gestured in the direction of a never-ending philosophical debate about what constitutes science, and what it means to falsify or verify.

Although most scientific papers are not written in strictly Popperian terms, the *Daubert* majority's citing Popper and Hempel is helpful. Those philosophers remain important and durable, not because of the details of their positions, but because of the general thrust of what they insist upon. The "testability" and "falsifiability" criteria are both useful to and used by scientists. These terms tell us something about how a proposition must be framed to be admissible as "scientific" in federal court. Propositions that are so loosely framed as to be untestable are very slippery indeed. Many a misuse of expert testimony in court involves a "nonfalsifiable" diagnosis of a disease that lacks well-defined, specific symptoms. There simply are no definite criteria for determining when patients have a disease and when they don't.

The diagnostic criteria for multiple chemical sensitivities, for example, are so loose as to make it impossible to decide when any person does not have the syndrome. Similarly, there now appear to have been spectacular miscarriages of justice in litigation concerning breast implants and their alleged (but very doubtful) link to immune-system disorders and in some criminal cases involving the alleged sexual abuse of very young children. The legal system performed very badly in those instances, precisely because the diagnoses employed criteria so imprecise that they didn't permit falsi-fication. Assertions that should have been specific were presented in sur-passingly vague terms. In the worst cases, "cause" and "effect" were replaced by "activated, precipitated into disabling manifestation," "aroused into disabling reality," and other lawyerly prevarications. In the testimony proffered by Shanna Swan in *Daubert*, the analysis was pre-sented so loosely that it did not lead to meaningful conclusions. The testi-mony proffered by Alan Done, in contrast, was verifiable—and easily shown to be rife with errors. The great but irascible physicist Wolfgang Pauli once remarked that a paper he had read wasn't even good enough to be wrong.

Testing and Falsification

Popper and Hempel serve a second, much more practical purpose: to set the stage for testing and falsification. Much of the time, the key issue is not whether theories and techniques can be "falsified" but whether they have been subjected to enough testing to establish their reliability.

This kind of scrutiny need not come only from other scientists. As we discussed in chapter 3, testing the internal logical consistency of a claim is something that any intelligent layperson does routinely when evaluating any claim about the world. And nonscientists are often perfectly able to determine how well a particular claim fits with other established knowledge. In contrast, the testing and falsification of more technical arguments and the evaluating of empirical data will usually require specialized knowledge.

The validation of experimental methods is a fundamental part of experimental research. The reliability of a theory is directly related to how many different ways have been concocted to test it. Using falsifiability as a philosophical criterion to define the boundaries of "science" is debatable. Equally debatable is any attempt to use "verifiability" as a philosophical test of meaning. But these problems have little bearing when similar criteria are used to evaluate the reliability of empirical claims made by scientists or by laypeople.

For example, Shanna Swan's Bendectin testimony was too loosely phrased ever to be tested at all. If she had been willing to state flatly that use of Bendectin during pregnancy increases by at least 50 percent (say) the risk of limb-reduction birth defects, that claim could have been systematically tested through new epidemiological studies. The accumulation of evidence could eventually have led to general acceptance of Swan's number—or to its general rejection. Either way, concrete claims about important issues (claims solid enough to satisfy Popper) eventually lead to the kind of "general acceptance" that *Frye* demands—either general acceptance that the claims are right or general acceptance that they are wrong. Only claims that are too loose to satisfy Popper will remain forever outside the ambit of *Frye*.

For practical purposes in court, "falsifiable" claims are simply claims that could, someday, become "generally accepted"—and will, if they are both correct and interesting. A judge concerned with falsifiability will weigh carefully whether claims are being set forth in a form that allows testing. *Daubert* paraphrases Popper to say that "scientific knowledge" is that which "can be (and has been) tested." This can be read as a signpost on the road that leads to *Frye*. Scientific views that are formulated in terms concrete enough to be falsified if in fact they are wrong are views that are likely to become "generally accepted" over time if in fact they are correct.

Errors in Science

In chapter 4 we considered the third factor emphasized in *Daubert*: the problem of scientific error. We explored various ways in which errors arise, and the nuts-and-bolts prescriptions that scientists try to follow to avoid them. Scientists are expected to estimate and report potential errors, and to consider their effects on the conclusions of a study. But scientists are notoriously prone to underestimate the errors in their studies and to overestimate the reliability of their results. This suggests that judges should remain skeptical of all experts, even those from the mainstream of science.

Any nonscientist trying to get a practical grip on possible errors in a claim or a study will almost inevitably have to look at the methods that other scientists in the field have used to analyze and report potential errors. That provides a benchmark by which to evaluate the methods of any individual scientist. The "error rates" inquiry is plainly not identical to *Frye*'s, but it is closely related to it. Claims based on experiments or methods that are fraught with errors or with conceptual difficulties win limited acceptance in the broader scientific community. As methods are continually refined through the normal, cumulative scientific process, they gradually become accepted in the relevant scientific community. An individual scientist's estimates of the reliability of his own work are generally unreliable. The only way to gauge how good a grip a scientist has on potential errors is to look at the track record of other scientists who do similar work.

There is a large literature on scientific error and there are standards for reporting errors in a study. Normative prescriptions for estimating and reporting errors come from the larger scientific community and are articulated by widely accepted standards. Any legal standard that focuses on error rates therefore points away from the individual scientist and toward the standards and practices of scientists collectively. Such a standard, in other words, again points back toward *Frye*.

"Reliability"

In chapter 5 we turned to the first of two positive criteria articulated in *Daubert*: that expert testimony must be "reliable." As the Supreme Court put it in *Daubert*, "*evidentiary reliability* will be based upon *scientific validity*."[12] The majority distinguished "reliable" science from mere "conjecture," "subjective belief," or "unsupported speculation."

As we discussed in chapter 5, however, scientific work commonly begins with conjecture. The problem that arises from this doesn't stem from conjecture itself, but from the untested and hence unreliable nature of conjecture. As Popper argued, a scientific theory is tested by comparing conclusions that can be deduced from the theory among themselves, by investigating the logical form of the theory, by comparing the theory with other theories, and by testing the theory empirically. These criteria are cumulative. The more thoroughly a theory has been tested in these ways, the more confidence one can have in its reliability. As a general (though not invariable) rule, what moves claims from the "conjecture" side of the continuum to the "scientific knowledge" side is the active involvement of a broader scientific community. The chief difference between *Frye* and *Daubert* is that under *Daubert* the judge is expected to undertake at least preliminary assessment along these lines, rather than relying entirely on the scientific community through application of a "general acceptance" criterion.

Furthermore, as we discussed in chapter 5, the overall reliability of any observation, scientific or otherwise, is determined by the confluence of two independent factors: (1) the reliability of observational tools (eyes, spectrometers, or diagnostic tests) and (2) the underlying probability of the reported observation (yellow taxis, chemical contaminants, or HIV infection).

The first factor inevitably includes some examination of both the observational tools used by an expert and the expert's observational skills. If this inquiry seems somewhat ad hominem, it is only because the business of admitting or excluding an expert's testimony invariably has a personal conclusion. (For similar reasons, courts routinely limit or exclude testimony from children, or from individuals who are mentally incompetent, on the ground that their individual and personal capabilities prevent them from giving reliable testimony.) This first factor seems to put legal practice squarely at odds with the scientific ethic. Scientists pride themselves on passing judgment on scientific theories, not on other scientists. A truly general scientific proposition—relativity, say, or quantum mechanics—is assessed without any reference to whether it originated in the mind of a saint, a schizophrenic, or a chronic drunk. The same doesn't hold for a very specific observation or datum. Biologists evaluating a report about an abominable snowman in the Andes may instinctively, and with some justification, inquire as to the sobriety and observational skill of the person who makes the report. *Daubert* is, of course, concerned with general "scientific" propositions, not narrow technical ones. But a judge applying the *Daubert* criteria to the testimony of a specific witness will often be forced to inquire, in some measure, as to the expert's personal reliability as an observer and as an interpreter of science. However objectively "valid" the substance, proffered testimony will not be accepted if the expert arrives to testify visibly intoxicated.

The second component of reliability centers on the objective probability of the thing being observed. As we discussed in some detail in chapter 5, determining this requires knowledge of the background incidence of the thing being tested for—HIV infection, say, or child abuse. Unfortunately, there is no expert-independent way of knowing the incidence of the thing being tested for in most scientifically interesting cases. No bureau supplies scientists with external and independent assessments of the background incidence of child abuse, for example. Thus, if an expert claims to be able to identify child abuse by interrogating the child in question, a judge needs data on the background incidence of child abuse in order to assess the overall "reliability" of the diagnosis. The more common child abuse actually is, the more likely it is that a positive diagnosis of child abuse is correct. A testifying expert who claims to have identified child abuse may maintain that child abuse is indeed very common. Other experts may disagree. To assess the overall reliability of the testifying expert's diagnosis, the judge still needs a background rate.

Daubert plainly does not contemplate that experts will certify their own reliability. In Bayesian terms, *Daubert* therefore requires courts to look beyond the individual expert to estimate the background rates needed to assess the reliability of the individual diagnosis. Two practical choices spring to mind: the court can appoint its own expert, or the court can make its own determination of what estimates are "generally accepted" among other experts in the field. Either way, *Daubert*'s reliability requirement has a profound and practical effect. The only way to assess the reliability of any single scientist's observation or opinion is to combine information about the observational tools used by that scientist with external information about the actual likelihood of the thing he or she claims to have observed and historical information about the reliability of scientific knowledge in a particular field. Some judges may reasonably conclude that the most convenient (and perhaps only) "external" information about "background" likelihoods is the view most generally accepted by other scientists in the field. Other approaches are possible, but all look to some external referent beyond the individual expert. Bayes' law impels an important legal conclusion: It is not possible to assess the "reliability" of an observation without some extrinsic measure of the background probability of the thing observed.

Thus, when an individual scientist testifies that a subject's birth defects were caused by the mother's use of a drug during pregnancy, there is no way to assess the reliability of the scientific proposition underlying that opinion without reliable information on background rates of similar birth defects in children of women who used the drug and in those of women who didn't. Absent such information (commonly presented in terms of statistical quantities such as relative risk), the reliability of the individual diagnosis cannot be gauged. That does not mean that the opinion or theory is inherently unreliable (or reliable); it simply means that we are missing a crucial input. One cannot measure the area of a rectangle by measuring only one side, no matter how carefully one measures it. In the case of Bendectin, which turned on epidemiological evidence, that would have involved making a case that the relative risk for the birth defect in question was greater than 2—an argument that was conspicuously missing from the testimony of Shanna Swan and other experts for the plaintiff.

Assessing the reliability of scientific testimony thus requires a two-dimensional measurement. One aspect involves the reliability of the observational tools and the skills of the observer. The other looks beyond the observer—possibly (though not necessarily) to methods accepted by other observers in the same field, and certainly to established scientific knowledge in the field.

If no such broader perspective is available, reliability cannot be gauged at all. Since the legal burden is on the party that proffers expert testimony to justify its admission, the absence of an external standard means that testimony cannot be admitted. The scrutiny of "reliability" under the *Daubert* standard requires either *Frye*-like "general acceptance" or some functional equivalent, such as textbook knowledge summarized by a court-appointed expert. Without that input, no expert evidence can properly be termed reliable. This is not a claim that only scientists have reliable knowledge—the straw man that sociologists of science delight in knocking down. It is simply a claim that reliability, like scientific knowledge, is a collective quantity.

"Scientific Validity"

The second positive criterion set out in *Daubert*, and undoubtedly the most important, is one that attempts to clarify what the Court means by scientific validity. "In a case involving scientific evidence, *evidentiary reliability* will be based upon *scientific validity*," the Court wrote, italicizing for emphasis.[13] The Court returned to the term "scientific validity" at numerous other points in its opinion. According to the Court, the "overarching subject" of the debate about admitting expert testimony is "the scientific validity—and thus the evidentiary relevance and reliability—of the principles that underlie a proposed submission."[14]

As we discussed in chapter 6, "validity" has several components. The first is logical validity. This is a matter of internal consistency. A mathematical proof is either valid or not valid. But less formal arguments can be tested for logical validity too. Arguments built on non sequiturs, ad hominem attacks, appeals to ignorance, begging the question, special pleading, and so on lack validity at a basic level of logic. A scientific argument built on logic that does not parse is invalid on its face and must fail *Daubert*'s validity requirement.

Logical issues aside, however, scientific validity is not a binary, yes-or-no quality that is intrinsic to a theory or a test without reference to larger issues. It depends on how the knowledge is to be used. Popper used the metaphor of science rising on piles above a swamp. There is never an utterly solid bedrock underneath—no "'natural' or 'given' base." Scientists simply stop driving deeper when they are satisfied that the piles "are firm enough to carry the structure, at least for the time being."[15] Stopping points are determined, instead, by considerations external to the instrument or theory itself. But Popper also listed various positive ways in which a theory can be tested. It can be tested for logical consistency, it can be compared with other theories, and it can be tested empirically. These criteria are cumulative; the more advanced the testing, the more confidence we can have in a theory's strength. Theories that are logically inconsistent, or that disagree with already established scientific principles, are not "valid" in the lay or the scientific sense of the word.

As we discussed in chapter 6, validity is also a term of art in science—particularly in epidemiology and in other sciences that rely heavily on statistics. In these contexts, at least, science itself offers more specific definitions of the term. In particular, statistics offers clear guidelines for valid uses of tests for statistical inference, determined by the assumptions that were made in developing the tests. It is safe to assume that the *Daubert* Court had no precise definition in mind when it used the term "scientific validity." But it is equally reasonable to assume that any statistical analysis that involves serious misuse of statistics fails the test of validity should be inadmissible under *Daubert*. The statistical tests have been formulated with an eye to issues entirely analogous to the "evidentiary reliability" that concerned the *Daubert* Court.

As we also discussed in chapter 6, a practical test for scientific validity is whether it has survived what Henry Bauer calls the "knowledge filter." Science is heterogeneous. Its growing margin—"proto-science," "frontier science," or something of that sort—interesting, but often wrong. Its core is much less interesting (because it is familiar) but very solid. There is a wide intermediate area. Data and theories are kept, modified, or discarded as the totality of knowledge accumulates. Given time, scientists and engineers develop a good sense of what works and learn to avoid what does not. Reliability, in both science and technology, develops in a collective way, as the relevant communities constantly diagnose and fix the failures.[16] Scientific ideas are constantly filtered and refined. Those that withstand the give and take among scientists and are adopted for use in the scientific community eventually come to be generally accepted by scientists as reliable and valid.

Judges operate their own "knowledge filter," roughly mimicking how a journal editor screens papers submitted for publication. But science offers no guidance to the judge as to how fine the filter should be or how the criteria should be applied. Those are legal issues that lie entirely outside the domain of science. As one legal commentator observes, "scientific matters are best left to scientific journals, and legal standards of admissibility of evidence better left to judges."[17]

Judges and journal editors do use broadly similar criteria, though they operate under quite different constraints. Both scientific and judicial "knowledge filters" operate largely in a negative way, excluding claims that are deemed to be flawed, unreliable, or not relevant to the intended audience and its interests. Science, John Ziman recently noted, is ruled not by the Invisible Hand but by the Royal Boot.[18]

Neither journal editors nor judges will ever feel comfortable certifying knowledge as valid for the world in general. But neither has to. A journal editor controls quality only within a single journal; a judge admits or excludes scientific evidence only in a single case. Both can identify badly flawed claims; both can examine how far the principles underlying a claim have progressed through the knowledge filter of science. A journal editor does not certify validity but does endeavor to promote the overall scientific quality of its contents. *Daubert*'s mandate likewise requires judges to determine whether proffered testimony somehow merits the label of "scientifically valid" at one specific point in time and in the context of one specific case. Journal editors and judges alike decide whether scientific knowledge is valid enough, for the time being, for present purposes. Nothing more.

As we argued above, testing the validity, error rate, and so forth of proffered testimony requires some examination of scientific knowledge apart from the specific observations that the witness offers. Judges, whether or not they are wholly comfortable with the role, must make preliminary evaluations of how well the facts, theories, and conclusions attested to by expert witnesses concord with knowledge that has passed through the knowledge filter of science. In practical terms, this is judged by examining how extensively the witness's methods and theories have been tested by the larger scientific community. If anything at all can be concluded from the scholarship discussed in this book, it is that reliability of empirical knowledge is a collective phenomenon, for which the term "knowledge filter" is a fitting metaphor.

Acceptance in the Scientific Community

In chapter 7 we addressed the last factor noted by the *Daubert* Court: peer review and the old *Frye* standard of "general acceptance."

One amicus brief filed with the Supreme Court on behalf of the *Daubert* plaintiffs argued vehemently that "the exclusion of scientific testimony that the respondent deems 'heresy' is inimical to the search for truth." (See box 9.2.) A second group of scientists responded: "It is a complete non sequitur, and false, to suggest . . . that the refusal of a court to receive testimony from a scientist has anything to do with the advancement or progress of science. . . . The problem is that non-scientists, whether judges or jurors, often cannot distinguish between 'good science' and 'bad science.'" (See box 9.3.) Other amicus briefs filed by scientific societies likewise emphasized the "consensus" perspective on "scientific knowledge." (See box 9.4.) The closest the Supreme Court comes to this concept is in its discussion of *Frye*. After concluding that the Federal Rules of Evidence did not simply codify *Frye*'s "general acceptance" standard, the Court declares that "general acceptance" remains "an important factor" in assessing the "reliability" of proffered scientific evidence—as does its absence. "[A] known technique that has been able to attract only minimal support within the community, may properly be viewed with skepticism."[19]

Black et al., along with other commentators, point out that "general acceptance" can be used as a conclusory label that simply ducks any real examination of the substantive scientific issues.[20] But science does have mechanisms for articulating what well-informed scientists generally accept to be true about issues ranging from how research should be conducted to health and disease.

Reports issued by well-constituted groups under the auspices of the National Academy of Sciences, the National Council on Radiation Protection and Measurements, and similar organizations set forth the best scientific thinking that is available about important issues. (See chapter 7.) Such reports often include minority statements or other indications of the

Box 9.2
Scientific Inquiry, Like the Fact-Finding Process in the Law, Is Undermined by a Categorical Refusal Even to Consider Views or Analysis That Challenge the Supposed Conventional Wisdom

Brief Amici Curiae of Physicians, Scientists, and Historians of Science in Support of Petitioners, *Daubert v. Merrell Dow Pharmaceuticals, Inc.*, Dkt. No. 92-102 (U.S. Dec. 2, 1992) (amici: Ronald Bayer, Stephen Jay Gould, Gerald Holton, Peter Infante, Philip Landrigan, Everett Mendelsohn, Robert Morris, Herbert Needleman, Dorothy Nelkin, William Nicholson, Kathleen Joy Propert, and David Rosner) (citations omitted)

The Ninth Circuit's almost cursory conclusion that the only science worth considering is that which reflects some undefined "consensus" in the field is predicated on two fallacious assumptions about the nature of scientific inquiry.

First, the court below assumes that science always progresses by the continuous accumulation of objective, irrefutable truths, which are gradually incorporated into a consensus reflected in the scientific literature. This is incorrect. . . . The conventional scientific wisdom is as often a stumbling-block as a stepping-stone to better understanding. . . .

The Ninth Circuit's second fallacy is the assumption that scientific truths, once discovered, are complete, universal, immutable and eternal. The defendants have urged this Court that the expert testimony excluded here was inadmissible because it supposedly challenged "universally recognized scientific truths." . . .

. . . As a consequence those who seek in science the immutable truth they find lacking in the law are apt to be disappointed:

One notable similarity [between law and epidemiology] is the dependence of both fields upon subjective judgments. . . .

In the end, a quality which lawyers should understand better than any—judiciousness—matters more than any. Scientists use both deductive and inductive inference to sustain the momentum of a continuing process of research. . . . The courts of law, and the courts of application, use inference to reach decisions about what action to take. Those decisions often cannot rest on certitudes, most especially when population risks are converted into individual risks. . . .

. . . [T]he exclusion of scientific testimony that the respondent deems "heresy" is inimical to the search for truth. Advancement in scientific understanding frequently comes from what was once denounced by many as unorthodox. . . .

. . . If a jury is asked to decide a question of fact on which qualified scientific testimony would be of assistance, we believe that the search for truth would be aided by allowing the jury to consider—as a practicing scientist would—*all* of the relevant evidence, not just that which a particular judge deems to reflect the consensus of scientific opinion.

Box 9.3
There Are Fundamental Differences in the Meaning of "Truth" in the Legal and Scientific Realms
Brief Amici Curiae of Nicolaas Bloembergen et al. in Support of Respondent, *Daubert v. Merrell Dow Pharmaceuticals, Inc.*, Dkt. No. 92-102 (Jan. 19, 1993) (amici: Nicolaas Bloembergen, Erminio Costa, Dudley Herschbach, Jerome Karle, Arthur Langer, Wassily Leontief, Richard S. Lindzen, William N. Lipscomb, Donald B. Louria, John B. Little, A. Alan Moghissi, Brooke T. Mossman, Robert Nolan, Arno A. Penzias, Frederick Seitz, A. Frederick Spilhaus, Dimitrios Trichopoulos, and Richard Wilson) (citations omitted)

It is common ground, we believe, that in science accepted "truth" is not a constant: that it evolves, either gradually or discontinuously. . . . An hypothesis can be falsified or disproved, but cannot, ultimately, be proven true because knowledge is always incomplete. An hypothesis that is tested and not falsified is corroborated, but not proved. Thus, scientific statements or theories are never final and are always subject to revision or rejection. . . .

All of this is also relevant to law, since the basic principles of reasoning or logic are no different in the field of law than in science. However, the functions of law, and thus the propositions to be established by evidence and logic in the legal process, are quite different. While science involves an effort to construct a system of descriptive general theories based on particular data, law consists of a system of normative general rules that are individualized to apply to particular cases. . . .

An important difference between science and law is that the propositions to be tested in science are predictive while the facts to be proved in the legal process arise out of situations that occurred in the past and which cannot be repeated exactly. . . .

The scientists on whose behalf this brief is filed believe that the Bayer brief [box 9.2] . . . although it may speak for one group of scientists, unfortunately embodies a fundamental misconception of the relationship between science and law, a misconception which permeates the brief and invalidates its conclusions. . . .

. . . United States courts do not have, and do not assert or claim to have, any authority whatsoever over the publication or promulgation of scientific observations, data or theories, and are not at all concerned with "heresy". . . .

There are two distinctly different areas of activity and authority. . . . First, there is the process of scientific research and publication which concerns the formulation, corroboration, and advancement of scientific principles and theories. . . . Second, there is an entirely separate area, which is the field of legal process that concerns the adjudication of rights between particular parties. In the course of litigation issues arise involving the admissibility of certain types of evidence from many fields, including science; but the legal process does not establish nor attempt to establish scientific theories, principles or "truth" for the purposes of science, but only for the purposes of adjudication. . . .

It is a complete *non sequitur*, and false, to suggest, as the Bayer brief does, that the refusal of a court to receive testimony from a scientist has anything to do with the advancement or progress of science. . . .

. . . The problem is that non-scientists, whether judges or jurors, often cannot distinguish between "good science" and "bad science". The expertise provided by the peer review process of experts in a field evaluating proposed theories and the procedures used to arrive at them is of great assistance in providing judges with a benchmark. . . .

It is *how* the conclusions are reached, not *what* the conclusions are, that makes them "good science" today. Conclusions, however divergent from conventional wisdom, that are arrived at by using sound scientific methods, should be considered both in the laboratory and in the courtroom. . . .

range of informed opinion. Any individual witness who holds views sharply at variance with statements like these should bear a heavy burden of explaining why the individual is right and the community, speaking through its committees, academies, or institutes, is wrong. Other expressions of general acceptance include the reports adopted by major medical societies that set forth diagnostic criteria for diseases, and the reports put out by the Association of Official Analytical Chemists describing analytical methods for chemicals with regulatory or health significance. Jasanoff has pointed out that such reports have been effective in reducing the impact in court of fringe groups, such as clinical ecologists.[21]

Peer review is one mechanism by which the scientific community detects and reduces errors, and publication in a peer-reviewed journal is an important step in gaining general acceptance of a theory within that community. Although it does not ensure the validity of a scientific finding, peer review usually weeds out flagrantly unscientific claims.

While *Daubert* triggered much discussion about peer review, the proffered testimony of Shanna Swan involved problems much more fundamental than a failure to publish. Swan could certainly have published a review of the Bendectin literature in a peer-reviewed journal; it would probably have been well received by scientists, insofar as it used scientifically standard methods and language to highlight the residual uncertainties about Bendectin. She also could have published an opinion piece in a scientific journal—perhaps even a peer-reviewed editorial—expressing her political view that Bendectin should not be marketed until its safety had been more fully investigated. The core problem with the testimony she

Box 9.4

Acceptance by the Scientific Community Is an Essential Guide to the Truth of Scientific Statements

Brief Amicus Curiae of the American College of Legal Medicine in Support of the Respondent Brief Amicus Curiae of the American College of Legal Medicine in Support of the Respondent, *Daubert v. Merrell Dow Pharmaceuticals, Inc.*, Dkt. No. 92-102 (U.S. Jan. 19, 1993) (citations omitted)

In considering whether the foundation of an expert's opinion is credible, scientists are concerned whether the opinion is properly supported. They invariably ask: (1) Whether a controlled study has been performed?; (2) Were the results of the study statistically significant?; and (3) Was the study published in a peer-reviewed journal?

1. Has a "controlled" study been performed? ... [T]he outcome must be compared to some standard in order to determine what effect, if any, may be attributed to the technique or substance under study. Without a basis of comparison, no serious conclusions may be drawn from the study. ...

Controls are important because, in every branch of science, precautions must be taken so that conclusions are not drawn on the basis of factors that are irrelevant to the study. ... In the evaluation of medications and therapeutic measures, the principal precaution taken is the use of a control group. ... What is essential is that the expert opinion be based on a comparison between those exposed and those not exposed to the substance or technique in question. Where a study is not controlled, there is no way of knowing to what to attribute the observations that result, and, hence, the scientific community will not seriously consider the findings of the study.

2. If the testimony is based upon a statistical study, were the results of the study statistically significant? ...

... While no particular threshold of statistical significance is implied by the Federal Rules of Evidence, a test of significance should be reported for all statistical studies upon which an expert relies as the basis of his or her testimony. Such tests of statistical significance should be made available to judges when they are determining the validity and reliability of the basis of an expert's testimony. If the results of a study are very likely due to chance, then such a study should not be considered valid and should not be admissible.

3. Was the study published in a peer-reviewed journal? Science does not generate exact knowledge with logical certainty. Instead, it relies on the give and take of criticism, testing, experimentation, and review to determine if it is valid. ... Acceptance is the fundamental test scientists use to decide validity of theories and reasoning in any given context. Because acceptance is predicated on a process of refinement and critical review, communication among scientists is a necessity; hence, the importance of publication and peer review cannot be disregarded. Publication and peer review serve as an evidentiary threshold of validity in science. If a theory is not accepted anywhere in the scientific literature, strong doubts about its validity inevitably arise among the scientific community. ...

> It is only through th[e] peer review process that courts can determine if
> an expert's opinion has a valid and reliable *basis*. . . . [N]o reputable scien-
> tist would credit a scientific result that had not gone through this peer review
> process. Publication in a peer-reviewed journal is thus a necessary element
> for scientific credibility.

proposed to offer in court was that it was naked opinion. The views framed
as scientific in her affidavit weren't. She substituted "might be a problem"
rhetoric for sober "is a problem" analysis.

The old *Frye* standard of "general acceptance" is, of course, much more
demanding than a requirement of peer review, though peer review may
help set new claims on the road to broad acceptance. And neither "peer
review" nor "general acceptance" is quite the same as "consensus"—a
word that does not appear once in *Daubert*. But when it exists, consensus
about an issue can be a powerful indication of reliable knowledge.
Scientists commonly emphasize the importance of mutual agreement in
establishing scientific reliability. In his 1993 book *Uncommon Sense*, Alan
Cromer writes: "The test of public consensus is severe. Private insights and
intuitions, no matter how strongly felt, won't do. Most of the traditional
knowledge that has guided and misguided humankind from its beginning
won't do." Truth in science is not "whatever the scientific consensus says
it is." The process, Cromer argues, works the other way around. The consensus of informed opinion does not form "unless there is something 'real'
out there." This consensus "is our only objective proof of that reality."[22]
(See box 9.5.)

Polanyi likewise emphasized the "consensual ground" of scientific judgment and the "tacit dimension of science" that allows scientists to reject
implausible scientific theories on the basis of a shared understanding of
the world.[23] But, as Polanyi notes, this tacit component depends on a common viewpoint among individuals who have similar educations and share
similar values. This emphatically does not preclude the review of an
expert's opinions by nonscientists. It does suggest that a nonscientist examining a scientist's opinion should carefully clarify the expert's terms of art
and scrutinize unstated assumptions in the expert's scientific argument.

"General acceptance," in contrast, is a legal concept not a scientific one.
"General acceptance" is certainly not established by the kind of peer

Box 9.5
Science and Nonsense
Alan H. Cromer

source: *Uncommon Sense: The Heretical Nature of Science* (Oxford University Press, 1993)

What distinguishes science from its imitators and rivals? . . . The British physicist John Ziman (1968) offered a very simple answer that works surprisingly well. Science is the search for a consensus of rational opinion among all competent researchers. . . .

Science, like democratic politics, is a social activity. . . .

With this understanding, then, we can also define science as the study of those things about which the scientific public can form a consensus. This isn't a circular definition, since the scientific public exists before the attempt to establish a new fact or principle. To be taken seriously as science, any new idea or assertion must, at the very least, be capable in principle of convincing the established scientific public. . . .   . . . Indeed, we can define objective reality as those matters about which the scientific public agrees. . . .

. . . I am *not* saying that truth in science is whatever the scientific consensus says it is. Rather, I am saying that, in general, there can't be a consensus of informed opinion unless there is something "real" out there and that this consensus is our only objective proof of that reality. . . .

Science doesn't ban egocentrism, intuition, or subjectivity. It can't because they are intrinsic parts of human nature. Science doesn't care how a scientist comes up with an idea: by hard work, in a dream, or from a fortune-teller. It does care, however, about the evidence the scientist uses to support the idea. It must be convincing to those who don't believe in Ouija boards, not just to those who do. . . .

In summary, then, scientific knowledge resides in the consensus of informed opinion. Reliable evidence and logical consistency are the two basic requirements for achieving such a consensus. These place a tight constraint on new knowledge, and scientists tend to be closed-minded about claims that aren't so constrained. This occasionally causes science to miss real knowledge for a time, as in the case of parity violation. But it helps guard against being swamped by a flood of nonexistent phenomena that result from the egocentric tendency toward self-deception. How wasteful this can be is shown by the case of cold fusion.

The fundamental conclusion of this book is that the social arrangement that is science is a new development in human history. It is, in fact, a sort of growing up, a putting aside of childish egocentrism and an acceptance of human responsibility in the face of human fallibility.

review that might accompany publication of a single article in a single journal. Science draws no bright line to separate "generally accepted" knowledge from the rest. Science simply supplies a process—the "knowledge filter" described by Bauer. The further knowledge successfully progresses through the filter of the scientific community, the more it may merit the shorthand (and strictly legal) label of "general acceptance." But the two concepts are different. The "knowledge filter" is a never-quite-final process within a community; "general acceptance" suggests a sort of Gallup poll taken at an instant in time. Any application of the shorthand "general acceptance" standard in court requires a clear understanding of who is doing the accepting and of how the presence (or absence) of acceptance is verified.

As David Hull remarks in his book *Science as a Process*, consensus among scientists supplies one operational definition of "truth" in science, but "it is only one operational definition of this emotionally charged term and it is only an operational definition."[24] Nonetheless, any expert who contradicts generally accepted scientific views or presents a novel scientific finding for the first time in the courtroom is most likely wrong. Judges are well justified in being skeptical of witnesses who choose a courtroom as an arena in which to present for the first time a new scientific principle or discovery. As we discussed in chapter 7, such skepticism is warranted in the case of any new scientific discovery, in whatever forum it is presented.

As we have emphasized throughout this book, there is no sharp line between valid and invalid science. In the end, the clearest guide to reliable scientific knowledge is whether it has been exposed to systematic scrutiny by the scientific community or, absent that, whether it has withstood examination by other critical observers—observers who have examined the work in the scientific arena as well as in the legal one. A statement of generally accepted views by a well-constituted panel is the most reliable opinion that exists about a given scientific matter.

Prejudicing, Confusing, or Misleading The Jury

In chapter 8 we turned to the distinct issues of jury prejudice and confusion. As we noted, even valid science may not be presented in ways likely to encourage valid inference by lay jurors. Rule 403 of the Federal Rules of Evidence requires exclusion of any evidence that presents too great a risk of "unfair prejudice, confusion of the issues, or misleading the jury." Judges routinely exclude photographs of an autopsy not because they somehow lack scientific or medical validity, but because they are more likely to provoke revulsion than rational thought.

Sophistic presentation of scientific data is a particular problem in court because science often relies on statistical reasoning, which is often counterintuitive or at least difficult to fathom for nonscientists. Moreover, a jury may incorrectly believe that an individual scientist speaks with the authority of science—that, in some sense, the individual represents a broad body of established scientific learning. A similar error is encouraged by pasting a doctor's picture on a bottle of medicine. The medicine may or may not work, but the picture of the doctor suggests not merely the individual endorsement of one physician but the approval of the medical community.

The issue here is legal, not scientific, except perhaps insofar as it implicates the science of psychology. A scientist comes to court with an impressive title. The title, and all it implies, often leads laypeople to put more faith in the scientist's claims and arguments than they merit, because science as a whole has high credibility and influence in society. The problem of prejudice, in other words, derives from the fact that the expert witness comes into court implicitly claiming (1) special status for scientists and scientific knowledge and (2) membership in the exclusive club that confers that status. In the minds of ordinary jurors, the special status of scientists derives from the perception that they have special education, special means of discovering scientific knowledge, and special procedures for checking one another's work. A juror may, thus, readily assume that an individual scientist represents a larger professional community. If the individual scientist presents views that have not been derived, shared, or checked by other scientists, there is a subtle but serious problem of misrepresentation. The question how best to protect against this points back, yet again, to the scientific community. Judges should make sure that the testimony of expert witnesses is grounded in theories or methods that have survived extensive testing in the scientific community. But gross misrepresentations are still possible if a witness makes unfounded or misleading claims about accuracy or precision. The basic methodology of "DNA fingerprinting," for example, is firmly accepted in the scientific community, but there is much considerable disagreement about how to collect DNA evidence, prevent contamination, and test the evidence properly in a laboratory.

"Scientific Knowledge"

The comparison of *Frye* and *Daubert* thus ends where it began: with the original, common-law standard of *Frye* and with the Federal Rules of Evidence that replaced it in 1975. *Frye* referred to "general acceptance" in a scientific community; the Federal Rules refer, more cryptically, to "scientific knowledge." For practical legal purposes, the two may not be so very different. The law is constructed out of language, and the key words in the Federal Rules are "scientific knowledge." The *Oxford English Dictionary* defines "science" as "the state or fact of knowing; knowledge or cognizance of something specified or implied" and as "knowledge acquired by study; acquaintance with or mastery of any department of learning." Most of the other alternative definitions offered in the *OED* also contain the word "knowledge." Thus, in strictly semantic terms, "scientific knowledge" means "knowledge of knowledge." This seems redundant, but it isn't. The *OED* also repeatedly refers to a science as a "department of learning" and a "recognized department of learning." On reflection, "knowledge of knowledge" implies much the same thing. It is not what the individual expert knows subjectively that matters. An expert scientific witness is admitted to testify about what *others* know—what the "department" (the scientific community) has learned collectively. Doctors, engineers, and other technical experts may of course be admitted to testify about much more specific diagnoses and analyses, and their views may be admissible under other clauses of Rule 702 of the Federal Rules of Evidence.[25] But a witness seeking admission to testify about "scientific knowledge" under Rule 702 must represent something more than purely technical findings. *Daubert* offers additional grounds on which scientific evidence may be excluded: when a theory underlying a claim is not framed in "falsifiable" terms, or when it is logically flawed. But even theories that meet these must be excluded if they are not sufficiently reliable; in practice, that means when they have never been submitted to, scrutinized, or tested by some larger scientific community. For judges applying Rule 702, "scientific knowledge" is reliable only if it is the knowledge of a community rather than an individual. This does not seem very different from what an appellate court wrote in *Frye* seven decades before *Daubert*.

"Reaching a quick, final, and binding legal judgment"

Whether the standard is labeled *Frye* or *Daubert*, it is clear that judges must decide whether to admit expert witnesses. Perhaps the greatest contribution of *Daubert* was to underscore this forcefully and to emphasize that judges must carefully scrutinize testimony proffered by scientific experts. Somehow, judges must draw lines between expert testimony that is "reliable enough" or "valid enough" and expert testimony that is "not reliable enough" or "not valid enough." The question is where the law should make these binary demarcations, given that reliability and validity in science are not yes-no propositions except in extreme cases of logical inconsistency or gross error. Fortunately, judges need only rule on the reliability or validity of specific testimony offered by a particular witness, not on that of the scientific claim.

Once one accepts that science is a collective enterprise with epistemic and cognitive goals that are quite different from those of the law, science can never be fairly represented or vindicated in a courtroom. Many scientists understand this intuitively, and therefore they make a point of steering clear of legal proceedings of any kind. In an important sense, there is no science in the courtroom. There are only scientists, with their opinions.

But neither *Frye* nor *Daubert* requires a judge to pass judgment on science itself. A judge only makes a strictly procedural call: whether or not to allow an individual scientist to speak up before a jury in court. Ruling on an individual's right to testify about particular data, opinions, and conclusions is quite different from "judging science." A judge who bars a witness from testifying is not passing any final judgment on the validity of the witness's views. The judge is simply ruling that those views are not sufficiently probative to be presented in court. Hearsay evidence is excluded for similar reasons—even though rumors and hearsay are quite often true.

Coerced confessions may quite often be true too, but not often enough to belong in court.

This difference between a scientist's mission and a judge's mission is fundamental to everything else discussed in this book. Science, by its very nature, is general and prospective, whereas a trial is particular and retrospective. Scientific knowledge, and its acceptance as such by scientists, both evolve with time. Everything is potentially mutable; nothing is ever absolutely final. At some deep level, science is the ultimate agnosticism. Law, in contrast, is judgmental; a court makes "findings of fact" with the solemnity and finality of an *ex cathedra* pronouncement. The purpose of a trial, as the Supreme Court pointed out in *Daubert*, is to resolve a dispute.

"Principles and methodology, not conclusions"

In the *Daubert* litigation, the plaintiffs' expert Shanna Swan had correctly pointed out that the epidemiological studies at hand did not eliminate the possibility that Bendectin still presented some risk that was below the statistical horizon.[26] Swan followed with a second doubly negative statement, to the effect that an epidemiologist would not rely only on epidemiology to "suggest" that Bendectin did not cause birth defects. The statement that followed this one, however, was the most revealing. In such a context, Swan opined, "the prudent epidemiologist would be concerned about the public safety and when there is data consistent with increased risks, as with Bendectin, conclude that it is more probable than not that Bendectin is associated with birth defects."[27]

Read carefully, Swan's extraordinary statement repudiates the very objectivity of scientific knowledge. Swan expressly declares that the personal sentiments of the expert shape the scientific conclusion. Her view implies that a prudent and concerned scientist would attach one degree of probability to the likelihood that Bendectin causes birth defects, an imprudent and indifferent scientist a different probability, and a reckless sociopathic scientist yet another probability.

Suppose that precisely the same body of evidence—including epidemiological evidence—had been collected exclusively from studies of rats exposed to a product (call it "Bendratin") not used by humans at all. Scientists, prudent or otherwise, would then have no cause to be "concerned about the public safety." According to Swan, the same body of scientific evidence would be interpreted differently in that social context. One supposes that if the product were intended to poison rats or their offspring, the "prudent" scientist "concerned about the public safety" (rats spread plague) might again conclude . . . what exactly? That Bendratin probably was effective at controlling pests, and therefore should be approved as effective by public health officials concerned about pest control? Or that Bendratin was not effective (the evidence of its effects being very weak) and that the public health officials should discourage its use in favor of some other product?

Or suppose that an exactly equivalent body of data, with the same degrees of uncertainty and imprecision, suggested that Bendectin marginally reduced the incidence of limb defects in humans. Swan's logic would then require that precisely the same body of scientific evidence somehow be interpreted differently because of the possibly important positive impacts on "the public safety." By this logic, the FDA should be especially quick to accept unreliable and statistically insignificant scientific data whenever there is some hint of public benefit, because in those circumstances the failure to approve the new, speculative therapy might deprive some mother and child of the chance to avoid a limb defect.

The "Bendratin" example is extreme but telling. It illustrates that how society regards scientific uncertainty depends greatly on the context. A doctor considering whether to use a test that has no convincing statistical evidence to support its use (e.g., a mammogram for an asymptomatic woman below the age of 40), a regulatory agency considering a drug that has not been conclusively proved to be effective (e.g., a novel AIDS drug), and a jury considering a claim for compensation for damage that has not been proved to occur all weigh scientific uncertainty differently. None of this, however, has anything to do with science, or epidemiology. It pertains to how scientific knowledge is used. That decision that is not a proper subject of expert testimony, at least in court.

In the Bendectin context, Swan is arguing that uncertain data should be interpreted in the most pessimistic way: that effects that are possible (i.e., may be hidden in the noise in the data) actually do exist. From the viewpoint of public safety that is a defensible position; regulatory agencies sometimes use "just in case" arguments in an attempt to protect the public against suspected but unproved hazards. But it is inappropriate in a tort case where the issue is not public safety but whether or not one private party has harmed another. It is exactly this kind of value-laden judgment masquerading as objective science that Jasanoff warns against.

In sum: Swan's statement is political, not scientific. She could quite reasonably have declared that a "prudent Commissioner of the FDA" is properly "concerned about the public safety" and should therefore ban Bendectin because it threatens some real harm, or, alternatively, approve it hastily because of possible benefits.[28] Such a statement would have been entirely admissible and proper in a policy debate or on a television talk show.

Swan's "scientific" opinions, in short, are directly shaped by the conclusions they generate. Her science works differently depending on whether the conclusions implicate rats or humans. For Dr. Swan, the science of "bad" effects is subtly but significantly different from the science of "good" ones. In the baldest possible terms: Swan's science varies depending on whether it favors plaintiffs or defendants in cases that pit users of drugs against manufacturers. This is politics, policy, activism, and perhaps even responsible public citizenship. But it is not "scientific knowledge" within the meaning of Rule 702. For that reason, it should not be admitted as expert testimony in court. Such a statement does not bear on the question as to which experts have special expertise. It is not about or derived from scientific knowledge. It is therefore wholly inadmissible as expert testimony. On this point, at least, the *Daubert* opinion is explicit and unambiguous. In determining whether proffered evidence constitutes scientific knowledge, the Supreme Court declared, the "overarching subject is the scientific validity—and thus the evidentiary relevance and reliability—of the principles that underlie a proposed submission," and "[t]he focus, of course, must be solely on principles and methodology, not on the conclusions that they generate."[29]

The Judgment in *Daubert*

The last word on the *Daubert* case was not written by the Supreme Court; it was written by the Ninth Circuit Court of Appeals, on remand. The *Daubert* plaintiffs relied on the testimony of three groups of scientific experts. One claimed there is a statistical link between the ingestion of Bendectin during pregnancy and limb-reduction defects. He based that conclusion on a reanalysis of studies published by other scientists, none of whom reported a statistically significant association between Bendectin and birth defects. Another claimed that Bendectin causes limb-reduction defects in laboratory animals. A third claimed that Bendectin has a chemical structure similar to those of other drugs suspected of causing birth defects. The defendants, in response, put forward an extensive body of published studies, and the conclusion of the FDA, all supporting the conclusion that "available data do not demonstrate an association between birth defects and Bendectin."

The Ninth Circuit noted that Bendectin litigation had been pending in the courts for more than 10 years, "yet the only review the plaintiffs' experts' work has received has been by judges and juries, and the only place their theories and studies have been published is in the pages of federal and state reporters. . . . Despite the many years the controversy has been brewing, no one in the scientific community—except defendant's experts—has deemed these studies worthy of verification, refutation or even comment. It's as if there were a tacit understanding within the scientific community that what's going on here is not science at all, but litigation."[30] At the very least, the appellate court concluded (citing *Daubert*), this persistent failure to publish seriously undermined the plaintiffs' claim "that the findings these experts proffer are 'ground[ed] in the methods and procedures of science' and 'derived by the scientific method.'"[31] The plaintiffs relied "entirely on the experts' unadorned assertions that the methodology they employed comports with standard scientific procedures"—but "under *Daubert*, that's not enough."[32] One witness offered "no tested or testable theory to explain how, from this limited information, he was able to eliminate all other potential causes of birth defects, nor [did] he explain how he alone [could] state as a fact that Bendectin caused plaintiffs' injuries."[33] He did not testify "'on the basis of the collective view of his scientific discipline, nor [did] he take issue with his peers and explain the grounds for his differences. Indeed, no understandable scientific basis is stated. Personal opinion, not science, is testifying here.'"[34] (Here the appellate court was citing another appellate court that had rejected the same witness's testimony.)

The rest of the expert testimony offered by the *Daubert* plaintiffs suffered from similar defects. Moreover, the plaintiffs' experts had not come close to showing that the injuries in question were caused by Bendectin rather than some other, independent factor, known or unknown.

Tort plaintiffs must not merely prove that an agent increased the likelihood of injury, they must establish that it probably caused their injury. In *Daubert* the plaintiffs' experts failed even to allege that the injuries in question were "more likely than not" caused by Bendectin rather than some other, independent factor, known or unknown. With purely statistical evidence, this means proving that Bendectin more than doubled the risk of the injury. But none of the plaintiffs' epidemiologist experts were willing to make so specific a claim. They were willing to testify only that Bendectin is "capable of causing" birth defects. As the district court had previously found, "the strongest inference to be drawn for plaintiffs based on the epidemiological evidence is that Bendectin could *possibly* have caused plaintiffs' injuries. . . ."[35] Whether or not these claims were true, they were not good enough to be admitted in court. The appellate court had no need to pass on the overall weight of the evidence offered by the plaintiffs, and did not do so. Swan's testimony was nonfalsifiable; Done's was simply wrong. These deficiencies would have been regrettable had they surfaced in only one lawsuit. But these and similar ones appeared again and again, in hundreds of Bendectin suits filed across the country. More recently, many tort suits have been filed over supposed injuries from silicone breast implants, based (it appears) on similarly specious scientific evidence. (See box 9.6.)

The *Daubert* plaintiffs asked the Supreme Court to review the case a second time. On October 2, 1995, the Supreme Court declined.[36]

Box 9.6
A Physician's Perspective
Marcia Angell, M.D.
source: Evaluating the health risks of breast implants: The interplay of medical science, the law, and public opinion (Shattuck Lecture), *New England Journal of Medicine* 334 (1996): 1513–1518 (citations omitted)

In my view, the most important implication of the breast-implant story is its reflection of what appears to be a widespread distrust and misunderstanding of science in American society. In the long run, this feeling will cause more damage than any other aspect of the controversy. Several jurors who participated in implant decisions, as well as the head of a powerful advocacy group, have publicly said that the results of scientific studies did not matter to them. In their view, medical research was irrelevant. All that mattered was what they believed, never mind why they believed it. Yet readers of the [*New England Journal of Medicine*] know that medicine is replete with instances of convictions being proved wrong by rigorous research. Only a commitment to evidence can test the hopes and fears and biases that otherwise would have full sway. Science is not perfect, but it is the best method we have to answer questions about the material world and to evaluate the myriad alleged health risks that continually capture public attention.

The breast-implant controversy is not the only example of the problem. Over the past 20 years, the public's attention has been caught in rapid succession by asbestos, diethylstilbestrol (DES), Bendectin, the Dalkon shield, Agent Orange, Alar-treated apples, radon, and electromagnetic fields, among other real or alleged health hazards. Each engendered a mix of fear, recriminations, and denials. There were also mass lawsuits, Congressional hearings, and demands for tighter government regulation. The scientific evidence was highly variable. Sometimes, as in the case of the connection between DES and vaginal cancer, it was solid. But in other cases, such as the alleged link between Bendectin and birth defects, the evidence was strongly against a connection. And in others, such as those of asbestos and radon, the risk was real but greatly exaggerated. The strength of the evidence seemed irrelevant to the public debate. Risks for which there was little evidence were taken as seriously as those for which there was good evidence, and small risks received as much attention as large ones.

Many people have become alienated from science and scientific habits of thought—at a time when we need science more than ever to help us find our way through an increasing number of serious and complicated questions involving risks to health and safety. To reverse the alienation we need a better public understanding of science, beginning with more and better science education in schools at all levels. That requires more than a field trip, a bug collection, and a computer. It also means attention to scientific thinking, including an understanding of the nature of evidence, the concepts of chance and error, and the value of skepticism. . . . Courts compound the problem by largely ignoring the rules of science and handing down verdicts that fly in the face of evidence. Given these conditions, it is no wonder that the public finds the scientific approach so foreign. And yet, without a better understanding of science, we stand to live out Carl Sagan's darkest vision: "It's a foreboding I have—maybe ill-placed—of an America in my children's generation, or my grandchildren's generation . . . when, clutching our horoscopes, our critical faculties in steep decline, unable to distinguish between what's true and what feels good, we slide, almost without noticing, into superstition and darkness."

Appendix A
Bendectin in the Press: The Misreporting of Law and Science

Peter Huber

In a one-line order issued on October 2, 1995, the Supreme Court wrote the final word in a seminal case, *Daubert v. Merrell Dow Pharmaceuticals*.[1] The litigation pitted Jason Daubert and his family against a major pharmaceutical company. A second plaintiff in the same case was Eric Schuller. The plaintiffs claimed that their birth defects had been caused by their mothers' prenatal ingestion of Bendectin, a drug once widely used by pregnant women to control morning sickness.

The Supreme Court's October 2 order came as no surprise to knowledgeable legal observers. What was surprising was that it received absolutely no coverage at all in the press. It should have. Partly because it finally resolved, unambiguously, just who "won" the landmark *Daubert* litigation. And partly because the final ruling reveals just how badly reporters sometimes misunderstand and misreport scientific controversies that fall into the hands of lawyers.

The main Supreme Court decision in *Daubert* was released on June 28, 1993.[2] The Supreme Court agreed to review the case to interpret the meaning of the Federal Rules of Evidence that govern the admission of expert testimony into federal courts.

The Supreme Court might simply, with little elaboration, have affirmed the 1991 ruling of the appellate court, which had affirmed the 1989 ruling of a trial court, which had thrown out the plaintiff's "expert" scientific testimony and ruled summarily in favor of Merrell Dow. But few serious observers expected *that* to happen. The Supreme Court had never before had occasion to interpret the critical words ("scientific knowledge") in the 1975 Federal Rules. Most observers familiar with Supreme Court practice expected it to write an opinion and then "vacate and remand" the case back to the lower courts. They would then take another look, in light of what was to be the Supreme Court's first-ever interpretation of the applicable words in the 1975 Rules.

That is what happened in 1993. The Supreme Court wrote a detailed opinion and sent the case back down.

The Supreme Court Decides

With the Supreme Court's work finished, the work of the legal reporters began. They now had to explain to the general public how the Court had ruled. Readers would inevitably expect an answer to the central question: Who won? Unfortunately for reporters, no one yet knew for sure.

In a narrow, technical sense, the *Daubert* plaintiffs had "won"—not because of *how* the Supreme Court ruled, but simply because the Supreme Court had written an opinion that directed the lower courts to take another look in light of that new decision. The case was indeed headed back down for further proceedings, in which the plaintiffs might yet prevail. But "remands" are very common in cases of this sort. In themselves, they establish no clear winner.

The important and much harder question was how the *Daubert* case was going to unfold on remand. Reporters had no choice but to read the opinion and understand its likely impact on federal appellate and trial judges. They had to predict its overall impact in *Daubert* itself and in other cases of similar character.

In effect, then, the Supreme Court had handed legal reporters an open-book test: Examine the evidence (in this case, a legal opinion), then tell the public what it really means. Will the expert witnesses assembled by Jason Daubert's lawyers ultimately be allowed to testify at a trial, or won't they? The tough part for the reporters was that their analysis was going to be graded, in effect, by federal judges. Sooner or later, anybody who bothered to follow these things could find out whether their favorite legal reporter had got it right, or mostly right, or miserably wrong.

Here was what the reporters had in hand as they filed their stories on June 28, 1993: Seven members of the Court had signed onto Justice Blackmun's majority opinion. Most of the majority opinion consisted of an intricate essay on the meaning of the words "scientific knowledge." It began with Karl Popper, Carl Hempel, and the philosophical meaning of "falsifiability." The opinion, which ran to 10 printed pages of dense prose, cited 37 *amicus* briefs and other secondary sources. In dissent, Chief Justice Rehnquist complained: "I defer to no one in my confidence in federal judges; but I am at a loss to know what is meant when it is said that the scientific status of a theory depends on its 'falsifiability,' and I suspect some of them will be, too." In the two concluding sentences of his dissent, the Chief Justice added: "I do not doubt that [the relevant Federal Rule of Evidence] confides to the judge some gatekeeping responsibility in deciding questions of the admissibility of proffered expert testimony. But I do not think it imposes on them either the obligation or the authority to become amateur scientists in order to perform that role."

Justice Blackmun had answered the Chief Justice in footnote 7 of his majority opinion: "The Chief Justice 'does not doubt that [the Federal Rule] confides to the judge some gatekeeping responsibility,' . . . but would neither say how it does so, nor explain what that role entails. We believe the better course is to note the nature and source of the duty." Six other Justices had agreed. Justice Blackmun's majority opinion had discussed, in some length and detail, just how federal judges were supposed to handle expert scientific testimony.

One might have expected reporters describing the *Daubert* majority opinion in 1993 to echo the Chief Justice's compact summary of it in his dissent. The majority opinion was not an easy read; the dissent's summary of it was. The Chief Justice surely had a pretty good idea of what seven of his colleagues really meant. He, after all, had sat in the conference chamber with them, where they had all chatted candidly about the case and their views. And, as the Chief Justice read it, the main thrust of the majority opinion was that it directed federal judges to become "amateur scientists" and perform "gatekeeping responsibilities" in screening scientific testimony.

Daubert in the Press

Among the mainstream commentators, Linda Greenhouse of the *New York Times* performed the best. Her story of June 29, 1993, was headlined "Justices put judges in charge of deciding reliability of scientific testimony."[3] Greenhouse described the *Daubert* majority opinion in almost exactly the same words the Chief Justice had used.[4] The Supreme Court's ruling was "likely in the long run to prove much more favorable to defendants than to plaintiffs."[5] In a separate account for the *Times* a few days later, Natalie Angier got it right too.[6] Joan Van's July 6 story in the *Chicago Tribune* earned a high grade as well.[7]

But readers who read the *Washington Post*'s report on *Daubert* must have wondered if the *Post* and the *Times* were reporting on the same case. Joan Biskupic's *Post* story, headlined "Judges get broader discretion in allowing scientific testimony," noted that the Supreme Court had "relaxed the standards."[8] Indeed, according to Ms. Biskupic, the ruling had been "unanimous" on the key issue, on which all nine Justices had sided with the plaintiffs. According to Ms. Biskupic, Merrell Dow's lawyers had tried to persuade the Supreme Court that looser standards "could result in a 'free-for-all' in which befuddled juries are confounded by absurd and irrational pseudoscientific assertions."[9] But Merrell Dow had lost. Paul Barrett of the *Wall Street Journal* reported the story much the same way. In a story headlined "Justices rule against business in evidence case,"[10] Barrett called the *Daubert* ruling "a defeat for business and the medical profession."[11] A reporter for the *Union-Tribune*—from San Diego, the home town of the Daubert family—performed even worse. "A trial is now expected for [Jason Daubert]," she wrote.[12]

But in the end there was no trial.[13] Judge Kozinski wrote the appellate court's opinion, which was released on January 4, 1995.[14] Applying the Supreme Court's *Daubert* opinion to the facts at hand, he again rejected all the "expert" testimony offered by the plaintiffs.

This was too late for many legal reporters, each of whom had filed his or her one *Daubert* story two years earlier. Many of them had declared victory for the plaintiffs. Most did not even report on the appellate court's remand decision of January 4, 1995, or on the Supreme Court's refusal on October 2, 1995, to review the case a second time.

Perhaps they didn't think the story important enough to revisit in 1995. But the *Daubert* ruling and in its aftermath have in fact had enormous legal consequences. We have here the legal equivalent of the "Dewey defeats Truman" headline—except that more than one paper ran it, and many of those that did failed to report the final outcome.

Daubert in the Federal Courts

Virtually every knowledgeable observer now agrees that the overall practical effect of the Supreme Court's *Daubert* opinion was to tighten the standards for "scientific" evidence offered in federal courts. A 1994 study by
David Bernstein, conducted almost a year before Judge Kozinski's remand
opinion was released, provided the first, comprehensive analysis of how
Daubert was playing out in the federal courts.[15] District judges, Bernstein
observed, were taking their new screening role very seriously: ". . . the
Bendectin plaintiffs' attorneys who declared victory after the *Daubert* battle were in error. . . . It is now clear beyond cavil that the most significant
command of *Daubert* is the trial judge's obligation to assume his gatekeeper's role when dealing with challenged scientific evidence."[16]

Bernstein first surveyed how judges were dealing with the evidence in
other Bendectin cases. The post-*Daubert* cases involved a wide range of
speculative scientific claims, including allegations linking ibuprofen to kidney disease, over-the-counter asthma medication to birth defects, and pes-
ticides to "multiple chemical sensitivities." Courts had rejected the
plaintiff's evidence in nine of the eleven major post-*Daubert* rulings available at the time of Bernstein's study. *Daubert* was not only being applied
strictly, it was being applied in an unexpectedly broad variety of cases.
Expert testimony had been rejected under the *Daubert* standard in two accident liability cases.[17] (See table A.1.) *Daubert* had been applied to expert
testimony on economics and statistics,[18] and to other forms of "technical"
(as opposed to "scientific") evidence.[19] Testimony based on psychological
theories had also been broadly excluded in the post-*Daubert* courts.

Bernstein concluded: "*Daubert* is causing judges to systematically and
carefully weigh the quality of expert scientific evidence proffered before
them." In toxic tort cases, "where evidence of causation tends to be most
speculative and unreliable, the courts have overwhelmingly rejected proffered evidence of causation challenged under *Daubert*." On the whole,
"*Daubert* has caused closer scrutiny of expert testimony than mere affir-
mance of the *Frye* rule [the pre-*Daubert* standard] would have permitted."
"It is clear that *Daubert* has ushered in a new era of judicial scrutiny of
scientific testimony and, more broadly of expert evidence in general." "The
parties who sought meaningful standards and proofs before expert testimony could be offered in evidence have carried the day."[20]

Table A.1
Source: David E. Bernstein, Daubert One Year Later (unpublished manuscript, 1994)

Bendectin cases	Exclusion: 1	Admission: 0
	Insufficient: 1	Sufficient: 0
Causation evidence in toxic	Exclusion: 6	Admission: 1
tort cases (including Bendectin)	Insufficient: 5	Sufficient: 1
"Traditional" tort cases	Exclusion: 2	Admission: 6
Pollution cases	Exclusion: 1	Admission: 1
Other civil cases	Exclusion: 2	Admission: 2
DNA identification	Exclusion: 0	Admission: 4
Polygraph	Exclusion: 2	Admission: 0
Other criminal forensic techniques	Exclusion: 1	Admission: 4
Psychological/psychiatric evidence	Exclusion: 3	Admission: 1

Daubert Back in the Press

None of the reporters who got *Daubert* badly wrong on the first round has ever expressly retracted his or her original story. However, the press did eventually catch up with legal reality.

The *Wall Street Journal*'s news pages had declared the plaintiffs the winners in 1993. But on January 19, 1995, after Judge Kozinski handed down his remand opinion, the *Journal*'s editorial page told precisely the opposite story. An editorial titled "Junk science is junked" characterized the Supreme Court's 1993 opinion as "a giant step toward returning sanity to our out-of-control tort liability system." The Supreme Court had, according to this editorial, "ruled that when it comes to scientific evidence, judges have a duty to distinguish between good science and bad science," and "the courts, it said, must act as 'gatekeepers' and exclude evidence that is not scientifically reliable. . . . Now the Ninth Circuit has done just that. . . ."

Most reporters for other papers now describe *Daubert* in similar terms, as a Supreme Court opinion that tightened the standards of scientific evidence greatly. After Judge Kozinski's remand, the *Chicago Tribune* ran a story in which Joan Beck noted that "by strengthening the hand of judges to throw out 'scientific' evidence that doesn't meet widely accepted scientific standards and to keep 'experts' with dubious scientific credentials from testifying, this case has accomplished something."[21] Marcia Barinaga's report in the January 13, 1995, issue of *Science* noted that "the *Daubert* case is one of some 200 in which the 1993 decision has been applied, and legal experts say the ruling has generally led courts to be more skeptical of unconventional scientific evidence."[22] Barinaga reported that the overall effect of *Daubert*, according to commentators not aligned with either party involved, was that "the Supreme Court's ruling has tightened standards for admitting evidence."

In the August 15 issue of *Business Week*, Linda Himelstein reported that the disposition of *Daubert* by the appellate court on remand "illustrates the tough new scrutiny science is under in the courtroom."[23] The plaintiffs' lawyers, who had loudly proclaimed victory in 1993, now "question whether jurists should play such pivotal roles in issues they don't fundamentally understand." But judges "are questioning the soundness of science in a growing number of cases. . . . They are also giving the boot to cases before trial when they find expert testimony inadequate."[24] Until *Daubert*, judges had generally refrained from excluding expert witnesses. The Supreme Court's *Daubert* opinion had put in place stricter standards, mandatory only in federal courts but also very influential in state courts.

Since *Daubert*, Himelstein reported, evidence had been "barred in nearly two dozen cases alleging everything from ibuprofen causing kidney disease to Retin-A leading to birth defects."[25] "Cellular-phone companies and utilities have flattened cases alleging that radiation from their products causes cancer. Computer keyboard makers have won rulings in cases alleging links to repetitive-stress injuries. . . . In one suit against Whitehall Laboratories Inc., the maker of Primatene asthma medication, all five of the plaintiff's experts were disqualified."[26] In a 1995 Louisiana case against Volkswagen, a $2 million verdict was set aside after an appellate court labeled expert testimony unreliable. The Texas Supreme Court had dismissed a case against DuPont involving the fungicide Benlate. A federal judge had barred testimony linking use of Unisys keyboards with carpal tunnel syndrome, calling the methodology unreliable. Another federal judge had thrown out a case against NEC in which the plaintiff alleged that cellular phone use caused his wife's brain tumor, declaring an expert's testimony inconclusive.

If the impact of *Daubert* is so clear today, to judges and reporters alike, how did so many reporters manage to misread the 1993 opinion so badly? One explanation is that many reporters clearly didn't understand how Supreme Court opinions on technical rules of evidence or procedure actually work. They understood that in 1991 the appellate court had ruled for Merrell, and that the words "vacated and remanded" appeared at the end of the Supreme Court's 1993 opinion. If the defendant's 1991 victory had been "vacated," that must surely mean that the plaintiffs now had won.

But it seems equally clear that many reporters were sympathetic to plaintiffs' claims, instinctively hostile to corporate defendants, and pleased to report the story line fed to them by the plaintiffs' lawyers when the *Daubert* ruling was announced. Barry J. Nace, then president-elect of the Association of Trial Lawyers of America, had praised the decision because "'it allows the jury to hear all relevant views, thus helping to ensure that injury victims . . . will get their day in court.'"[27] Kenneth Chesebro, one of the lawyers for the Daubert family, had called the ruling "a clear victory for consumers."[28]

What Nace and Chesebro knew, but weren't saying, was what so many legal reporters completely missed. The Supreme Court had *not* "reversed." A *reversal* would indeed have been a victory for the plaintiffs. But the Supreme Court had simply "vacated"—a quite different legal matter. The "vacating" of the appellate court's 1991 opinion was utterly routine. Once nine Justices of the Supreme Court have delivered a detailed, new opinion on a technical legal subject, prior views expressed in the same case by three judges on an appellate court aren't "law" any more—except in the rather rare case where the Supreme Court agrees not only with the appellate court's conclusion but with all its logic too. The Supreme Court had *not* rejected the appellate court's ruling. It had simply articulated a new logic.

Daubert ultimately means what federal judges say it means. The final legal reality is unambiguous. Either expert testimony is admitted into court or it isn't. Parties either win or lose. The *Daubert* plaintiffs, and many others like them, lost. Reporters writing about scientific evidence today now see that plainly enough.

Creating the Bendectin Crisis

And yet newspaper readers are still waiting for one final and even more important correction of the Bendectin story in the popular press. The mis-reporting of Bendectin didn't begin in 1993 with the Supreme Court's *Daubert* opinion. It is, in fact, only a modest exaggeration to say that the Supreme Court had to take a Bendectin case because many reporters had so badly misreported the science of Bendectin a decade earlier. The press had manufactured a real legal crisis out of a phantom medical one. It required a trip to the Supreme Court to clean up the ensuing mess.

Much of the early manufacturing was done by the *Washington Post*'s Morton Mintz. His February 11, 1980, story strongly implied that Bendectin was dangerous and Merrell knew it.[29] Almost line by line, Mintz paraphrased the legal claims that the plaintiffs' lawyers were just begin-ning to press in court. "One charge is that Merrell did no premarketing animal or clinical tests of safety for the unborn," Mintz wrote, "even though women in the sensitive first trimester of pregnancy were the sole sales target." Merrell had been accused of withholding "troubling animal test data from the Food and Drug Administration and of concealing reports on human birth deformities from inquiring physicians.[30] Merrell had failed to inform physicians "that adequate safety testing wasn't done." Bendectin was associated with limb-reduction birth defects at a rate "great-ly exceeding that for any other drug." Bendectin was perhaps causing "approximately five malformations per thousand women."

Mintz and the *Post* followed with another major Bendectin story on August 23, 1980. Three new unpublished studies indicated a link with birth defects, Mintz reported, and "world-renowned experts were split" on whether Bendectin caused birth defects.[31] One study indicated that Bendec-tin more than doubled the overall risk of birth defects, and more than tripled it among mothers who had had more than one Bendectin prescription.

A third Mintz story ran on June 25, 1982, this time on the *Post*'s front page. The FDA was going to require a new warning, because studies "raise questions about possible birth defects." A "recent lab study" had "indi-cated a possible link between Bendectin and a life-threatening hole in the diaphragm called diaphragmatic hernia. FDA statistics indicate the defect occurs in about 40 of each 10,000 babies exposed to the drug in the first three months of pregnancy." "A second preliminary study . . . disclosed a possible link between Bendectin and a hole in the wall of the heart called ventricular septal defect."[32] "Striking" though still "inconclusive" findings suggested that infants of Bendectin users experienced diaphragm hernias almost 8 times as often as babies of non-users. Yet another analysis found a 64 percent increase. Merrell's study of 4,000 pregnancies, which had found "no correlation between Bendectin and fetal abnormalities," was now found to have "gaps in the back-up data." It had "practically no value," and it "actually could be misleading."[33]

The *Post* ran its third major Bendectin story by Mintz on December 16, 1982. A new federally funded study, according to Mintz, indicated that Bendectin quadrupled the risk of a birth defect of the stomach. Bendectin was "strongly associated" with this disorder (pyloric stenosis). Bendectin also had "a possible association . . .with a three-fold increase in the risk of defective heart valves."[34]

The Associated Press ran a similar sequence of stories, and a small but influential cluster of other reporters took the same tack. With few exceptions, their stories were all carefully crafted. No reporter purported to make any definite scientific calls. They were all just reporting the remarks of a scientist, or an FDA bureaucrat, or a plaintiff's lawyer. In retrospect, one cannot point to a single sentence in these stories that is baldly wrong. Yet, taken as a whole, the stories were as false and misleading as journalism can be. Their strongly implied message was that the evidence against Bendectin was converging. Bendectin was dangerous. Merrell, its manufacturer, had prevaricated on, concealed, or simply ignored the underlying problems. Journalists and lawyers were simply ahead of the scientists.

This journalism had its inevitable effect. Tens of millions of women had used Bendectin. Birth defects are tragically common. In larger numbers, Bendectin mothers who had borne children with birth defects read the stories, responded to the lawyers' advertisements, and lined up to sue. The decade-long march to the Supreme Court had begun.

A Scientific Consensus Emerges

But it was a march toward a scientific mirage. The hazards of Bendectin existed in the press, most vividly in the pages of the *Washington Post*. They existed nowhere else. In 1995 Robert Brent published a review of the scientific literature on Bendectin in the journal *Reproductive Toxicology*. The somewhat ponderous title of the analysis summarizes its main conclusion: "Bendectin: Review of the medical literature of a comprehensively studied human nonteratogen and the most prevalent tortogen-litigen." A teratogen is a substance that causes birth defects; a "tortogen-litogen" is a substance that causes lawsuits.

Brent concludes that his very intensive study of a large volume of Bendectin data, including epidemiology, animal studies, and an analysis of "biologic plausibility," "clearly indicates that the therapeutic use of Bendectin has no measurable human teratogenic potential."[35] Quoting another scientist, Brent concludes: "The hysteria manifested in litigation associating [Bendectin] with birth defects before its removal from the market are a sad commentary [*sic*], given the available knowledge we have concerning its teratogenic potential. All evidence to date indicates a notable absence of malformation induction."[36] Brent also quotes from a report presented to the British Parliament: ". . . to suggest that the Health Minister of this country should act in response to scare mongering or the verdict of a lay jury in the United States rather than of the advice of expert committees, is to align oneself with a movement that is at heart antiscience, antiprogress, antimedicine and anti- the welfare of the people of this country."[37]

The most telling summary of the evidence in Brent's piece appears in a graph (figure A.1) showing the incidence of limb-reduction defects (the alleged injury in *Daubert*) and the fraction of pregnant women who took Bendectin.

Until the early 1980s, Bendectin had been prescribed in 10–30 percent of pregnancies. If Bendectin doubled the risk of limb-reduction defects, it would have accounted for 10–30 percent of all the reported cases during that period. Bad press and a concomitant deluge of litigation drove Bendectin from the market. American women haven't used Bendectin for a decade. If one assumes a doubling of risk, that should have led to a small but detectable decrease in the number of reported cases, to about 25 or 30 cases per 100,000 live births. But the incidence of the birth defects that Bendectin was alleged to cause has not changed at all. If anything, the trend has been in the opposite direction.

Who are the "experts" who were retained by the Bendectin plaintiffs and so widely cited by Morton Mintz and other reporters ? According to Brent, they are fringe players who have "failed to meet the scientific

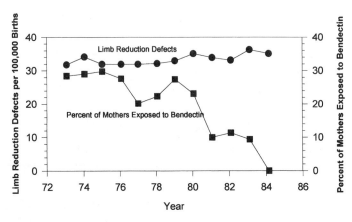

Figure A.1
Limb-reduction defects per 100,000 births (circles) and percentage of US mothers exposed to Bendectin (squares). Adapted, with permission, from Robert J. Brent, Bendectin: Review of the medical literature of a comprehensively studied human nonteratogen and the most prevalent tortogen-litigen, *Reproductive Toxicology* 9 (1995): 337–350.

standards that should be expected of scientists knowledgeable in the fields of teratology, embryology, genetics and epidemiology."[38] None of them has published a single scientific review of Bendectin. "There are many factors that contribute to the pursuit of nonmeritous litigation," states Brent. "The experts for the plaintiff have had a major role in this process by presenting to the courts partisan presentations rather than an objective scientific analysis."[39] "Bendectin litigation could not have proceeded without the participation of scientists who failed in their role as objective experts during the Bendectin litigation."[40]

After a decade of indecision, and a trip all the way to the Supreme Court, federal judges have at last converged on the same conclusion. The reporters who did so much to fan the unscientific flames of the Bendectin crisis in the early 1980s have reported almost nothing about the scientists who finally extinguished the conflagration.

Notes to Appendix A

1. *William Daubert, et al. v. Merrell Dow Pharmaceuticals*, 64 U.S.L.W. 3245 (U.S. Oct. 2, 1995).

2. *William Daubert, et al. v. Merrell Dow Pharmaceuticals*, 113 S. Ct. 2786 (1993).

3. Linda Greenhouse, Justices put judges in charge of deciding reliability of scientific testimony, *New York Times*, June 29, 1993.

4. *Daubert* required federal judges to serve as "active gatekeepers charged with insuring that 'any and all scientific testimony or evidence admitted is not only relevant, but reliable.'" Judges, Greenhouse reported, had been invited "to be aggressive in screening out ill-founded or speculative scientific theories" (ibid.).

5. Ibid. A month later Greenhouse wrote: "In its first ruling on the place of scientific evidence in Federal courtrooms, the Court placed judges firmly in charge of keeping bad science out and letting good science in. The 7-to-2 decision in *Daubert v. Merrell Dow*, No. 92-102, held that while an expert witness's actual conclusions need not be 'generally accepted' in the scientific community, the 'methods and procedures' used in reaching those results must be valid. The judge should limit the jury's consideration to testimony or evidence that is 'not only relevant, but reliable,' Justice Blackmun said for the Court." (Linda Greenhouse, The Court's counterrevolution comes in fits and starts, *New York Times*, July 4, 1993.

6. ". . . The United States Supreme Court has assured that a great many judges will be frantically playing catch-up on the basics of scientific method. . . . The Court rejected the most rigid arguments from the defendant that scientific testimony could be dismissed just because it had not been previously published in scientific journals or was not widely accepted by mainstream scientists. But the Justices insisted that this somewhat liberal allowance did not mean that the courts should serve as circuses for any crackpot scientific theory a self-described expert witness might care to offer. The Court said that Federal judges must assume strong responsibility for the quality of the scientific evidence presented in their courts. . . ." (Natalie Angier, Ruling on scientific evidence: A just burden, *New York Times*, June 30, 1993)

7. "In a complex ruling last week, the U.S. Supreme Court clarified the rules of jurisprudence by charging lower-court judges to become 'gatekeepers' who weed out witnesses whose work and ideas are clearly outside orthodox science." (Joan Van, Ruling on 'junk science' may affect jury awards, *Chicago Tribune*, July 6, 1993) On June 28, 1993, the Reuters news service supplied a compact and legally precise description of what the Supreme Court had done: U.S. High Court orders more Merrell Dow hearings.

8. Joan Biskupic, Judges get broader discretion in allowing scientific testimony, *Washington Post*, June 29, 1993.

9. Ibid.

10. Paul M. Barrett, Justices rule against business in evidence case, *Wall Street Journal*, June 29, 1993.

11. Ibid. Steve Marshall, in *USA Today*, likewise reported only the plaintiffs' perspective on *Daubert*. The opinion "threw out a strict rule," he wrote (Scientific testimony gets boost, June 29, 1993). The reporter for *Business Wire* read *Daubert* that way too. While the wording of the wire service's report avoided saying anything too

precise or definite, the story clearly implied that the plaintiffs had won a solid victory. Their expert testimony "could be admitted as evidence in court" and "the High Court had agreed with [the plaintiff] Daubert." (U.S. Supreme Court rules on admissibility of scientific evidence, *Business Wire*, June 28, 1993)

12. Dori Meinert, San Diego families may get trial after Justices' ruling on evidence, *San Diego Union-Tribune*, June 29, 1993.

13. Ibid. Immediately after the Supreme Court released its 1993 *Daubert* opinion, many of us flatly predicted there wouldn't be a trial. It seemed apparent to us that on remand the Ninth Circuit would end up reaffirming its original conclusion. If anything, we were too pessimistic. We expected the Ninth Circuit Court of Appeals to give the trial judge a first crack at applying the *Daubert* opinion to the facts at hand. "The Bendectin plaintiffs won a narrow technical battle in *Daubert*, but they plainly lost the war. On remand, when the district judge applies the standard the U.S. Supreme Court has articulated, he will most probably once again exclude the evidence the plaintiffs originally sought to present at trial. If the judge does admit the evidence, he will almost certainly use one of the two other tools the court pointed to—summary judgment or directed verdict—to resolve the case once again for the defense. In the very unlikely event that the plaintiffs somehow emerge from the trial court with a verdict in their favor, the U.S. Court of Appeals for the Ninth Circuit will almost certainly apply *Daubert* to overturn it." (David E. Bernstein and Peter W. Huber, *Daubert* plaintiffs won technical battle but plainly lost the war, *Product Safety and Liability Reporter*, summer/fall 1993, p. 16)

14. *William Daubert, et al. v. Merrell Dow Pharmaceuticals*, 43 F.3d 1311 (9th Cir. 1995).

15. The study was sponsored by the Manhattan Institute.

16. David E. Bernstein, *Daubert* One Year Later (unpublished manuscript, 1994).

17. In one of these cases, testimony from a mechanical engineer regarding the design of a saw was excluded. See *Stanczyk v. Black & Decker, Inc.*, 836 F. Supp. 565 (N.D. Ill. 1993); see also *Clement v. Griffin*, 1994 WL 65134 (La. App. 1994) (testimony regarding cause of tire blowout).

18. *United States v. Daccarett*, 6 F.3d 37 (2d Cir. 1993) (admissible).

19. *Tamarin v. Adam Caterers, Inc.*, 13 F.3d 51 (2d Cir. 1993) (*Daubert* not relevant to payroll review by accountant).

20. All the quotes in this paragraph are from Bernstein, *Daubert* One Year Later.

21. Joan Beck, Junk science strikes out at the courts and pregnant women, *Chicago Tribune*, January 22, 1995.

22. Marcia Barinaga, Bendectin case dismissed, *Science*, January 13, 1995.

23. Linda Himelstein, Putting science on trial, *Business Week*, August 15, 1995, p. 76.

24. Ibid. Throughout her story, Himelstein makes clear that her own sympathies lie with plaintiffs. She argues that judges are now freezing out *legitimate* claims. Astonishingly, she cited as examples silicone breast implants, the Norplant con-

traceptive device, which uses a silicone base, and tobacco. The former two are hotbeds of junk science, while with tobacco the key legal battles revolve not around science but around the issue of fair warning and private choice. "In the end," Himelstein declares, "the new rules are likely to tilt in favor of deep-pocketed corporate defendants, who have the money to back studies and fund drawn-out disputes over evidence."

25. Ibid. Himelstein cites Bernstein's study.

26. Ibid.

27. Joan Van, Ruling on "junk science" may affect jury awards, *Chicago Tribune*, July 6, 1993.

28. Steve Marshall, Scientific testimony gets boost, *USA Today*, June 29, 1993.

29. Morton Mintz, Drug for "morning sickness" is suspected in birth defects, *Washington Post*, February 11, 1980.

30. Ibid.

31. Morton Mintz, FDA to study "morning sickness" drug link to birth defects, *Washington Post*, August 23, 1980.

32. Morton Mintz, Warning eyed on anti-nausea drug Bendectin, *Washington Post*, June 25, 1982.

33. Ibid. On June 26 the *Post* ran yet another Mintz followup story: Drug linked to birth defect; group seeks halt to sales of Bendectin.

34. Morton Mintz, Medicine for morning sickness is newly linked to birth defect, *Washington Post*, December 16, 1982.

35. Robert L. Brent, Bendectin: Review of the medical literature of a comprehensively studied human nonteratogen and the most prevalent tortogen-litigen, *Reproductive Toxicology* 9 (1995): 337–350.

36. Ibid.

37. Ibid., quoting G. Young, speech before Parliament about Debenox (Bendectin), April 23, 1980.

38. Ibid.

39. Ibid.

40. Ibid. In other articles, Brent urges medical societies to take responsibility for teaching physicians and scientists the appropriate and inappropriate functions of an expert witness, and to monitor the testimony experts give in court. "Just as a faculty member expects to have peer review of his clinical, research, teaching, and writing activities. . . ." (Robert L. Brent, Improving the quality of expert witness testimony, *Pediatrics* 82 (1988): 511f.) Brent also promotes the submission of scholarly review articles in the fields currently involved in litigation. "Such a document," he writes, "can raise the quality of expert testimony, discourage nonmeritous suits, and precipitate pretrial settlements in meritorious suits." (Robert L. Brent, The irresponsible expert witness: A failure of biomedical graduate education and profession accountability, *Pediatrics* 70 (1982): 754ff.)

Appendix B

William Daubert et al. v. Merrell Dow Pharmaceuticals, Inc.

United States Supreme Court (509 U.S. 579, 1993)

Justice Blackmun delivered the opinion of the Court.

In this case we are called upon to determine the standard for admitting expert scientific testimony in a federal trial.

I

Petitioners Jason Daubert and Eric Schuller are minor children born with serious birth defects. They and their parents sued respondent in California state court, alleging that the birth defects had been caused by the mothers' ingestion of Bendectin, a prescription antinausea drug marketed by respondent. Respondent removed the suits to federal court on diversity grounds.

After extensive discovery, respondent moved for summary judgment, contending that Bendectin does not cause birth defects in humans and that petitioners would be unable to come forward with any admissible evidence that it does. In support of its motion, respondent submitted an affidavit of Steven H. Lamm, physician and epidemiologist, who is a well-credentialed expert on the risks from exposure to various chemical substances.[1] Doctor Lamm stated that he had reviewed all the literature on Bendectin and human birth defects—more than 30 published studies involving over 130,000 patients. No study had found Bendectin to be a human teratogen (i.e., a substance capable of causing malformations in fetuses). On the basis of this review, Doctor Lamm concluded that maternal use of Bendectin during the first trimester of pregnancy has not been shown to be a risk factor for human birth defects.

Petitioners did not (and do not) contest this characterization of the published record regarding Bendectin. Instead, they responded to respondent's motion with the testimony of eight experts of their own, each of whom also possessed impressive credentials.[2] These experts had concluded that Bendectin can cause birth defects. Their conclusions were based upon "in vitro" (test tube) and "in vivo" (live) animal studies that found a link between Bendectin and malformations; pharmacological studies of the chemical structure of Bendectin that purported to show similarities between the structure of the drug and that of other substances known to cause birth defects; and the "reanalysis" of previously published epidemiological (human statistical) studies.

The District Court granted respondent's motion for summary judgment. The court stated that scientific evidence is admissible only if the principle upon which it is based is "'sufficiently established to have general acceptance in the field to which it belongs.'" 727 F. Supp. 570, 572 (SD Cal. 1989), quoting *United States v. Kilgus*, 571 F.2d 508, 510 (CA9 1978). The court concluded that petitioners' evidence did not meet this standard. Given the vast body of epidemiological data concerning Bendectin, the court held, expert opinion which is not based on epidemiological evidence is not admissible to establish causation. 727 F. Supp., at 575. Thus, the animal-cell studies, live-animal studies, and chemical-structure analyses on which petitioners had relied could not raise by themselves a reasonably disputable jury issue regarding causation. Ibid. Petitioners' epidemiological analyses, based as they were on recalculations of data in previously published studies that had found no causal link between the drug and birth defects, were ruled to be inadmissible because they had not been published or subjected to peer review. Ibid.

The United States Court of Appeals for the Ninth Circuit affirmed. 951 F.2d 1128 (1991). Citing *Frye v. United States*, 54 App. D.C. 46, 47, 293 F. 1013, 1014 (1923), the court stated that expert opinion based on a scientific technique is inadmissible unless the technique is "generally accepted" as reliable in the relevant scientific community. 951 F.2d, at 1129–1130. The court declared that expert opinion based on a methodology that diverges "significantly from the procedures accepted by recognized authorities in the field . . . cannot be shown to be 'generally accepted as a reliable technique.'" Id., at 1130, quoting *United States v. Solomon*, 753 F.2d 1522, 1526 (CA9 1985).

The court emphasized that other Courts of Appeals considering the risks of Bendectin had refused to admit reanalyses of epidemiological studies that had been neither published nor subjected to peer review. 951 F.2d, at 1130–1131. Those courts had found unpublished reanalyses "particularly problematic in light of the massive weight of the original published studies supporting [respondent's] position, all of which had undergone full scrutiny from the scientific community." Id., at 1130. Contending that reanalysis is generally accepted by the scientific community only when it is subjected to verification and scrutiny by others in the field, the Court of Appeals rejected petitioners' reanalyses as "unpublished, not subjected to the normal peer review process and generated solely for use in litigation." Id., at 1131. The court concluded that petitioners' evidence provided an insufficient foundation to allow admission of expert testimony that Bendectin caused their injuries and, accordingly, that petitioners could not satisfy their burden of proving causation at trial.

We granted certiorari, 56 U.S. 914 (1992), in light of sharp divisions among the courts regarding the proper standard for the admission of expert testimony. Compare, e.g., *United States v. Shorter*, 257 U.S. App. D.C. 358, 363–364, 809 F.2d 54, 59–60 (applying the "general acceptance" standard), cert. denied, 484 U.S. 817 (1987), with *DeLuca v. Merrell Dow Pharmaceuticals, Inc.*, 911 F.2d 941, 955 (CA3 1990) (rejecting the "general acceptance" standard).

II

A

In the 70 years since its formulation in the *Frye* case, the "general acceptance" test has been the dominant standard for determining the admissibility of novel scientific evidence at trial. See E. Green & C. Nesson, Problems, Cases, and Materials on Evidence 649 (1983). Although under increasing attack of late, the rule continues to be followed by a majority of courts, including the Ninth Circuit.[3]

The *Frye* test has its origin in a short and citation-free 1923 decision concerning the admissibility of evidence derived from a systolic blood pressure deception test, a crude precursor to the polygraph machine. In what has become a famous (perhaps infamous) passage, the then Court of

Appeals for the District of Columbia described the device and its operation and declared:

> Just when a scientific principle or discovery crosses the line between the experimental and demonstrable stages is difficult to define. Somewhere in this twilight zone the evidential force of the principle must be recognized, and while courts will go a long way in admitting expert testimony deduced from a well-recognized scientific principle or discovery, *the thing from which the deduction is made must be sufficiently established to have gained general acceptance in the particular field in which it belongs.* 54 App. D.C., at 47, 293 F., at 1014 (emphasis added).

Because the deception test had "not yet gained such standing and scientific recognition among physiological and psychological authorities as would justify the courts in admitting expert testimony deduced from the discovery, development, and experiments thus far made," evidence of its results was ruled inadmissible. Ibid.

The merits of the *Frye* test have been much debated, and scholarship on its proper scope and application is legion.[4] Petitioners' primary attack, however, is not on the content but on the continuing authority of the rule. They contend that the *Frye* test was superseded by the adoption of the Federal Rules of Evidence.[5] We agree.

We interpret the legislatively enacted Federal Rules of Evidence as we would any statute. *Beech Aircraft Corp. v. Rainey*, 488 U.S. 153, 163(1988). Rule 402 provides the baseline:

> All relevant evidence is admissible, except as otherwise provided by the Constitution of the United States, by Act of Congress, by these rules, or by other rules prescribed by the Supreme Court pursuant to statutory authority. Evidence which is not relevant is not admissible.

"Relevant evidence" is defined as that which has "any tendency to make the existence of any fact that is of consequence to the determination of the action more probable or less probable than it would be without the evidence." Rule 401. The Rules' basic standard of relevance thus is a liberal one.

Frye, of course, predated the Rules by half a century. In *United States v. Abel*, 469 U.S. 45 (1984), we considered the pertinence of background common law in interpreting the Rules of Evidence. We noted that the Rules occupy the field, id., at 49, but, quoting Professor Cleary, the Reporter, explained that the common law nevertheless could serve as an aid to their application:

> 'In principle, under the Federal Rules no common law of evidence remains. "All relevant evidence is admissible, except as otherwise provided . . . ." In reality, of course, the body of common law knowledge continues to exist, though in the some-

what altered form of a source of guidance in the exercise of delegated powers.' Id., at 51–52.

We found the common-law precept at issue in the Abel case entirely consistent with Rule 402's general requirement of admissibility, and considered it unlikely that the drafters had intended to change the rule. Id., at 50–51. In *Bourjaily v. United States*, 483 U.S. 171 (1987), on the other hand, the Court was unable to find a particular common-law doctrine in the Rules, and so held it superseded.

Here there is a specific Rule that speaks to the contested issue. Rule 702, governing expert testimony, provides:

If scientific, technical, or other specialized knowledge will assist the trier of fact to understand the evidence or to determine a fact in issue, a witness qualified as an expert by knowledge, skill, experience, training, or education, may testify thereto in the form of an opinion or otherwise.

Nothing in the text of this Rule establishes "general acceptance" as an absolute prerequisite to admissibility. Nor does respondent present any clear indication that Rule 702 or the Rules as a whole were intended to incorporate a "general acceptance" standard. The drafting history makes no mention of *Frye*, and a rigid "general acceptance" requirement would be at odds with the "liberal thrust" of the Federal Rules and their "general approach of relaxing the traditional barriers to 'opinion' testimony." *Beech Aircraft Corp. v. Rainey*, 488 U.S., at 169 (citing Rules 701 to 705). See also Weinstein, Rule 702 of the Federal Rules of Evidence is Sound; It Should Not Be Amended, 138 F.R.D. 631, 631 (1991) ("The Rules were designed to depend primarily upon lawyer-adversaries and sensible triers of fact to evaluate conflicts"). Given the Rules' permissive backdrop and their inclusion of a specific rule on expert testimony that does not mention "general acceptance," the assertion that the Rules somehow assimilated *Frye* is unconvincing. *Frye* made 'general acceptance' the exclusive test for admitting expert scientific testimony. That austere standard, absent fromand incompatible with the Federal Rules of Evidence, should not be applied in federal trials.[6]

B

That the *Frye* test was displaced by the Rules of Evidence does not mean, however, that the Rules themselves place no limits on the admissibility of purportedly scientific evidence.[7] Nor is the trial judge disabled from screening such evidence. To the contrary, under the Rules the trial judge must ensure that any and all scientific testimony or evidence admitted is not only relevant, but reliable.

The primary locus of this obligation is Rule 702, which clearly contemplates some degree of regulation of the subjects and theories about which an expert may testify. "*If scientific*, technical, or other specialized *knowledge will assist the trier of fact* to understand the evidence or to determine a fact in issue" an expert "may testify *thereto*." (Emphasis added.) The subject of an expert's testimony must be "scientific . . . knowledge."[8] The adjective "scientific" implies a grounding in the methods and procedures of science. Similarly, the word "knowledge" connotes more than subjective belief or unsupported speculation. The term "applies to any body of known facts or to any body of ideas inferred from such facts or accepted as truths on good grounds." Webster's *Third New International Dictionary* 1252 (1986). Of course, it would be unreasonable to conclude that the subject of scientific testimony must be "known" to a certainty; arguably, there are no certainties in science. See, e.g., Brief for Nicolaas Bloembergen et al. as *Amici Curiae* 9 ("Indeed, scientists do not assert that they know what is immutably 'true'—they are committed to searching for new, temporary, theories to explain, as best they can, phenomena"); Brief for American Association for the Advancement of Science et al. as *Amici Curiae* 7–8 ("Science is not an encyclopedic body of knowledge about the universe. Instead, it represents a *process* for proposing and refining theoretical explanations about the world that are subject to further testing and refinement" (emphasis in original)). But, in order to qualify as "scientific knowledge," an inference or assertion must be derived by the scientific method. Proposed testimony must be supported by appropriate validation—i.e., "good grounds," based on what is known. In short, the requirement that an expert's testimony pertain to "scientific knowledge" establishes a standard of evidentiary reliability.[9]

Rule 702 further requires that the evidence or testimony "assist the trier of fact to understand the evidence or to determine a fact in issue." This condition goes primarily to relevance. "Expert testimony which does not relate to any issue in the case is not relevant and, ergo, non-helpful." 3 Weinstein & Berger ¶ 702[02], p. 702–18. See also *United States v. Downing*, 753 F.2d 1224, 1242 (CA3 1985) ("An additional consideration under Rule 702—and another aspect of relevancy—is whether expert testimony proffered in the case is sufficiently tied to the facts of the case that it will aid the jury in resolving a factual dispute"). The consideration has been aptly described by Judge Becker as one of "fit." Ibid. "Fit" is not always obvious, and scientific validity for one purpose is not necessarily scientific validity for other, unrelated purposes. See Starrs, *Frye v. United States* Restructured and Revitalized: A Proposal to Amend Federal Evidence Rule 702, 26 *Jurimetrics* J. 249, 258 (1986). The study of the phases of the moon, for example, may provide valid scientific "knowledge" about whether a certain night was dark, and if darkness is a fact in issue, the knowledge will assist the trier of fact. However (absent creditable grounds supporting such a link), evidence that the moon was full on a certain night will not assist the trier of fact in determining whether an individual was unusually likely to have behaved irrationally on that night. Rule 702's "helpfulness" standard requires a valid scientific connection to the pertinent inquiry as a precondition to admissibility.

That these requirements are embodied in Rule 702 is not surprising. Unlike an ordinary witness, see Rule 701, an expert is permitted wide latitude to offer opinions, including those that are not based on firsthand knowledge or observation. See Rules 702 and 703. Presumably, this relaxation of the usual requirement of firsthand knowledge—a rule which represents "a 'most pervasive manifestation' of the common law insistence upon 'the most reliable sources of information,'" Advisory Committee's Notes on Fed. Rule Evid. 602, 28 U.S.C. App., p. 755 (citation omitted)—is premised on an assumption that the expert's opinion will have a reliable basis in the knowledge and experience of his discipline.

C

Faced with a proffer of expert scientific testimony, then, the trial judge must determine at the outset, pursuant to Rule 104(a),[10] whether the expert is proposing to testify to (1) scientific knowledge that (2) will assist the trier of fact to understand or determine a fact in issue.[11] This entails a preliminary assessment of whether the reasoning or methodology underlying the testimony is scientifically valid and of whether that reasoning or methodology properly can be applied to the facts in issue. We are confident that federal judges possess the capacity to undertake this review. Many factors will bear on the inquiry, and we do not presume to set out a definitive checklist or test. But some general observations are appropriate.

Ordinarily, a key question to be answered in determining whether a theory or technique is scientific knowledge that will assist the trier of fact will be whether it can be (and has been) tested. "Scientific methodology today is based on generating hypotheses and testing them to see if they can be falsified; indeed, this methodology is what distinguishes science from other fields of human inquiry." Green 645. See also C. Hempel, *Philosophy of Natural Science* 49 (1966) ("[T]he statements constituting a scientific explanation must be capable of empirical test"); K. Popper, *Conjectures and Refutations: The Growth of Scientific Knowledge* 37 (5th ed. 1989) ("[T]he criterion of the scientific status of a theory is its falsifiability, or refutability, or testability") (emphasis deleted).

Another pertinent consideration is whether the theory or technique has been subjected to peer review and publication. Publication (which is but one element of peer review) is not a *sine qua non* of admissibility; it does not necessarily correlate with reliability, see S. Jasanoff, *The Fifth Branch: Science Advisors as Policymakers* 61–76 (1990), and in some instances well-grounded but innovative theories will not have been published, see Horrobin, The Philosophical Basis of Peer Review and the Suppression of Innovation, 263 *JAMA* 1438 (1990). Some propositions, moreover, are too particular, too new, or of too limited interest to be published. But submission to the scrutiny of the scientific community is a component of "good science," in part because it increases the likelihood that substantive flaws in methodology will be detected. See J. Ziman, *Reliable Knowledge: An Exploration of the Grounds for Belief in Science* 130–133 (1978); Relman & Angell, How Good Is Peer Review?, 321 *New Eng. J. Med.* 827 (1989). The fact of publication (or lack thereof) in a peer reviewed journal thus will be a relevant, though not dispositive, consideration in assessing the scientific validity of a particular technique or methodology on which an opinion is premised.

Additionally, in the case of a particular scientific technique, the court ordinarily should consider the known or potential rate of error, see, e.g., *United States v. Smith*, 869 F.2d 348, 353–354 (CA7 1989) (surveying studies of the error rate of spectrographic voice identification technique), and the existence and maintenance of standards controlling the technique's operation, see *United States v. Williams*, 583 F.2d 1194, 1198 (CA2 1978) (noting professional organization's standard governing spectrographic analysis), cert. denied, 439 U.S. 1117 (1979).

Finally, "general acceptance" can yet have a bearing on the inquiry. A "reliability assessment does not require, although it does permit, explicit identification of a relevant scientific community and an express determination of a particular degree of acceptance within that community." *United States v. Downing*, 753 F.2d, at 1238. See also 3 Weinstein & Berger ¶ 702[03], pp. 702–41 to 702–42. Widespread acceptance can be an important factor in ruling particular evidence admissible, and "a known technique that has been able to attract only minimal support within the community," *Downing*, 753 F.2d, at 1238, may properly be viewed with skepticism.

The inquiry envisioned by Rule 702 is, we emphasize, a flexible one.[12] Its overarching subject is the scientific validity—and thus the evidentiary relevance and reliability—of the principles that underlie a proposed submission. The focus, of course, must be solely on principles and methodology, not on the conclusions that they generate.

Throughout, a judge assessing a proffer of expert scientific testimony under Rule 702 should also be mindful of other applicable rules. Rule 703 provides that expert opinions based on otherwise inadmissible hearsay are to be admitted only if the facts or data are "of a type reasonably relied upon by experts in the particular field in forming opinions or inferences upon the subject." Rule 706 allows the court at its discretion to procure the assistance of an expert of its own choosing. Finally, Rule 403 permits the exclusion of relevant evidence "if its probative value is substantially outweighed by the danger of unfair prejudice, confusion of the issues, or misleading the jury . . . ." Judge Weinstein has explained: "Expert evidence can be both powerful and quite misleading because of the difficulty in evaluating it. Because of this risk, the judge in weighing possible prejudice against probative force under Rule 403 of the present rules exercises more control over experts than over lay witnesses." Weinstein, 138 F.R.D., at 632.

III

We conclude by briefly addressing what appear to be two underlying concerns of the parties and *amici* in this case. Respondent expresses apprehension that abandonment of "general acceptance" as the exclusive requirement for admission will result in a "free-for-all" in which befuddled juries are confounded by absurd and irrational pseudoscientific assertions. In this regard respondent seems to us to be overly pessimistic about the capabilities of the jury and of the adversary system generally. Vigorous cross-examination, presentation of contrary evidence, and careful instruction on the burden of proof are the traditional and appropriate means of attacking shaky but admissible evidence. See *Rock v. Arkansas*, 483 U.S. 44, 61 (1987). Additionally, in the event the trial court concludes that the scintilla of evidence presented supporting a position is insufficient to allow a reasonable juror to conclude that the position more likely than not is true, the court remains free to direct a judgment, Fed. Rule Civ. Proc. 50(a), and likewise to grant summary judgment, Fed. Rule Civ. Proc. 56. Cf., e.g., *Turpin v. Merrell Dow Pharmaceuticals, Inc.*, 959 F.2d 1349 (CA6) (holding that scientific evidence that provided foundation for expert testimony, viewed in the light most favorable to plaintiffs, was not sufficient to allow a jury to find it more probable than not that defendant caused plaintiff's injury), cert. denied, 506 U.S. 826 (1992); *Brock v. Merrell Dow Pharmaceuticals, Inc.*, 874 F.2d 307 (CA5 1989) (reversing judgment entered on jury verdict for plaintiffs because evidence regarding causation was insufficient), modified, 884 F.2d 166 (CA5 1989), cert. denied, 494 U.S. 1046 (1990); Green 680–681. These conventional devices, rather than wholesale exclusion under an uncompromising "general acceptance" test, are the appropriate safeguards where the basis of scientific testimony meets the standards of Rule 702.

Petitioners and, to a greater extent, their *amici* exhibit a different concern. They suggest that recognition of a screening role for the judge that allows for the exclusion of "invalid" evidence will sanction a stifling and repressive scientific orthodoxy and will be inimical to the search for truth. See, e.g., Brief for Ronald Bayer et al. as *Amici Curiae*. It is true that open debate is an essential part of both legal and scientific analyses. Yet there are important differences between the quest for truth in the courtroom and the quest for truth in the laboratory. Scientific conclusions are subject to perpetual revision. Law, on the other hand, must resolve disputes finally and quickly. The scientific project is advanced by broad and wide-ranging consideration of a multitude of hypotheses, for those that are incorrect will eventually be shown to be so, and that in itself is an advance. Conjectures that are probably wrong are of little use, however, in the project of reaching a quick, final, and binding legal judgment—often of great consequence—about a particular set of events in the past. We recognize that in practice, a gatekeeping role for the judge, no matter how flexible, inevitably on occasion will prevent the jury from learning of authentic insights and innovations. That, nevertheless, is the balance that is struck by Rules of Evidence designed not for the exhaustive search for cosmic understanding but for the particularized resolution of legal disputes.[13]

IV

To summarize: "general acceptance" is not a necessary precondition to the admissibility of scientific evidence under the Federal Rules of Evidence, but the Rules of Evidence—especially Rule 702—do assign to the trial judge the task of ensuring that an expert's testimony both rests on a reliable foundation and is relevant to the task at hand. Pertinent evidence based on scientifically valid principles will satisfy those demands.

The inquiries of the District Court and the Court of Appeals focused almost exclusively on "general acceptance," as gauged by publication and the decisions of other courts. Accordingly, the judgment of the Court of Appeals is vacated and the case is remanded for further proceedings consistent with this opinion.

It is so ordered.

Chief Justice Rehnquist, with whom Justice Stevens joins, concurring in part and dissenting in part.

The petition for certiorari in this case presents two questions: first, whether the rule of *Frye v. United States*, 54 App. D.C. 46, 293 F. 1013 (1923), remains good law after the enactment of the Federal Rules of Evidence; and second, if *Frye* remains valid, whether it requires expert scientific testimony to have been subjected to a peer review process in order to be admissible. The Court concludes, correctly in my view, that the *Frye* rule did not survive the enactment of the Federal Rules of Evidence, and I therefore join Parts I and II-A of its opinion. The second question presented in the petition for certiorari necessarily is mooted by this holding, but the Court nonetheless proceeds to construe Rules 702 and 703 very much in the abstract, and then offers some "general observations." Ante, at 593.

"General observations" by this Court customarily carry great weight with lower federal courts, but the ones offered here suffer from the flaw common to most such observations—they are not applied to deciding whether or not particular testimony was or was not admissible, and therefore they tend to be not only general, but vague and abstract. This is particularly unfortunate in a case such as this, where the ultimate legal question depends on an appreciation of one or more bodies of knowledge not judicially noticeable, and subject to different interpretations in the briefs of the parties and their *amici*. Twenty-two *amicus* briefs have been filed in the case, and indeed the Court's opinion contains no fewer than 37 citations to *amicus* briefs and other secondary sources.

The various briefs filed in this case are markedly different from typical briefs, in that large parts of them do not deal with decided cases or statutory language—the sort of material we customarily interpret. Instead, they deal with definitions of scientific knowledge, scientific method, scientific validity, and peer review—in short, matters far afield from the expertise of judges. This is not to say that such materials are not useful or even necessary in deciding how Rule 702 should be applied; but it is to say that the unusual subject matter should cause us to proceed with great caution in deciding more than we have to, because our reach can so easily exceed our grasp.

But even if it were desirable to make "general observations" not necessary to decide the questions presented, I cannot subscribe to some of the observations made by the Court. In Part II-B, the Court concludes that reliability and relevancy are the touchstones of the admissibility of expert testimony. Ante, at 590–592. Federal Rule of Evidence 402 provides, as the Court points out, that "[e]vidence which is not relevant is not admissible." But there is no similar reference in the Rule to "reliability." The Court constructs its argument by parsing the language "[i]f scientific, technical, or other specialized knowledge will assist the trier of fact to understand the evidence or to determine a fact in issue, . . . an expert . . . may testify thereto. . . ." Fed. Rule Evid. 702. It stresses that the subject of the expert's testimony must be "scientific . . . knowledge," and points out that "scientific" "implies a grounding in the methods and procedures of science," and that the word "knowledge" "connotes more than subjective belief or unsupported speculation." Ante, at 590. From this it concludes that "scientific knowledge" must be "derived by the scientific method." Ibid. Proposed testimony, we are told, must be supported by "appropriate validation." Ibid. Indeed, in footnote 9, the Court decides that "in a case involving scientific evidence, *evidentiary reliability* will be based upon *scientific validity*." Ante, at 591, n. 9 (emphasis in original).

Questions arise simply from reading this part of the Court's opinion, and countless more questions will surely arise when hundreds of district judges try to apply its teaching to particular offers of expert testimony. Does all of this *dicta* apply to an expert seeking to testify on the basis of "technical or other specialized knowledge"—the other types of expert knowledge to which Rule 702 applies—or are the "general observations" limited only to "scientific knowledge"? What is the difference between scientific knowledge and technical knowledge; does Rule 702 actually contemplate that the phrase "scientific, technical, or other specialized knowledge" be broken down into numerous subspecies of expertise, or did its authors simply pick general descriptive language covering the sort of expert testimony which courts have customarily received? The Court speaks of its confidence that federal judges can make a "preliminary assessment of whether the reasoning or methodology underlying the testimony is scientifically valid and of whether that reasoning or methodology properly can be applied to the facts in issue." Ante, at 592–593. The Court then states that a "key question" to be answered in deciding whether something is "scientific knowledge" "will be whether it can be (and has been) tested." Ante, at 593. Following this sentence are three quotations from treatises, which speak not only of empirical testing, but one of which states that "'the criterion of the scientific status of a theory is its falsifiability, or refutability, or testability.'" Ibid.

I defer to no one in my confidence in federal judges; but I am at a loss to know what is meant when it is said that the scientific status of a theory depends on its "falsifiability," and I suspect some of them will be, too.

I do not doubt that Rule 702 confides to the judge some gatekeeping responsibility in deciding questions of the admissibility of proffered expert testimony. But I do not think it imposes on them either the obligation or the authority to become amateur scientists in order to perform that role. I think the Court would be far better advised in this case to decide only the questions presented, and to leave the further development of this important area of the law to future cases.

Notes to Appendix B

1. Doctor Lamm received his master's and doctor of medicine degrees from the University of Southern California. He has served as a consultant in birth-defect epidemiology for the National Center for Health Statistics and has published numerous articles on the magnitude of risk from exposure to various chemical and biological substances. App. 34–44.

2. For example, Shanna Helen Swan, who received a master's degree in biostatics from Columbia University and a doctorate in statistics from the University of California at Berkeley, is chief of the section of the California Department of Health and Services that determines causes of birth defects, and has served as a consultant to the World Health Organization, the Food and Drug Administration, and the National Institutes of Health. Id. at 113–114, 131–132. Stewart A. Newman, who received his bachelor's degree in chemistry from Columbia University and his master's and doctorate in chemistry from the University of Chicago, respectively, is a professor at New York Medical College and has spent over a decade studying the effect of chemicals on limb development. Id. at 54–56. The credentials of the others are similarly impressive. See id. at 61–66, 73–80, 148–153, 187–192, and Attachments 12, 20, 21, 26, 31, and 32 to Petitioners' Opposition to Summary Judgment in No. 84-2013-G(I) (SD Cal.).

3. For a catalogue of the many cases on either side of this controversy, see P. Gianelli & E. Imwinkelried, *Scientific Evidence* § 1–5, pp. 10–14 (1986 and Supp. 1991).

4. See, e.g., Green, Expert Witnesses and Sufficiency of Evidence in Toxic Substances Litigation: The Legacy of *Agent Orange* and Bendectin Litigation, 86 Nw. U. L. Rev. 643 (1992) (hereinafter Green); Becker & Orenstein, The Federal Rules of Evidence After Sixteen Years—The Effect of "Plain Meaning" Jurisprudence, the Need for an Advisory Committee on the Rules of Evidence, and Suggestions for Selective Revision of the Rules, 60 Geo. Wash. L. Rev. 857, 876–885 (1992); Hanson, "James Alphonso Frye is Sixty-Five Years Old; Should He Retire?," 16 West St. U. L. Rev. 357 (1989); Black, A Unified Theory of Scientific Evidence, 56 Ford. L. Rev. 595 (1988); Imwinkelried, The "Bases" of Expert Testimony: The Syllogistic Structure of Scientific Testimony, 67 N.C. L. Rev. 1 (1988); Proposals for a Model Rule on the Admissibility of Scientific Evidence, 26 *Jurimetrics J.* 235 (1986); Gianelli, The Admissibility of Novel Scientific Evidence: *Frye v. United States*, A Half-Century Later, 80 Colum. L. Rev. 1197 (1980); The Supreme Court, 1986 Term, 101 Harv. L. Rev. 7, 119, 125–127 (1987). Indeed, the debates over *Frye* are such a well-established part of the academic landscape that a distinct term—"*Frye*-ologist"—has been advanced to

describe those who take part. See Behringer, Introduction, Proposals for a Model Rule on the Admissibility of Scientific Evidence, 26 *Jurimetrics J.*, at 239, quoting Lacey, Scientific Evidence, 24 *Jurimetrics J.* 254, 264 (1984).

5. Like the question of *Frye*'s merit, the dispute over its survival has divided courts and commentators. Compare, e.g., *United States v. Williams*, 583 F.2d 1194 (CA2 1978) (*Frye* is superseded by the Rules of Evidence), cert. denied, 439 U.S. 1117 (1979), with *Christophersen v. Allied-Signal Corp.*, 939 F.2d 1106, 1111, 1115–1116 (CA5 1991) (en banc) (*Frye* and the Rules coexist), cert. denied, 503 U.S. 912 (1992), 3 J. Weinstein & M. Berger, Weinstein's Evidence ¶ 702[03], pp. 702–36 to 702–37 (1988) (hereinafter Weinstein & Berger) (*Frye* is dead), and M. Graham, Handbook of Federal Evidence § 703.2 (3d ed. 1991) (*Frye* lives). See generally P. Gianelli & E. Imwinkelried, Scientific Evidence § 1–5, at 28–29 (citing authorities).

6. Because we hold that *Frye* has been superseded and base the discussion that follows on the content of the congressionally enacted Federal Rules of Evidence, we do not address petitioners' argument that application of the *Frye* rule in this diversity case, as the application of a judge-made rule affecting substantive rights, would violate the doctrine of *Erie R. Co. v. Tompkins*, 304 U.S. 64 (1938).

7. THE CHIEF JUSTICE "do[es] not doubt that Rule 702 confides to the judge some gatekeeping responsibility," *post*, at 600, but would neither say how it does so, nor explain what that role entails. We believe the better course is to note the nature and source of the duty.

8. Rule 702 also applies to "technical, or other specialized knowledge." Our discussion is limited to the scientific context because that is the nature of the expertise offered here.

9. We note that scientists typically distinguish between "validity" (does the principle support what it purports to show?) and "reliability" (does application of the principle produce consistent results?). See Black, 56 *Ford. L. Rev.* at 599. Although "the difference between accuracy, validity, and reliability may be such that each is distinct from the other by no more than a hen's kick," Starrs, *Frye v. United States Restructured and Revitalized: A Proposal to Amend Federal Evidence Rule 702*, 26 *Jurimetrics J.* 249, 256 (1986), our reference here is to *evidentiary* reliability—that is, trustworthiness. Cf., e.g., Advisory Committee's Notes on Fed. Rule Evid. 602, 28 U.S.C. App., p. 755 ("'[T]he rule requiring that a witness who testifies to a fact which can be perceived by the senses must have had an opportunity to observe, and must have actually observed the fact' is a 'most pervasive manifestation' of the common law insistence upon 'the most reliable sources of information.'" (citation omitted)); Advisory Committee's Notes on Art. VIII of Rules of Evidence, 28 U.S.C. App., p. 770 (hearsay exceptions will be recognized only "under circumstances supposed to furnish guarantees of trustworthiness"). In a case involving scientific evidence, *evidentiary reliability* will be based upon *scientific validity*.

10. Rule 104(a) provides: "Preliminary questions concerning the qualification of a person to be a witness, the existence of a privilege, or the admissibility of evidence shall be determined by the court, subject to the provisions of subdivision (b)

[pertaining to conditional admissions]. In making its determination it is not bound by the rules of evidence except those with respect to privileges." These matters should be established by a preponderance of proof. See *Bourjaily v. United States*, 483 U.S. 171, 175–176 (1987).

11. Although the *Frye* decision itself focused exclusively on "novel" scientific techniques, we do not read the requirements of Rule 702 to apply specially or exclusively to unconventional evidence. Of course, well-established propositions are less likely to be challenged than those that are novel, and they are more handily defended. Indeed, theories that are so firmly established as to have attained the status of scientific law, such as the laws of thermodynamics, properly are subject to judicial notice under Federal Rule Evidence 201.

12. A number of authorities have presented variations on the reliability approach, each with its own slightly different set of factors. See, e.g., *Downing*, 753 F.2d, at 1238–1239 (on which our discussion draws in part); 3 Weinstein & Berger ¶ 702[03], pp. 702–41 to 702–42 (on which the *Downing* court in turn partially relied); McCormick, Scientific Evidence: Defining a New Approach to Admissibility, 67 *Iowa L. Rev.* 879, 911–912 (1982); and Symposium on Science and the Rules of Evidence, 99 F.R.D. 187, 231 (1983) (statement by Margaret Berger). To the extent that they focus on the reliability of evidence as ensured by the scientific validity of its underlying principles, all these versions may well have merit, although we express no opinion regarding any of their particular details.

13. This is not to say that judicial interpretation, as opposed to adjudicative factfinding, does not share basic characteristics of the scientific endeavor: "The work of a judge is in one sense enduring and in another ephemeral. . . . In the endless process of testing and retesting, there is a constant rejection of the dross and a constant retention of whatever is pure and sound and fine." B. Cardozo, The Nature of the Judicial Process 178–179 (1921).

Appendix C

William Daubert et al. v. Merrell Dow Pharmaceuticals, Inc.

United States Court of Appeals for the Ninth Circuit (43 F.3d 1311, 1995)

Kozinski, Circuit Judge.

On remand from the United States Supreme Court, we undertake "the task of ensuring that an expert's testimony both rests on a reliable foundation and is relevant to the task at hand." *Daubert v. Merrell Dow Pharmaceuticals, Inc.*, __ U.S. __, __, 113 S. Ct. 2786, 2799, 125 L. Ed. 2d 469 (1993).

I

A.   Background

Two minors brought suit against Merrell Dow Pharmaceuticals, claiming they suffered limb reduction birth defects[1] because their mothers had taken Bendectin, a drug prescribed for morning sickness to about 17.5 million pregnant women in the United States between 1957 and 1982. See Resp't's Br. on Writ of Cert. at 2; *Turpin v. Merrell Dow Pharmaceuticals, Inc.*, 959 F.2d 1349, 1350 (6th Cir. 1992). This appeal deals with an evidentiary question: whether certain expert scientific testimony is admissible to prove that Bendectin caused the plaintiffs' birth defects.

For the most part, we don't know how birth defects come about. We do know they occur in 2–3% of births, whether or not the expectant mother has taken Bendectin. See Jose F. Cordero and Godfrey P. Oakley, Jr., Drug Exposure During Pregnancy: Some Epidemiologic Considerations, 26 *Clinical Obstetrics and Gynecology* 418, 424–25 (June 1983). Limb defects are even rarer, occurring in fewer than one birth out of every 1000. *Turpin*, 959 F.2d at 1353. But scientists simply do not know how teratogens (chemicals known to cause limb reduction defects) do their damage:

They cannot reconstruct the biological chain of events that leads from an expectant mother's ingestion of a teratogenic substance to the stunted development of a baby's limbs. Nor do they know what it is about teratogens that causes them to have this effect. No doubt, someday we will have this knowledge, and then we will be able to tell precisely whether and how Bendectin (or any other suspected teratogen) interferes with limb development; in the current state of scientific knowledge, however, we are ignorant.

Not knowing the mechanism whereby a particular agent causes a particular effect is not always fatal to a plaintiff's claim. Causation can be proved even when we don't know precisely *how* the damage occurred, if there is sufficiently compelling proof that the agent must have caused the damage *somehow*. One method of proving causation in these circumstances is to use statistical evidence. If 50 people who eat at a restaurant one evening come down with food poisoning during the night, we can infer that the restaurant's food probably contained something unwholesome, even if none of the dishes is available for analysis. This inference is based on the fact that, in our health-conscious society, it is highly unlikely that 50 people who have nothing in common except that they ate at the same restaurant will get food poisoning from independent sources.

It is by such means that plaintiffs here seek to establish that Bendectin is responsible for their injuries. They rely on the testimony of three groups of scientific experts. One group proposes to testify that there is a statistical link between the ingestion of Bendectin during pregnancy and limb reduction defects. These experts have not themselves conducted epidemiological (human statistical) studies on the effects of Bendectin; rather, they have reanalyzed studies published by other scientists, none of whom reported a statistical association between Bendectin and birth defects. Other experts proffered by plaintiffs propose to testify that Bendectin causes limb reduction defects in humans because it causes such defects in laboratory animals. A third group of experts sees a link between Bendectin and birth defects because Bendectin has a chemical structure that is similar to other drugs suspected of causing birth defects.

The opinions proffered by plaintiffs' experts do not, to understate the point, reflect the consensus within the scientific community. The FDA—an agency not known for its promiscuity in approving drugs—continues to approve Bendectin for use by pregnant women because "available data do not demonstrate an association between birth defects and Bendectin." U.S. Department of Health and Human Services News, No. P80-45 (Oct. 7, 1980). Every published study here and abroad—and there have been many—concludes that Bendectin is not a teratogen. *Turpin*, 959 F.2d at 1353–56. In fact, apart from the small but determined group of scientists testifying on behalf of the Bendectin plaintiffs in this and many other cases, there doesn't appear to be a single scientist who has concluded that Bendectin causes limb reduction defects.

It is largely because the opinions proffered by plaintiffs' experts run counter to the substantial consensus in the scientific community that we affirmed the district court's grant of summary judgment the last time the case appeared before us. *Daubert v. Merrell Dow Pharmaceuticals, Inc.*, 951 F.2d 1128, 1131 (9th Cir. 1992). The standard for admissibility of expert testimony in this circuit at the time was the so-called *Frye* test: Scientific evidence was admissible if it was based on a scientific technique generally accepted as reliable within the scientific community. *Frye v. United States*, 293 F. 1013, 1014 (D.C. Cir. 1923).[2] We found that the district court properly applied this standard, and affirmed. The Supreme Court reversed, holding that *Frye* was superceded by Federal Rule of Evidence 702, __ U.S. at __, 113 S. Ct. at 2794, and remanded for us to consider the admissibility of plaintiffs' expert testimony under this new standard.

B. Procedural Issues

First, however, we address plaintiffs' argument that we should simply remand the case so the district court can make the initial determination of admissibility under the new standard announced by the Supreme Court. There is certainly something to be said for this position, as the district court is charged with making the initial determination whether to admit evidence. In the peculiar circumstances of this case, however, we have determined that the interests of justice and judicial economy will best be served by deciding those issues that are properly before us and, in the process, offering guidance on the application of the *Daubert* standard in this circuit.

The district court already made a determination as to admissibility, albeit under a different standard than we apply on remand, and granted summary judgment based on its exclusion of plaintiffs' expert testimony.

Daubert v. Merrell Dow Pharmaceuticals, Inc., 727 F. Supp. 570, 575–76 (S.D. Cal. 1989). A grant of summary judgment may be sustained on any basis supported by the record, *Leonard v. Clark*, 12 F.3d 885, 889 (9th Cir. 1993), so we shall consider whether the district court's grant of summary judgment can be sustained under the new standard announced by the Supreme Court. Our review here is, of course, very narrow: We will affirm the summary judgment only if, as a matter of law, the proffered evidence would have to be excluded at trial. The district court's power is far broader; were we to conclude that the expert testimony is not per se inadmissible, the district court on remand would nevertheless have discretion to reject it under Rule 403 or 702. *Daubert*, __ U.S. at __, 113 S. Ct. at 2798. Such a ruling would be reviewed under the deferential abuse of discretion standard.

One other procedural matter detains us. According to plaintiffs, they weren't required to come forward with *any* evidence to survive summary judgment because the affidavit of Merrell's expert was itself inadmissible under *Daubert*; the burden thus never shifted to plaintiffs to demonstrate a genuine issue as to causation. Plaintiffs not only fail to mention the many other exhibits offered by Merrell, they also misunderstand the moving party's burden on summary judgment. Because plaintiffs bear the ultimate burden of proof on causation, Merrell had only to point to the absence of a genuine issue of material fact; it wasn't required to produce any evidence at all. See *Maffei v. Northern Insulation of New York*, 12 F.3d 892, 899 (9th Cir. 1993). Thus, the admissibility of Merrell's expert's affidavit is beside the point; the question is whether plaintiffs adduced enough admissible evidence to create a genuine issue of material fact as to whether Bendectin caused their injuries. See *Elkins v. Richardson-Merrell, Inc.*, 8 F.3d 1068, 1071–72 (6th Cir. 1993). It is to that question we now turn.

II

A. Brave New World

Federal judges ruling on the admissibility of expert scientific testimony face a far more complex and daunting task in a post-*Daubert* world than before. The judge's task under *Frye* is relatively simple: to determine whether the method employed by the experts is generally accepted in the scientific community. *Solomon*, 753 F.2d at 1526. Under *Daubert*, we must engage in a difficult, two-part analysis. First, we must determine nothing less than whether the experts' testimony reflects "scientific knowledge," whether their findings are "derived by the scientific method," and whether their work product amounts to "good science." __ U.S. at __, __, 113 S. Ct. at 2795, 2797. Second, we must ensure that the proposed expert testimony is "relevant to the task at hand," id. at __, 113 S.Ct. at 2797, i.e., that it logically advances a material aspect of the proposing party's case. The Supreme Court referred to this second prong of the analysis as the "fit" requirement. Id. at __, 113 S.Ct. at 2796.

The first prong of *Daubert* puts federal judges in an uncomfortable position. The question of admissibility only arises if it is first established that the individuals whose testimony is being proffered are experts in a particular scientific field; here, for example, the Supreme Court waxed eloquent on the impressive qualifications of plaintiffs' experts. Id. __ n.2, 113 S.Ct. at 2791 n.2. Yet something doesn't become "scientific knowledge" just because it's uttered by a scientist; nor can an expert's self-serving assertion that his conclusions were "derived by the scientific method" be deemed conclusive, else the Supreme Court's opinion could have ended with footnote two. As we read the Supreme Court's teaching in *Daubert*, therefore, though we are largely untrained in science and certainly no match for any of the witnesses whose testimony we are reviewing, it is our responsibility to determine whether those experts' proposed testimony amounts to "scientific knowledge," constitutes "good science," and was "derived by the scientific method."

The task before us is more daunting still when the dispute concerns matters at the very cutting edge of scientific research, where fact meets theory and certainty dissolves into probability. As the record in this case illustrates, scientists often have vigorous and sincere disagreements as to what research methodology is proper, what should be accepted as sufficient proof for the existence of a "fact," and whether information derived by a particular method can tell us anything useful about the subject under study.

Our responsibility, then, unless we badly misread the Supreme Court's opinion, is to resolve disputes among respected, well-credentialed scientists about matters squarely within their expertise, in areas where there is no scientific consensus as to what is and what is not "good science," and occasionally to reject such expert testimony because it was not "derived by the scientific method." Mindful of our position in the hierarchy of the federal judiciary, we take a deep breath and proceed with this heady task.

B.   Deus ex Machina

The Supreme Court's opinion in *Daubert* focuses closely on the language of Fed. R. Evid. 702, which permits opinion testimony by experts as to matters amounting to "scientific . . . knowledge." The Court recognized, however, that knowledge in this context does not mean absolute certainty. __ U.S. at __, 113 S.Ct. at 2795. Rather, the Court said, "in order to qualify as 'scientific knowledge,' an inference or assertion must be derived by the scientific method." Id. Elsewhere in its opinion, the Court noted that Rule 702 is satisfied where the proffered testimony is "based on scientifically valid principles." Id. at __, 113 S.Ct. at 2799. Our task, then, is to analyze not what the experts say, but what basis they have for saying it.

Which raises the question: How do we figure out whether scientists have derived their findings through the scientific method or whether their testimony is based on scientifically valid principles? Each expert proffered by the plaintiffs assures us that he has "utiliz[ed] the type of data that is generally and reasonably relied upon by scientists" in the relevant field, see, e.g., Newman Aff. at 5, and that he has "utilized the methods and methodology that would generally and reasonably be accepted" by people who deal in these matters, see, e.g., Gross Aff. at 5. The Court held, however, that federal judges perform a "gatekeeping role," *Daubert*, __ U.S. at __, 113 S. Ct. at 2798; to do so they must satisfy themselves that scientific evidence meets a certain standard of reliability before it is admitted. This means that the expert's bald assurance of validity is not enough. Rather, the party presenting the expert must show that the expert's findings are based on sound science, and this will require some objective, independent validation of the expert's methodology.

While declining to set forth a "definitive checklist or test," id. at __, 113 S.Ct. at 2796, the Court did list several factors federal judges can consider in determining whether to admit expert scientific testimony under Fed. R. Evid. 702: whether the theory or technique employed by the expert is generally accepted in the scientific community; whether it's been subjected to peer review and publication; whether it can be and has been tested;

and whether the known or potential rate of error is acceptable. Id. at __, 113 S.Ct. at 2796–97.[3] We read these factors as illustrative rather than exhaustive; similarly, we do not deem each of them to be equally applicable (or applicable at all) in every case.[4] Rather, we read the Supreme Court as instructing us to determine whether the analysis undergirding the experts' testimony falls within the range of accepted standards governing how scientists conduct their research and reach their conclusions.

One very significant fact to be considered is whether the experts are proposing to testify about matters growing naturally and directly out of research they have conducted independent of the litigation, or whether they have developed their opinions expressly for purposes of testifying. That an expert testifies for money does not necessarily cast doubt on the reliability of his testimony, as few experts appear in court merely as an eleemosynary gesture. But in determining whether proposed expert testimony amounts to good science, we may not ignore the fact that a scientist's normal workplace is the lab or the field, not the courtroom or the lawyer's office.[5]

That an expert testifies based on research he has conducted independent of the litigation provides important, objective proof that the research comports with the dictates of good science. See Peter W. Huber, *Galileo's Revenge: Junk Science in the Courtroom* 206–09 (1991) (describing how the prevalent practice of expert-shopping leads to bad science). For one thing, experts whose findings flow from existing research are less likely to have been biased toward a particular conclusion by the promise of remuneration; when an expert prepares reports and findings before being hired as a witness, that record will limit the degree to which he can tailor his testimony to serve a party's interests. Then, too, independent research carries its own indicia of reliability, as it is conducted, so to speak, in the usual course of business and must normally satisfy a variety of standards to attract funding and institutional support. Finally, there is usually a limited number of scientists actively conducting research on the very subject that is germane to a particular case, which provides a natural constraint on parties' ability to shop for experts who will come to the desired conclusion. That the testimony proffered by an expert is based directly on legitimate, preexisting research unrelated to the litigation provides the most persuasive basis for concluding that the opinions he expresses were "derived by the scientific method."

We have examined carefully the affidavits proffered by plaintiffs' experts, as well as the testimony from prior trials that plaintiffs have introduced in support of that testimony, and find that none of the experts based his testimony on preexisting or independent research. While plaintiffs' scientists are all experts in their respective fields, none claims to have studied the effect of Bendectin on limb reduction defects before being hired to testify in this or related cases.

If the proffered expert testimony is not based on independent research, the party proffering it must come forward with other objective, verifiable evidence that the testimony is based on "scientifically valid principles." One means of showing this is by proof that the research and analysis supporting the proffered conclusions have been subjected to normal scientific scrutiny through peer review and publication.[6] Huber, *Galileo's Revenge* 209 (suggesting that "[t]he ultimate test of [a scientific expert's] integrity is her readiness to publish and be damned").

Peer review and publication do not, of course, guarantee that the conclusions reached are correct; much published scientific research is greeted with intense skepticism and is not borne out by further research. But the test under *Daubert* is not the correctness of the expert's conclusions but the soundness of his methodology. See n.11 *infra*. That the research is accepted for publication in a reputable scientific journal after being subjected to the usual rigors of peer review is a significant indication that it is taken seriously by other scientists, i.e., that it meets at least the minimal criteria of good science. *Daubert*, __ U.S. at __, 113 S. Ct. at 2797 ("[S]crutiny of the scientific community is a component of 'good science'"). If nothing else, peer review and publication "increase the likelihood that substantive flaws in methodology will be detected." *Daubert*, __ U.S. at __, 113 S. Ct. at 2797.[7]

Bendectin litigation has been pending in the courts for over a decade, yet the only review the plaintiffs' experts' work has received has been by judges and juries, and the only place their theories and studies have been published is in the pages of federal and state reporters.[8] None of the plaintiffs' experts has published his work on Bendectin in a scientific journal or solicited formal review by his colleagues. Despite the many years the controversy has been brewing, no one in the scientific community—except defendant's experts—has deemed these studies worthy of verification, refutation or even comment. It's as if there were a tacit understanding within the scientific community that what's going on here is not science at all, but litigation.[9]

Establishing that an expert's proffered testimony grows out of pre-litigation research or that the expert's research has been subjected to peer review are the two principal ways the proponent of expert testimony can show that the evidence satisfies the first prong of Rule 702.[10] Where such evidence is unavailable, the proponent of expert scientific testimony may attempt to satisfy its burden through the testimony of its own experts. For such a showing to be sufficient, the experts must explain precisely how they went about reaching their conclusions and point to some objective source—a learned treatise, the policy statement of a professional association, a published article in a reputable scientific journal or the like—to show that they have followed the scientific method, as it is practiced by (at least) a recognized minority of scientists in their field. See *United States v. Rincon*, 28 F.3d 921, 924 (9th Cir. 1994) (research must be described "in sufficient detail that the district court [can] determine if the research was scientifically valid").[11]

Plaintiffs have made no such showing. As noted above, plaintiffs rely entirely on the experts' unadorned assertions that the methodology they employed comports with standard scientific procedures. In support of these assertions, plaintiffs offer only the trial and deposition testimony of these experts in other cases. While these materials indicate that plaintiffs' experts have relied on animal studies, chemical structure analyses and epidemiological data, they neither explain the methodology the experts followed to reach their conclusions nor point to any external source to validate that methodology. We've been presented with only the experts' qualifications, their conclusions and their assurances of reliability. Under *Daubert*, that's not enough.

This is especially true of Dr. Palmer—the only expert willing to testify "that Bendectin did cause the limb defects in each of the children." Palmer Aff. at 8. In support of this conclusion, Dr. Palmer asserts only that Bendectin is a teratogen and that he has examined the plaintiffs' medical records, which apparently reveal the timing of their mothers' ingestion of the drug. Dr. Palmer offers no tested or testable theory to explain how, from this limited information, he was able to eliminate all other potential causes of birth defects, nor does he explain how he alone can state as a fact that Bendectin caused plaintiffs' injuries. We therefore agree with the Sixth Circuit's observation that "Dr. Palmer does not testify on the basis of the collective view of his scientific discipline, nor does he take issue with his peers and explain the grounds for his differences. Indeed, no understandable scientific basis is stated. Personal opinion, not science, is testifying here." *Turpin*, 959 F.2d at 1360. For this reason, Dr. Palmer's testimony is inadmissible as a matter of law under Rule 702.

The failure to make any objective showing as to admissibility under the first prong of Rule 702 would also fatally undermine the testimony of plaintiffs' other experts, but for the peculiar posture of this case. Plaintiffs submitted their experts' affidavits while *Frye* was the law of the circuit and, although they've not requested an opportunity to augment their experts' affidavits in light of *Daubert*, the interests of justice would be disserved by precluding plaintiffs from doing so. Given the opportunity to augment their original showing of admissibility, plaintiffs might be able to show that the methodology adopted by some of their experts is based on sound scientific principles. For instance, plaintiffs' epidemiologists might validate their reanalyses by explaining why they chose only certain of the data that was available, or the experts relying on animal studies might point to some authority for extrapolating human causation from teratogenicity in animals.[12]

Were this the only question before us, we would be inclined to remand to give plaintiffs an opportunity to submit additional proof that the scientific testimony they proffer was "derived by the scientific method." *Daubert*, however, establishes two prongs to the Rule 702 admissibility inquiry. See pp. 1315–16 supra. We therefore consider whether the testimony satisfies the second prong of Rule 702: Would plaintiffs' proffered scientific evidence "assist the trier of fact to . . . determine a fact in issue"? Fed. R. Evid. 702.

C. No Visible Means of Support

In elucidating the second requirement of Rule 702, *Daubert* stressed the importance of the "fit" between the testimony and an issue in the case: "Rule 702's 'helpfulness' standard requires a valid scientific connection to the pertinent inquiry as a precondition to admissibility." __ U.S. at __, 113

S. Ct. at 2796. Here, the pertinent inquiry is causation. In assessing whether the proffered expert testimony "will assist the trier of fact" in resolving this issue, we must look to the governing substantive standard, which in this case is supplied by California tort law.

Plaintiffs do not attempt to show causation directly; instead, they rely on experts who present circumstantial proof of causation. Plaintiffs' experts testify that Bendectin is a teratogen because it causes birth defects when it is tested on animals, because it is similar in chemical structure to other suspected teratogens, and because statistical studies show that Bendectin use increases the risk of birth defects. Modern tort law permits such proof, but plaintiffs must nevertheless carry their traditional burden; they must prove that their injuries were the result of the accused cause and not some independent factor. In the case of birth defects, carrying this burden is made more difficult because we know that some defects—including limb reduction defects—occur even when expectant mothers do not take Bendectin, and that most birth defects occur for no known reason.

California tort law requires plaintiffs to show not merely that Bendectin increased the likelihood of injury, but that it more likely than not caused *their* injuries. See *Jones v. Ortho Pharmaceutical Corp.*, 163 Cal. App. 3d 396, 403, 209 Cal. Rptr. 456 (1985). In terms of statistical proof, this means that plaintiffs must establish not just that their mothers' ingestion of Bendectin increased somewhat the likelihood of birth defects, but that it more than doubled it—only then can it be said that Bendectin is more likely than not the source of their injury. Because the background rate of limb reduction defects is one per thousand births, plaintiffs must show that among children of mothers who took Bendectin the incidence of such defects was more than two per thousand.[13]

None of plaintiffs' epidemiological experts claims that ingestion of Bendectin during pregnancy more than doubles the risk of birth defects.[14] To evaluate the relationship between Bendectin and limb reduction defects, an epidemiologist would take a sample of the population and compare the frequency of birth defects in children whose mothers took Bendectin with the frequency of defects in children whose mothers did not. See *DeLuca*, 911 F.2d 941 at 946. The ratio derived from this comparison would be an estimate of the "relative risk" associated with Bendectin. See generally Joseph L. Fleiss, *Statistical Methods for Rates and Proportions* (2d ed.

1981). For an epidemiological study to show causation under a preponderance standard, "the relative risk of limb reduction defects arising from the epidemiological data . . . will, at a minimum, have to exceed '2'." *DeLuca*, 911 F.2d at 958.[15] That is, the study must show that children whose mothers took Bendectin are more than twice as likely to develop limb reduction birth defects as children whose mothers did not.[16] While plaintiffs' epidemiologists make vague assertions that there is a statistically significant relationship between Bendectin and birth defects, none states that the relative risk is greater than two. These studies thus would not be helpful, and indeed would only serve to confuse the jury, if offered to prove rather than refute causation. A relative risk of less than two may suggest teratogenicity, but it actually tends to *dis*prove legal causation as it shows that Bendectin does not double the likelihood of birth defects.[17]

With the exception of Dr. Palmer, whose testimony is inadmissible under the first prong of the Rule 702 analysis, see p. 1319 supra,[18] the remaining experts proffered by plaintiffs were equally unprepared to testify that Bendectin caused plaintiffs' injuries; they were willing to testify only that Bendectin is "capable of causing" birth defects. Crescitelli Aff. at 3, 8; Glasser Aff. at 6, 8; Gross Aff. at 9; Newman Aff. at 5, 9; Swan Aff. at 7. Plaintiffs argue "these scientists use the words 'capable of causing' meaning that it does cause. This is an ambiguity of language . . . . If something is capable of causing damage in humans, it does." Tape of Oral Arg. Mar. 22, 1994. But what plaintiffs must prove is not that Bendectin causes some birth defects, but that it caused *their* birth defects. To show this, plaintiffs' experts would have had to testify either that Bendectin actually caused plaintiffs' injuries (which they could not say) or that Bendectin more than doubled the likelihood of limb reduction birth defects (which they did not say).

As the district court properly found below, "the strongest inference to be drawn for plaintiffs based on the epidemiological evidence is that Bendectin could *possibly* have caused plaintiffs' injuries." 727 F. Supp. at 576. The same is true of the other testimony derived from animal studies and chemical structure analyses—these experts "testify to a possibility rather than a probability." *Turpin*, 959 F.2d at 1360. Plaintiffs do not quantify this possibility, or otherwise indicate how their conclusions about causation should be weighted, even though the substantive legal standard has always required proof of causation by a preponderance of the evidence.[19] Unlike these experts' explanation of their methodology, this is not a shortcoming that could be corrected on remand; plaintiffs' experts could augment their affidavits with independent proof that their methods were sound, but to augment the substantive testimony as to causation would require the experts to change their conclusions altogether. Any such tailoring of the experts' conclusions would, at this stage of the proceedings, fatally undermine any attempt to show that these findings were "derived by the scientific method." Plaintiffs' experts must, therefore, stand by the conclusions they originally proffered, rendering their testimony inadmissible under the second prong of Fed. R. Evid. 702.

Conclusion

The district court's grant of summary judgment is AFFIRMED.

Notes to Appendix B

1. Limb reduction defects involve incomplete development of arms, legs, fingers and toes, such as the defects associated with the Thalidomide disaster of the 1960s.

2. We had adopted *Frye* as the law of the circuit in *United States v. Solomon*, 753 F.2d 1522, 1526 (9th Cir. 1985).

3. These factors raise many questions, such as how do we determine whether the rate of error is acceptable, and by what standard? Or, what should we infer from the fact that the methodology has been tested, but only by the party's own expert or experts? Do we ask whether the methodology they employ to test their methodology is itself methodologically sound? Such questions only underscore the basic problem, which is that we must devise standards for acceptability where respected scientists disagree on what's acceptable.

4. Two of the four factors mentioned by the Supreme Court would be difficult or impossible to apply to the expert testimony in this case. Only one of plaintiffs' experts has done original research. Dr. Crescitelli mentions that he "specifically performed studies" on Bendectin and its antihistamine component, Aff. at 3, but does not explain the nature of those studies or the methodology employed. The others have examined the available literature and studies within their respective fields and drawn different conclusions than the scientists who performed the original work. As to such derivative analytical work, it makes little sense to ask whether the technique employed "can be (and has been) tested," *Daubert*, __ U.S. at __, 113 S. Ct. at 2796, or what its "known or potential rate of error" might be, id. at __, 113 S.Ct. at 2797.

5. There are, of course, exceptions. Fingerprint analysis, voice recognition, DNA fingerprinting and a variety of other scientific endeavors closely tied to law enforcement may indeed have the courtroom as a principal theater of operations. See, e.g., *United States v. Chischilly*, 30 F.3d 1144, 1153 (9th Cir. 1994) (admitting expert testimony concerning a DNA match as proof the defendant committed sexual abuse and murder). As to such disciplines, the fact that the expert has developed an expertise principally for purposes of litigation will obviously not be a substantial consideration.

6. We refer, of course, to publication in a generally recognized scientific journal that conditions publication on a bona fide process of peer review. See *Daubert*, __ U.S. at __, 113 S. Ct. at 2797 ("The fact of publication (or lack thereof) in a peer-reviewed journal thus will be . . . relevant . . . .") (emphasis added). See generally The Journal's Peer-Review Process, 321 *New Eng. J. Med.* 837 (1989).

7. For instance, peer review might well have brought to light the more glaring arithmetical errors in the testimony presented by plaintiffs' experts in other Bendectin cases. See *DeLuca v. Merrell Dow Pharmaceuticals, Inc.*, 791 F. Supp. 1042, 1048 (D.N.J. 1992), *aff'd*, 6 F.3d 778 (3d Cir. 1993).

8. As Judge Frank Johnson has succinctly noted, "the examination of a scientific study by a cadre of lawyers is not the same as its examination by others trained in the field of science or medicine." *Perry v. United States*, 755 F.2d 888, 892 (11th Cir. 1985).

9. There may well be good reasons why a scientific study has not been published. For example, it may be too recent or of insufficiently broad interest. *Daubert*, __ U.S. at __, 113 S. Ct. at 2797. These reasons do not apply here. Except with respect to the views expressed in this litigation, plaintiffs' experts have been well-published, see, e.g., Crescitelli Aff. at 3 (authored 125 formal papers, 80–100 short notes or abstracts, a half-dozen reviews, and articles concerning antihistamines and related compounds), and the opinions they proffer, if supported by sound methodology, would doubtless be greedily devoured by the machinery of peer review. A conclusion that Bendectin causes birth defects would be of significant public interest both in this country (where millions of women have taken Bendectin and the FDA continues to approve its use) and abroad (where Bendectin is still widely used). That plaintiffs' experts have been unable or unwilling to publish their work undermines plaintiffs' claim that the findings these experts proffer are "ground[ed] in the methods and procedures of science" and "derived by the scientific method." *Daubert*, __ U.S. at __, __, 113 S. Ct. at 2795, 2796.

10. This showing would not, of course, be conclusive. Proffering scientific testimony and making an initial showing that it was derived by the scientific method enables a party to establish a prima facie case as to admissibility under Rule 702. The opposing party would then be entitled to challenge that showing. This it could do by presenting evidence (including expert testimony) that the proposing party's expert employed unsound methodology or failed to assiduously follow an otherwise sound protocol. Where the opposing party thus raises a material dispute as to the admissibility of expert scientific evidence, the district court must hold an in limine hearing (a so-called *Daubert* hearing) to consider the conflicting evidence

and make findings about the soundness and reliability of the methodology employed by the scientific experts. See Fed. R. Evid. 104(a) ("In making its determination [the court] is not bound by the rules of evidence."); Fed. R. Evid. 706 (on the use of court-appointed experts).

11. This underscores the difference between *Daubert* and *Frye*. Under *Frye*, the party proffering scientific evidence had to show it was based on the method generally accepted in the scientific community. The focus under *Daubert* is on the reliability of the methodology, and in addressing that question the court and the parties are not limited to what is generally accepted; methods accepted by a minority in the scientific community may well be sufficient. However, the party proffering the evidence must explain the expert's methodology and demonstrate in some objectively verifiable way that the expert has both chosen a reliable scientific method and followed it faithfully. Of course, the fact that one party's experts use a methodology accepted by only a minority of scientists would be a proper basis for impeachment at trial.

12. Dr. Palmer could not similarly bolster his testimony. Unlike the other experts, who speak in terms of probabilities, Dr. Palmer goes so far as to conclude that plaintiffs' injuries were in fact caused by Bendectin rather than another cause. The record in this case categorically refutes the notion that anyone can tell what caused the birth defects in any given case. See p. 1313 supra.

13. No doubt, there will be unjust results under this substantive standard. If a drug increases the likelihood of birth defects, but doesn't more than double it, some plaintiffs whose injuries are attributable to the drug will be unable to recover. There is a converse unfairness under a regime that allows recovery to everyone that *may* have been affected by the drug. Under this regime, all potential plaintiffs are entitled to recover, even though most will not have suffered an injury that can be attributed to the drug. One can conclude from this that unfairness is inevitable when our tools for detecting causation are imperfect and we must rely on probabilities rather than more direct proof. In any event, this is a matter to be sorted out by the states, whose substantive legal standards we are bound to apply. See *O'Melveny & Myers v. FDIC*, __ U.S. __, __, 114 S. Ct. 2048, 2053, 129 L. Ed2d 67 (1994).

14. The only exception is Dr. Done, who in another case presented metaanalysis studies purporting to show a relative risk greater than two. But his conclusion in that case rested on a demonstrably faulty methodology, see *DeLuca*, 791 F. Supp. at 1047–59, and perhaps for that reason was not proffered here.

15. For a more complete explanation of the relationship between the burden of proof and relative risk, see Robert P. Charrow and David E. Bernstein, *Scientific Evidence in the Courtroom: Admissibility and Statistical Significance after* Daubert 28–33 (Wash. Legal Found., 1994).

16. A statistical study showing a relative risk of less than two could be combined with other evidence to show it is more likely than not that the accused cause is responsible for a particular plaintiff's injury. For example, a statistical study may show that a particular type of birth defect is associated with some unknown causes, as well as two known potential causes—e.g., smoking and drinking. If a study

shows that the relative risk of injury for those who smoke is 1.5 as compared to the general population, while it is 1.8 for those who drink, a plaintiff who does not drink might be able to reanalyze the data to show that the study of smoking did not account for the effect of drinking on the incidence of birth defects in the general population. By making the appropriate comparison—between non-drinkers who smoke and non-drinkers who do not smoke—the teetotaller plaintiff might be able to show that the relative risk of smoking for her is greater than two. Here, however, plaintiffs' experts did not seek to differentiate these plaintiffs from the subjects of the statistical studies. The studies must therefore stand or fall on their own.

17. The Supreme Court recognized that the "fit" requirement "goes primarily to relevance," *Daubert,* __ U.S. at __, 113 S. Ct. at 2795, but it obviously did not intend the second prong of Rule 702 to be merely a reiteration of the general relevancy requirement of Rule 402. In elucidating the "fit" requirement, the Supreme Court noted that scientific expert testimony carries special dangers to the fact-finding process because it "'can be both powerful and quite misleading because of the difficulty in evaluating it.'" Id. at __, 113 S.Ct at 2798 (quoting Weinstein, *Rule 702 of the Federal Rules of Evidence Is Sound; It Should Not Be Amended,* 138 F.R.D. 631, 632 (1991)). Federal judges must therefore exclude proffered scientific evidence under Rules 702 and 403 unless they are convinced that it speaks clearly and directly to an issue in dispute in the case, and that it will not mislead the jury.

18. Dr. Palmer's testimony would easily meet Rule 702's fit requirement, were it not rendered inadmissible by the total lack of scientific basis for his conclusions. See pp. 1319–20 and n. 12 supra. Dr. Palmer's testimony thus illustrates how the two prongs of Rule 702 work in tandem to ensure that junk science is kept out of the federal courtroom.

19. Several circuits have conducted a similar analysis in finding plaintiffs' expert testimony insufficient to prove causation as a matter of law. See *Elkins,* 8 F.3d at 1071–72; *Turpin,* 959 F.2d at 1359–61; *Ealy v. Richardson-Merrell, Inc.,* 897 F.2d 1159, 1163 (D.C. Cir. 1990); *Brock v. Merrell Dow Pharmaceuticals, Inc.,* 874 F.2d 307, 311–15 (5th Cir. 1989); *Lynch v. Merrell-Nat'l Labs.,* 830 F.2d 1190, 1195–97 (1st Cir. 1987).

Notes

Chapter 1

1. A. I. Marcus, *Cancer from Beef* (Johns Hopkins University Press, 1994); L. Cole, *The Politics of Radon* (AAAS Press, 1994). See also *Phantom Risk*, ed. K. Foster et al. (MIT Press, 1993), p. 101.

2. *Daubert v. Merrell Dow Pharmaceuticals, Inc.*, 509 U.S. 579 (1993). The majority opinion and the dissenting opinion are reproduced in their entirety in appendix B below.

3. *Daubert*, 509 U.S. at 592–593.

4. Ibid. at 598–599.

5. E. Green and C. Nesson, *Problems, Cases, and Materials on Evidence* (Little, Brown, 1983), p. 649; *Webster's Third New International Dictionary* (1986), p. 1252 ('scientific'); B. Black, A unified theory of scientific evidence, *Fordham Law Review* 56 (1988): 595–599; J. Starrs, *Frye v. United States* restructured and revitalized: A proposal to amend Federal Evidence Rule 702, *Jurimetrics J.* 26 (1986): 249–256; Advisory Committee's Notes on Fed. Rule Evid. 602; Advisory Committee's Notes on Art. VIII of the Rules of Evidence; 3 J. Weinstein and M. Berger, Weinstein's Evidence P 702[03], pp. 702–718 (1988); ibid., P 702[03], pp. 702-741–702-742; S. Jasanoff, *The Fifth Branch: Science Advisors as Policymakers* (Harvard University Press, 1990), pp. 61–76; M. McCormick, Scientific evidence: Defining a new approach to admissibility, *Iowa Law Review* 67 (1982): 879, 911–912; Symposium on science and the Rules of Evidence, 99 F.R.D. 187, 231 (1983) (statement by Margaret Berger); J. Weinstein, Rule 702 of the Federal Rules of Evidence is sound; It should not be amended, *Federal Rules Decisions* 138 (1991): 631–632; B. Cardozo, *The Nature of the Judicial Process* (Yale University Press, 1921), pp. 178–179.

6. *Daubert*, 509 U.S. at 590 (citing and quoting from Brief for Nicolaas Bloembergen et al. as amici curiae 9); ibid. (citing and quoting from Brief for American Association for the Advancement of Science and the National Academy of Sciences as amici curiae 7–8); ibid. at 2798 (citing Brief for Ronald Bayer et al. as amici curiae).

7. Nicolaas Bloembergen (physics, 1981), Dudley Herschbach (chemistry, 1986), Jerome Karle (chemistry, 1980), Wassily Leontief (economics, 1973), William Lipscomb (chemistry, 1976), and Arno Penzias (physics, 1978).

8. 727 F. Supp. 570 (S.D. Cal. 1989), aff'd, 951 F.2d 1128 (9th Cir. 1991), vacated and remanded, 509 U.S. 579 (1993), aff'd, 43 F. 3d 1311 (9th Cir. 1995), cert. denied, 116 S. Ct. 189 (1995).

9. See *Phantom Risk*, ed. Foster et al.

10. *Daubert v. Merrell Dow Pharmaceuticals, Inc.*, 727 F. Supp. 570 (S.D. Cal. 1989).

11. *Daubert v. Merrell Dow Pharmaceuticals, Inc.*, 951 F.2d 1128 (9th Cir. 1991).

12. *Daubert v. Merrell Dow Pharmaceuticals, Inc.*, 506 U.S. 914 (1993).

13. Board of Trustees of the American Medical Association, Impact of product liability on the development of new medical technologies, Report A-88, Resolution 6, A-87 (1988), p. 11.

14. Quoted in C. Skrzycki, The risky business of birth control, *U.S. News and World Report*, May 26, 1986, p. 42.

15. D. C. Paterson, Congenital deformities, *Canadian Medical Association Journal* 101 (1969): 175–176.

16. Public Health Service, Hearing before the Fertility and Maternal Health Drugs Advisory Committee, Department of Health and Human Services, Public Health Service, Food and Drug Administration (Government Printing Office, 1990).

17. C. A. Bunde and D. M. Bowles, A technique for controlled survey of case records, *Current Therapeutic Research* 5 (1963): 245–248.

18. K. J. Rothman et al., Exogenous hormones and other drug exposures of children with congenital heart disease, *American Journal of Epidemiology* 109: (1979): 433–439.

19. L. Lasagna and S. R. Shulman, Bendectin and causation, in *Phantom Risk*.

20. R. L. Brent, Bendectin: Review of the medical literature of a comprehensively studied human nonteratogen and the most prevalent tortogen-litigen, *Reproductive Toxicology* 9 (1995): 337–349.

21. See, e.g., J. Golding, S. P. Vivian, and J. A. Baldwin, Maternal anti-nauseants and clefts of lip and palate, *Human Toxicology* 2 (1983): 63–73.

22. Dr. Swan is currently providing expert testimony for plaintiffs in breast implant litigation.

23. *Frye v. United States*, 293 F. 1013, 1014 (D.C. Cir. 1923).

24. See *Phantom Risk* and P. W. Huber, *Galileo's Revenge: Junk Science in the Courtroom* (Basic Books, 1991). One notorious case was *Wells v. Ortho Pharmaceutical Corp.*, 615 F. Supp. 262 (N.D. Ga. 1985), which resulted in a $4.7 million award for birth defects allegedly resulting from the mother's use of spermicide (*Phantom Risk*, pp. 137–138).

25. See, e.g., *Christopherson v. Allied Signal Corp.*, 939 F. 2d 1106 (5th Cir. 1991) (en banc).

26. A physician who testifies that he or she relied on a standard laboratory test to diagnose a disease in a specific patient is presenting some pure science and some applied knowledge. The scientific proposition is that the test is a reliable, valid indicator of the disease. The technical half of the testimony involves the specific application of the test to a specific patient. "Our discussion is limited to the scientific context," the *Daubert* majority stated, "because that is the nature of the expertise offered here" (*Daubert*, 113 S. Ct. at 2795 n.8).

27. *Daubert*, 509 U.S. at 597.

28. Ibid. at 590.

29. Ibid. and n.9.

30. Ibid. at 593.

31. Ibid. at 594.

32. Ibid. at 593.

33. Ibid. at 594 (citing *United States v. Downing*, 753 F.2d 1224, 1238 (3d Cir. 1985)).

34. Ibid. at 594–595.

35. Ibid. at 596.

36. See K. Chesebro, Taking *Daubert*'s focus seriously: The methodology/conclusion distinction, *Cardozo Law Review* 15 (1994): 1745.

37. Huber, *Galileo's Revenge*.

38. An interesting and accessible discussion of the issues for laypeople is A. F. Chalmers's *What Is This Thing Called Science?* (second edition: Hackett, 1982).

39. *Daubert*, 509 U.S. at 593–594.

40. Ibid.

41. The Federal Judicial Center's recent *Reference Manual on Scientific Evidence* (West, 1994) serves the latter purpose quite well.

42. 727 F. Supp. 570 (S.D. Cal. 1989), aff'd, 951 F.2d 1128 (9th Cir. 1991), vacated and remanded, 509 U.S. 579 (1993), aff'd, 43 F. 3d 1311 (9th Cir. 1995), cert. denied, 116 S. Ct. 189 (1995).

43. J. Baron, *Thinking and Deciding*, second edition (Cambridge University Press, 1994).

44. *Daubert*, 509 U.S. at 597.

45. Ibid.

46. See H. Margolis, *Paradigms and Barriers: How Habits of the Mind Govern Scientific Beliefs* (University of Chicago Press, 1993), p. 178.

Chapter 2

1. *Daubert v. Merrell Dow Pharmaceuticals, Inc.*, 509 U.S. 579, 591 (1993). With perhaps an excess of lawyerly caution, the opinion adds "absent creditable grounds supporting such a link."

2. Ibid., at 591.

3. This reinforces the more general mandate of Rule 402, that testimony of any kind must be "relevant" to be admissible. Rule 402 provides: "All relevant evidence is admissible, except as otherwise provided by the Constitution of the United States, by Act of Congress, by these rules, or by other rules prescribed by the Supreme Court pursuant to statutory authority. Evidence which is not relevant is not admissible."

4. *Daubert*, at 592.

5. Ibid., at 591, quoting *United States v. Downing*, 753 F.2d 1224, 1242 (9th Cir. 1985).

6. *Daubert*, 509 U.S. at 593.

7. Ibid., at 591, quoting *Downing*. That word now has unfortunate (and irrelevant) connotations in the aftermath of a notorious criminal trial in which a glove was said not to fit the hand of the alleged murderer.

8. S. J. Gould, *The Mismeasure of Man* (Norton, 1981). Gould argues that some of the nineteenth century's best-known studies of brain volume and race manipulated their data in such a way as to place white males at the top of the brain-volume (intelligence) hierarchy.

9. See Testing medicines to death, *The Economist*, January 30, 1988, p. 54.

10. In 1897 the House of the Indiana Legislature approved, by a vote of 67–0, a measure that would change the value of π. The bill was killed by the Indiana Senate after the protests of a math professor who was at the State House to lobby for more appropriations for education. See J. Walsh, *The Centennial History of the Indiana General Assembly, 1816–1978* (Indiana Historical Bureau, 1984). (Walsh writes: "The legislation was the result of the work of Edwin J. Goodwin, who concluded he had disproved the theories of Euclid, the father of geometry. Goodwin was willing to offer his new value for pi free of charge for use in Hoosier schools, but wanted to collect a royalty if it was used out of state.").

11. T. S. Kuhn, *The Structure of Scientific Revolutions* (University of Chicago Press, 1970).

12. We know in retrospect that the disease, and the species of mosquito that is its vector, had been introduced into the city that spring by an influx of immigrants from what is now Haiti. See J. M. Powell, *Bring Out Your Dead* (University of Pennsylvania Press, 1949; reprinted in 1993 with an introduction by K. Foster et al.).

13. A. B. Hill, The environment and disease: Association or causation? *Proceedings of the Royal Society of Medicine* 59 (1965): 295.

14. M. Susser, Falsification, verification and causal inference in epidemiology: Reconsiderations in the light of Sir Karl Popper's philosophy, in *Causal Inference*, ed. K. Rothman (Epidemiology Resources, 1988).

15. The Risk Assessment Guidelines of 1986, Report EPA/600/8-87/046, 51 Fed. Reg. 33992 (1986).

16. Final Guidelines for Developmental Toxicity Risk Assessment, 56 *Fed. Reg.* 63798 (1991).

17. Guidelines for Reproductive Toxicity Risk Assessment (external review draft, February 1994), Report EPA/600/AP-94/001.

18. D. E. Lilienfeld and P. D. Stolley, *Foundations of Epidemiology* (Oxford University Press, 1994), p. 267.

19. W. H. Farland, The U.S. Environmental Protection Agency's risk assessment guidelines: Current status and future direction, *Toxicology and Industrial Health* 8 (1992): 205.

20. Ibid.

21. J. V. Rodricks, Some observations on *Daubert* by a toxicologist, *Shepards Expert and Scientific Evidence Quarterly* 1 (fall 1993): 337–344.

22. An example might be a hypothetical witness in a Bendectin case who cites three positive epidemiology studies linking Bendectin to birth defects but not the two dozen other negative studies on this question. See chapter 4.

Chapter 3

1. M. D. Green, Expert witnesses and sufficiency of evidence in toxic substances litigation: The legacy of Agent Orange and Bendectin litigation, *Northwestern University Law Review* 86 (1992): 643–645.

2. *Daubert v. Merrell Dow Pharmaceuticals, Inc.*, 509 U.S. 579, 593 (1993) .

3. *Daubert*, at 593, citing C. Hempel, *Philosophy of Natural Science* (1966) (emphasis omitted).

4. *Daubert*, at 593, citing K. Popper, *Conjectures and Refutations: The Growth of Scientific Knowledge*, fifth edition (Routledge, 1989).

5. *Daubert*, at 600 (Rehnquist, C.J., dissenting).

6. Green, Expert witnesses (notes omitted).

7. K. Popper, *The Logic of Scientific Discovery* (Basic Books, 1959), pp. 40–41.

8. K. Popper, *Conjectures and Refutations* (Routledge, 1992), pp. 36–37.

9. Ibid., p. 35.

10. This was the basic assumption of the Hempel-Popper-Carnap group. But the situation is far more complex than they thought. As Thomas Kuhn pointed out in his *Structure of Scientific Revolutions* (1962), and as is now widely accepted by philosophers, scientific belief is substantially underdetermined by objective factors. It is interesting to note that Einstein's prediction of the bending of light by the sun (one of Popper's favorite examples) was initially wrong by a factor of 2; Einstein promptly corrected the theory. See A. Pais, *The Science and the Life of Albert Einstein* (Oxford University Press, 1982), p. 255.

11. K. Popper, Reason or revolution, in *The Myth of the Framework* (Routledge, 1994).

12. C. Hempel, Laws and their role in scientific explanation, in *Philosophy of Natural Science* (Prentice-Hall, 1966), p. 48.

13. C. Hempel, Laws and their role in scientific explanation, in *Philosophy of Natural Science*, p. 49.

14. M. J. Mahoney, *Scientist as Subject: The Psychological Imperative* (Ballinger, 1976), p. 155; M. J. Mahoney and B. G. DeMonbreun, Psychology of the scientist: An analysis of problem-solving bias, *Cognitive Therapy and Research* 1 (1977): 229–238.

15. See M. Garry et al., Memory: A river runs through it, *Consciousness and Cognition* 3 (1994): 438–451.

16. Michelson himself had pointed out that the ether might perhaps have been trapped in the basements in which he did his experiments. And in 1926, D. C. Miller received an award from the prestigious American Association for the Advancement of Science for a paper of his that claimed that a drift of the ether had definitely been established. See Abraham Pais, *Subtle is the Lord: The Science and Life of Albert Einstein* (Oxford University Press, 1982), p. 113.

17. For a devastating critique of Popper, see T. S. Kuhn, Logic of discovery or psychology of research, in *Criticism and the Growth of Knowledge*, ed. I. Lakatos and A. Musgrave (Cambridge University Press, 1970), pp. 1–22.

18. T. F. Gieryn, Boundaries of science, in *Handbook of Science and Technology Studies*, ed. S. Jasanoff et al. (Sage, 1994).

19. D. L. Hull, *Science as Process* (University of Chicago Press, 1988), pp. 342–343.

20. Interview with R. Giere, in *Taking the Naturalistic Turn, or How Real Philosophy of Science Is Done*, ed. W. Callebaut (University of Chicago Press, 1993).

21. Interview with Kitcher in *Taking the Naturalistic Turn, or How Real Philosophy of Science Is Done*, ed. W. Callebaut (University of Chicago Press, 1993), p. 128.

22. P. Kitcher, *The Advancement of Science* (Oxford University Press, 1993), p. 187.

23. F. Franks, *Polywater* (MIT Press, 1981).

24. L. C. Allen and P. A. Kollman, A theory for anomalous water, *Science* 167 (1970): 1443–1454; L. C. Allen and P. A. Kollman, What can theory say about the existence and properties of anomalous water? *Journal of Colloid and Interface Science* 36 (1970): 469–482.

25. P. Kitcher, *The Advancement of Science* (Oxford University Press, 1993), p. 196.

26. *McLean v. Arkansas Board of Education*, 529 F. Supp. 1255, 1267 (E.D. Ark. 1982).

27. L. Laudan, *Beyond Positivism and Relativism* (Westview, 1996), p. 227.

28. See, e.g., S. Kondo, *Health Effects of Low-Level Radiation* (Kinki University Press, 1993).

29. L. Cole, *The Politics of Radon* (AAAS Press, 1994).

30. H. H. Bauer, *Beyond Velikovsky* (University of Illinois Press, 1984), pp. 314–315.

31. See generally A. M. Harvey and J. Bordley III, *Differential Diagnosis* (Saunders, 1970).

32. Experienced physicians seem to use an intuitive version of this approach in practice, using a style of reasoning that the medical decision experts Peter Szolovits and Stephen Pauker have termed "categorical decision making" ("Categorical and probabilistic reasoning in medical diagnosis, *Artificial Intelligence* 11 (1978): 115–144). "Because so many diagnostic possibilities appear to be available for the expert to consider," they note, "we suspect that the rapid generation and equally rapid modification or elimination of many explicit hypotheses play a significant role in his or her reasoning."

33. J. I. Balla, *The Diagnostic Process: A Model for Clinical Teachers* (Cambridge University Press, 1985), p. 8.

34. Ibid., pp. 9–10.

35. Ibid., p. 10.

36. American College of Physicians, Position paper: Clinical ecology, *Annals of Internal Medicine* 111 (1989): 168.

37. J. Benveniste et al., Human basophil degranulation triggered by very dilute antiserum against IgE, *Nature* 333 (1988): 816–818.

38. J. Maddox et al., High-dilution experiments a delusion, *Nature* 334 (1988): 287–290.

39. D. Reilly et al., Is the evidence for homoeopathy reproducible? *Lancet* 344 (1994): 1601–1606.

40. Ibid.

41. Affidavit of Shanna Helen Swan, submitted as part of Joint Appendix at 116, *Daubert v. Merrell Dow Pharmaceuticals, Inc.*, No. 92-102 (U.S. Dec. 2, 1992).

42. Ibid.

43. *Daubert v. Merrell Dow Pharmaceuticals, Inc.*, 116 S. Ct. 189 (1995).

44. *Daubert v. Merrell Dow Pharmaceuticals, Inc.*, 43 F.3d 1311, 1322 (9th Cir. 1995).

45. Dori Meinert, San Diego families may get trial after justices' ruling on evidence, *San Diego Union-Tribune*, June 29, 1993.

Chapter 4

1. E. G. Carmines and R. A. Zeler, *Reliability and Validity Assessment* (Sage, 1979), p. 11.

2. Ibid.

3. E. Bright Wilson Jr., *An Introduction to Scientific Research* (Dover, 1990), p. 232.

4. Ibid., pp. 232–234.

5. International Organization for Standardization, *Guide to the Expression of Uncertainty in Measurements* (ISO, 1995).

6. A. M. Finkel, *Confronting Uncertainty in Risk Management* (Resources for the Future, 1990).

7. K. J. Rothman, *Modern Epidemiology* (Little, Brown, 1986), p. 128.

8. E. L. Carstensen, *The Biological Effects of Transmission Line Fields* (Elsevier, 1987).

9. B. MacMahon et al., Coffee and cancer of the pancreas, *New England Journal of Medicine* 304 (1981): 630–633; Coffee and cancer of the pancreas (chapter 2), ibid. 315 (1986): 587–589.

10. M. Henrion and B. Fischhoff, Assessing uncertainty in physical constants, *American Journal of Physics* 54 (1986): 791–798.

11. A. Shlyakhter, Uncertainty estimates in scientific models: Lessons from trends in physical measurements, population, and energy projections, in *Uncertainty Modelling and Analysis: Theory and Applications*, ed. B. Ayuub and M. Gupta (North-Holland, 1994).

12. There is, however, considerable ambiguity in how these false-positive detection rates should be calculated. For an extensive discussion of the difficulties in applying population genetics to forensic DNA evidence, see P. Kitcher, *The Lives to Come* (Simon and Schuster, 1996), pp. 170–172. To minimize the problem of incorrect analysis, Kitcher stresses the importance of sharing samples and repeating analyses in different laboratories.

13. J. J. Koehler, A. Chia, and S. Lindsey, The random match probability in DNA evidence: Irrelevant and prejudicial? *Jurimetrics Journal* 35 (1995), winter: 201–219.

14. C. Babbage, *Reflections on the Decline of Science in England* (1830; reprinted by Augustus M. Kelley in 1970), p. 178ff.

15. Quoted by Billy Goodman, Scientists are split over findings of research integrity commission, *The Scientist*, January 22, 1996: 1, 8–9.

16. James Mills, Data torturing, *New England Journal of Medicine* 329 (1993): 1196–1199.

17. J. K. Baldwin and B. K. Hoover, Quality assurance for epidemiologic studies, *Journal of Occupational Medicine* 33 (1991): 1250–1252.

18. D. V. Voiss, Occupational injury: Fact, fantasy or fraud? *Neurologic Clinics* 13 (1995): 431–446.

19. *Deluca v. Merrell Dow Pharmaceuticals, Inc.*, 131 F.R.D. 71 (D.N.J. 1990), *rev'd and remanded*, 911 F.2d 941 (3d Cir. 1990), rev'd, 791 F. Supp. 1042 (D.N.J. 1992), *aff'd without opinion*, 6 F.3d 778 (3d Cir. 1993), *cert. denied*, 114 S. Ct. 691 (1994).

20. Affidavit of Shanna H. Swan at 1, *Deluca v. Merrell Dow Pharmaceuticals, Inc.*, No. 87-226 (D.N.J. Mar. 29, 1991).

21. "Dr. Done testified that he calculated the relative risk of 13 by taking 3/23 as the numerator and dividing by 1/28. Done Test., Tr. 7/10/91, at 116–18. Simple arithmetic reveals, however, that 3/23 divided by 1/28 equals 3.65, not 13." *Deluca v. Merrell Dow Pharmaceuticals, Inc.*, 791 F. Supp. 1042, 1048 (D.N.J. 1992).

22. "Dr. Done purports to have taken the numbers he entered in the boxes on his chart from either the underlying studies themselves, or in the articles where no calculations were made, Dr. Done claims to have calculated the numbers himself. In many cases, this is simply not true." Ibid., 1047.

23. "Dr. Done admitted that he transposed the entries for the Newman and Greenberg studies on his chart and so noticed during cross-examination. . . . The odds ratio of 3.3 reported by Dr. Done for limb reduction defects in the Kullander study related to women who took promethazine (an ingredient not found in Bendectin) and only to children with congenital dysplasia of the hip (a condition Amy DeLuca does not have)." Ibid., 1049. "Dr. Done included the Shapiro/ Heinonen study twice, although it is only one single study printed in two separate versions." Ibid., 1050.

24. See *Deluca*.

25. *Deluca*, 1047–1051.

Chapter 5

1. *Daubert v. Merrell Dow Pharmaceuticals, Inc.*, 509 U.S. 579, 590 (1993).

2. *Daubert*, 509 U.S. at 597.

3. August Kekulé, *Chemische Berichte* 23 (1890): 1306 (English translation from R. T. Morrison and R. N. Boyd, *Organic Chemistry*, third edition (Allyn and Bacon, Inc., 1973), p. 319).

4. J. C. Polanyi, Understanding discovery, in *Science and Society*, ed. M. Moskovits (House of Anansi Press, 1995), p. 6.

5. The following discussion is based on the third edition of S. H. Gehlbach's *Interpreting the Medical Literature* (McGraw-Hill, 1993), a clear and comparatively nontechnical reference that we recommend to laypeople.

6. Some authors define this as the accuracy of a test.

7. D. M. Kammen, A. I. Shlyakhter, and R. Wilson, What is the risk of the impossible? *Technology: Journal of the Franklin Institute* 331A (1994): 97–116.

8. See P. D. Cleary et al., Compulsory premarital screening for human immunodeficiency virus, *Journal of the American Medical Association* 258 (1987): 1757–1782.

9. Thus, out of 100 reports, Mrs. Smith has correctly identified 16 yellow taxis as "yellow" and has incorrectly identified 16 yellow taxis as "not yellow."

10. C. Howson and P. Urbach, *Scientific Reasoning: The Bayesian Approach*, second edition (Open Court, 1993).

11. J. Baron, *Thinking and Deciding* (Cambridge University Press, 1994).

12. P. Kitcher, *The Advancement of Science: Science Without Legend, Objectivity Without Illusions* (Oxford University Press, 1993).

13. Howson and Urbach, *Scientific Reasoning*, p. 11.

14. M. J. Saks and J. J. Koehler, What DNA "fingerprinting" can teach the law about the rest of forensic science, *Cardozo Law Review* 13 (1991): 361–371.

15. Although the most common source of error in DNA testing, errors by the testing labs, were overlooked by scientists until quite recently.

16. Saks and Koehler, What DNA "fingerprinting" can teach the law.

17. Kitcher, *The Advancement of Science*, p. 293.

18. Even people who purport to grasp the statistical issues often bungle them. In the trial of O. J. Simpson, the prosecution established that the defendant had a history of assaulting his wife. A defense attorney (Alan Dershowitz) responded that only about 0.1 percent of men who batter their wives go on to murder them. A statistician (I. J. Good) responded in a letter published in the scientific journal *Nature*. If Dershowitz's statistics are right, a woman whose husband batters her can take comfort in the knowledge that he probably will not end up murdering her. But murder itself is rare. A consistent use of statistics (a correct application of Bayes' theorem) shows that, when a woman is first battered and then murdered, the odds are better than even that the murderer was also the batterer. Dershowitz did not say how many women are battered by their husbands but end up murdered by someone else. See I. J. Good, When batterer turns murderer, *Nature* 375 (1995): 541.

19. See, for example, J. J. Koehler and D. N. Shaviro, Veridical verdicts: Increasing verdict accuracy through the use of overtly probabilistic evidence and methods, *Cornell Law Review* 75 (1990): 247–279, and references cited therein.

20. It is easy to imagine some of the difficulties that can arise in the law. Bayes' theorem demands that one consider base rate information when calculating the probability that a hypothesis is true given evidence. Thus, if certain forensic evidence suggests that an inner city, minority teenager shoplifted from a store, Bayes' theorem demands that the reliability of the evidence be assessed in light of the known frequency with which similar individuals commit similar crimes. This might seem to require presenting evidence on shoplifting rates among inner-city minority teenagers and different data for cases involving prosperous suburban whites. A statistician, a judge, or a jury cannot assess "reliability" properly without access to good "base-rate" data. But it is unlikely that other principles of American law would permit even judges to rely on "base-rate" data that distinguished sharply on the basis of race, class, economic circumstance, and so forth. It seems even less likely that juries could use the information intelligently, even if it were to be accurately presented to them.

21. M. Piattelli-Palmarini, *Inevitable Illusions: How Mistakes of Reason Rule Our Minds* (Wiley, 1994).

22. D. Kahneman and A. Tversky, On the psychology of prediction, *Psychological Review* 80 (1973): 237–251.

23. Some academics disagree. For example, Jonathan Koehler (The base rate fallacy reconsidered: Descriptive, normative, and methodological challenges, *Behavioral and Brain Research* 19 (1996): 1–53) has argued that "base rate information does not map unambiguously into the Bayesian framework in most real world problems."

24. See *Phantom Risk: Scientific Inference and the Law*, ed. K. Foster et al. (MIT Press, 1993).

25. J. D. Graham, L. C. Green, and M. J. Roberts, *In Search of Safety; Chemicals and Cancer Risk* (Harvard University Press, 1988).

26. See *Biomarkers and Occupational Health*, ed. M. Mendelsohn et al. (National Academy Press, 1995).

27. See J. C. Bailar III, J. Needleman, B. L. Berney, and J. M. McGinnis, *Assessing Risks to Health* (Auburn House, 1993).

28. S. Jasanoff, *Science at the Bar: Law, Science, and Technology in America* (Harvard University Press, 1995), p. 210.

Chapter 6

1. *Daubert v. Merrell Dow Pharmaceuticals, Inc.*, 509 U.S. at 599–600. (Rehnquist, C.J., dissenting) (citations omitted). To his string of broken quotes, the chief justice might have added "rests on a reliable foundation" (id. at 2799), "accepted as truths on good grounds" (id. at 2795), "derived by the scientific method" (ibid.), and "evidentiary reliability"—that is, trustworthiness (ibid.).

2. Perhaps Justice Blackmun added this key footnote to his opinion at the behest of another justice in the majority.

3. There is a fair chance that this language was not written by Justice Blackmun, but by one of the other justices joining his opinion. It is not unusual for important language to find its way into footnotes when a concurring justice insists that it be included as a condition for joining the opinion.

4. *Daubert*, 509 U.S. at 594–595.

5. K. Popper, *Logic of Scientific Discovery* (Hutchinson, 1972), p. 111.

6. "I am a Professor of Scientific Method—but have a problem: there is no scientific method. . . . However there are some simple rules of thumb, and they are quite helpful."—Popper, quoted by Paul Feyerabend in *Killing Time: The Autobiography of Paul Feyerabend* (University of Chicago Press, 1995), p. 88.

7. K. Popper, A survey of some fundamental problems, in *The Logic of Scientific Discovery* (Basic Books,1992), pp. 32–33.

8. R. B. Marcus, in *Oxford Companion to Philosophy*, ed. T. Honderich (Oxford University Press, 1995), p. 894.

9. For a recent and quite good example see T. Schick Jr. and L. Vaughn, *How to Think about Weird Things: Critical Thinking for a New Age* (Mayfield, 1995).

10. J. Baron, *Thinking and Deciding*, second edition (Cambridge University Press, 1994).

11. D. Faust, *The Limits of Scientific Reasoning* (University of Minnesota Press, 1984).

12. A. R. Feinstein, *Clinical Epidemiology* (Saunders, 1985), p. 58.

13. S. H. Gehlbach, *Interpreting the Medical Literature*, third edition (McGraw-Hill, 1993), p. 112.

14. E. G. Carbines and R. A. Zeller, *Reliability and Validity Assessment* (Sage, 1979), p. 12.

15. S. J. Gould, *The Mismeasure of Man*, second edition (Norton, 1996).

16. Mental testing, of sorts, was for many years performed on would-be immigrants to the United States. For the first half of the twentieth century the large immigration center on Ellis Island in New York Harbor processed thousands of immigrants a day. People who were uncooperative or who appeared confused were given a "mental test" consisting of a few verbal questions and a simple wooden puzzle. Those who failed the test were labeled mental defectives and were likely to be shipped back home. Such tests were undoubtedly valid for identifying uncooperative and confused individuals (most of whom had just completed a horrific transatlantic voyage in steerage), but we question their validity for identifying mental defectives. The wooden puzzles are now on display at Ellis Island, where the reception center is now a museum.

17. Choosing an appropriate test is often a difficult matter that depends on the design of the study and the nature of the hypothesis one wants to test. The scientific journals are filled with advertisements for computer programs for statistical analysis of data. "Don't base your journal article on the wrong statistical test," one cautions. "Award-winning SigmaStat is the first and only statistical program that guides and counsels you through your entire statistical analysis. Its 'expert system' design handles messy data, automatically checks that your data fits the underlying assumptions of your statistical model and automatically prints a detailed report complete with an explanation of your results." (*American Scientist* 84 (1996): 218)

18. G. D. Murray, The task of a statistical referee, *British Journal of Surgery* 75 (1988): 664–447.

19. P. G. Goldschmidt and T. Colton, The quality of medical literature: An analysis of validation assessments, in *Medical Uses of Statistics*, ed. J. C. Bailar and F. Mosteller (New England Journal of Medicine Books, 1986), pp. 370–391.

20. J. M. Yancey, Ten rules for reading clinical research reports, *American Journal of Surgery* 159 (1990): 533–534.

21. Ibid.

22. J. C. Bailar, Research on the health effects of electromagnetic fields: Science, uncertainty, and stopping rules, paper presented at ASA Conference on Radiation and Health, Alexandria, Virginia, 1989.

23. See P. Brodeur, *The Great Power-Line Cover-Up* (Little, Brown, 1993). See also P. Brodeur, Annals of radiation (cancer and power lines), *New Yorker*, July 9, 1990, p. 38; P. Brodeur, Annals of radiation (part 1—power lines), *New Yorker*, June 12, 1989, p. 51; P. Brodeur, Annals of radiation: The cancer at Slater School, *New Yorker*, December 7, 1992, p. 86.

24. R. Doll and A. B. Hill, A study of aetiology of carcinoma of the lung, *British Medical Journal* 2 (1952): 1271–1286

25. American Physical Society, Statement on Power Line Fields and Public Health, April 23, 1995. ("The scientific literature and the reports of reviews by other panels show no consistent, significant link between cancer and power line fields. . . . No plausible biophysical mechanisms for the systematic initiation or promotion of cancer by these power line fields have been identified.")

26. This recommendation is intensely controversial; most expert panels that have examined the issue have concluded that the available evidence is too weak to make any policy recommendations. Contrast this with the recommendation of the medical establishment to avoid giving children aspirin for fever because of the risk of Reye's syndrome. The difference between these cases reflects differences in the strength of the evidence, the availability of other options, the scientists' estimate of possible consequences of the risk (if it should exist)—mostly nonscientific considerations.

27. D. A. Savitz et al., Scientific standards of criticism: A reaction to "Scientific standards in epidemiologic studies of the menace of daily life" by A. R. Feinstein, *Epidemiology* 1 (1990): 78–82.

28. Ibid.

29. Consider the amount of effort the National Transportation Safety Board has spent in investigating the crash of a Boeing 737 near Pittsburgh in 1994, and the remedial steps taken by the Department of Defense after the crash of the airplane carrying Commerce Secretary Ron Brown near Dubrovnik in 1996.

30. H. H. Bauer, *Scientific Literacy and the Myth of the Scientific Method* (University of Illinois Press, 1992).

31. For example, the physicist Robert Adair has made a second (or perhaps third or fourth) career in recent years of debunking theories that other scientists have proposed that "explain" biological effects of magnetic fields. In a series of papers, Adair has shown that many of these theories are grossly inconsistent with well-established principles of physics. Unless his adversaries successfully counter Adair's criticisms (and so far their track record in this regard is dismal) the theories are doomed to fail, even though they passed normal peer review and were published in good journals in the first place.

32. Most scientific papers go uncited. Four years after publication, almost 40 percent of all physics papers, 72 percent of all engineering, 75 percent of papers in the social sciences, and 98 percent of papers in the arts and humanities remain

uncited. Source: D. P. Hamilton, Research papers: Who's uncited now? *Science* 251 (1991): 25.

33. For example: When the Soviet Union was a workers' paradise, Soviet doctors published numerous reports in their medical literature of a "microwave sickness" among workers in radar factories. The reports were based on nonspecific symptoms such as headache and anxiety, and the syndrome is not accepted by Western physicians. The reports, still available, will no doubt provide grist for litigation in the future. (The cure was most often a visit to a rest spa; this might help explain the high incidence of the disease.)

Chapter 7

1. *Daubert v. Merrell Dow Pharmaceuticals, Inc.*, 509 U.S. 579, 593 (1993).

2. Ibid.

3. *Daubert*, 509 U.S. at 594.

4. *Daubert*, 509 U.S. at 593.

5. J. Ziman, *Reliable Knowledge: An Exploration of the Grounds for Belief in Science* (Cambridge University Press, 1978), pp. 130–133.

6. J. Ziman, *Public Knowledge: The Social Dimension of Science* (Cambridge University Press, 1968), p. 9.

7. See also D. Horrobin, The philosophical basis of peer review and the suppression of innovation, *Journal of the American Medical Association* 263 (1990): 1438–1441. Charles McCutchen (Peer review: Treacherous servant, disastrous master, *Technology Review*, October 1991: 29–40) takes a more provocative view, describing the political factors that can distort the editorial decisions.

8. See also M. Angell and A. S. Relman, How good is peer review? *New England Journal of Medicine* 321 (1989): 827–829.

9. Brief Amicus Curiae of Professor Alvan R. Feinstein in Support of Respondent at 7–8, *Daubert v. Merrell Dow Pharmaceuticals*, No. 92-102 (U.S. Jan. 19, 1993).

10. S. W. Lagakos, B. J. Wessen, and M. Zelen, An analysis of contaminated well water and health effects in Woburn, Massachusetts, *Journal of the American Statistical Association* 81 (1986): 583–596.

11. B. MacMahon, Comment on the article "An analysis of contaminated well water and health effects in Woburn, Massachusetts," *Journal of the American Statistical Association* 81 (1986): 597–599.

12. S. Jasanoff, *Science at the Bar: Law, Science, and Technology in America* (Harvard University Press, 1995), p. 208.

13. The Institute of Electrical and Electronics Engineers, for example, issues numerous position papers on issues of national importance. It has (as of this writing) no formal peer-review process for these reports, but relies on members of the committees that develop the papers to carry out the reviews.

14. See *The Velikovsky Affair: The Warfare of Science and Scientism*, ed. A. de Grazia (University Books Inc., 1966).

15. H. H. Bauer, *Beyond Velikovsky* (University of Illinois Press, 1984), p. 147.

16. P. Feyerabend, Realism and instrumentalism: Comments on the logic of factual support, in *The Critical Approach to Science and Philosophy*, ed. M. Bunge (Free Press, 1964), p. 114.

17. M. Polanyi, The growth of science in society, *Minerva* 5 (1967): 533–545.

18. T. Kuhn, *The Structure of Scientific Revolutions*, third edition (University of Chicago Press, 1996).

19. R. D. Laing, *The Divided Self* (Pantheon, 1969).

20. For a comprehensive survey of STS studies, see *Handbook of Science and Technology*, ed. S. Jasanoff et al. (Sage, 1995).

21. S. Jasanoff, *Science at the Bar* (Harvard University Press, 1995), p. 52.

22. D. Callahan, *New York Times Book Review*, April 9, 1995, p. 15.

23. B. Martin and E. Richards, Scientific knowledge, controversy, and public decision making, in *Handbook of Science and Technology*.

24. S. Jasanoff, What judges should know about the sociology of science, *Judicature* 77 (1993): 77–82.

25. D. Edge, Reinventing the wheel, in *Handbook of Science and Technology*, ed. S. Jasanoff et al. (Sage, 1995), p. 41.

26. Does ideology stop at the laboratory door? A debate on science and the real world, *New York Times*, October 22, 1989, p. E24.

27. N. Kraus, T. Malmfors, and P. Slovic, Intuitive toxicology: Expert and lay judgments of chemical risks, *Risk Analysis* 12 (1992): 215–232.

28. The Frankfurt School was a collection of leftist philosophers and social thinkers who gathered in the Institute of Social Research at the University of Frankfurt in the 1920s and the 1930s and then again after World War II. The group is known for neo-Marxist writings and for "Critical Theory," a form of analysis that was aimed at putting philosophic ideas to the task of diagnosing social problems. Among the prominent members were Theodor Adorno, Max Horkheimer, Ernst Bloch, and Herbert Marcuse.

29. K. Popper, Reason or revolution? in *The Myth of the Framework* (Routledge, 1993), p. 69.

30. If it really is true that "the most significant insight that has emerged from sociological studies of science in the past 15 years is the view that science is socially constructed" (see box 7.11), Popper's criticism might apply to modern sociology of science as well.

31. W. G. McBride, Doxylamine succinate-induced dysmorphogenesis in the marmoset, *IRCS Medical Science* 13 (1985): 225–226.

32. R. L. Brent, Bendectin: Review of the medical literature of a comprehensively studied human nonteratogen and the most prevalent tortogen-litigen, *Reproductive Toxicology* 9 (1995): 337–350.

Chapter 8

1. *Daubert v. Merrell Dow Pharmaceuticals, Inc.*, 509 U.S. 579, 595 (1993) (quoting Weinstein, Rule 702 of the Federal Rules of Evidence is sound; It should not be amended, 138 F.R.D. 631, 632 (1991)).

2. *Daubert v. Merrell Dow Pharmaceuticals, Inc.*, 43 F.3d 1311, 1321 n. 17 (1995).

3. R. A. Posner, *Overcoming Law* (Harvard University Press, 1995), p. 525.

4. Ibid., p. 526.

5. M. Angell, *Science on Trial* (Norton, 1996).

6. *In re Agent Orange Product Liability Litigation*, 611 F. Supp. 1223, 1243–1248 (D.C.N.Y. 1985), *aff'd on other grounds*, 818 F.2d 187 (2d Cir. 1987), *cert. denied sub nom.*, *Lombard v. Dow Chem.*, 487 U.S. 1234 (1988).

7. Affidavit of Dr. Samuel S. Epstein, *In re Agent Orange Product Liability Litigation*, MDL No. 381 (D.C.N.Y. Mar. 12, 1985).

8. S. Epstein, *The Politics of Cancer* (Sierra Club Books, 1978).

9. J. Baron, *Thinking and Deciding*, second edition (Cambridge University Press, 1994), p. 177.

10. S. Jasanoff, *Science at the Bar* (Harvard University Press, 1995), p. 52. Judges do not, of course, "certify an expert's credibility." They do not decide whether a jury can or may or should believe an expert's testimony. Under Rule 703, judges make a threshold "gatekeeper" decision about whether testimony is so inherently unreliable that it should not be presented to a jury at all. Under Rule 403, they make an additional call about whether testimony is so confusing, misleading, or prejudicial that it should not be admitted even though it may be reliable.

11. T. Porter, *Trust in Numbers: The Pursuit of Objectivity in Science and Public Life* (Princeton University Press, 1995).

12. The Court pointed out that Dr. Swan "received a master's degree in biostatistics from Columbia University and a doctorate in statistics from the University of California at Berkeley" and "is chief of the section of the California Department of Health and Services that determines causes of birth defects, and has served as a consultant to the World Health Organization, the Food and Drug Administration, and the National Institutes of Health." (*Daubert*, 509 U.S. at 583 n.2)

13. Affidavit of Shanna Helen Swan, submitted as part of Joint Appendix at 115–116, *Daubert v. Merrell Dow Pharmaceuticals, Inc.*, No. 92-102 (U.S. Dec. 2, 1992).

14. In this regard, a civil trial is different from an application for FDA approval of a new drug. The pharmaceutical company "loses," and the FDA "wins," when there is not enough evidence to support issuance of a license.

15. Swan, in her testimony, actually made a slightly stronger statement: Bendectin "more probably than not does increase the risk of birth defects." However, unless the increase in risk is quantified, this statement too is inadequate.

16. *Daubert v. Merrell Dow Pharmaceuticals, Inc.*, 43 F.3d 1311, 1321 (9th Cir. 1995).

17. *Daubert*, 43 F.3d at 1322.

Chapter 9

1. For a historical account of *Frye*, see J. Starrs, "A still-life watercolor": *Frye v. United States, Journal of Forensic Sciences* 27 (1982): 684–694.

2. B. Black, F. J. Ayala, and C. Saffran-Brinks, Science and the law in the wake of *Daubert*: A new search for scientific knowledge, *Texas Law Review* 72 (1994): 715–802.

3. Compare A. F. Chalmers, *What Is This Thing Called Science?* second edition (Hackett, 1994), p. 169.

4. Ibid.

5. Richard Posner, Chief Judge of the United States Court of Appeals for the Seventh Circuit, has complained that "to select as one's theme the celebration of reason can have the side effect of making one's rhetoric invisible" (R. A. Posner, *Overcoming Law* (Harvard University Press, 1995), p. 525).

6. P. Kitcher, *Abusing Science: The Case against Creationism* (MIT Press, 1982), p. 48; M. Polanyi, The growth of science in society, *Minerva* 5 (1967): 533–545.

7. A. B. Hill, The environment and disease: Association or causation? *Proceedings of the Royal Society of Medicine* 59 (1965): 295-300; I. Langmuir, "Pathological science," *Physics Today*, October 1989: 36-48; J. V. Rodricks, Some observations on *Daubert* by a toxicologist, *Shepards Expert and Scientific Evidence Quarterly* 1 (fall 1993): 337-344. The Henle-Koch postulates were originally conceived by Jakob Henle. His pupil Robert Koch further developed them and presented them as part of lectures given in 1884 and 1890. See R. Koch, Ueber bakteriologische Forschung, in *Verh. X. Int. Med. Congr. Berlin*, 1890 (1892), p.35.

8. S. Jasanoff, *Science at the Bar: Law, Science, and Technology in America* (Harvard University Press, 1995), p. 79.

9. *Daubert v. Merrell Dow Pharmaceuticals, Inc.*, 509 U.S. 579, 595 (1993).

10. *Daubert*, 509 U.S. at 592.

11. Ibid. at 600.

12. Ibid. at 591 n.9.

13. Ibid. at 591 n.9.

14. Ibid. at 594–595.

15. K. Popper, *Logic of Scientific Discovery* (Hutchinson, 1972), p. 111.

16. The complexity of modern technology complicates this process. The logic built into a computer chip is too complex to test completely, and bugs can be subtle and hard to trace. The recent difficulty with the Pentium chip is surely just the tip of the iceberg. Surely many other subtle bugs lie hidden in this and other computer chips,

undetected by vendors and users. The need for extensive testing to identify and "fix the failures" accounts for a large part of the $400 million claimed by the drug industry as the cost of developing a new drug.

17. G. J. Annas, Nothing but the truth? *Nature* 379 (1996): 501–502.

18. J. Ziman, *Of One Mind: The Collectivization of Science* (AIP Press, 1995), p. 135.

19. *Daubert*, 509 U.S. at 594 (quoting *United States v. Downing*, 753 F.2d 1224, 1238 (3rd Cir. 1985)).

20. Black et al., Science and the law in the wake of *Daubert*.

21. Jasanoff, however, interprets this as an example of successful boundary setting by professional groups, not as a result of the loose and nonfalsifiable nature of the medical theories upon which clinical ecology are based. See S. Jasanoff, Judicial construction of new scientific evidence, in *Critical Perspectives on Nonacademic Science and Engineering*, ed. P. Durbin (Lehigh University Press, 1991).

22. A. H. Cromer, *Uncommon Sense: The Heretical Nature of Science* (Oxford University Press, 1993), pp. 147–148.

23. Polanyi, The growth of science in society.

24. D. L. Hull, *Science as a Process: An Evolutionary Account of the Social and Conceptual Development of Science* (University of Chicago Press, 1988), p. 342.

25. As we noted in chapter 1, *Daubert* addresses only "scientific knowledge," not "technical, or other specialized knowledge." The Supreme Court expressly noted that its "discussion is limited to the scientific context because that is the nature of the expertise offered here" (*Daubert*, 509 U.S. at 590 n. 8).

26. As we discussed in chapter 3, she might also have added that no mountain of data, no matter how high, can ever eliminate such a possibility.

27. Affidavit of Shanna Helen Swan, submitted as part of Joint Appendix at 116, *Daubert v. Merrell Dow Pharmaceuticals, Inc.*, No. 92-102 (U.S. Dec. 2, 1992).

28. If Swan had concerns about the safety of Bendectin, she should have voiced them in more appropriate forums. Her arguments would have carried little weight in the regulatory arena, however. The burden of proof of safety she requires—showing that a drug does not double the risk of any adverse outcome, no matter how rare, to any user, is impossible to meet. No drug has been "proven safe" by Swan's standard, and regulatory agencies do not require such proof. Moreover, before Swan submitted her affidavit, an FDA panel had examined the data relevant to the safety of Bendectin, and found no reason for concern. We have no indication that she participated in that review.

29. *Daubert*, 509 U.S. at 594–595.

30. *Daubert v. Merrell Dow Pharmaceuticals, Inc.*, 43 F.3d 1311, 1318 (9th Cir. 1995).

31. *Daubert*, 43 F.3d at 1318 n.9.

32. Ibid. at 1319.

33. Ibid.

34. Ibid. at 1319 (citing *Turpin v. Merrell Dow Pharmaceuticals, Inc.*, 959 F.2d 1349, 1360 (6th Cir. 1992).

35. *Daubert v. Merrell Dow Pharmaceuticals, Inc.*, 727 F. Supp. 570, 576 (S.D. Cal. 1989).

36. *Daubert v. Merrell Dow Pharmaceuticals, Inc.*, 116 S. Ct. 189 (1995).

Index